Branded

*How Italian Immigrants
Became 'Enemies'
During World War II*

Branded

How Italian Immigrants
Became 'Enemies'
During World War II

Lawrence W. DiStasi

Sanniti Publications
Bolinas, CA
2016

BRANDED: HOW ITALIAN IMMIGRANTS BECAME 'ENEMIES' DURING WWII
Copyright © 2016, by Lawrence W. DiStasi

For further information, contact Sanniti Publications, P.O. Box 533, Bolinas, California 94924.

ISBN: 978-0-9652714-3-1

Cover Photograph: Enemy Aliens from Pittsburg, CA. Courtesy of the Pittsburg Historical Society Museum. Title photograph: Courtesy NARA II.

Cover/Interior Design: Lawrence W. DiStasi

Library of Congress Control Number: 2016902842

Printing and Binding by Sheridan Books Inc., Chelsea, Michigan.

ACKNOWLEDGMENTS

First, I should like to thank all those who contributed to this story over the years, either by telling their stories, or by contibuting information in the form of photographs, documents, or records. After going so long untold, their accounts and others in this book comprise yet another attempt to bring the full 'secret' story into the light and correct the historical record.

Next, I should like to thank all those colleagues--both in the Italian American Studies Association's Western Regional Chapter, and throughout the nation --who have contibuted not just scholarship and enthusiasm, but often physical settings for hosting the *Una Storia Segreta* exhibit, all of which critically aided our efforts to tell this story. Any project this large and sustained cannot ever hope to succeed without such cooperation and coordination. It would take another book to detail them all, but I hope they know who they are and find satisfaction in what we have accomplished together.

I must mention my daughter, Mia Theis, whose encouragement and suggestions pushed this book to be better; and my sister, Mia R. DiStasi, whose support and aid in distribution has been invaluable. I must also thank Frank Gado, long-lost fellow traveler from Dartmouth, for his advice and counsel in seeing this book through to completion. Finally, I owe a debt of gratitude to Layla Smith Bockhorst for her expert advice regarding matters of design.

And then there are those stalwarts who contributed to the crowd-sourcing campaign to make this book possible. I am deeply indebted to them all, both those whose names are listed below, and those whose names are not. It is no exaggeration to say that without them, this book would not exist.

Last, but by no means least, come those whose generous contributions deserve special mention. They are what, in the old days of publishing, would have been called "Angels."

Patrons: John Calvelli
                  Mia R. DiStasi
                  Maria Gloria
                  Italian Cultural Society of Sacramento

Sponsors: Frank Bruno
                  Anthony Rosati

Donors: Doris Giuliotti
                  Julianna Galli Kleppe
                  Adele Negro

CONTENTS

ILLUSTRATIONS

INTRODUCTION

One of the patterns of my life, including my writing life, has been a pronounced inclination to avoid repeating myself. Like most humans, in a situation where I have a choice I tend to prefer novelty, to explore areas that I have not explored before. What, then, can justify the book that follows which does, in fact, treat a subject (the restrictions on and internment of Italian immigrants during World War II) that, while neglected for decades, has in the past few years been written about by me and several others?

To begin with the most obvious reason, no historical period can ever be fully plumbed by one or two or a dozen books, no matter how complete. The mass of detail and the variety of human experience that fills even a year can never be reduced to words, or sentences, or chapters or books, or indeed, whole libraries. There is always something more to say or to write about any period, and for a time as rich as the days and years leading up to, including, and following World War II, this is especially true. So much that was unique and original and noteworthy took place that whole libraries of books have been devoted to it. This is another.

More specifically with regard to the plight of Italian Americans, this period was especially pregnant with development and meaning, not only for the 600,000 immigrants directly branded as enemy aliens, and hence subject to all the restrictions associated with that designation, but also for those not so targeted but who were related to or knew or have recently heard about what happened to them. And even more specifically, the books and articles that have so far addressed these developments have never, to my knowledge, put the entire range of government measures—the general restrictions, the temporary detentions, the internments, the evacuations from prohibited zones, the restrictions on fishermen, the exclusions of naturalized citizens from coastal states, the seizure of contraband and arrests nationwide—in comprehensible, chronological context. That is what this book seeks to do. It aims to present the entire range of measures arrayed against the 600,000 enemy aliens of Italian descent (including some aimed at naturalized citizens as well) in a comprehensive narrative from start to finish. Each phase of the restrictions is treated separately, and then distinguished from the others to which it is related. It is my hope that by so doing, many of the confusions that pertain even now, even among those who were directly affected, can be eliminated, or at least clarified to the point where the proper questions can be asked.

One of those confusions tripped up even those of us who prepared the seminal exhibit, *Una Storia Segreta: When Italian Americans Were "Enemy Aliens."* Based on what we knew in 1994, the events relating to the major restrictions were attributed to the President's now infamous Executive Order 9066. It was that order, promulgated on February 19, 1942, that was devised to provide the legal basis (not legal to all, it should be noted, which is why it was successfully challenged in court cases such as the Korematsu case) for relocating and interning 70,000 American-born citizens of Japanese descent. Given its historical importance, and the dearth of other information, EO 9066 was thus considered the legal basis for interning and evacuating Italian and German enemy aliens as well. But further research, which I try to elucidate here, and which is buttressed by the Department of Justice's 2001 *Report to the Congress of the United States*, establishes beyond any doubt that EO 9066 was simply not needed to intern and evacuate and otherwise restrict enemy aliens. The legal basis for doing so, as well as most other expedients aimed at enemy aliens, was already contained in the executive orders issued months before, on December 7 & 8, 1941, when war first broke out: EO 2525 for the Japanese, EO 2526 for the Germans and EO 2527 for the Italians. The detailed legal basis for these actions is thus clearly laid out in Chapters Two, Three and Four below so I won't go into them here. All I mean to emphasize now is that it is critical to understand that once a population is designated "enemy aliens," little more needs to be done in order to impose on them whatever the government wishes to impose, up to and including deporting them without further justification. As the Immigration and Naturalization Service noted in one of its training lectures: "These individuals then technically lose all their constitutional rights and privileges, and find that 'what others do confidently and of right, they [enemy aliens] do by sufferance and doubtfully, uncertain of the restrictions of tomorrow.'"[1]

One other aspect of the following study bears emphasis here, partly for its own uniqueness and partly for its relevance to our own time. Adam Curtis in his recent documentary, *The Power of Nightmares*, has labeled the procedural pattern followed by the government anticipating war as the "paradigm of prevention." By this is meant the general strategy engaged in by governments, in what they perceive to be a crisis, to target and control individuals or, more commonly, whole populations *before* any criminal or hostile action has been committed. That is, government agencies, like the FBI prior to World War II, made lists of those who it thought might be preparing, or were simply capable of preparing to take some action against the United States once the war it had long been expecting broke out. The entire intelligence apparatus thereby focused its considerable manpower and intelligence-gathering capabilities on people who had done nothing wrong, who had done nothing at all, who were not yet even enemy aliens, but who the FBI believed *might* intend (if they had the capacity) to take some hostile action. The main reasons for its belief were the usual ones: birth in the country now, or soon to be at war with the United States; opportunity or inclination to do something inimical to the war effort; presumed beliefs that, if true, would align a person with the aims of the enemy; associations with groups that were assumed to be capable of hostile actions. Nor were government efforts limited to suspicion and surveillance, though that is bad enough. The FBI's lists were specifically labeled with the intention they bore, i.e., custodial detention; which is why the main one was called the Custodial Detention Index, or CDI. That is to say, those who were considered suspect, if they were considered suspect enough, were slated to be detained or interned or moved in some way to *prevent* them from doing what the government thought they *might* want to do. Well before war even broke out. This cannot be emphasized enough: directly contrary to the basic due process rights contained in the U.S. Constitution, people were slated to be seized and separated from the rest of the population based *not* on an action they had committed or even planned to commit, but to prevent them from acting on what they were thought to believe. And most importantly, they were thought to believe such things primarily because of where they had been born.

It does not take much thought to realize that such a paradigm can, if carried far enough, put just about anyone at risk. As legal scholar David Cole has noted, there is no way to disprove such suspicion—it is based on speculation about a person's future actions, and speculation is impossible to disprove—no way to keep oneself safe from such preventive detention. Kings and despots have routinely employed such tactics to pre-empt any action or imagined action by their enemies. But in a democracy, and specifically in the American democracy, such tactics have always been seen as violations of basic rights, the rights enumerated primarily in that part of the Constitution called the Bill of Rights. During World War II, however, those rights were suspended on the home front for those categorized as enemy aliens, and in the most extreme case, against those of Japanese descent who were American born. For that reason alone, it seems to me, this book and this episode deserve the attention of every American who values his or her freedom. For the paradigm of prevention has continued to be used right up to the present day, as the recent experiences since 9/11 and even before, make clear.

A final note. We who put together the exhibit that started most of the uncovering of these events employed the name *Una Storia Segreta* to indicate that the defining mark of those restrictions and the people who suffered them was secrecy: secrecy by the government imposing them and secrecy by those who endured the shame associated with them. For my part, in the course of the exhibit's travels, I spoke to numerous audiences about this secret history and was often asked what had inspired me to begin my research into these events. This was a logical question because I routinely made a part of my presentation what I thought was noteworthy and even astonishing: that many Italian Americans whose own families had suffered one or more of these restrictions had no idea of what had happened until our exhibit exposed the truth. 'Yes, but what drove *you*?' was a common follow-up. Usually I would fall back upon my interest in history, or an encounter with a friend of mine whose grandfather's radio had been hidden under his bed during the war, or simply my astonishment when I first heard that such dramatic events had taken place, events about which I, during my own experience growing up in Connecticut and in all my study of Italian American history, had heard or read nothing.

Then a few years ago, my daughter was looking into the possibility of getting Italian citizenship, and found that in order to do so, she needed my father's birth certificate to prove that he had been born in Italy. I emailed a colleague in the Department of Homeland Security I had consulted before, and asked her if she could find the documents pertaining to my father's naturalization. And then came the shock: my father had become naturalized alright, but not until 1944! This meant that he had been, completely unknown to me or any of my living relatives, an enemy alien during the war. I had in fact speculated that perhaps the older people in my family had been enemy aliens—my grandfather, or grandmother, or great aunt. But it turned out that my grandfather had himself become naturalized in 1928, and that was the problem for my father. My father apparently thought that he was covered by his father's naturalization, in a process called 'derivative citizenship.' The problem was, in 1928 my father was twenty-six years old, several years too old for derivative citizenship (the cutoff age is eighteen). So when the wartime came, my father was informed that he had to register as an enemy alien because he had never applied for citizenship on his own.

Suddenly it became clear to me not only why we had rightly called our project *Una Storia Segreta*, but also what the underlying (one might almost say subconscious) reasons were for my persistent interest in this story. Some subterranean part of me must have known, when I first heard of these events on the West Coast, that they related to me not only as an Italian American, but as one who was directly, albeit unknowingly, affected. It took an accidental search to confirm that unknown knowing. And to me, that is another reason, perhaps the most important reason this book needed to be written. Whether or not we, as Italian Americans, or as Americans in general, were directly affected by the secret wartime measures, their effects, whether we know it or not, have extended to us all.

Lawrence DiStasi
Bolinas, CA   2016

----

1. Thomas B. McDermott, *INS Training Lecture,* 1943, p. 5. The quote is attributed to Techt v. Hughes, 229 U.S. 222 (1920).

I: PRELUDE TO WAR

The Italian relationship to America goes back to its "discovery" (from Europe's point of view) by Cristoforo Colombo, a navigator from Genoa sailing for the Spanish Crown in 1492. He was followed in 1497 by the Florentine, Amerigo Vespucci, whose descriptions of South America as a "new world" led to the use of his Italian first name to describe what he saw: America. Other Italian explorers, such as Giovanni Caboto and Giovanni da Verrazano soon followed, exploring the northern reaches of the new continent's east coast, while Alessandro Malaspina, also in the employ of Spain, in 1775 explored the coast of the Pacific Northwest, stopping, among other places, at Monterey, California to make detailed observations about it. Filippo Mazzei arrived in Virginia in 1773, lived near his close friend Thomas Jefferson, and provided the writer of the Declaration of Independence with both extensive horticultural information and his most famous line, All men are created equal. Mazzei had put it, "All men are by nature equally free and independent..."[1]

Following these and other notable early Italian forays into the new nation, including a significant Italian presence in California during and after the gold rush of 1849 (the Italian 49ers were largely immigrants from Genoa who journeyed to California by way of South America, most of them rather quickly abandoning gold-prospecting to enter related support trades: fruit and vegetable farms, groceries, vineyards, transport firms, hotels and restaurants)[2], there continued sporadic immigration from Italy until after the

Risorgimento—Italy's long fight for independence, which finally, thanks to Giuseppe Garibaldi's liberation of southern Italy in 1861, freed most of Italy from foreign rule and initiated its modern period as a self-governing nation. Ironically, liberation did little to improve the lives of the masses of Italians, particularly in the south, where most peasants continued to exist in a kind of modern serfdom that national unification often enough tended to make worse.[3]

By the late 1870s, with farm imports from America contributing to the worsening lot of Italian farmers unable to compete with subsidized American products, and American companies promising Italians a new world of plentiful work at unheard-of pay, the modern phase of Italian emigration to the Americas began. It was a movement almost without parallel in history, a virtual hemorrhage of mostly, but not exclusively, peasants, the majority of them from southern Italy, who pulled up stakes to risk their luck and lives in an America said to have streets paved with gold. Since that time, upwards of 12.5 million Italians have emigrated permanently, with nearly 5 million settling in the United States (as of 1970)[4] and millions more making the passage only to work and save enough money to return to their homeland. Some Italian villages nearly emptied. The villagers left behind mourned the loss of their men, and eventually women, who followed the first pioneers to the cities they wrote home about in the process known as "chain migration." It was a wrenching process that saw millions leaving villages their families had inhabited since time immemorial for an ocean voyage that not only took them thousands of miles but hundreds of years from the life they had always known.

Once in the new world, most Italian immigrants settled near their *paesani* from the home village—friends or relatives who were expected to help the newcomers find work. Enormous numbers lived in the Little Italys forming in their main port of entry: New York City's Greenwich village, East Harlem, the Bronx, Brooklyn, and eventually Queens, Staten Island and the surrounding suburbs. Depending on their village of origin, others moved on, as they could afford it, to similar clusters of Italian immigrants in Newark, NJ's first ward, South Philadelphia, Boston's North End, Bridgeport, New Haven and Waterbury in Connecticut, Providence in Rhode Island, Chicago, Detroit, Cleveland, and St. Louis in the Midwest, New Orleans in the South, and even farther west to Denver, San Francisco, and every large city and rural area in between. They worked as pick-and-shovel men building roads, railroads, sewers, and the New York City subway. They labored as coal and copper miners, garment workers, bricklayers, concrete finishers and garbage men (known, in the West, as 'scavengers'). The more skilled among them found jobs or opened businesses as barbers, tailors, hairdressers, shoemakers, un-

dertakers, butchers, and importers of the traditional foods their paesani found it absolutely necessary to have. Some few, especially in California, found work as truck farmers
or fishermen. And everywhere they faced the deep prejudice known as 'nativism.'

Italians as the 'nightmare of the American Dream.'

According to John Higham,[5] nativism encompassed three volatile ingredients: a
belief in the superiority of the Anglo-Saxon heritage, a suspicion of the authoritarian
tendencies of the Roman Catholic Church, and a fear of the subversive influence of European political radicalism. In essence, the doctrine maintained that the only immigrants
truly suited to become Americans were of Anglo-Saxon or northern European stock
similar to that of America's revolutionary founders. All others, particularly those stream-
ing into Ellis Island from eastern and southern Europe in the late 19th century, looking
as if they had just emerged from the Middle Ages (which many of them had), were considered unfit—a "cursed rabble," as Woodrow Wilson once put it, in a term that not only
suggested hordes who threatened to overwhelm the capacity of America to house or feed
or employ them, but also mobs that could never be assimilated into American culture.
To nativists, the essence of America as a mostly white, Protestant, freedom-loving nation
(always excepting, of course, the Native Americans herded onto reservations, and the
Africans shipped to the new colonies as slaves) was in danger of being transformed, if not
destroyed, by what was perceived as a wholly other race of people. They believed that this
'effluvium' of which Europe was ridding itself could never be salvaged, not even by the
great natural and democratic capacities of the United States.

Italians were at the core of this threat—both the most numerous and the most visibly foreign of the new immigrants. They were considered in every sense the 'nightmare of
the American dream'—dark-skinned idol worshippers, who not only drank wine freely
and openly, and lived in crowded tenements no civilized person could bear to enter, but
who were prone to sudden, uncontrollable outbursts of emotion and savage crimes of
passion. As John Diggins notes,

> If "Rum, Romanism, and Rebellion" was the unfortunate anti-Irish shibboleth of the
> election of 1884, "Chianti, Catholicism, and Crime" could as easily have been the in-
> delible stigma borne by the Italian immigrant.[6]

Their increasing numbers in American cities raised more and more alarm that this
was an unacceptable, even diseased perversion of the 'noble' immigration that had built
the nation, and it had to be stopped. And that was what nativists set out to do.

In public, nativists attacked Italian workers as wage-depressers and strike-breakers.

Behind the scenes, they lobbied their representatives to change immigration laws to stem the hemorrhage from southern Europe. Eventually, all this pressure, aided by the anti-foreign sentiments unleashed by World War I and the Russian revolution, led to the Immigration Act of 1924, also known as the National Origins Law. This law based immigration quotas for each country on two percent of the 1890 census, i.e. when northern European representation was far higher. At a stroke, this expanded the allowable immigration for northern Europeans, while dramatically lowering it for Italians and other Mediterranean groups. Other laws[7] penalized American-born women who married Italian immigrants, by stripping them of their citizenship. Though this latter procedure was actually ended in 1922, it resulted in the loss of citizenship for thousands of women while it was in effect (from 1907 to 1922), and had dramatic results when so-called 'enemy aliens' were targeted in World War II (see Chapter 4: "Evacuation & Curfew").

In the most extreme cases of nativist hatred, Italian immigrants were attacked and sometimes lynched. Indeed, the largest single lynching in United States history targeted Sicilian immigrants in New Orleans in October 1890, after the police chief there was murdered, and witnesses claimed to have heard the dying Chief Hennessey say, "The Dagos did it." Eleven Sicilian immigrants were rounded up and tried for the murder. Nine were soon acquitted, with two still awaiting trial, but outrage over the acquittals inflamed popular sentiment for some form of 'justice,' and demands for punishment mounted. On March 11, 1891, a mob, goaded on by civic leaders, stormed the jail where the acquitted men were being held, and overwhelmed those in charge. All eleven Italians, including the two who had not yet been tried, were subsequently killed in an act that Theodore Roosevelt, prior to his presidency, actually characterized as "a rather good thing."[8] The mayor of New Orleans, Joseph Shakspeare (sic), agreed: "These men deserved hanging... They were punished by lawful means. The men who did it were all peaceable and law-abiding. The Italians had taken the law into their own hands and we had to do the same."[9] A similar lynching took place in Hahnville, Louisiana in 1896, when three Italian immigrants were lynched. Nor was Louisiana the only place of danger for Italian immigrants. In Walsenburg, Colorado in 1895, five Italian mine workers were murdered. Then, four years before passage of the 1924 Immigration Act,

> On the evening of August 5, 1920, mobs in West Frankfurt, a small mining town in
> Illinois, stormed into the Italian district, dragged frightened occupants from their
> houses, clubbed and stoned them, and set their dwellings aflame.[10]

Lynchings, racism and discrimination notwithstanding, the economic and political conditions in Italy guaranteed that immigration to America would actually increase just before World War I. During the peak years of 1901 through 1910, more than 2 million Italians left their homeland for the United States. This lifted the total Italian immigration to the United States from 1870 to 1920 to well over 4 million,[11] most of them peasants fleeing their native land for economic reasons, but also including significant numbers fleeing political persecution. One result was that the period between the war's end in 1917 and the shutting off of immigration in 1924 uncovered an additional focus for anti-Italian sentiment: Italian radicalism. Socialists in Italy had been preaching labor and land reform for years before and after the turn of the century. Many, both socialists and anarchists, emigrated to America to help their co-nationals there fight for related reforms in the industries they stocked: the garment trades, silk manufacture, and mining.[12] Italian-born radicals took part in and led several strikes, most notably the major actions in Lawrence, Massachusetts and Patterson, New Jersey. By the post-World War I period, socialist leaders like Carlo Tresca of the International Workers of the World (IWW) had become notorious, and American law-enforcement agencies, including the fledgling FBI (originally called the Bureau of Investigation), set out to investigate them and others. It wasn't long before the stereotyped image of the Italian immigrant grew from, at best, that of an illiterate and harmless organ-grinder or fruit peddler, to, worse, a stiletto-wielding sociopath drunk on wine, to, worst of all, a bomb-throwing revolutionary motivated by Karl Marx and Errico Malatesta. In fact, Malatesta briefly visited Paterson, New Jersey in 1899, where he was shot in the leg at an anarchist meeting.[13] All this allowed Nativists to accuse Italian immigration of being not just a conduit for moral, intellectual and emotional defectives, but a medium for exporting revolution. Such suspicions culminated in the Palmer Raids of the early 1920s, named for the Attorney General, A. Mitchell Palmer, whose house had been bombed, and who thereafter led a series of unconstitutional raids and mass arrests in Italian neighborhoods in the search for "reds." This resulted not only in mass deportations, but also in cooperation between American law enforcement and the Fascist Police of the newly-empowered Benito Mussolini.[14]

The fear of Italian radicals reached its apogee at about this same time when a robbery and murder in South Braintree, Massachusetts was laid at the doorstep of two Italian-born anarchists, Nicola Sacco and Bartolomeo Vanzetti. Though the Sacco-Vanzetti case and trial became a *cause celebre* for not only Italian immigrants, but also for the American Left and intellectuals worldwide, not even global protests or the many questions about the impartiality of the trial and the validity of the evidence could save the two immigrants. Convicted in 1921, the Italian-born shoemaker and his fisherman comrade were finally executed in 1927.

The Rise of Mussolini

By 1922, the serious economic and political dislocations in Italy following her severe losses during World War I, and Italian popular outrage at what was perceived to be
Italy's paltry share of territories won by the Allies (Woodrow Wilson at Versailles rejected the notion of Italian control over the Adriatic port city of Fiume), led to the ascen-
sion of Benito Mussolini as leader of the nation. A former socialist and newspaperman,
the man who insisted on being called Il Duce had such a genius for public relations that
he is often credited with inventing the modern art of propaganda.[15] Within a very short
time, his clever sloganeering and strong-arm tactics had silenced or exiled or murdered
his leftist opposition, reduced his parliament to a rubber stamp, and molded the Italian
government to the form of state corporatism he called "Fascism" after a Roman symbol,
the fascio.[16] From the outside, Italy appeared to change into a modern, efficient, industrialized nation with such rapidity that nations and leaders the world over looked to the
Italian "miracle" as a model of development. Much of the American press agreed. Mussolini was hailed as the heroic figure who had saved Italy from communism (commonly
called "bolshevism" at that time), the leader who could tame the ancient unruliness of
the Italian people and turn them into obedient workers and citizens—like Americans,
presumably. Ironically, even American nativists approved of fascism: they thought, basically, that Italians "deserved" a dictatorship because of their "deliberate" vices.[17] As John
Diggins summarizes it:

> Fascism seemed to stand for property and filial values, social mobility with a social
> order, and for God and country. To businessmen especially, Italy's corporatism dis-
> played all the benefits of coherent national planning without the threat of wholesale
> collectivism.[18]

One reason for this perception of order was that alone among modern Italian leaders, Mussolini appeared to have successfully controlled not just the disorderly Italian
masses but even organized crime by ruthlessly rounding up known Mafia leaders and
exiling them to remote islands, or to the United States. He was praised in poetry by the
January 23, 1923 *Wall Street Journal*:

> On formula and etiquette
>   He seems a trifle shy;
> But when it comes to 'go and get,'
>   He's some two-fisted guy!...

Red nonsense and its mischief proved;
  His black-shirts curbed and quelled,
Perhaps in ways not graced or grooved—
  How the reins be held?

A blacksmith's son to purple Rome
  A brusque command he brought;
Italia, cleansed and rescued home—
  But more than her he's taught! ...

History maybe holds a chance
  Of more for blacksmith's son,--
If he, 'twixt Germany and France,
  Sees justice kindly done.

Whate-er that outcome, write his name
  That history may not shirk,--
A new Columbus with his fame
  New world of will and work!

Not long afterward, the "new Columbus" was featured, complete with his enco-
miums on the glories of war, in a five-part series that started May 5, 1928 in the hugely
popular mass magazine, *The Saturday Evening Post.*

Collage of *Saturday Evening Post* issues featuring Mussolini.

Major American journalists visited Italy and wrote glowing reports about the rapid expansion of Italian roads, railroads, industries, and schools. Few suspected that much of what they saw had been staged, including the much-sought-after personal interviews with the great leader, or that the entire nation had become a kind of stage set for Il Duce's fake exploits (as Luigi Barzini points out in *The Italians*)[19]. Even Franklin Roosevelt wrote that he would be keeping in close touch with "that admirable gentleman,"[20] and in fact sent several of his advisers, including Harry Hopkins, Hugh Johnson and Rexford Tugwell, to see if they might "pick up some ideas" from observing Mussolini's programs for combating worldwide depression.[21] Some commentators went so far as to suggest that the United States itself, having in the Depression lost its own bearings and its commitment to its core values, might be in need of a Mussolini of its own "to save us from the American equivalent of a Lenin."[22]

In short, Mussolini appeared to be making Italy into another America. As John Diggins points out, Mussolini seemed to stand for two constantly mythologized American values: rational intelligence and human willpower. Citing the ongoing love affair with Italy and the "happy" Italian people of such trenchant American observers as the reporter Lincoln Steffens and the philosopher George Santayana, Diggins notes that their simultaneous critique of Italian apathy and lack of American-style discipline demonstrates that "In the end America's apologia for Fascism would betray an inevitable desire to see the Americanization of Italy."[23] Such sentiments might be borne in mind when contemplating the actual Americanization of both Italy and the Italian immigrants in America that followed World War II.

All this praise of their native country's leader by American journalists, thinkers, politicians and businessmen was music to the ears of most Italian immigrants in America. Where Italy had always been treated as a pathetic laggard among modern nations, unable to truly unite, and incapable of changing the abysmal poverty that had oppressed its masses for so long, she now appeared to be garnering universal respect as a global leader. Mussolini seemed to have found the formula not only to defeat the specter of violent revolution espoused by communists and anarchists both, but also to build a modern, prosperous nation out of nothing but his inexhaustible will. With all the approbation he was receiving, the designation 'Italian' seemed to be recovering some of the glory it had not known since the days of the Roman Empire. That glory appeared to be reflected upon those of Italian heritage in the United States (at least in the eyes of the immigrants themselves), for Mussolini himself made it plain that the Italian spirit, no matter where it migrated, retained its strength and power unto the seventh generation. Such stirring ideas were trumpeted repeatedly in Italian publications in America—in Italian-language newspapers like *Il Progresso* of New York and *L'Italia* of San Francisco, in popular American magazines like *McCall's* and *The Saturday Evening Post,* and most fervidly in language texts supplied by the Fascist government for the Italian language schools that proliferated in Little Italys throughout the nation, and on radio programs hosted by Italian-speaking broadcasters. This was because Mussolini, ever the great propagandist, made sure that every avenue for spreading his message to those he considered his subjects abroad was exploited. His government, mainly through consular officials, directed the formation of fascios with heroic Italian names in cities such as New York, Boston and San Francisco. Through its control of the Italian Chambers of Commerce, the Italian government made clear to Italian immigrants who wished to do business in Italy, such as importers, that open loyalty to the Fascist government was required. Italian Consulates let it be known that maintaining Italian citizenship was useful and probably necessary to any Italian immigrant anxious to be secure about relatives still in Italy, or to eventually return to a beloved village. Italian veterans of World War I, the *Ex-Combattenti,* were made to understand that continued receipt of their meager pensions depended upon Fascist Party membership. Italian American organizations such as the Sons of Italy and the Dante Alighieri Society, as well as Italian American newspapers with direct wires to Italy, were left in no doubt that the subsidies and praise and nourishment—and sometimes direction—they received from Italy depended upon continuing enthusiasm for their Italian fascist source.[24]

Fencers at the San Francisco Doposcuola

Nor were more direct methods ignored. Shortly after he took power, Mussolini and his administration set out to spread Fascism abroad as well as at home. His consular officials found a ready audience in American cities, in many of which fascist organizations were already being formed. In 1924, Mussolini sent Count Thaon di Revel to New York to bring some fascist order to these fledgling organizations and Revel, as President, formed the Fascist League of North America (FLNA). Before long it had over 70 branches with some 6,000 members. Advertising itself as opposed to "atheism, internationalism, free-love, communism, and class hatred," it stated that its primary objective was to enlighten the American people about the "ideals of Fascism."[25] Such open advocacy, however, soon proved too brazen even for a hero-worshipping America, and in 1929, an article in *Harper's Magazine* by Marcus Duffield exposed what it called "The Fascist Invasion of the U.S." Within weeks Congress was asking for an investigation, and Count di Revel was announcing that the Fascist League—by now up to 80 branches and over 12,000 members—would be disbanded. Though it would be replaced by Domenico Trombetta's Lictor Federation, and though Mussolini himself would remain highly popular, organized fascism in the United States would never again be so openly prominent or influential.

Still, all this publicity and propaganda meant that approval for Benito Mussolini in the Italian "colonies" of American cities equaled, and often outstripped the leader's popularity at home. For while many Italians in Italy could see the iron fist behind the universal compliance with fascist orders and the stage props behind the fascist bombast, those an ocean away saw mainly the heroics. This was partly due to the efficiency of the propaganda, but perhaps moreso to what Italian immigrants in America wanted to see, needed to see. Living in a Great Depression that would not resolve, and in an America that still treated them with contempt, they hungered for something to save at least their pride, and Mussolini seemed to be that savior. He managed a Concordat with the Vatican in 1929, impressing many devout Italians and the leading prelates of the American Catholic Church, including the Rev. Joseph Hickey (who called Mussolini "a superman who has solved order out of chaos") and Monsignor Fulton J. Sheen, who said he saw in Mussolini's movement a spiritual "resurrection."[26] According to the anti-fascist immigrant Max Ascoli,[27] Fascism was what gave Italian Americans an ethnic identity: no longer parochial emigrants from their village alone, they were now, for the first time, "Italians;" and though that designation still left them, in many American eyes, simply "wops," Mussolini had now even raised the value of that slur, for he had become the "wop on the front page." More than that, he had managed to create an unbreakable link between being 'Italian' and his fascist government, to the degree that, in much of Italian America, attacking fascism became equivalent to attacking Italy itself, to being un-Italian. This identification, along with the unbroken string of successes they heard and read about, convinced Italian Americans, desperate for convincing, that here at last was an Italy and an Italianism that would buoy their spirits in exile, provide them with their much-longed-for respect, and perhaps even help to support their return to a still-loved village one day.

Mussolini on the cover of *Newsweek*, June 17, 1940.

This is not to say that Mussolini's victory among Italians in America was total. Even as he bludgeoned his way to power in 1922 there were those, mainly Italian immigrants on the Left, especially those in organized labor, who opposed and tried to expose him at every turn. Luigi Antonini of the ILGWU and Frank Bellanca, who organized the anti-fascist magazine, *Il Nuovo Mondo,* fought hard to counter the propaganda of the pro-

Mussolini newspapers and the demonstrations held by American blackshirts. Renowned anarchist and labor militant Carlo Tresca often led his groups to attack fascist meetings and celebrations, while his compatriots attacked parades of blackshirts marching on Italian and American holidays. Often these confrontations turned into pitched battles where casualties could be significant: Diggins estimates that at least a dozen deaths resulted from these battles. In the most serious incident, in 1933 the home of Sons of Italy president John de Silvestro was bombed, resulting in the death of his wife and injuries to four of his children. The perpetrator was never found, but since de Silvestro and his organization vociferously supported Il Duce, and de Silvestro himself had publicly pledged the allegiance of his organization to Fascism, most assumed the attack was the work of anti-Fascist leftists.

This Italian American opposition to Fascism was joined, fitfully in the 1920s and 1930s, and then in a rush in the late 1930s, by anti-fascist exiles from Italy. Many of these exiles, known in Italian as *fuorusciti*, had had no choice but to flee Italy, and significant numbers made their way to the United States where they were determined to continue the fight by educating all Americans, including Italian Americans, to the truth about Fascism. While radical activists like Carlo Tresca marched and battled in opposition to Fascist gatherings, scholars like Max Ascoli, Carlo Sforza and Gaetano Salvemini wrote tirelessly and fiercely to expose the true intentions and perfidy of the pro-Fascist organizations in America. Though they had trouble joining themselves to the local opposition or reaching the average immigrant, partly because of the gulf between these intellectual exiles on the one hand and the mainly working-class-oriented labor leaders on the other, their constant writing and lecturing began to have its effect, especially on those who formed the thinking and governing elite. So did the formation, in 1940, of the Mazzini Society—an organization founded by Max Ascoli and others that not only created a magazine, *Nazioni Unite*, but also worked on forming a plan to aid the partisans in Italy resisting Fascism on the ground.

The result was that after Italy's brutal attack on the African nation of Ethiopia in 1935, the admiration for Mussolini among America's opinion-makers shifted dramatically. Mussolini's musings about the glory of war and violence were turning to brutal, lethal, embarrassing actions. His aid to Generalissimo Franco's Spain in the Spanish dictator's war against Spanish communists prefigured an even greater perfidy that would stun the world: in 1938, his Italian Fascist government allied itself with Hitler's Nazi Germany in a union that threatened another worldwide conflagration.

Thus, Mussolini's actions ended up exacerbating the dual, even schizophrenic attitude of America towards Italian immigrants (as well as giving many of those immigrants severe doubts about his value). On the one hand, there was the national celebration of the courage of the foundational explorers Christopher Columbus and Amerigo Vespucci, leading to all those positives of immigration: the ability of America to bring out the best in any immigrant, no matter how humble his origins; all of this testified to by an Italian community that even then seemed on the verge of success and acceptance with major writers, judges, and even politicians holding mayoral office in both New York and San Francisco (both Fiorello LaGuardia and Angelo Rossi were unthreatening, appealing figures who seemed to embody a kind of Italianate joy). On the other hand, there remained the deep and lingering prejudice against Italians, now reinforced by their bombastic leader, as a basically un-American group—one that evoked images of Italians as superstitious, untrustworthy, excessively pleasure-loving buffoons at best, and volatile, dangerous revolutionaries and/or gangsters at worst—whose ability to assimilate into American life was questionable if not hopeless. Indeed, this same opposition would be reflected shortly afterward in the American President's schizoid attitude toward Italians. On the one hand, when Italy joined Germany's invasion of France in 1940, Franklin Roosevelt made his notorious "stab in the back" statement—"The hand that held the dagger has thrust it into the back of its neighbor"—evocative of the suspicion that all Italians were treacherous, dangerous gangsters. At the other extreme was the President's remark when discussing with Attorney General Biddle in December 1941 how Biddle would handle the enemy aliens; the President, in a sentence dripping with condescension said: "I'm not worried so much about the Italians; they're a lot of opera singers."[28]

This was not unimportant, for by the 1940 census, Italians constituted the largest foreign-born group in the nation—a largely unassimilated population of four to six million people,[29] many living in Italian "colonies" where the Italian way of life still largely prevailed. Indeed, of all immigrant groups from the WWII enemy nations, Italians had the lowest percentage of naturalizations—28 percent[30]--as compared with about 75 percent of the Germans (the Japanese, of course, *could not* naturalize, due to discriminatory laws against Asians). In California in 1940, for example, there resided about 100,000 foreign-born Italians, less than half of whom were naturalized – leaving the 52,000 others to become enemy aliens when war broke out.[31] In the nation as a whole in 1940, 694,000 Italian immigrants—again, the largest group by far of those who would be suspect, that is, the 330,000 enemy aliens of German descent, and the 130,000 of Japanese descent— would register as non-citizen aliens to comply with the Alien Registration Act of that year.[32] Though in the end it would turn out to be highly overblown (Italian Americans proved their loyalty by joining the US armed forces in record numbers during World War II, estimates running from 528,000[33] to as many as 1 million under arms), this dual citizenship—and Mussolini made much of the fact that Italians, no matter where they were, always remained Italians first of all—led to some influential and widespread alarm bells about the danger of fifth-column activity among Italian immigrants. As early as November 1929 Marcus Duffield, in that month's issue of *Harper's Magazine* cited above,[34] had asserted that Mussolini could turn Italian Americans into soldiers and saboteurs overnight. Though this was quickly refuted by then-Secretary of State Henry Stimson,[35] the accusation led to others.

Suspicion of Italian-language media, for example, led many to fear the danger of Fascist propaganda in the 135 Italian newspapers publishing in immigrant colonies in 1940,[36] as well as in the many radio broadcasts. Though most Italian editors and broadcasters maintained a public position that Italian Americans could be for Italy under Mussolini and for America at the same time, American authorities remained suspicious. *Fortune* magazine, after the Ethiopian war, reported that "there is dynamite on our shores."[37] Then in 1940, the same magazine reported authoritatively that Mussolini could, in case of war, muster 25,000 Fascists in the United States, and count on another 100,000 for support.[38] Carlo Sforza, the leading anti-fascist figure in the United States, agreed, telling President Roosevelt that Italian Americans were predominantly pro-Fascist (it should be noted that Sforza also considered Wendell Wilkie an "unconscious fascist").[39] So did Gaetano Salvemini, who, from his professorial post at Harvard, inundated government officials with lists of those he considered pro-fascists and potential fifth columnists. Carmelo Zito, an ardent anti-fascist editor of the newspaper *Il Corriere del Popolo* in San Francisco, denied Sforza's generalization, maintaining that in his state of California perhaps ten percent of the immigrants were pro-fascist.[40] Still, American authorities had their doubts, particularly when reading the reports insisting that Europe, especially Norway and the Low Countries like Belgium and Holland, had fallen to the Nazi onslaught due mainly to fifth-column activity by ethnic Germans. Though more recent authoritative studies have proven these conclusions about fifth-column effectiveness to be "virtually all fantasies,"[41] in the days leading up to American involvement in the war, the possibility of a powerful anti-American force among Italian immigrants would not die. "Wild Bill" Donovan, soon to initiate what would become the CIA, along with journalist Edgar Mowrer, published a pamphlet, "Fifth Column Lessons for America," that predicted the German colony in the United States would work with the Nazi Gestapo when war came. Harold Ickes, Secretary of the Interior, fully subscribed to this theory. In

May 1941, when the House UnAmerican Activities Committee (HUAC) heard Richard Krebs, a reformed Comintern agent, describe Nazi espionage techniques, and assert that to be released by the Gestapo and become a refugee to the United States, Germans had to pledge to work for the Gestapo, authorities were frightened and ramped up their policies for spying on, and controlling anyone with roots in enemy nations.[42]

The Government Prepares for War

For United States government agencies, the likelihood of another global conflict had long been anticipated. U.S. Naval planners as early as 1935 had adopted code words for anticipated wars with Japan, Germany and Italy, ORANGE being the color code for war with Japan. Such code words were used to plan not only for naval battles, but also for measures to secure the home front, such as requisitioning fishing and/or pleasure boats for military use. Nor was it only the military that was making plans to control potential home-front problems in the event of war. In August of 1936, not long after the Italian invasion of Ethiopia the previous year, President Franklin Roosevelt summoned J. Edgar Hoover, head of the Bureau of Investigation (soon to become the Federal Bureau of Investigation, or FBI), to the White House to begin planning for domestic intelligence measures.

At the outset, it should be noted that virtually all of the information available on these critical White House meetings (critical because they initiated what was to become a deeply controversial policy, i.e., investigations of Americans that were undertaken *not* in connection with any violation of law—which in 1924 then-Attorney General Harlan Fiske Stone had said Bureau of Intelligence operations should be solely concerned with—but rather for what came to be known as "pure" or "preventive" intelligence) comes from the memos preserved by the head of the FBI, J. Edgar Hoover.[43] With that caveat, we "know" that Hoover had prepared the ground for this meeting by relating to the President information he had received from General Smedley Butler in 1934 about two alleged right-wing plots, one related to an expedition to Mexico, the other a coup against the president's New Deal. Since FDR had been shot at by an anarchist named Zangara even before he took office, he would have been inclined to credit either or both plots, though it is not clear how seriously he took them.[44] What *is* clear is that J. Edgar Hoover had predisposed the President, if he needed predisposing, to agree that espionage, sabotage and propaganda against the United States from within its own borders were real threats, especially in view of the war that appeared to be imminent.

Also noteworthy is the fact that where the President seemed to be initially concerned with obtaining information about specific activities—that is, foreign-based espionage, sabotage, or propaganda to influence public opinion so as to aid the Nazis or Fascists in their attempt to thwart America's ability to wage war or aid its allies—the FBI director expressed most concern about internal "subversion" of the government by Communists and radicals. Accordingly, Hoover's memos record that in this August 1936 meeting, he warned President Roosevelt about the potential "paralyzing" of the U.S. government and its industries by communist influence in labor unions, specifically in the persons of Harry Bridges of the west coast Longshoreman's Union, John L. Lewis of the United Mine Workers, and others with similar influence in the Newspaper Guild. Whether or not the president needed to be persuaded, he apparently (again, according to Hoover's memo) responded by asking Hoover to commence intelligence measures to provide a "broad picture" of all such activities that might be implemented by Fascists, Communists or their sympathizers in the country. As to how authorization for such domestic spying could be undertaken legally, that is, *absent any specific violations of existing law*, Hoover suggested that if the U.S. State Department requested such information, that request, plus the appropriations statute under which the FBI operated, could provide legal cover for his intelligence-gathering activities. More than that, it could do so without the need to go public with a separate request from Congress—and if there was one thing the FBI director was obsessed with, it was keeping such potentially unconstitutional activities secret from Congress. The President agreed, and the next day called then-Secretary of State Cordell Hull to a meeting at the White House. As Ralph deToledano, one of Hoover's biographers, describes it, Hull, upon hearing of the alleged dangers, including the probable espionage of a Soviet consular official named Oumansky, and the intelligence plan to combat such activities, authorized it by saying something like, "investigate the hell out of those cocksuckers."[45] The machinery for large-scale *domestic spying* on Americans was thus set in motion.

This is not to say that J. Edgar Hoover had not, prior to this time, been seeking out and recording secret information on his fellow Americans. For many years, in spite of the admonition from Attorney General Stone, the FBI director had been ordering his special agents in charge of field offices (SACs) to submit reports on organizations such as the Communist Party of the USA and the American Civil Liberties Union, as well as many individuals suspected of "radical activities."[46] But the pre-war intelligence operation he entered upon in 1936 was of another order entirely. As Hoover put it in a memo:

> In talking with the Attorney General today concerning the radical situation, I in-

formed him of the conference which I had with the President on September 1, 1936 [sic], at which time the Secretary of State, at the President's suggestion, requested of me, the representative of the Department of Justice, to have investigation made of the subversive activities in this country, including communism and fascism.[47]

The important words here are "subversive activities," and the fact that rather than focusing, as the President would almost always do, primarily on the possible dangers of espionage and sabotage, especially if they were foreign-directed, the FBI director fore-grounded the term "subversive." He would do it again and again in the coming months and years. To understand the significance of this, it is instructive to refer to the warning given in 1940 by then-Attorney General Robert Jackson regarding the term "subversion." Jackson maintained that subversion was a dangerous concept because there were "no definite standards to determine what constitutes a 'subversive activity', such as we have for murder or larceny." The Attorney General expanded on this problem with more examples:

> Activities which seem benevolent or helpful to wage earners, persons on relief, or those who are disadvantaged in the struggle for existence may be regarded as "subversive" by those whose property interests might be burdened thereby. Those who are in office are apt to regard as "subversive" the activities of any of those who would bring about a change of administration. Some of our soundest constitutional doctrines were once punished as subversive.[48]

In other words, what J. Edgar Hoover did was use the broadest possible definition of what his "intelligence operation" should or could involve, in order that he and the FBI would be free to investigate virtually anything or anyone deemed threatening to a concept of order that could not help but shift with the prevailing political winds. As just one concrete example of how this might work in practice, the term "downright subversive activity" actually appeared in the file of one of the Italian immigrants, Federico Dellagatta, who was interned as an allegedly "dangerous" enemy alien during WWII. And what was this "subversive" activity for which Dellagatta was arrested? It was talk, "irresponsible talk about the greatness of the Italian people and the Italian army." These were the words used to describe Dellagatta's offense by his hearing board, a group of three reputable citizens deputized by the Justice Department to judge those taken into custody, and which, in its conclusions, said it did NOT think Dellagatta's "talk" was dangerous to the people and safety of the United States. The board therefore recommended that he be paroled.

The Department of Justice reviewer of Dellagatta's case disagreed, however, in the following terms:

> In the opinion of this reviewer, subject's persistent talk in praising and boasting of the greatness of the Italian people and of the Italian army while employed in a shoe shining shop constitutes *downright subversive activity..*"[49] [Emphasis added].

In this way, a Justice Department official in Washington, disputing the finding of the hearing board on site, found Dellagatta's "loose talk" about the greatness of the Italian people "subversive." And, in a demonstration of precisely the type of elasticity concerning the term that Attorney General Jackson had warned about, Federico Dellagatta was ordered to be incarcerated behind barbed wire for the looseness of his talk while shining shoes in Providence, Rhode Island's Union Station.

When one examines more closely what was set in motion by the August 1936 meeting in the White House, we can see even more clearly what the attorney general's warning meant. Armed with what he interpreted as presidential approval and authority, J. Edgar Hoover sent orders to all his bureau stations to make collecting information about any alleged Nazi, Communist, Fascist or subversive individuals or organizations their highest priority. He made a point of the fact that all information should be gathered and recorded, regardless of the source:

> The Bureau desires to obtain from all possible sources information concerning subversive activities conducted in the United States by Communists, Fascisti, and representatives or advocates of other organizations or groups advocating the overthrow or replacement of the Government of the United States....you should immediately transmit to the Bureau any information relating to subversive activities on the part of any individual or organization, *regardless of the source* from which this information is received.[50] [Emphasis added.]

And it was. With the same zeal he had displayed during World War I and in the Red Scare that followed, Hoover and his FBI by 1939 had assembled a wide-ranging collection of lists and dossiers on nearly 10 million Americans, large numbers of whom had been born in foreign countries, unknown numbers of whom had been informed upon by confidential sources of all kinds.

Nor, it should be noted, was everyone in government indifferent to the dangers of such domestic spying. Senator McKellar of Tennessee had complained about the FBI's growing power as early as 1934. In 1940, Senator George Norris of Nebraska did likewise, asserting that without controls, "there will be a spy behind every stump and a detective in every closet in our land."[51] But the growing peril of Axis aggression in Europe and Asia (Japan invaded China in 1937, while Hitler marched into the Sudetenland in October 1938), together with alarming reports that early Nazi invasions had been substantially aided by a "fifth column" made up of ethnic Germans within various nations,[52] soon trampled all objections to the pre-emptive gathering of intelligence in the United States. Even before war broke out, in fact, Congress seemed eager to pass laws providing for the detention of those who might pose security risks in the event of trouble. The Hobbs Bill of 1939 was the first. Not content with the fact that the government already had the authority to deport aliens, Representative Sam Hobbs of Alabama introduced a bill allowing for the detention of such aliens in camps run by the Labor Department while they awaited deportation. Complaints that such camps were a "thinly disguised attempt to establish concentration camps," and therefore un-American, fell upon deaf ears, and on May 5, 1939, the Hobbs Bill passed the House of Representatives by a vote of 289 to 61.[53] It thereby became legal, even absent a conflict, to lock up 'suspicious foreigners' in America.

Meantime, the process of searching out and recording intelligence on Americans, and its consolidation in the FBI under J. Edgar Hoover continued, with Hoover fiercely combating any "chiseling in" by other agencies, especially the State Department, on what he now considered his territory. By 1939, he had persuaded the president not only of his department's efficacy, but of its right to near-exclusive jurisdiction in intelligence. The outbreak of war in Europe in September 1939 changed only the Director's demand for secrecy, especially when he learned that even the New York City Police Department had "created a special sabotage squad."[54] In order to head off further poaching on his territory, he asked President Roosevelt to go public, by issuing a formal statement to all police officials, directing them to turn over to the FBI any information regarding potential espionage, sabotage or like matters. On September 6, 1939 the president did just that:

> The Attorney General has been requested by me to instruct the Federal Bureau of Investigation of the Department of Justice to take charge of investigative work in matters relating to espionage, sabotage, and violations of the neutrality regulations....
>
> To this end I request all police officers, sheriffs, and other law enforcement officers in the United States promptly to turn over to the nearest representative of the Federal Bureau of Investigation any information obtained by them relating to espionage, counterespionage, sabotage, subversive activities and violations of the neutrality laws.[55]

Two days later on September 8, the President went further, proclaiming a national emergency "in connection with and to the extent necessary for the proper observance, safeguarding, and enforcing of the neutrality of the United States and the strengthening of our national defense within the limits of peacetime authorizations." Though nothing in either statement overtly mentioned spying on Americans, much less using that information as a basis for detention, J. Edgar Hoover interpreted both statements to mean that his authority to investigate, and, if necessary, arrest and detain the persons on his lists, had been granted. He immediately sent orders to all FBI offices to cull through their now-voluminous files, obtain still more information from "reliable contacts," all in order to generate reports on "persons of German, Italian, and Communist sympathies," as well as others "whose interests may be directed primarily to the interest of some other nation than the United States." The persons reported on should include not just the editors, owners and reporters of "all German and Italian language newspapers in the United States," but "lists of subscribers" to those newspapers as well.[56] Also to be investigated were members of all German and Italian societies, "whether they be of a fraternal character or of some other nature." And despite the public nature of the President's proclamations, agents were instructed to keep the purpose of their inquiries into "public and private records, confidential sources of information, newspaper morgues [sic], public libraries, school records, etc" strictly confidential, using as a cover story the fiction that the investigations were being conducted in connection with "the Registration Act requiring agents of foreign principals to register with the State Department [the Foreign Agents Registration Act of 1938, ed.]."[57]

If one wonders why, with presidential authority backing him, the FBI Director continued to insist on secrecy, a hint comes from the previously-referenced Church Committee Report and its comments on what has already been referred to: the concepts of "pure" and "preventive" intelligence. "Pure" intelligence is built on the theory of "subversive infiltration." That is, it refers to intelligence gathered not to "assist in the enforcement of criminal laws," as Attorney General Harlan Stone had originally mandated for his new intelligence bureau, but rather to "supply the President and other executive officials with information believed to be of value for making decisions and developing governmental policies." It can easily be seen how elastic such a function might be: there is almost no limit to information that might prove useful in making policy decisions. As to "preventive" intelligence, it was designed to gather information useful in the event of a future national emergency or war. It would provide the grounds for taking measures against individuals or groups who *might* be disposed, *at some future date*, to interfere with national defense. Again, if such interference involved specific crimes like sabotage or espionage, such intelligence was clearly related to the enforcement of legal statutes.

The problem was, "the relationship was often remote and highly speculative, based on political affiliations and group membership rather than any tangible evidence of preparation to commit criminal acts."[58] In short, both pure and preventive intelligence could, and did provide the basis for what have been called "fishing expeditions," whereby not illegal actions or even words, but simply the most tenuous and tangential connections to suspect groups can be used to smear and possibly imprison individuals of little value or danger. Thus was set in motion, in the run-up to World War II, the means to compile mountains of data on groups and individuals who had done nothing, but who were anticipated to be *potential* dangers when and if the United States entered the war, as well as the procedures for intelligence gathering that have proved increasingly controversial and of doubtful legality in the years since.

The Preparation of Lists

Controversial or not, all this enormous inflow of information to the FBI was then distilled to produce a list that became known, in June 1940, as the Custodial Detention Index (CDI). This was a list of those persons from the prospective enemy nations (war did not start until eighteen months later) characterized as "dangerous"—i.e. whose "presence at liberty in this country in time of war or national emergency would constitute a menace to the public peace and safety of the United States Government." Such people were separated by the FBI into two classes:

> Class #1. Those to be apprehended and interned immediately upon the outbreak of hostilities between the Government of the United States and the Government they serve, support, or owe allegiance to.
>
> Class #2. Those who should be watched carefully at and subsequent to the outbreak of hostilities because their previous activities indicate the *possibility but not the probability* that they will act in a manner adverse to the best interests of the Government of the United States.[59] [Emphasis added.]

Aside from alleged Communists, the people on this list were, in Hoover's summary, those who held "official positions in organizations such as the German-American Bund" or Fascist groups, those who distributed "literature and propaganda favorable to a foreign power," and "agitators who are adherents of foreign ideologies...which in time of war would be a serious handicap in a program of internal security and national defense." While there is little doubt that some of the many reports on such individuals and groups were based in legitimate concerns for national security, some were also reports on "lawful domestic political activities" by groups such as the League for Fair Play, which furnished "speakers to Rotary and Kiwanis Clubs and to schools and colleges." Its purpose was reported by the FBI itself to be the furthering of "fair play, tolerance, adherence to the Constitution, democracy, liberty, justice, understanding and good will." Yet it appeared on the CDI. The National Association for the Advancement of Colored People, or NAACP, was also one of the organizations to be investigated and held in suspicion, because it was believed by Hoover to be infiltrated by Communists.[60]

What is not known is how often information on individuals was based on legitimate concerns, and how often it was based on hearsay and/or accusations from unreliable sources, such as vengeful ex-spouses, disgruntled former business partners, or political enemies. Neither is it known how many on the lists were U.S. citizens, and how many were aliens. All that is known is that the FBI took all accusations seriously, that its lists grew and grew with each accusation, and that the FBI itself admitted that in 1939 alone it had received some 78,000 such accusations,[61] all of which were followed up by interviews with employers, family, friends and neighbors. Most disconcerting of all, once a person's name appeared on a card comprising the CDI, no matter what the source or the reasons, nothing could get it expunged save the death of the individual listed.

Perhaps having some sense that his investigations and growing lists might need somewhat firmer support, and knowing that his intelligence gathering was rapidly moving from simple information to preventive action (such as arrest and detention) based on that information, Director Hoover in June 1940 asked his superior in the Justice Department for policy guidance regarding the list of those who might actually be arrested in the event of war. Then-Attorney General Robert Jackson assigned this responsibility to a new unit in the Justice Department headed by Lawrence M.C. Smith. Originally called the Neutrality Laws Unit, it was later known as the Special War Policies Unit or simply the Special Unit. Jackson charged it with reviewing and evaluating the FBI's reports, as well as the names on the Custodial Detention Index. Eventually, this unit would also "initiate such wartime measures as the internment of several thousand enemy aliens, the denaturalization of members of the German-American Bund who had become American citizens, sedition prosecutions, exclusion of publications from the mails, and prosecution of foreign propaganda agents."[62] Though this was rather more than Director Hoover had asked for, and led him to complain that sharing his sensitive information might compromise the secrecy and confidentiality of both his lists and his informants, he had no choice but to go along for a time, and agreed to turn over his secret "dossiers" to the Special Unit for oversight (though it took him until April of 1941 to do so).[63]

For its part, the Special Unit decided on procedures for what it anticipated might be numerous arrests, insisting as well that arrests of alien enemies could proceed only on the basis of warrants issued by the Attorney General, and carried out by the FBI (though as it turned out, the very first arrests on December 8, 1941 were initiated by the FBI *without warrants*, presumably based on its own lists and its own determination of "dangerousness.")[64] The Special Unit also began to create its own list of those thought to be serious security risks, as well as its own classification system. This list, dubbed the ABC list, separated security risks into three categories of dangerousness based on their ethnic affiliations. The most dangerous, Category A, were persons thought to have the greatest commitment to their nation of birth by reason of their being leaders of ethnic organizations, be they cultural, social or political. Those in Category B simply belonged to those organizations, while Category C people were known to support those now-suspect organizations in some way.[65]

As Attorney General Francis Biddle later admitted, the problem with such lists was twofold: if commitment to the country of one's birth becomes the criterion for placing someone on a suspect list, then how would the government distinguish between normal ethnic affection for one's birthplace, and disloyalty?[66] A related and no less important question was how, in a democracy, does one justify locking up a person based not on an action he has committed but on the mere suspicion that he might at some future date do something—especially given the fact that large numbers of people on the list were not aliens at all, but American citizens? Writer Jerre Mangione referred to precisely this dilemma when, years later, he wrote about his government-mandated inspection tour of the WWII camps in which alien enemies had been interned: "The war had thrust us into the shameful position of locking up people for their beliefs."[67]

All such questions would come back to haunt those who implemented the policies stemming from the FBI's Custodial Detention Index. Indeed, even before the outbreak of war and the implementation of such policies, the Justice Department demonstrated that it was keenly aware of the potential for problems. In late 1941, for example, the Attorney General indicated his sensitivity to the irony of classifying people as "enemy aliens" in a country which boasted of its commitment to immigration, when he pointedly referred to them as "American aliens." Shortly thereafter, Earl Harrison, newly appointed Commissioner of the Immigration and Naturalization Service, went even further when he wrote:

> The 'American Alien,' for much the greater part, is neither a refugee, nor, at any time, an enemy alien. He is, in reality, an immigrant—a product of American history." [68]

Harrison was pointing to the fact that calling someone an "enemy alien" was to put him in the category of a visitor, a diplomat, an infiltrator or a spy—someone who, by reason of his temporary or illicit presence inside enemy borders, can act on behalf of his homeland from within. The 'American alien,' by contrast, had, as an immigrant, abandoned his homeland to become a permanent resident of a new nation (the term "permanent resident alien" acknowledges this fact and the commitment it represented.) In other words, to brand and then treat immigrants—those who had chosen America as their adopted country—in the same way that nations at war have always treated the enemies actually attacking them from within (i.e., via espionage or sabotage), was to ignore America's history. It was to ignore the fact that thousands of those who were thus branded had lived upright lives in established communities for as many as fifty years; and that most now being labeled 'enemies' had numerous American-born children, some of whom were already serving in the Armed Forces of the country their parents had freely chosen.[69]

This was no idle debate. As the lawyers in the Justice Department well knew, the legal justification for America's power to violate, in time of war, the constitutional protections afforded the American alien's person and property rested with the 1798 Alien and Sedition Acts, and with the legal decision of the Supreme Court in Brown v. United States rendered in 1814. In that 1814 case, Chief Justice Marshall had said:

> Respecting the power of Government no doubt is entertained. That war gives to the sovereign the full right to take the person and confiscate the property of the enemy wherever found, is conceded....[70]

The emphasis here is clearly on the word "enemy," with all it implies about those who are attacking a nation with arms from without, or espionage/sabotage from within. To apply it to an entire group of immigrants who have chosen to live permanently in that nation, with children born in that nation, many of whom were already in uniform defending that nation, is to make precisely the error which Earl Harrison had addressed: ignoring American history and the fundamental place in that history of immigration itself. Nonetheless, in World War I and again in World War II, the United States government took the position that any immigrant with roots in an enemy nation who had failed to complete the citizenship process was henceforth an 'alien enemy' of the United States, and was subject to whatever the governmental authorities chose to do to him, including the confiscation of his person and property. About this, as Justice Marshall had written, "no doubt was entertained." As the Immigration and Naturalization Service, apparently forgetting Earl Harrison's early sentiments about "American aliens," put it shortly afterward,

> ..the declaration of war effects a great transformation in the status of aliens who are
> designated as alien enemies. These individuals then technically lose all their consti-
> tutional rights and privileges, and find that "what others do confidently and of right,
> they do by sufferance and doubtfully, uncertain of the restrictions of tomorrow."[71]

Ezio Pinza, the great Italian-born opera star who was arrested as an enemy alien in
March of 1942, learned from his lawyers exactly this. As he put it in his autobiography
years later:

> To understand the full gravity of my situation, you must bear in mind that the Bill of
> Rights, not always applicable to U.S. citizens in time of war, is nonexistent so far as an
> enemy alien is concerned. In being summoned to a hearing, he is presumed guilty until
> he can prove his innocence...[72]

In the days and months to come, more than one million permanent resident aliens
in the United States would learn the same lesson: with war, their rights as Americans had
vanished, had in fact been reversed. If they ran afoul of the FBI or other authorities (and
many on the CDI, unbeknownst to them, already had), they would be *presumed guilty*
unless and until they could prove their innocence.

Rights vs. Security

Indeed, well before war had been declared, the mounting concern over the "aliens"
in America's midst coalesced in yet another act of Congress, the 1940 Alien Registration Act, commonly known as the Smith Act after its author, Representative Howard
Smith of Virginia. This act, signed into law on June 28, 1940, was initiated when Senator Harry Byrd (also of Virginia) suggested that all aliens in the United States should
be photographed and fingerprinted.[73] At about the same time, states like Georgia began
demanding registration of their aliens, while the LaFollette Civil Liberties Bill included
an amendment from Senator Reynolds of North Carolina imposing fines and possible
imprisonment on employers who gave more than one job in ten to aliens.[74] President
Roosevelt's move in the Spring of 1940 to transfer the Immigration and Naturalization
Service (INS) from the Department of Labor to the Department of Justice also signaled
a new era of toughness toward immigrants. With passage of the Alien Registration Act,
the new policy of suspicion towards foreigners took definite shape. Not only did the
Act require all adult non-citizens to register (answering 42 specific questions about their
lives, children and birthplaces), be fingerprinted and carry a card, it also contained harsh

new regulations to control sedition, or speech. The act made it a criminal offense for anyone to

> ...knowingly or willfully advocate, abet, advise or teach the duty, necessity, desirability or propriety of overthrowing the Government of the United States or of any State by force or violence, or for anyone to organize any association which teaches, advises or encourages such an overthrow, or for anyone to become a member of or to affiliate with any such association.[75]

Alien Registration Card required by the Smith Act of 1940

This meant, to many, a throwback to the World War I era, when thousands of German aliens were arrested and jailed not for plotting the government's overthrow, but for simply speaking or being overheard to speak negatively about the U.S. government, or its entry into the war. The problem with such regulations, as then-Attorney General Robert Jackson and his successor, Francis Biddle, knew, was their conflict with the bedrock First Amendment right to free speech, which gave all Americans the constitutional right to criticize their government or its leaders. As Biddle later wrote,

> History showed that sedition statutes—laws addressed to what men said—invariably had been used to prevent and punish criticism of the government, particularly in time of war. I believed them to be unnecessary and harmful.[76]

Accordingly, Biddle (then Solicitor General) and Attorney General Jackson prepared a statement, to be issued by the President, explaining that the new law "was designed to protect the country and the loyal aliens who were its guests; no stigma was carried with the requirement of registration, most aliens were loyal, and were entitled to receive full protection of the law, without harassment."[77] It would not be the last time the President had to reassure the enemy aliens and warn the nation (and his own agencies) that no stigma attached to alien status.[78]

Neither would it be the last time the Smith Act came into prominence, for its prohibition on seditious speech applied not just to aliens, but to "all persons." Accordingly, the first persons considered for custodial detention immediately after Pearl Harbor included not just enemy aliens but a surprising number of American citizens. J. Edgar Hoover's December 1941 memo[79] to Major Lemuel Schofield of the INS about such people and their possible arrest gave these figures as:

German aliens	636
American citizens sympathetic to Germany	1,393
Persons of German descent whose citizenship is unknown	1,694
Italian aliens	77
American citizens sympathetic to Italy	49
Persons of Italian descent whose citizenship is unknown	211
TOTAL	4,060

The question was, under what statutory authority would, or could such arrests be made? The Justice Department's Special Unit had clearly anticipated this problem, and noted that a special committee would decide whether American citizens "not subject to internment" might be prosecuted under the Smith Act of 1940 or "some other appropriate statute."[80] But the fact that in February 1942 the President felt the need to issue Executive Order 9066 providing specific authority for American citizens of Japanese descent to be relocated to internment camps indicates that the problem was far from resolved. In this regard, it might be useful at this point to review the sequence of events, each a small step, that led to the Custodial Detention Index and its inevitable result, the arrest during World War II of more than 60,000 Americans and the detention and/or internment of thousands (not counting the 120,000 persons of Japanese descent, two-thirds of them American-born, who were forced into 'relocation' camps).

1) the FBI director and the President meet in August of 1936, with the President agreeing that the probability of war makes it desirable that information be gathered regarding possible spies, saboteurs, or propagandists working on behalf of foreign governments.

2) the FBI director begins large-scale spying on Americans, particularly those he classifies as Communists, Nazis, Fascists, and "subversives," though, absent any crime, there is no specific statutory authority for such domestic spying. The United States Congress is kept in the dark about such spying and the lists stemming from it to forestall troublesome questions about its legality.

3) in September 1939, with the outbreak of war in Europe, the President goes public with his instructions that all information regarding national security be consolidated in the FBI. He also declares a national emergency regarding the nation's determination to maintain its neutrality, aid its allies, and protect its defense capabilities.

4) now (September 1939) considering the nation to be on a war footing, the FBI ramps up its collection of information on what it considers potential "subversives."

5) in June 1940 Congress passes the Alien Registration Act (aka the Smith Act), requiring all aliens to register, and, perhaps more significantly, making it a crime for any American to say or write anything that can be construed as advocating the overthrow of government, or associate with anyone who does.

6) in June 1940 the FBI Director labels his growing list the Custodial Detention Index (CDI), and seeks guidance from his boss, the Attorney General, for what now appears likely: that many on his CDI will be taken into custody (arrested and detained).

7) in response, the Attorney General establishes an entire unit in the Justice Department to review the lists, decide on prosecutions, establish the need for arrest warrants, and determine how to prosecute those who are American citizens.

In all this, there is *no statute*—that is, no Congressionally-passed legislation signed by the President, save the Smith Act's statute concerning sedition—that specifically authorizes either spying on, arresting, or detaining Americans.

It is for this reason that Francis Biddle, who became Attorney General in September 1941, weighed in twice on this issue. First, on September 25, 1942, he defined the duties of several divisions in his Department of Justice, specifically identifying the FBI's duties as investigating criminal offenses against the United States, and acting only as a "clearing house" for information pertaining to "espionage, sabotage, and other subversive matters" to carry out the president's September 6, 1939 directive.[81] Second, on July 16, 1943 Biddle wrote a memo to Hugh Cox, Assistant Attorney General, and J. Edgar Hoover, Director of the FBI, to be placed in the file of every foreign-born American citizen who had been excluded from military zones during the war; it says:

> There is no statutory authorization or other present justification for keeping a "custodial detention" list of citizens. The Department fulfills its proper function by investigating the activities of persons who may have violated the law. It is not aided in this work by classifying persons as to "dangerousness."[82]

In short, though the director of the FBI (and possibly the President[83]) seemed unperturbed and undeterred by the lack of legal authority for the government's World War II spying activities, or by the pre-emptive action implied by characterizing FBI lists as a

Custodial Detention Index, Justice Department lawyers consistently raised issues regarding the legal and constitutional rights of the Americans—both aliens and citizens—who would be affected by such governmental activities.[84]

War Department Plans

While the Justice Department was aware of and concerned about preserving the vanishing legal rights of Americans in wartime, the War Department was focused on its mission to protect the nation by any means necessary. Therefore, as it had been doing for several years, it began to make preparations to control the home front, even if it had to usurp that control from a Justice Department it saw as inadequate to the task. What resulted was a struggle between these two powerful departments over who would take charge of the people surveilled, arrested, detained, and interned, be they alien enemies, or even American citizens with roots in the enemy nations. The expedients that the War Department was quite ready to consider ranged from the mass internment of whole groups based on nationality or ethnicity, to martial law imposed over entire geographical areas (as occurred in Hawaii), both of which would give the military full authority over all persons whom it might consider dangerous in time of war. In this contest, the military in almost all instances would prove more powerful and more adept at the bureaucratic infighting that was involved, both because of its clearer idea of its mission and the plans to accomplish it, and because its cabinet-level head, Henry Stimson as Secretary of War, was a more seasoned veteran of government than the newly-appointed head of the Justice Department, Attorney General Francis Biddle. Stimson was a virtual icon in Washington, having served at cabinet level in several previous administrations.[85] His and his department's ability to impose their will on the alien enemy program would have serious consequences for those who were unlucky enough to have earned the designation "alien enemy."

Thus, while the Department of Justice worried about not repeating the wholesale arrests and internments that had been imposed on German resident aliens during World War I, especially the resultant vigilantism that German Americans had been subjected to, the War Department had already begun, in 1940, to inquire into its ability to intern not just aliens but American citizens. The man who was to become Provost Marshal General, Major General Allen Gullion, as early as August 1940, drew up a memo asking two questions that would prove to be both vital and prophetic:

a. In the zone of the interior, as differentiated from the theatre of operations under military control, to what extent can the Military legally, actually control through

Provost Marshal Generals, local forces, police or constabulary, any operations against 'Fifth Columnists'?

b. Can the Military in the zone of the interior participate in the arrest and temporary holding of civilians who are not alien enemies but citizens of the United States?[86]

In fact, the creation of the office he was to occupy, Provost Marshal General, on July 3, 1941, totally dedicated to domestic operations relating to prisoners of war and alien enemies, testified not only to the Army's future plans, but also to its distrust of the Justice Department's ability to handle the operation which, by right and precedent, belonged to Justice alone: the control over American civilians. The War Department repeatedly made clear its opinion that the Department of Justice lacked the facilities, the personnel, and the will to handle domestic enemies who might be dangerous. Harold Ickes, Secretary of the Interior, concurred, considering Attorney General Biddle a "dilettante" regarding subversion. Therefore, the War Department began early on to insist that, first, alien enemies be treated not as individuals but en masse, and, second, that the U.S. military be allowed to use its facilities and personnel to contain them.

The initial result of this struggle was a compromise, partly brokered by the State Department, involving a split in responsibilities. To begin with, alien enemies under government control would be treated according to the Geneva Convention, essentially as prisoners of war. Their initial arrests would be undertaken by the FBI, a division of the Justice Department, and their initial custody and the determination of their release, parole or internment would remain within Justice Department rules, jurisdictions and facilities. The Immigration and Naturalization Service (the INS, recently made part of the Justice Department) had, in fact, already set up facilities and procedures for interning enemy nationals: when, in December 1939, the German merchant ship Columbus was scuttled off the American coast, the rescued German seamen were taken into custody and eventually interned as "alien enemies" in former CCC camps taken over by the INS, first at Fort Stanton in New Mexico, then at Fort Lincoln, in Bismarck, North Dakota. Similarly, the Italian crews of several merchant ships caught in American ports shortly after the outbreak of war in Europe were, by April 1941, sent as "alien enemies" to the internment camp at Fort Missoula, Montana (they, too, had sabotaged their ships to prevent their use by the American navy). All three camps, Stanton, Lincoln and Missoula, were under INS control and manned by members of the Border Patrol, with Willard Kelly as its head.

The Army was content with this arrangement, i.e. allowing those who were arrested to be detained by the INS to begin with. It insisted, however, that once a formal order of internment had been issued by the Attorney General, all male resident aliens had to be turned over to the tougher custody of the War Department. In this, the War Department won its point that it, not the Justice Department, had the facilities and the know-how to handle "dangerous" civilians. Thus, the Aliens' Division of the Provost Marshal General's Office (the PMGO), with Major Karl Bendetsen at its head, within the War Department, and the Immigration and Naturalization Service (INS) within the Department of Justice, were to supply locations and staff for the two phases: first, arrest and initial detention by the INS; and then formal internment by the PMGO in Army-run facilities (usually sections of existing army bases). For women, the INS would maintain control of both temporary detention and internment, mostly at its facility in Seagoville, Texas. The INS alone would also run the camps for families—Crystal City and Camp Kenedy, both in Texas—which also held a number of internees from Latin America.[87] A Joint Committee made up of members from each department was to coordinate all operations.

All this seemed logical enough in theory. In practice, however, the chaos of war and the enormous number of those, both enemy aliens and American citizens, picked up in the first weeks after Pearl Harbor, threw many of these preparations into disarray. Much of what happened might have been avoided if less suspicion between the two contending departments, War and Justice, had prevailed. But no one knew at the outset either how confusing the initial arrests would prove, nor how the burgeoning number of arrests would tax the facilities that had been prepared for them. Neither did the military anticipate the enormous job it would face in "relocating" the entire Japanese American population of the West Coast, nor the large numbers of enemy prisoners of war (POWs) that would be transferred from the European theatre to the United States for incarceration, nor the extent to which these additional charges would stretch its personnel and the facilities to care for them. Finally, no one seems to have anticipated the wave of anti-Axis feeling that would be unleashed with the Japanese bombing of Pearl Harbor, a public antagonism that was first ignited by public officials such as General John DeWitt of the Western Defense Command, and then fanned into flames by local pressure groups calling for entire populations to be locked up. The result was a far greater number of arrests—60,000 persons of enemy nationality were rounded up for questioning by the Department of Justice, as many as 120,000 Japanese Americans were interned, and over 50,000 Italian POWs were kept in U.S. confinement—than either department had anticipated, and the related confusion and unnecessary hardship that prevailed for those rounded up.

1. Charles Guzzetta, "Mazzei in America," in *Dream Streets: The Big Book of Italian American Culture,* ed. Lawrence DiStasi, (New York, NY: Harper & Row, 1989), p. 13. (Paperback reprint as *The Big Book of Italian American Culture*, (Berkeley, CA: Sanniti Publications, 1996).

2. See, among others, the Nostra Storia exhibit sponsored by the Italian Cultural Society of Sacramento, http://italiancenter.net/goldcountry/.

3. See, among others, Jane Schneider, ed., *Italy's Southern Question: Orientalism in One Country,* (Oxford: Berg Publishing, 1998); and Pino Aprile, *Terroni: Tutto quello che é stato fatto perche gli italiani del sud diventassero meridionali,* (Milan: Piemme, 2010).

4. Stephanie Bernardo, *The Ethnic Almanac,* (Garden City, NY: Doubleday, 1981), p. 29. Census figures (Statistical Abstract of the United States) for Italians in America as of 1930 indicate a population of some 1,781,000. http://www2.census.gov/prod2/statcomp/documents/1941-02.pdf, p. 34.

5. John Higham, *Strangers in the Land: Patterns of American Nativism,* (New York: Atheneum, 1963), cited in John Diggins, *Mussolini and Fascism: The View From America,* (Princeton NJ: 1972) 12.

6. Ibid.

7. The 1907 Nationality Act, also called the Expatriation Act, said in part: "[A]ny American who married a foreigner shall take the nationality of her husband." By means of this act, countless American-born women were penalized for marrying foreigners by being stripped of their American citizenship. It was not until 1922 that the Expatriation Act was repealed by the Cable Act, which ended "derivative citizenship" for women. See Lawrence DiStasi, "Derived Aliens: Derivative Citizenship and Italian American Women during World War II," *Italian Americana*, Winter: 2010.

8. Richard Gambino, *Blood of My Blood: The Dilemma of the Italian Americans,* (Garden City, NY: Anchor Books, 1974) 118. See also Patrizia Salvetti, *Corde e Sapone: Storie di linciaggi degli italiani negli Stati Uniti,* Roma: Donzelli Editore, 2003. Salvetti counts no less than 39 Italians lynched in the United States, including five more Sicilians in Tallulah, LA in 1899.

9. Tom Smith, *The Crescent City Lynchings,* (Guilford CT: Lyons Press, 2007), 246.

10. Diggins, op cit, p. 78.

11. Bernardo, op cit, p. 29.

12. See especially Jennifer Guglielmo, *Living the Revolution: Italian Women's Resistance and Radicalism in New York City, 1880-1945,* (Chapel Hill: U of North Carolina Press, 2010).

13. See website: http://dwardmac/pitzer.edu/Anarchist_Archives/malatesta/malatestabio.html.

14. According to historian Paul Avrich, J. Edgar Hoover, who, during World War II, would arrest many enemy aliens suspected of being pro-fascist, in 1924, "assisted the Fascist Police, supplying reports about (Luigi) Galleani and the anarchists." Paul Avrich, *Sacco & Vanzetti: The Anarchist Background* (Princeton, NJ: Princeton U Press, 1991), 445.

15. In fact, of course, propaganda was probably invented in the United States in the runup to World War I, when President Woodrow Wilson had to combat the widespread resistance to American involvement in the European conflict. In 1917, a week after he declared war, Wilson

created the Committee for Public Information, or CPI, commonly known as the Creel Commission after its head, George Creel. According to Chris Hedges in *Death of the Liberal Class* (Nation Books: 2010), the Creel Commission "would become the first modern mass propaganda machine," its goal not "simply to impart pro-war messages but to discredit those who attempted to challenge the nation's involvement in the conflict" (p. 69).

16. Guglielmo, op. cit., notes that the term fascio was used by socialists in Sicily in 1892, when, after an uprising, women in Piana dei Greci formed a "fascio delle lavoratrici (union of workers) to denote "a solidarity of peasants, miners, or artisans" (p. 10). Such fasci spread throughout Sicily in subsequent years.

17. As one example, Kenneth Roberts, in his novel *Black Magic,* says that Mussolini's dictatorship was not only a "national necessity," but that his brutal methods are "what Italy deserved and must continue to have before she can climb from the hole in which she deliberately sank herself." cited in Diggins, 18.

18. Diggins, 37.

19. Luigi Barzini, *The Italians*. Barzini as a young man also had a hand in Mussolini's autobiography: as he related it to John Diggins, "as a boy I collaborated with Richard Washburn Child (American ambassador to Rome) in 'writing' Mussolini's 'autobiography'...I did the translation." (quoted in Diggins, op. cit, p. 28, note 9).

20. Franklin Roosevelt to John Lawrence, July 27, 1933, cited in Diggins, 279.

21. see Diggins, 276ff.

22. Irving Babbitt, *Democracy and Leadership* (Boston, 1924), 313.

23. Diggins, op cit, 21.

24. Gaetano Salvemini's *Italian Fascist Activities in the United States*, (New York: Center for Migration Studies, 1977), cites, with Salvemini's characteristic passion and thoroughness, the numerous activities engaged in by what he terms these "fascist transmission belts" throughout the United States.

25. Diggins, 91.

26. Diggins, 183. Diggins devotes an entire chapter to Mussolini's reception by the American church, including the adoration by Father Coughlin, the pro-Fascist, anti-semitic radio priest of Detroit. Like many others on the right, the church considered that Mussolini's "triumph" over pagan communism and liberalism covered many of his other sins.

27. Max Ascoli, "On the Italian Americans," February 4, 1942, RG 208, NARA II, (cited in Guido Tintori, "New Discoveries, Old Prejudices," in *Una Storia Segreta: The Secret History of Italian American Evacuation and Internment During World War II*, ed. Lawrence DiStasi, (Berkeley: Heyday Books, 2001), 247-48.

28. Francis Biddle, *In Brief Authority*, (New York: Doubleday, 1962), 207.

29. Diggins, 116, refers to the Italian population in America in 1930 as 4,600,000; again, on p. 342, Generoso Pope, publisher of *Il Progresso of New York*, refers to the 6 million Italians and 4 million Jews in the United States ("For a Better Understanding," *Il Progresso*, Dec. 25, 1938.)

30. Stephen R. Fox, *The Unknown Internment: An Oral History of the Relocation of Italian Americans during World War II* (Boston: Twayne Publishers, 1990), 4.

31. Ibid.

32. *Personal Justice Denied: Report of the Commission on Wartime Relocation and Internment of Civilians,* notes that "A total of 4,921,452 aliens registered." p. 372, note 66, from Donald R. Perry, "Aliens in the United States," Annals of the American Academy of Political and Social Science, vol. 223 (Sept 1942), 1-9.

33. This estimate is based on Francis Biddle's comment in his Columbus Day 1942 speech

that Italian Americans fought in the Armed Forces at a rate of "five hundred on the average in every division." This amounts to .033% (a division averaging 15,000 men), and when that number is applied to the 16,000,000 Americans under arms, the number of Italian Americans who served comes to approximately 528,000. See Biddle, *In Brief Authority,* 230, and the figures on http://www.historyshots.com/usarmy/backstory.cfm,

34. Marcus Duffield, "Mussolini's American Empire: The Fascist Invasion of the United States," *Harper's Magazine*, November 1929.

35. Fox, 33.

36. Ibid.

37. Fox, 34.

38. Fox, 35.

39. Fox, 37.

40. Fox, 35.

41. Bradley Smith, *The Shadow Warriors: The OSS and the Origins of the CIA*, (New York, Basic Books: 1983), 12, 15, 21, 23.

42. Fox, 38.

43. Regarding these memos, Curt Gentry in *J.Edgar Hoover: the Man and His Secrets,* (New York NY: W.W. Norton, 1991), calls what Hoover did a coup d'etat: "J. Edgar Hoover had managed to stage his own coup d'etat, by memorandum." 210.

44. Gentry devotes the chapter, "Coup d'Etat," to this story.

45. Ralph deToledano, *J. Edgar Hoover: The Man in His Time* (New Rochelle, NY: Arlington House, 1973) 40.

46. Gentry, 208.

47. *Supplementary Detailed Staff Reports on Intelligence Activities and the Rights of Americans. Book III. Final Report of the Select Committee to Study Governmental Operations with Respect to Intelligence Activities,* U.S. Senate. April 23, 1976. "The Development of FBI Intelligence Investigations." Hereafter cited as "Church report". See http://www.icdc.com/~paulwolf/cointelpro/churchfinalreportIII.htm.

48. Church report, Section E. Congress and FBI Intelligence.

49. Dellagatta file, RG 389, Entry 4661—Records Relating to Italian Civilian Internees During WWII, Box 10, NARA II.

50. U.S. Senate, Select Committee to Study Governmental Operations with Respect to Intelligence Activities, Hearings on Intelligence Activities, 94th Cong., 1st sess., 1975, vol 6, FBI, 562.

51. Arnold Krammer, *Undue Process: The Untold Story of America's German Alien Internees,* (New York: Rowman & Littlefied, 1997) 2.

52. Bradley Smith, 23.

53. New York Times, "Alien Internment is Voted by House," May 6, 1939, p. 8.

54. Church report, Section D: FBI Intelligence Authority and "Subversion."

55. Ibid.

56. Church Report, Section F: The Scope of FBI Domestic Intelligence.

57. Ibid.

58. Ibid.

59. Church Report, Section F, op cit.

60. Ibid.

61. Krammer, op. cit., 11.

62. Church Report, Section G, The Custodial Detention Program.

63. Athan Theoharis, *Spying on Americans: Political Surveillance from Hoover to the Huston Plan,* (Philadelphia: Temple Univ. Press, 1978), 42.

64. Francis Biddle, In Brief Authority, (New York: Doubleday, 1962), 206.

65. Fox, op. cit., 152. The ABC classification was probably based on a similar classification employed by the British to classify their alien enemies.

66. Assistant Attorney General James Rowe believed that lack of citizenship literally meant retention of devotion to the fatherland—never considering that being illiterate, and/or being busy supporting a family might also be a factor.

67. Jerre Mangione, *An Ethnic at Large: Memoirs of America in the Thirties and Forties* (New York: Putnam, 1978), 352.

68. Earl Harrison, "Axis Aliens in an Emergency," Survey Graphic, Sept. 1941, 467-68.

69. The number of Italian Americans serving in the U.S. Armed Forces during World War II has been variously estimated at from 500,000 to 1.5 million.

70. Quoted in INS training Lecture, "Aliens of Enemy Nationality," by Thomas D. McDermott, 1943.

71. Ibid, 5. Quote from Techt v Hughes, 229 U.S. 222 (1920).

72. Ezio Pinza (with Robert Magidoff), *Ezio Pinza: An Autobiography,* (New York: 1958), pp 211-12.

73. Biddle, op. cit, 107.

74. Ibid. It should be noted, in passing, that the "aliens" mentioned in these acts are not illegal, but rather are legal immigrants who have not yet become American citizens.

75. http://en.wikipedia.org/wiki/Smith_Act

76. Biddle, op cit, 151.

77. Biddle, op cit, 110.

78. On January 2, 1942, the President issued a statement voicing his concern over discrimination against enemy aliens: "I am deeply concerned over the increasing number of reports of employers discharging workers who happen to be aliens or even foreign-born citizens..." cited in Report to the Congress of the United States: A Review of the Restrictions on Persons of Italian Ancestry During World War II, (Dept of Justice: Nov. 2001), 39.

79. J. Edgar Hoover to Major Lemuel B. Schofield, Immigration and Naturalization Service, "On Various Individuals Being Considered for Custodial Detention," 8 Dec. 1941, doc. 14, cited in Krammer, 31-32.

80. Church Report, Section G. The Custodial Detention Program. (also cited in Theoharis, op cit, 42)

81. Francis Biddle, Attorney General's Order No. 3732, 9/25/42, cited in Church Report, Section D. FBI Intelligence Authority and "Subversion."

82. File of Nino Guttadauro, excludee, FBI file # 100-15901.

83. However, as Athan Theoharis exhaustively proves, President Roosevelt's Sept. 6, 1939 directive did NOT authorize the FBI to investigate "subversive activity." FDR actually issued a statement in January 1943 clarifying this, conspicuously leaving out any mention of "subversive" activity. He said: "On September 6, 1939, I issued a directive providing that the Federal Bureau of Investigation of the Department of Justice should take charge of investigative work in matters relating to espionage, sabotage, and violations of the neutrality regulations....I am again calling the attention of all enforcement officers to the request that they report all such information promptly to the nearest field representative of the Federal Bureau of Investigation, which is charged with the responsibility of correlating this material..." Theoharis, op cit, 75. Theoharis also cites the repeated instances where Hoover referred back to this Sept. 6, 1939 non-authori-

zation as each new president came into office, until, with no one bothering to check, it became accepted dogma that it provided authorization for spying. Furthermore, Theoharis points out, in 1973, recognizing that the Sept. 6, 1939 presidential directive "did not convey any authority or jurisdiction" to the FBI beyond its clearing-house responsibility for espionage, sabotage and neutrality matters, then-FBI Director Clarence Kelley asked for "an up-to-date Executive Order" that would clearly establish "a need for intelligence-type investigations, (and) delineating clear authority for the FBI to conduct such investigations." (see Chapter 3: "Authorizing Political Surveillance," in Athan Theoharis, *Spying on Americans*).

84. Though Attorney General Biddle called for an end to the Custodial Detention Index, FBI director Hoover cannot be said to have complied. He simply changed its name to the Security Index and continued adding names to its rolls. We know this because of the recently released FBI file of radical historian Howard Zinn. As Chris Hedges noted in *Death of the Liberal Class*.op. cit., Zinn's file contains several entries that refer to the updated CDI. On Jan. 10, 1964, Director Hoover sent a memo to SAC Boston concerning Zinn, indicating that Zinn's name was being "included in Reserve Index, Section A." Another memo in Zinn's file, on May 18, 1964, explained in the Observation section the difference between the Reserve Index and the Security Index from which Zinn's name had been deleted in July 1955 "because of absence of evidence of CP [Communist Party] membership within the past five years..." The memo further explains that "the Reserve Index represents a special group of individuals scheduled to receive priority attention with respect to investigation, interrogation, or detention under the terms of the Emergency Detention Program following invoking of the Program and arrest of all Security Index subjects." In other words, those on the Security Index would be arrested immediately in an emergency, while those on the Reserve Index would be subjected to "priority attention" and then possibly detention. For all practical purposes, in short, Howard Zinn was on the updated Custodial Detention Index, which had persisted through the 1960s, and may still persist to the present day. (Zinn files at https://archive.org/details/Howard.Zinn_FBI.file_pt.1, accessed May 25, 2014).

85. Indeed, Francis Biddle himself notes in his autobiography (op cit, 184) that of all FDR's cabinet members, he most admired Secretary of War Henry Stimson.

86. See Guido Tintori, "The Internment of Italian Americans During World War II," in *Una Storia Segreta*, op. cit.

87. Facilities. INS: Fort Missoula, MT; Fort Lincoln, ND; Fort Stanton, NM; Crystal City, TX; Camp Kennedy, TX; Seagoville, TX; Ellis Island, NY; Gloucester City, NY; E. Boston, MA; Sharp Park, CA (SEE PHOTO), Tujunga Canyon, CA; numerous local police stations. PMGO: Camp Upton, NY; Fort Meade, MD; Fort McAlester, OK; Camp Forrest, TN; Fort Sam Houston, TX; Camp McCoy, WI; Fort McDowell, CA (Angel Island). See INS Administrative History of the Immigration and Naturalization Service during World War II, Prepared by the General Research Unit, Hugh Carter, Supervisor, August 19, 1946.)

II: WAR AND RESTRICTIONS

On December 7, 1941, Japanese forces attacked the United States Naval Base at Pearl Harbor in Hawaii with fighter planes that had taken off from a nearby Japanese fleet. The attack and the news of this "day of infamy," as President Roosevelt characterized it, not only set in motion the full involvement of the United States in a war against the Axis powers of Japan, German and Italy, but also inaugurated a series of events on the American home front that would deeply affect more than a million Americans with roots in those now enemy nations. Among them were the 694,000 Italian resident aliens who had recently registered to comply with the Alien Registration Act of 1940, and their families.

Events moved swiftly. Though war with Italy would not be formally declared until December 11, the President, on December 8, 1941, issued Proclamation 2527 declaring that some 600,000 Italian immigrants who had not yet become American citizens—referred to in the Proclamation as "natives, citizens, subjects, and denizens of Italy"—were now "alien enemies" and hence subject to various "regulations which are found necessary in the premises and for the public safety." To begin with, the proclamation contained several sections outlining the "Conduct to be Observed by Alien Enemies," to wit:

> All alien enemies are enjoined to preserve the peace towards the United States and to
> refrain from crime against the public safety, and from violating the laws of the United
> States...and to refrain from actual hostility or giving information, aid or comfort to
> the enemies of the United States or interfering by word or deed with the defense of
> the United States or the political processes and public opinion thereof; and to comply

strictly with the regulations which are hereby or which may be from time to time promulgated by the President.[1]

The proclamation designated the Attorney General as the authority charged "with the duty of executing all the regulations hereinafter prescribed regarding the conduct of alien enemies within the continental United States, Puerto Rico, the Virgin Islands and Alaska," and the Secretary of War with the same duty for the Panama Canal Zone, the Hawaiian Islands, and the Philippine Islands. The Proclamation then noted that the regulations in Proclamation 2525 of December 7, issued for Japanese alien enemies, "are hereby incorporated in and made part of this proclamation," meaning that Italian alien enemies would have to abide by the same regulations as the Japanese.

After specifying areas such as the Canal Zone, the Hawaiian Islands, Alaska and elsewhere that might be prohibited to alien enemies, the regulations in Proclamation 2525 had detailed thirteen paragraphs of restrictions on alien enemy possessions and/or activities, the most relevant of which are cited below:

> (5) No alien enemy shall have in his possession, custody or control at any time or place or use or operate any of the following enumerated articles:
>> a. Firearms.
>> b. Weapons or implements of war or component parts thereof.
>> c. Ammunition.
>> d. Bombs.
>> e. Explosives or material used in the manufacture of explosives.
>> f. Short-wave radio receiving sets.
>> g. Transmitting sets.
>> h. Signal devices.
>> i. Codes or ciphers.
>> j. Cameras.
>> k. Papers, documents or books in which there may be invisible writing; photograph, sketch, picture, drawing, map or graphical representation of any military or naval installations or equipment or of any arms, ammunition, implements of war, device or thing used or intended to be used in the combat equipment of the land or naval forces of the United States or of any naval post, camp or station.
>
> All such property found in the possession of any alien enemy in violation of the forgoing regulations shall be subject to seizure and forfeiture.
>
> (6) No alien enemy shall undertake any air flight or ascend into the air in any airplane, aircraft or balloon of any sort, whether owned governmentally, commercially or privately, except that travel by an alien enemy in an airplane or aircraft may be authorized by the Attorney General...or the Secretary of War...

(7) Alien enemies deemed dangerous to the public peace or safety of the United States by the Attorney General or the Secretary of War, as the case may be, are subject to summary apprehension...Alien enemies shall be subject to confinement in such place of detention as may be directed by the officers responsible for the execution of these regulations...and there confined until he shall have received such permit as the Attorney General or the Secretary of War...shall prescribe.

(10) With respect to the continental United States, Alaska, Puerto Rico, and the Virgin Islands, an alien enemy shall not change his place of abode or occupation or otherwise travel or move from place to place without full compliance with any regulations as the Attorney General of the United States may, from time to time, make and declare...

(12) No alien enemy shall enter or be found in or upon any highway, waterway, airway, railway, railroad, subway, public utility, building, place or thing not open and accessible to the public generally, and not generally used by the public.

(13) No alien enemy shall be a member or an officer of, or affiliated with, any organization, group or assembly hereafter designated by the Attorney General, nor shall any alien enemy advocate, defend or subscribe to the acts, principles, or policies thereof, attend any meetings, conventions or gatherings thereof or possess or distribute any literature, propaganda or other writings or productions thereof.[2]

These proclamations took their authority from the Alien Enemy Act of 1798, granting the President of the United States broad powers to deal with enemy aliens during wartime. The Act had previously been employed by President James Madison to remove aliens from coastal areas during the War of 1812, and again by President Woodrow Wilson to intern some 4,000 German immigrants designated enemy aliens during World War I.[3] It had also been employed, via its sedition statute, against the political enemies of President John Adams (2d U.S. president, 1797 to 1801). As Attorney General Francis Biddle noted in warning about sedition statutes:

> ...critics of the administration of John Adams, particularly newspaper editors, were sent to jail, sometimes for merely jeering at the President; and one outspoken Republican was fined for expressing a hope that the wad from the cannon to be fired in a presidential salute might hit President Adams on the seat of his pants![4]

Notwithstanding this warning, the basic restrictions on enemy aliens were published in newspapers nationwide. For example, the December 10, 1941 *San Francisco Examiner*, in addition to reporting the arrests of enemy aliens by the FBI, in a paragraph on "Wartime Steps" noted that

> the Department of Justice clamped wartime restrictions on 1,100,000 persons of enemy alien—meaning German and Italian, as well as Japanese—citizenship. These re-

strictions forbid possession of firearms, explosives, short wave radio sending or receiving sets, cameras, or any other device or thing of possible military importance. They are forbidden to enter any area or place of "military importance," or any place not open to the general public.[5]

On December 11, the *San Francisco Chronicle* announced in a column headlined, "2303 Aliens Seized Since Last Sunday," that "the United Press reported the Justice Department suspended for the duration citizenship applications filed by German and Italian nationals."[6] Anyone who had not completed the citizenship process by then was consigned to enemy alien limbo. Perhaps as a counter to the increasing animosity towards enemy aliens being stimulated by all this publicity, including a December 12 *San Francisco Examiner* article noting the closure of three Italian language schools in San Francisco accused of teaching "obedience to Il Duce," the December 15 *San Francisco Chronicle* carried a photo of Tony Barbagelata of the Scavengers' Protective Association pointing to a sign that read: "Italian Blood is in Some of our Veins, BUT AMERICA IS IN OUR HEARTS. WE HAVE ENLISTED FOR THE DURATION. GOD BLESS AMERICA." Identifying Barbagelata as "100 percent American," meaning, apparently, that he was a U.S. citizen, the caption reported that Tony had volunteered his truck and services to "distribute anti-incendiary bomb sand throughout the city."[7]

Still, the alarm bells about these presumptive enemies kept ringing. On December 28, a column in the *San Francisco Chronicle* headlined "Aliens Must Surrender Their Radios," described a crackdown on so-called contraband by "counter-espionage forces" in seven Western states. In an order that came from Attorney General Francis Biddle, all alien Japanese, Italians and Germans were ordered to turn in to local police "short wave radio equipment and cameras" by 11 AM the next morning. The article noted that failure to surrender such articles would result in "their seizure, and internment of the alien in an Army concentration camp for the duration of hostilities."[8] The Italian press added to the alarm with, in the December 29 issue of *L'Italia*, the San Francisco Italian daily, an article about the previous day's order by the Attorney General regarding "*le machine fotografiche ed i radios degli emigrati*" (the cameras and radios of immigrants). Dating the order 27 December 1941, it said the new order extended from the presidential proclamations of December 8 concerning enemy aliens (*stranieri nemici*). It reported that all foreign-born German, Italian and Japanese residents of California, Oregon, Washington, Montana, Idaho, Utah and Nevada were obligated to turn in to police authorities, by 11 PM Monday, December 29, all radio transmitting and receiving equipment with short wave, and all photographic equipment and cameras. The penalty for failure to turn in such articles would be confiscation of the articles and arrest or detention of the enemy alien.[9]

To add to the confusion, a December 29 *San Francisco Chronicle* article featured a photograph of the insides of a short-wave radio set with a police Lieutenant and two Japanese men hunched over it, and a report saying that though many aliens had showed up to turn in their contraband items, only a few were able to leave them because "police refused to accept them, saying they had 'no orders.'" The photo showed the one station where Lieutenant Dan Collins *was* accepting contraband and issuing receipts for it.[10] By the next day, however, the December 30 *Oakland Tribune* reported that ALIEN CAMERAS, RADIOS, GUNS DELUGE POLICE. Calling it a "veritable mountain," the paper reported that Oakland police "had to call in 10 extra officers last night to meet the rush," with a total of 448 aliens meeting the 11 PM deadline. The rush at one time numbered "more than 100 aliens" lined up at Central Station "waiting to turn in their cameras, radios, and guns." The article also reported that, according to U.S. Attorney Frank Hennessey of San Francisco,

> not only must aliens not possess the equipment, but they must not be kept in a house where aliens reside. That, he pointed out, would prevent many Japanese-Americans from having radio receiving sets with short wave bands because their parents live in the same house.[11]

The same, of course, would apply to U.S. citizens of Italian and German descent, many of whom lived with their non-citizen, now enemy alien, parents.

What was not pointed out in any of the official orders or news reports was the simple fact that almost all good radios at that time were equipped with a short-wave receiving capability. Many Italian families had saved up to buy such a radio—a prized possession around which family members would gather to hear favorite American (and *Americanizing*) programs such as "The Shadow," "Amos 'n Andy," and "Jack Benny," not to mention the famous "fireside chats" of President Roosevelt. No matter, for, as a final warning to underline the importance of depriving families of radios and cameras, the *Oakland Tribune* reported on January 3, 1942 that not only aliens but all American citizens of western states "were advised to avoid taking photographs of any military and industrial operations and structures that are vital to National defense." The Western Defense Command issuing the order listed not only such off-limits facilities as "Army units, headquarters, transports, camps, buildings, installations, and weapons" but also "railway and highway bridges, tunnels, shipping and railroad yards, reservoirs and water systems, and telephone, telegraph and radio installations."[12]

With regard to Proclamation 2525's last item, No. 13 cited above, virtually all Italian American organizations, such as the Sons of Italy, the Dante Alighieri Society, and many others had been put on the proscribed list of possibly disloyal groups. To be a leader of such a group could land one in an internment camp. Even to be a member or contributor to such a group would place one under suspicion, as, indeed, the Department of Justice's list of dangerous persons had made clear. Separated into A, B, and C categories (see Chapter I, Prelude to War), this list specifically made any connection to "ethnic" organizations sufficient cause to suspect or detain or arrest those so connected:

> The most dangerous, Category A, were those thought to have the greatest commitment to their nation of birth by reason of their being *leaders* of ethnic organizations, be they cultural, social or political. Those in Category B simply *belonged* to those organizations, while Category C people were known to *support* those now-suspect organizations in some way.[13]

By early January of 1942, after it had become clear that the surrender-of-contraband orders were being generally complied with, newspapers began focusing on another facet of the restrictions, the ban on travel. The January 3 *Oakland Tribune* reported on its front page that "Aliens Here Can't Travel." The subhead stated that "U.S. Ban Immobilizes Axis Citizens; Even Bay Trips Forbidden."[14] What initially bears notice here is the appellation applied to the aliens—"Axis Citizens." This couples the hatred of the word "Axis" with the residents described as "citizens" of Axis countries, a coupling that completely obscures the fact that most such people were permanent resident aliens, immigrants who had *chosen* to live in the United States, but had not yet completed the citizenship process, now suspended for them. The article then made the point that such presumptive "enemies" had been "immobilized" in their cities of residence, and "could not even cross the Bay to San Francisco legally." This was true. The implication, however, was that every move of such potentially dangerous people had to be watched, and seriously circumscribed. If they had a legitimate reason for traveling, the article noted, they had to "apply seven days in advance to U.S. District Attorneys for permits to travel outside of the limits of the city in which they are located." Scores of aliens, many of them traveling salesmen, were already applying for such permits, said the article, but permits would be issued "only for 'necessary business' trips," in the words of the local U.S. Attorney, Frank Hennessey. The article ended by noting that "Violations will bring a possible 10-year prison term, or a $10,000 fine, or both."

Thousands of these permits to travel must have been issued to accommodate the many kinds of emergencies that demanded a trip. A few examples will suffice here. Mrs. Teresa Bologna, of 123 Pearl Street, Waterbury, CT was a "48-year-old housewife" in

June of 1942 when she applied for a permit to travel. The form she filled out stated that she had been in the United States for "27 years," residing in the same home for "8 years,"

Bologna Travel Permit, courtesy Sando Bologna

and wanted to go to Boston, starting on "June 22, 1942" and returning on "July 1, 1942." The purpose of the trip, she indicated, was "to visit nieces and nephew who are orphans." The address she would be visiting was "3 Baldwin Place, Boston, MA" to which she expected to travel by "train." Accompanying her on the trip would be "Mrs. Sebastiana Lantieri," who also lacked American citizenship. Mrs. Bologna signed the application with her mark, an "X," indicating that she could not write. Her name is filled out by Santo Bologna, presumably her son, later known as Sando. At the bottom of the form, permission is granted for the trip by Robert P. Butler, U.S. Attorney, dated June 15, 1942.[15]

Perhaps the most ironic issuance of permits took place when California enemy aliens were forced to leave prohibited zones (see Chapter 4, Evacuation). Caterina Cardinale, of York St., Pittsburg CA, for example, applied for a travel permit on or about February 17, 1942, the reason being anything but frivolous. She needed it, she certified, to travel to 111 South Main St., in Centerville, CA. This was the address of the home she would rent after she was ordered out of her Pittsburg home (it was within the zone prohibited to enemy aliens)—and to get there, she was required to apply for a travel permit. Though one might have thought that the government order to move would be deemed sufficient justification, in and of itself, for traveling, apparently it was not. Mrs. Cardinale had to have permission from one government agency to do what another government agency had ordered her to do.[16]

One final irony regarding travel. Many of the enemy aliens—Louis Berizzi, Caterina Buccellato, Celestina Loero come to mind—had sons serving in the United States Armed Forces. With the ban on their travel to or near military installations of any kind, no enemy alien could visit a son serving in the United States military. The unfairness of branding "Gold Star Mothers" with this mark of suspicion and possible disloyalty was not lost on those sons risking their lives to defend the country their immigrant parents had adopted as their own.

Nicky Buccellato on leave with his mother in Pittsburg, CA

Re-Registration of Enemy Aliens

All the while that the Special Defense Unit of the Justice Department had been creating its regulations and enforcing them, the War Department under Provost Marshal General Allen Gullion was preparing its own plans to control enemy activity on the home front. The quarrel between these two departments, and its resolution regarding control of the civilian internees, has already been discussed in Chapter 1. The pre-war agreement concerning internment did not end the quarrel, however, but rather set the stage for further conflict. Specifically, the head of the Western Defense Command, Lt. General John DeWitt, was convinced that enemy aliens were preparing to aid their home countries in inflicting serious damage upon the West Coast of the United States. From very early on, General DeWitt had complained that, despite the massive manhunt for and arrests of thousands of those enemy aliens deemed "dangerous,"[17] many more thousands of these non-citizens remained at large and therefore free to commit espionage, sabotage, and who knew what else. DeWitt wanted these enemy aliens more strictly surveilled and controlled, and kept badgering the civilian authorities in Washington DC to this effect.

Beginning especially around the middle of December in 1941, no doubt sparked by the handful of attacks on American merchant shipping by four Japanese submarines, which had managed to sink two tankers and damage one freighter,[18] General DeWitt concluded that "signals" to these enemy submarines from alien elements in his military zone must have been responsible for the attacks. At one point, and without evidence, he told Assistant Attorney General James Rowe:

> I have reason to believe that there isn't a ship leaving that they don't know about...I am personally convinced that there is a portable sending set operating in the Monterey Bay area. I am pretty convinced that there is one operating in the Columbia River area.[19]

Accordingly, the General began to demand that the government "collect all alien subjects fourteen years of age and over...and remove them to the Zone of the Interior."[20] His plan, already in process by his staff, envisioned designating a 100-mile strip along the entire west coast as a combat zone, and therefore a zone from which all persons considered "undesirable" should be removed. In a series of telephone conversations with San Francisco FBI agent Nat Pieper in late December of 1941, DeWitt more and more stridently repeated his urgings to clear this zone, known as the Pacific Slope, reinforcing his demands with alleged reports of an imminent major attack by the Japanese, and numerous reports of attempted sabotage. FBI Director Hoover kept putting the General off, especially in light of the military's own findings that many such reports were false alarms: a report about the Bonneville Dam turned out to be "power lines sabotaged by cattle scratching their backs on the wires," while an "arrows of fire" report near Seattle turned out to be a "farmer burning brush as he has done for years."[21] Moreover, V. Ford Greaves, the Federal Communications Commissioner in California, estimated that "there would not be more than ten to twenty-five cases of reasonably probable illegal operation of radio sending sets on the entire Pacific Coast," adding that there were "no active cases on file indicating the possession of radio transmitters by alien enemies."[22]

Still, General DeWitt kept firing off telegraphic messages to Washington with new demands, initially berating the Justice Department for failing to draft the regulations necessary to implement the contraband and travel restrictions. When the Department of Justice issued these regulations near the end of December 1941, and thousands of enemy aliens had complied with them, DeWitt raised his demands to a new level. He told Nat Pieper of the San Francisco FBI office that he now needed "raids on all alien homes to see that the articles are picked up."[23] When this, too, was met with skepticism— some 200,000 homes occupied by alien enemies would have to be raided—the General warned that if the Justice Department continued to resist taking the necessary measures, the Army would request that the President transfer authority over enemy aliens from the Department of Justice to the War Department. In all this, it is clear that in the early days of the war, General DeWitt was focusing his concern mainly on the enemy aliens—the non-citizens born in Axis nations whom he considered potentially disloyal—and not on the German-, Italian- or Japanese-Americans who had been born in the United States. In fact, in a conversation with the Provost Marshal General regarding the Los Angeles Chamber of Commerce's suggestion to evacuate all Japanese residents of Los Angeles, including those born in the U.S., General DeWitt firmly resisted, noting that such a move would be likely to "alienate the loyal Japanese..." More than that, the General emphasized that while he wanted to ferret out those who were disloyal, he could not imagine acting against the native born: "An American citizen, after all, is an American citizen."[24]

Nonetheless, the General's persistence had its effect, and the Attorney General not only issued orders to enemy aliens to turn in contraband, but on January 1, 1942, also decreed that warrants to search the premises of any enemy alien could be issued, so long as the FBI found "reasonable cause" to believe that contraband could be found there. That is to say, such searches had to roughly comply with the 4th Amendment to the U.S. Constitution. More important, perhaps, and despite the Justice Department's general conclusion that the "dangerous" enemy aliens, the ones FBI director J. Edgar Hoover called his "bad boys," were being investigated and interned as quickly as was practical, while the others were well under control, the Attorney General agreed to send his assistant, James Rowe, to California in early January to confer with General DeWitt and work out some compromises regarding future measures.

This crucial meeting took place at the Presidio in San Francisco starting on January 4. The main difficulty for Assistant Attorney General James Rowe was that he arrived with no plan of his own. General DeWitt, by contrast, had a specific three-point plan that had already been drafted by Major Bendetsen at the urging of Provost Marshal General Gullion, including an overall plan to transfer authority over all alien enemies to the War Department. Though he kept this latter part of the plan under wraps for the time being, the General presented his three main demands almost immediately. First, he demanded "blanket authority" to enter alien homes and "search and seize immediately without waiting for normal processes of law." Stunned by this, James Rowe said he did not have the power to agree to such a violation of the 4th Amendment and would have to consult with the Attorney General. Undeterred by this appeal to a bedrock provision of the U.S. Constitution, General DeWitt added that he not only wanted to search every alien home, but also wanted to "stop every car on the highway and search it." His reasons were simple: the kind of spot raids the Attorney General had recently authorized meant that warrants were required, which in turn required going to court to provide reasonable cause for the search, and "We don't want to go to court."[25]

DeWitt's second demand was equally breathtaking: the Justice Department, he said, needed to initiate a new, full-scale alien-registration program. The recent registration of August 1940 required by the Smith Act, wherein the million or so enemy aliens had been forced to register, be fingerprinted, and reregister each year, was not thorough enough, DeWitt maintained. The army wanted new, more detailed information sufficient to implement the mass raids he felt were needed to find contraband hidden by enemy aliens. More than that, in order to keep track of the aliens at all times, he demanded that new identity booklets containing photos, fingerprints, and other information result from this registration. Alien enemies would be required, under penalty of immediate internment, to carry the ID booklets at all times, and produce them when asked. Though this system reminded some in the Justice Department of the infamous pass system required of Jews in Nazi Germany, Rowe offered no immediate objection.

Finally, General DeWitt demanded the authority to exclude all enemy aliens from vast "restricted zones" on the West Coast. This, the General explained, was necessary so that his troops would be able to more easily guard the great number of key defense installations and factories in his military area. Once the alien enemies were out of such zones, he argued, his troops could concentrate on other more critical missions.

In the face of all this, the ill-prepared James Rowe said he would have to consult with Washington, and respond the next day. Rowe spoke to the Attorney General that evening by phone, and next day received a memo, which he presented to General De-Witt. Ever after, Rowe referred to the points in this memo as his department's "first capitulations," for he saw them as preparing the way for all the violations that followed, including the mass relocation of the Japanese. Answering DeWitt's demands in detail, they stated the following:

> RESTRICTED AREAS.
> The Department of Justice tonight will by wire direct the United States Attorneys in the Western Theater of Operations, with particular emphasis on Washington, Oregon, and California, to telephone Major General BENEDICT for recommendations as to what areas should be regarded as restricted. The U.S. Attorney will automatically accept the General's recommendations, and these areas will immediately become restricted areas pending confirmation by the Attorney General. As soon as possible, a press release ordering all enemy aliens to evacuate restricted areas by a certain date and hour will be issued....
>
> SEARCH WARRANTS.
> New forms for search and seizure of prohibited articles in homes controlled by, or inhabited by, alien enemies, are to be received tomorrow morning by FBI teletype. The question of probable cause will be met only by the statement that an alien enemy is resident in such premises. The U.S. Attorney will issue a search warrant upon a statement by an FBI Agent that an alien enemy is resident at certain premises.
>
> ALIEN ENEMY REGISTRATION.
> The Department feels it can conduct an alien enemy registration in the Western Theater of Operations within a week or ten days. The Department feels it can conduct such a registration, through the local police authorities, much faster than the Army itself...
>
> SPOT RAIDS.
> The Department is willing to make spot-raids on alien enemies tomorrow or at any time after the registration, anywhere within the Western Theater of Operations, providing that such raids are confined to premises controlled by enemy aliens, or where enemy aliens are resident. In other words, the Department cannot raid a specific locality, covering every house in that locality, irrespective of whether such houses are inhabited by enemy aliens or citizens. Under no circumstances will the Department of Justice conduct mass raids on alien enemies. It is understood that the term "mass raids" means, eventually, a raid on every alien enemy within the Western Theater of Opera-

tions. The Attorney General will oppose such raids and, if overruled by the President, will request the Army to supersede the Department of Justice in the Western Theater of Operations.[26]

Though General DeWitt continued to castigate the Justice Department for its alleged inaction in acceding to his demands, in early January 1942 he agreed to the basic positions outlined above. What is noteworthy is the degree to which the Attorney General had agreed to abrogate the 4th Amendment's protections against unreasonable search and seizure. Though he continued to resist demands for "mass raids," Francis Biddle had reduced the requirement for "probable cause" to the simple fact that an alien enemy lived in a place. In other words, simply being born in Italy, Germany or Japan now constituted probable cause to believe that a crime might have been committed, and hence sufficient justification to search any home—*including homes owned by American citizens*. The following month, accordingly, would become a time of massive search-and-seizure raids of enemy alien homes up and down the West Coast, and nationwide.

Even before that, President Roosevelt on January 14 implemented another element of the "capitulations" by issuing Proclamation 2537 for a new nationwide registration, or re-registration of all alien enemies. To be conducted starting the week of February 2 on the West Coast, the re-registration would continue a week later in the rest of the nation. All enemy aliens would be required to bring with them (to local post offices) two thumbnail photographs, answer detailed questions about their date and place of birth, residence, physical description, and so on, and then be fingerprinted. All this information would be incorporated into the new identity cards—in this case, identity booklets with pink covers—duly signed and stamped with an official seal of registration. Enemy aliens had to carry these pink ID booklets at all times, and produce them on demand to investigating authorities, policemen, or other officials. Failure to register, or to produce the booklet on demand, could be met with arrest and internment for the duration of hostilities.

In addition to notices in newspapers announcing the re-registration, the Justice Department printed notices to be posted in immigrant neighborhoods. The notices, including printed sections in Italian, German and Japanese, advised those on the West Coast to register on February 2 through 7.

Newspapers carried more details. The January 28 *Alameda Times Star* noted that Alameda postmaster Ford Samuel had explained that "When enemy aliens go to the post office to register, they must carry on their person their alien registration receipt card [i.e. the one from August 1940, issued when an alien complied with the Smith Act, ed.] and three 2-inch-by-2-inch photographs of themselves taken within 30 days of the time of registration. The photos must have light backgrounds." Samuel further explained that "the Identification Certificates will be delivered to the enemy aliens at their specified address by registered mail shortly after the registration week ends." Those who "for any reason do not have their card should report to the Office of Immigration and Naturalization, Department of Justice, Oakland post office."[27]

Immediately, Italian Americans began to line up outside post offices to begin their re-registration. Prior to arriving, of course, most had to visit photography studios in

UNITED STATES DEPARTMENT OF JUSTICE

★

NOTICE TO ALIENS OF ENEMY NATIONALITIES

★ The United States Government requires all aliens of German, Italian, or Japanese nationality to apply at post offices nearest to their place of residence for a Certificate of Identification. Applications must be filed between the period February 2 through February 7, 1942. *Go to your postmaster today for printed directions.*

FRANCIS BIDDLE,
Attorney General.

EARL G. HARRISON,
Special Assistant to the Attorney General.

AVVISO

Il Governo degli Stati Uniti ordina a tutti gli stranieri di nazionalità Tedesca, Italiana e Giapponese di fare richiesta all' Ufficio Postale più prossimo al loro luogo di residenza per ottenere un Certificato d'Identità. Le richieste devono essere fatte entro il periodo che decorre tra il 2 Febbraio e il 7 Febbraio 1942.
Andate oggi dal vostro Capo d'Ufficio Postale (Postmaster) per ricevere le istruzioni scritte.

BEKANNTMACHUNG

Die Regierung der Vereinigten Staaten von Amerika fordert alle Auslaender deutscher, italienischer und japanischer Staatsangehoerigkeit auf, sich auf das ihrem Wohnorte naheliegende Postamt zu begeben, um einen Personalausweis zu beantragen. Das Gesuch muss zwischen dem 2. und 7. Februar 1942 eingereicht werden.
Gehen Sie noch heute zu Ihrem Postmeister und verschaffen Sie sich die gedruckten Vorschriften.

敵國外人注意

日獨伊諸國國籍ヲ有スル在留外人ハ二月二日ヨリ七日マデノ間ニ其居所ニ一番近イ郵便局デ自分證明書ヲ申シ込ム可シ會モ早速郵便局ヘ行キ説明書願様ニ願ヒマス．

Post This Side in States of
Arizona, California, Idaho, Montana, Nevada, Oregon, Utah, Washington

Notice to Register, Courtesy Japanese American Library

Pink Registration Booklet, Inside, required of all enemy aliens.

order to get the requisite photos. Then, often accompanied by their English-speaking children to serve as interpreters, and dressed in their Sunday best, they furnished the required information. The result was a pink ID booklet mailed to each enemy alien. It bore the alien's name on the front cover as well as the location of the postmaster from whom it was issued. Inside was the subject's Alien Registration Number, name, fingerprint, photo, and signature. Other information included date and place of birth, length of residence in the United States, address, height, weight, hair color, distinctive marks if any, the signature of the identification official, and the FBI office where a copy was filed. The back cover contained information about the regulations that had to be obeyed, warning that "It is your duty to learn about and obey the regulations and instructions controlling the conduct of holders of these certificates." It mentioned the travel restrictions, the contraband items such as short-wave radios that were forbidden, requirements for any changes of name, residence or place of employment, and notification that alien children, "upon reaching the age of 14 years, are required to apply for a Certificate of Identification." The final warning stated that "Violation of the regulations and instructions may subject you to detention and internment for the duration of the war."[28]

It didn't take long for newspapers to report that there were holdouts disobeying the orders. The February 13, 1942 *San Francisco Chronicle*, for example, under a headline announcing "Alien Crack-Down" said in its subhead that "35,000 Not Registering Face Drastic U.S. Action." The article reported that "Federal records had indicated 185,000 Japanese, German and Italian nationals were living in the eight Western States. By the registration deadline last Monday night, it was disclosed, only about 150,000 of these aliens had signed up." The article then went on to offer a partial explanation for the deficit in registration, to wit, that "Some aliens have already been interned, and others have left the country," while some "have undoubtedly moved to other parts of the United States."[29] Authorities scoffed at these explanations, however, saying the result was "extremely suspicious" and warning that they were "ready to act." U.S. Attorney Frank Hennessey granted that "if an enemy alien can show his failure was not willful, he will be allowed to register now," but only after presenting his valid reason directly to the U.S. Attorney. Officials in other areas recommended more extreme measures. The article noted that "especially in Southern California, aroused organizations were planning reprisals against all enemy aliens" as well as citizens of Japanese parentage.[30]

The above raises the point that even before any evidence of failure to register, newspapers were urging their readers to be alert to the dangers allegedly represented by enemy aliens. On December 25, 1941, for example, Stockton, California's newspaper, *The Stockton Daily Record,* ran a front page 'call to arms' with the headline, "Every Citizen Called to Look, Listen, Tell Authorities." Here is some of what the article said:

> "A call to arms of every private citizen to report suspicious actions by any person or persons, and otherwise help peace authorities to guard against possible sabotage and espionage, was sounded today by Charles H. Epperson, Stockton attorney and chairman of the propaganda sub-committee of the Stockton Defense Council.
>
> ...The constituted authorities are doing all they can to combat sabotage and espionage, but their best will be inadequate unless assisted by the eyes and ears of the people, Epperson stated...Epperson offered the following tips on how every citizen may aid America's war effort:
>
> 'Watch for and report any unexplained concentration of gasoline, oil or other fuel or combustible materials and food supplies. Treat similarly any appearance of traffic into a new part of the mountains or desert! Someone may be constructing a secret landing field.'
>
> 'Watch for any suspicious actions by persons working in factories engaged in any kind of manufacturing even remotely connected with national defense, including canneries and other plants dealing with food supplies.'
>
> 'Listen to and report any unexplained meetings or gatherings, especially among foreign elements....'

'Listen to and report all utterances of opinion in favor of the European dictators or against any phase of Americanism...'

'Do not be afraid of reporting too often.'"[31]

Thus, despite government warnings to avoid hasty conclusions about immigrants
or foreigners, the continuing publicity about alien enemy arrests, and the constraints on
their movements, their possessions, and their ability to conduct themselves like other
Americans inspired the inevitable reactions to and suspicion of those who looked, or
acted, or sounded different.

Cartoon from *Pittsburg Post Dispatch*, March 3, 1942.

Raids and Arrests

Once the government had its regulations in place, with each enemy alien under orders to carry a pink Certificate of Identification, it began the process of making sure that
all its rules and obligations were being complied with. The investigations were generally
carried out by FBI agents, local constabularies, or even, in some cases, local members of
fire departments. Needless to say, most Italian immigrants were terrified of any involve-

ment with government authorities, partly because many did not speak English well, if at all, and partly because their experience in Italy had educated them to the perilous and often disastrous nature of any such contact. Still, whether by accident or by design, many enemy aliens ran afoul of the law, and though most emerged relatively unscathed, all were seared by the experience in a way that numbers alone do not address.

As to those numbers, researchers who prepared *The Report to the Congress of the United States*,[32] mandated by the *Wartime Violation of Italian American Civil Liberties Act* (Public Law #106-451, November 2000), searched Justice Department records and found the following figures. Spot searches were conducted in almost 2,900 homes nationwide where aliens of Italian birth lived. Of these, 1,632 individuals had contraband confiscated. About two-thirds of these searches were conducted in four states: New York, Pennsylvania, California, and Louisiana. In these four states, 1,907 searches resulted in 1,077 instances where contraband was confiscated. Records also revealed that among Italian enemy aliens, there were 442 violations of regulations relating to failure to file a change of residence notice, failure to obtain a travel permit, and failure to obtain a certificate of identity.[33] An additional 500 persons were questioned about various infractions, but were not arrested or taken into custody.

Behind the numbers, of course, are people, and what follows are some of their stories, taken either from personal interviews, or from FBI records. These stories do not include curfew violations, as those cases will be cited in Chapter 4 on the evacuation from West Coast prohibited zones, to which the dusk-to-dawn curfew was related, nor to internment arrests, which will be treated separately in Chapter 3.

Lee Pernich, of El Cerrito, CA, wrote to this author to relate the story of his mother, Carolina Garbari Pernich. Pernich remembered the episode as taking place in early September of 1942, the date being significant because it occurred *after* those who had been forced to leave prohibited zones had already been allowed to re-enter them. Here is Lee Pernich's recollection:

> *I want to tell you a short story. My mother, brother and I came to El Cerrito, Calif. in 1935. My father was already here 7 years. My father was helped to become a citizen by Emily Axtel, in 1940.*
> *In 1942, my brother (20 years old) joined the navy. About a month after he was gone, 2 FBI agents were at our house. I came home from school and they told me that she [mother] was an alien and must move. I asked to wait for my father to come home from work, which they did. They explained that although <u>he</u> was a naturalized citizen, she was still an alien and must be moved from El Cerrito to*

Oakland, Calif.

 During her stay we were allowed to see her Sat. or Sun.

 After the 4th or 5th week, she said that her eyes were going bad (40 years old).

 We contacted Dr. Frasier, a well-known doctor in Richmond. He told us she was going into temporary blindness.

 My father contacted a friend, Victor Perero (El Cerrito Electric Co.). He went to Judge A. J. Bray and he went to work and got her back home. She was gone approximately 8 weeks. From that time on she recovered her blindness (sic)—and became a citizen of America in 1943.

 I was born in Rozzo, Italy, 1928.

 P.S. Excuse my writing—when I think of those days, I shake.[34]

Having never heard of such an arrest and detention, I contacted Pernich by phone and found out more. Carolina Garbari Pernich, his mother, was taken to some sort of detention facility in Oakland. Her son remembered it as a hotel near 19th street, near the old Roxie Theater. He remembered from visits that she was there with four other women, also detained there.

Neither the records, nor the hotel have turned up as yet. But what emerges from Pernich's story is that Caterina Pernich's infraction involved either failing to move out of a prohibited zone (though the date would seem to eliminate that reason), or failing to re-register in February of 1942 when all enemy aliens were ordered to obtain their pink booklets (Certificates of Identification). She had registered as an alien in 1940, and may have thought that was sufficient, especially since her husband was a citizen. It was not. When the authorities caught up with her, they arrested her for the violation. At least that is an informed guess, absent the specific records. Nonetheless, what bears emphasis here is that a middle-aged woman, born in Italy, but married to a U.S. citizen, apparently assumed that, as a wife, she was protected by his citizenship. This was a common belief at the time, the term being "derivative citizenship."[35] Her failure to register (or move) eventually caught the attention of authorities (or of an informant), and the FBI was sent to investigate. They detained her at a facility in Oakland until her medical condition persuaded authorities to release her. More important, that condition—a kind of hysterical blindness, or perhaps a stroke that resulted in blindness—was caused by the fear and distress of separation from her family. It is noteworthy that when she was allowed to return home, she recovered her vision.

Another case lends some credence to this conclusion. **Joe Bentivegna** of Loretto, Pennsylvania related an incident that happened to his mother in May of 1942. Mrs. Bentivegna was stopped one day on the street by a Loretto police officer. He asked her for her Certificate of Identification, and she reached into her pocketbook to withdraw it. At that point, the officer asked, "Do you have a gun in there?" Since Mrs. Bentivegna understood almost no English, she misunderstood the question and indicated, "Yes," at which point the officer drew his weapon and told her to "freeze." Terrified, she fainted, and, according to her son, ended up with a lifelong facial distortion.[36]

In sum, two terrified women, when confronted by authorities, both responded with symptoms that appear to be akin to stroke. In the one case, blindness occurred, and was cured by the return home. In the other, there was a kind of hysterical syncope, or fainting, which left the facial distortion characteristic of stroke. In both cases, the initiating incident seemed to be overwhelming fear connected to being treated by authorities as an "enemy." It will be seen below that several other Italian Americans responded in similar ways to this fearsome classification.

Regularly over the next months, authorities raided Italian homes searching for contraband, often arresting enemy aliens who had failed to turn in banned items. Edward Ennis, Director of the Alien Enemy Control Unit of the Justice Department, in an April 14, 1942 Memorandum to the Attorney General, made a review of these practices— "Disposition of alien enemies seized with prohibited articles".[37] The memo contested the view of J. Edgar Hoover of the FBI that "all such violations should be considered wilful and violators interned in the absence of extenuating circumstances." Noting that the raid procedure using "executive warrants" had been extended throughout the nation, with great publicity given to the persons apprehended and the articles seized, Ennis suggested that since most persons apprehended "proved to be ignorant of the regulations and harmless," they should not be held for long periods pending action by an internment hearing board, but rather be immediately given preliminary hearings by local U.S. Attorneys and "released if the violation did not appear to involve the national security." As justification, the Memo noted that

> A very large number of articles seized might reasonably be thought *not* to have been prohibited. Nothing in any of the Proclamations or regulations indicates to an alien enemy that he is forbidden to possess the binoculars, opera glasses, flashlights and the like, which have been seized. Automatic internment for possession of prohibited articles would be erroneously based upon a presumption of wilfulness which is not reasonable under the circumstances.[38]

Ennis also addressed the problem of "Articles Owned by Citizens," writing that

> A great many of the cases involved radios, cameras or other property of citizens, wife, husband, or children of an alien enemy, kept in the household with the alien enemy. The Proclamation and regulations do not require a citizen to give up his property. On

the other hand they forbid an alien enemy to have such articles in his control as well as in his possession...Obviously alien enemies were justified in believing that they were not required to turn in other people's property.[39]

Ennis attached to his memo abstracts of a number of cases that he thought notable, all picked randomly on April 9, 1942. Some of those abstracts follow:

Salvatore Rosetti. *Italian. 72 years old. Resided in the United States for 51 years. Employed as a laborer. Possessed a revolver. No other evidence of dangerousness. This man was arrested on an emergency warrant, and was held for several weeks while his case was put through the machinery devised for dangerous aliens.*[40]

Antonio Orsini. *Italian. 70 years old. Resident of the United States for 13 years. He is unable to read or write in any language and has been employed as a common laborer. He boarded with his son and his son's wife. The son is an American citizen. Subject was arrested on the theory that he had access to a radio and a gun. The radio belonged to the son. The gun had been the property of the son's wife's father, who had died in 1931. At the time of that man's death, his widow threatened to commit suicide, and the gun was hidden in the bottom of a chest to keep her from using it. The evidence indicated that it remained there from 1931 until the FBI agents discovered it. There was no evidence whatever to indicate that the subject knew of its existence.*

Mary Ferrante. *American citizen of Portland, Maine. Reported to the U.S. Attorney there to surrender a radio, due to the fact that she was residing with her parents, both alien enemies who had lived in the United States for 28 years. The attorney accepted the radio as contraband, but judged that further action was not authorized.*

Annie Messina. *This Italian alien enemy is 60 years old, having resided in the United States for 39 years. She resided in a house which was also occupied by her daughter and a son-in-law, both of whom were American citizens. Her husband has been absent for 11 years. She was apprehended and charged with possession of a pistol, a camera, 3 cartridges, a broken revolver, and a pair of field glasses. The pistol was the property of her husband... She admitted ownership of the camera, stating that it had been given to her. The field glasses, which were broken, the broken revolver, and the shells were found in parts of the house not occupied by her. Subject told the United States Attorney that she had never heard of the Presidential Proclamation, and that she had made no attempt to conceal the property. It is to be observed that she has four children who are citizens. The United States Attorney determined that she should be released.*

Joseph Greco. *Resident of Syracuse, NY came to the United States in 1908 at age 4. He has four children, all American citizens. Works at the* Post Standard *of Syracuse [a* *newspaper]. He was arrested on March 6, 1942 for possession of a camera, four photo flash lamps, one photo finishing unit, and five rolls of film. The U.S. Attorney authorized holding him for a hearing board procedure [i.e. to determine if the arrested alien were dangerous and should be interned, ed.]*

John Belpedio. *This Italian alien was apprehended on March 23 in the residence of Mrs. Barbara Krizan, where he resided. It appears that the alien has resided in the United States since 1911, and since 1918 he has boarded with Mrs. Krizan, who is an American citizen. It appears that Mrs. Krizan's husband, some years previously, had constructed a cabinet especially for the purpose of keeping firearms locked up away from the children. It was the custom of Mrs. Krizan's two citizen sons and the alien all to keep their guns in this cabinet, which was in the room occupied by the alien. When it was required that alien enemies deposit their firearms, the alien removed his guns and took them to the Sheriff of Deer Lodge County. On March 23 the premises were searched and five guns were found in the cabinet and confiscated. In addition, a radio with a short-wave band and a camera were found and confiscated. These belonged to Mrs. Krizan. The guns belonged to Mrs. Krizan's two sons. The Assistant United States Attorney who had this case states "from all of the testimony it is my opinion that the alien enemy had endeavored to comply with the regulations...It was further my opinion that the radio and camera taken were not the property of the alien enemy, and it was my opinion that if a violation of the regulations governing the possession, control or custody of firearms by an alien enemy has occurred, it was a technical violation and one such that the release of said alien enemy will not endanger the national security—that the said violation occurred due to excusable ignorance of the regulations."*

In a section of the Ennis memo entitled "Cases on which the Attorney General Has Requested a Report," a letter from U.S. Attorney T. Hoyt Davis of Marion, Georgia, reporting on "spot searches" for short-wave radios in his area, states that "one alien was apprehended because of a subway map of New York City which was found in some discarded papers. The alien stated that he had bought it at a newsstand when he made a trip to New York City." Another alien enemy was apprehended because of photographs of Fort Benning Military Reserve. The alien was a commercial photographer in Columbus, and it appeared that the photographs had been left with him for development by a commercial company. Mr. Davis further states that "in each case the alien was a Jewish refugee, and in almost every case the alien had relatives in Columbus who was supporting him or assisting him to get started."

Additional portraits of raids and arrests of residents of Italian descent, both enemy aliens and naturalized citizens, can be found in the FBI's reports of its activities in and around San Francisco, and the West.[41] Among these reports are accounts of numerous apprehensions of enemy aliens (and sometimes naturalized citizens) for moving without notifying authorities, changing jobs without notification, traveling without permission, and various other violations and/or suspicious activities. A few examples from those FBI reports follow:

James Capra. *American citizen residing on Hyde Street in San Francisco. Arrested for making "alleged pro-fascist remarks." Having worked as a waiter on a ship and a night janitor, he was then employed as a waiter at the Fairmont Hotel. Records revealed that he had been arrested once before, in 1941, for shoplifting. Also weighing against him was the fact that his daughter, Rosette, had attended the now-closed Italian Language School in San Francisco, and had received a free trip to Italy six years prior to his arrest. After investigation, the case against Capra was closed because there were no activities for which he could be held, but his file states, without explanation, that "denaturalization proceedings" [stripping a person of his American citizenship, ed.] were being pursued.*

Mrs. Emma Manfredi Lupi. *Enemy alien residing at Ney Street in San Francisco. Arrested for espionage and interviewed on October 5, 1942 [two weeks before all restrictions on Italian enemy aliens were lifted, ed.] Mrs. Lupi had sent a letter to her sister-in-law, in Argentina, allegedly to be forwarded to Italy on behalf of her friend, Rose Podesta, to inquire after Podesta's aging mother. This was judged to be an attempt to circumvent the restriction on enemy aliens sending mail to Italy. The FBI report noted that despite the violation, no action needed to be taken.*

Angelo Bobbio. *Enemy alien arrested drunk by a Healdsburg, CA police officer. Subject had no permit to travel although, when asked, he produced an April 16, 1942 permit to travel to Linden [near Stockton, ed.] to work picking cherries. No action.*

Enrico Compostrini. *Owner of a "dive" at Gazas Creek nine miles out of Pescadero, CA, arrested for using an invalid travel permit to drive to San Francisco for vegetables and to Santa Cruz for groceries. No action.*

Teresa Baronti. *Eureka, CA enemy alien arrested for possession of short-wave equipment. The equipment had belonged to her ex-husband, no longer living with her. Baronti had two sons serving in the U.S. Armed Forces. Short-wave equipment seized.*

Louis Mancini. *American-born citizen of Weed, CA. In Custodial Detention, 8/28/42. Judge J.P. Bradley alleges that Subject is author of controversial Italian article, "Stupidity and Intollerance (sic)," published in the Italian paper,* La Concordia, *at Weed, CA on 4/1/39. Alfred M. Cremer, superintendent of construction, Long Bell Lumber Company, Weed, CA, advised that subject stated to him that the "cripple (vulgarity) in Wash-*

ington is no good", meaning President Roosevelt. Article in question concerns a film, "The Meeting of the Two Powers," and argues against the attempt to "hinder the presenting" of this film in Weed. Text of article says: "As everyone knows, this film has no aim at propaganda, nor does it in any way have a character subversive to our form of republican government or to any other policy of this Nation. But it is simply a reproduction of various aspects of Italian life...Some of the super-patriots of this country, headed by the thus-far esteemed (ones) from the High School Football Coach, Al Nichelini, H.G. Anderson, Al Matthews, and a few members of the American Legion, through their ignorance, stupidness, and prejudice have done everything possible to have this show cancelled, and we must give credit to the Director of the Weed Theater for refusing to yield to this request. That, however, which chiefly offends us Italians is the fact that Mr. Nichelini as an Italian has shown himself as having repudiated his race....In the sight and judgment of the Italian people, he should be considered as a traitor and treated as such, and those who, like us, are proud of their nationality, should remember this insult and should repay him with interest." Despite all of the publicity surrounding the article, published two years before the war, no witness could ever positively attribute it to Louis Mancini, who, as an American citizen born in Weed, could not be charged as an enemy alien. The FBI report concludes: "In view of the fact that investigation herein has failed to furnish information indicating that the subject is or was engaged in any suspicious or subversive activity at any time covered by the investigation, this case is being closed by the San Francisco Field Division."[42]

Hugo Giulio Dellagnola. *Bingham Canyon, UT. Salt Lake County Deputy Sheriff Jack Householder reported Subject was keeping 5 or 6 short-wave radio sets as part of his radio business, in violation of regulations. On August 26, 1942, Special Agent Nugent and Bingham Canyon Chief of Police Centratto searched Dellagnola's premises at 389½ Main St., with negative results. Subject stated he had been born in Italy in 1908, at 18 months sailed with parents to United States, arriving in New York City on July 10, 1910, and traveling with them to Bingham Canyon. Attended local schools through 8th Grade, took correspondence course in electrical engineering and later one in radio. Employed since 1923 with Utah Copper Co. as an electrician. In April 1934 opened a radio and electrical appliance shop, which he operates after leaving day job at 5 PM. Subject stated he had filed declaration of intention to become U.S. citizen in 1931, renewed it in 1938, but then let it slip due to being "very busy." Subject also stated he did not think it necessary to turn in radios as he had reported them to Sheriff Householder, and to U.S. Attorney Dan Shields, who said "go on about your business and if anything comes up, call me." After search, facts were presented to U.S. Attorney John S. Boyden. When Boyden called U.S. Attorney Shields, Shields stated* *that he meant that "Subject could stay in the business long enough to dispose of his short-wave radio receiving sets." U. S. Attorney Boyden then held informal hearing, and ordered Subject to immediately dispose of the radio receiving sets and to report the following morning, which Subject did. U.S. Attorney Boyden then advised that he would decline further prosecution inasmuch as Subject was in the radio business and was not using the radios "for pleasure or personal purposes."[43]*

Pietro Vigno Casassa. *Italian alien arrested August 16, 1942, on drunk charge at the Oak Grove Picnic Grounds, Menlo Park, CA, thirty miles from his residence in San Francisco. Subject had no travel permit. Interviewed at San Mateo County Jail, Subject said he was employed at a saloon on Market St. as a janitor. Born in Torino, Italy in 1889, Subject came to United States in 1923, traveling cross-country to work in New Mexico mines, and then to San Francisco. In 1937, Subject enlisted in the International Brigade and traveled to Spain to fight for Loyalist forces from 1937 to 1939. Returned to San Francisco in 1940, working at various jobs in and around San Francisco. Subject stated that he left Italy because even in 1923 he did not like Mussolini, and that the reason he had gone to Spain was to "fight against Mussolini, Hitler and Franco." He stated that he is not a communist, and that the only organizations to which he belongs are the Dishwashers' Union and the International Workers' Order. He knew he was not supposed to travel more than five miles from San Francisco; however, he explained that the International Workers' Order gave a picnic at Menlo Park, and in view of the fact that the theme of the picnic was "Victory for the Allies," he felt a patriotic urge to attend. Confidential Informant SF-613 reported that George Anderson, Attorney for the Communist Party of San Francisco, was approached by Sam Jay of the Dishwasher's Union in an effort to secure Anderson's assistance in effecting Subject's release. These facts were presented to Assistant U.S. Attorney Wilbur Mathewson, who authorized maintaining custody over Subject.[44]*

Joe Antonio Nandi, alias Joe Savona. *Italian alien of Stockton, CA. Born 1891 in Savona, Italy, entered United States in 1908 and employed in Stockton area since 1910 as laborer on ranches and in canneries. Married to an American citizen. Subject was reported to Detective Sergeant R.C. Parker of Stockton police by a Leonard Walter, who alleged that around July 2, 1942, an unidentified individual was soliciting funds for Italian Relief from Louie Martini, a farmer at Linden. Subsequently, no one, including Mary L. Smith, Postmistress of Linden, was able to confirm a Leonard Walter in the vicinity. Smith also stated that she had never heard anyone speak of soliciting funds for Italian War Relief. Louie Martini of Linden affirmed that to the best of his knowledge no one had at any time approached him soliciting funds, adding that he had never heard of a person by the name of Leonard*

Walter. Further FBI searches failed to locate the person known as Leonard Walter. Among those interviewed, Mrs. Angela Pagano, manager of the Savona Place bar, said she had formerly been in business selling liquors with a person by the name of Joe Nandi, who had probably been referred to as Joe Savona, adding she had never heard of him soliciting funds. Joe DeLorenzi, owner of the Roma Bar, said he was acquainted with Joe Nandi, who at present worked at Morpak Cannery outside Stockton. He added that he had been acquainted with Joe Nandi for twenty years and that in his estimation he was a very fine, reputable and honest man. Agent O'Farrell interviewed Joe Nandi on September 2, 1942 and confirmed the information previously obtained. Nandi stated that he had not at any time appeared on the fruit ranch of Louie Martini at Linden, and had at no time solicited any funds from Martini or any other Italians or persons. Nandi stated that his wife's name was Jennie Denevi, who had been born in Calaveras County, CA, and that she had had three children by a former marriage. He stated that he had no relatives in Italy, had not at any time served in the Italian army, and had not at any time been a member of any lodges, organizations, or activities of any kind participated in by Italians. He said he was a member of the Cannery Union. He explained that he was not an American citizen for he had been advised by a lawyer that he had no papers on which to base his birth certificate, and it would be difficult to ascertain the exact time of his birth and other necessary information. He also added that he had been very careful and quite respectful of the alien regulations, and had turned in all of his contraband, which consisted of one radio with a short-wave band. The Alien Registration files of the San Francisco Field Division were checked and reflected that Joe Antonio Nandi had filed his application for Certificate of Identification. Case was closed.[45]

※

Sometimes newspapers sensationalized enemy alien raids, as in the January 7, 1942 *Stockton Record* in its front-page article titled "Jackpot Hit as Police Investigate Alien." The article reported that two detectives went to the home of Matteo Gosso, a gardener residing at 338 West Market Street in Stockton, "to investigate a shotgun owned by another resident of the home. Although Gosso is a naturalized citizen, Pete Darunga, 58, alleged owner of a shotgun, is registered as an alien." The detectives found Gosso "in the attic, admittedly attempting to conceal a pistol and a box of shells," but because Gosso was a citizen, "possession of the weapon was not illegal." However, in Gosso's bedroom, police *did* find a shotgun previously owned by Darunga, and given to Gosso to "evade the regulations" forbidding such possession by an enemy alien. Further search of Gosso's basement revealed 300 gallons of wine, which Gosso admitted "owning without a license." And finally, in the room of another boarder and non-citizen, Giuseppe Cardoni,

55, police found "complete barber equipment and evidence that Cardoni was carrying on a barber's business without a license."

Thus the "jackpot" found in the home of an American citizen: a pistol that was *not* illegal, a shotgun which may have been, a barber operating without a license, and 300 gallons of home-made wine. Police confiscated the shotgun, charged Gosso with illegal possession of wine, charged Cardoni with unlicensed barbering, and jailed Darunga for failing, as an enemy alien, to surrender his shotgun. Darunga was subsequently released with a warning that further "suspicious actions" would bring down upon him the "wrath" of federal officers.[46]

On February 21, 1942, the same *Stockton Record* bore a front-page headline that read: "Raids Extend Through All West Coast." Its first sentence, terming the raids "fifth column and espionage raids," emphasized the drama and danger: "Federal agents swept down on enemy aliens in the three Pacific Coast states and Arizona today in the greatest series of fifth column and espionage raids since the Pacific war broke out. Hundreds of Germans, Italians and Japanese were questioned. Scores of the aliens were taken into custody." The article continued in this vein:

> Striking almost simultaneously, FBI agents and local authorities assisting them moved into virtually every large city of California, Oregon, Washington and Arizona. They aimed particularly at seizing enemy nationals identified with secret societies and propaganda groups directed by Berlin, Tokio [sic] and Rome.

> Northern California raiders, numbering 300 or more, were directed by Nat J.L. Pieper, San Francsico FBI chief. FBI agents and local law enforcement authorities assisting them arrested Italian, German and Japanese nationals in Redding, Stockton, San Jose, Berkeley, Alameda, Monterey, Sacramento, Watsonville, Santa Rosa, Castroville, Santa Cruz, Salinas, the Richmond-Contra Costa area and the San Mateo-Redwood City Peninsula area.

> Within a few hours 54 aliens were in custody in the north. Some of them were identified as members of an Italian organization said to have fostered a Fascist program in this country.[47]

The latter reference to the Italian organization 'fostering Fascism,' the *Ex-Combattenti*, reinforced the sensationalizing tone of the report: the *Ex-Combattenti* were Italian veterans of World War I, during which Italy had fought on the Allied side. Though the organization, a kind of Italian VFW, had been disbanded since 1941, U.S. government authorities insisted on treating it as a subversive organization, and interning many of its members as "dangerous." A subsequent article from the same paper on March 24, created a similar impression: "20 Are Seized by FBI in Weed Alien Raids:"

> Federal agents directed by Nat J.L. Pieper, San Francisco, raided an Italian colony here today and seized 20 men and a quantity of contraband. Pieper said the raids were based on information that many aliens in the colony had pro-Fascist leanings, and in addition failed to turn in radios, cameras, guns and other contraband....
>
> Raiders said some of the men seized were veterans of the Italian armed forces—one has two sons still serving in the Italian army. Those arrested were removed to the Siskiyou County Jail at Yreka.[48]

It is notable that although the report says that "the raids were based on information that many aliens had pro-Fascist leanings" [i.e. the information about pro-Fascism came from informants, ed.], the article strongly suggests that a dangerous den of subversion has been uncovered. Taken together, both articles might well persuade the public that the government had succeeded in wiping out widespread "fifth column" and "espionage" activity that had presented a serious danger to the war effort. The truth, of course, is quite other: records reveal that not a single case of espionage or sabotage was ever brought against an Italian enemy alien. In fact, as Attorney General Francis Biddle wrote in a memorandum to President Roosevelt in May 1942:

> We have not uncovered through these searches any dangerous persons that we could not otherwise have known about...We have not found among all the sticks of dynamite and gunpowder any evidence that any of it was to be used in a manner helpful to our enemies. We have not found a camera which we have reason to believe was for use in espionage.[49]

❋

As for the effects of such raids on individuals, a more complete picture can be gleaned from the testimony of a few of those who endured them, presented below.[50]

Joan DiGregorio of Detroit, Michigan: "My father, Adamo E. Di Gregorio was arrested and questioned by the FBI in Detroit, Michigan circa December 8-10, 1941. At the time, he had derivative US citizenship, due to my paternal grandfather's naturalized citizenship quite a few years prior. My father was also registered and employed at Ford Motor Company in the manufacture and engineering of defense equipment. He was born in Cansano, Provincia L'Aquila, Abruzzo region, in 1913 and came to the USA in 1929 after completing military, polytechnical secondary school in Fermo, Italy. The arrest occurred in the middle of the night at much distress to the family; my eldest brother was four years old and my mother was pregnant with my older sister. My father indicates that he was released, after a rather strident examination, due to having received confirmation from his superiors at Ford Motor Company, both of his employment status and as to having a defense clearance."

Frank Brogno of Gary, Indiana: "I do not recall the exact day, but I do remember clearly what happened one evening at our home in Gary, Indiana a few days after Japanese planes bombed Pearl Harbor on Dec. 7, 1941. The three of us, Mamma, Papa and myself were listening to a program on our new Philco radio—a Philco console which was delivered to us just two or three weeks before. It was the very first radio we owned and it was purchased on a lay-away plan over several months at Kobacker's Department Store in Gary. It was our family Christmas present and we were very proud to have our own radio. We often sat together after supper to enjoy the music, the news and entertainment from the nearby Chicago stations. Our new radio also had a short-wave band which could receive programs from Europe. Papa, especially, was thrilled at listening to Italian voices and music late in the evening from Rome. Then it happened—the moment when smiles turned into stiff stares of shocking disbelief, and fear. A Gary Fire Department truck parked in front of our home. Two firemen came, one with a list of names and addresses in hand. This was the residence of Peter Brogno? Yes. They had orders to search the house for short-wave radios, for guns and other non-specified items. They searched the entire house from basement to second floor, as well as the small storage shanty in the side yard. They took the radio. They took my Papa's automatic revolver—a Spanish-made automatic which was given to him by his captain in the Italian Army when Papa was discharged at the end of WWI as a prize for having been an excellent member of the elite *Undicesimo Regimento Bersaglieri* (sharpshooters rifle regiment). Then came the tears and the anxiety about what would happen next. Would someone come to take us away? Papa's cheeks were awash in tears. I was a dumbfounded and speechless teenager, trying to reassure Papa and quiet my fiery and angry Mamma, who went to hover over my baby brother John in his crib (he was 18 months old) when she was not blasting away at the "mean and stupid firemen" with unrelenting anger and painful moans.

"I believe it was three or four weeks later that the fire department came back to return the radio and the prized revolver. The firemen who returned the radio said nothing—not a thing—about what happened or why it happened. They came and went just as they had when they took away the radio and gun. In the first encounter they presented no court orders, no explanations. They left no signed receipts for what they took. They came only with a list of Italian American names and addresses, period. They gave no apologies when they came to search and no apologies when they returned the items. They said nothing. And no one has said anything to Papa, to Mamma or to me ever since.

"My Papa, my Mamma and I were, all three, naturalized citizens of the United States. We were very proud of being American citizens. I can still hear Papa proudly telling people how he attained his citizenship status 'six months ahead of time.' He was a very good student in his citizenship class at the International Institute in Gary. He had also helped dozens of Italian immigrants obtain their papers, and assisted the staff of the Institute with interpreting and translating letters and documents presented to them in Italian at no charge. He had learned to read and write English quite well in five years and had taught his father—who had never set foot in a schoolroom in either Italy or America—to read the daily newspaper in English. I personally felt deep pain in reaction to the cold and harsh rejection of my Italian origin. Like Papa, I also had become a good student. I had graduated as the valedictorian of my high school class just a few months prior to the sledge-hammer blow to my Italian American self esteem. Yes, I began to feel shame. I felt growing concern and anxiety about who I was, where I came from, and very worried about belonging and being accepted as a 'real American.' I even entertained thoughts of changing my name. Perhaps, I thought, I could make my Italian name appear to be a 'French' name: 'French' because they were 'on our side;' because I was about to join the Navy; because to be 'French' was OK. I thought I would change my name just a bit, like this: BROGNO to 'BROGNE.' But I never took the step and I'm happy I did not. Finally, I must say it was a hurtful and difficult period for our Italian American family. The image of my Papa crying and my Mamma wailing is etched deeply in my memory. And they were such good and proud American citizens. *Che vergogna*!" [what shame!]

Ferdinando Ghibaudo. In October 1942, Ghibaudo filed for a permit to move from Richmond, CA to Santa Rosa, CA for a new job (he had been working at a Richmond poultry market). The FBI went to check on his new address, and he was not there. The FBI found him outside at midnight, when he should have been inside (an 8 PM curfew for enemy aliens being in effect at this time) and arrested him on October 2 for that violation. On October 8, 1942, he was taken to the Immigration station on Silver Avenue in San Francisco. Interrogation and a check of Ghibaudo's records revealed that he was in the United States illegally, having jumped ship in San Francisco in 1925, and thereby being in violation of the Immigration Act of 1924. A warrant was issued for his arrest on the immigration violation. Arrested, he was transferred to the Detention Center at Sharp Park on October 21, 1942. Another hearing around November 6 revealed that he had complied with all alien laws, registering in 1940, then again in February 1942 when he got his enemy alien Certificate of Identification, and applying for the permit to change his residence. Nonetheless, since he was in the U.S. illegally, he would be processed for deportation. On November 10, Ghibaudo was released from the Sharp Park Detention Center after posting a $500 bond, guaranteeing that he would appear at his deportation proceeding. Hiring a lawyer, Ghibaudo entered upon a series of legal delays and maneuvers, which eventually allowed him to go to Canada, re-enter the United States legally, and then apply for U.S. citizenship, which he acquired some time after 1948. Allowed to stay, he moved to Ferndale, CA and remained there until his death.[51]

Finally, there are stories from people who remain confused to this day about what happened to their parents or grandparents during World War II, and why. These are stories that may be the most painful of all—like Lee Pernich's story about his mother. One knows something traumatic took place, one spends most of one's life either suppressing it, or wondering about it, or concocting explanations—could it have been the work of informants? someone who might have wanted to ignite suspicion with a false accusation?—to make sense of what remains mysterious. And even when a general explanation emerges, the specific behavior or trait that led authorities in a specific place to intervene remains obscure, for the actions of authorities in different parts of the nation at different times during World War II varied wildly.

Gloria Micheletti Sylvernale. "I read the book about the internment of Italian Americans in California during WWII. This story was of much interest to me as my family in Galveston, Texas experienced something similar to this. My father failed to become naturalized even though he had been in this country for many years—too busy feeding a large family and trying to make a success of his grocery store. Early one morning (5 or 6 AM) we were awakened by several FBI agents with a search warrant. They entered our home, tore the house apart and left it that way. Took my father into custody even though they had no reason to other than the fact that he was considered an enemy alien. The search of the home did not result in any findings, other than a flashlight, a household radio, and a Brownie box camera. Of course, my mother was devastated; she was left with 10 children and the breadwinner had been taken away. My father was taken first to Fort Sam Houston, and then to Kelly Field*, San Antonio, TX where he was held for 6 months or so, investigated and finally released with no apology from the government. My brothers subsequently served in the U.S. military and my father worked at the Galveston Dry Docks. As we were growing up we were taught to be proud to be an American. My husband was a pilot in the USAF during WWII and a career officer in the

Air Force. This is an experience my family and I will never forget."

* *"Kelly AFB during the early 1940's was used as a camp to intern many, not sure of the numbers, Japanese, German, and Italian immigrants from Galveston and Friendswood County. Friendswood County had a large concentration of Japanese who were cotton farmers. Also, among many other missions, Kelly was an advanced flight cadet training base. I was 13 years old when my father was taken away from our home. I visited my father while he was at Fort Sam Houston with several members of my family and remember that the internees were housed in tents, in a double fenced enclosure made of heavy cyclone fencing with barbed wire across the top. Also 2 armed guards were sitting in towers at each corner of the enclosure. After investigation my father was released along with several other people being held, but with restrictions imposed on him, i.e. no travel without permission, could not move from his residence, and had to report to the Immigration Dept every week. His only "crime" was his Italian ancestry. My father was drafted into the Italian army during WW1 and served from 1918-1921. He was a telegraph operator. My father arrived in Galveston TX from Santa Maria del Guidice, Lucca, Italy in April 1921. He was a member, and at one time secretary of the Sons of Italy, which he considered a social organization. Other than that, he was too busy trying to make a success of his business and taking care of his family."*

[Ed. note: Kelly AFB may have served as an INS Detention Center, rather than an internment facility. Micheletti was probably detained there during the Government's attempt to determine whether to formally intern him or not. On the other hand, his being kept at Fort Sam Houston (which had a facility for internees) suggests internment there on the basis of his position with the Sons of Italy, a suspect organization, and/or on the basis of his earlier service in the Italian Army, especially for having been a member of the Ex-Combattenti, of which he was secretary before it was disbanded in 1936. Either or both positions would have made him suspect. His release on parole would be consistent with such an internment, but no record of a Micheletti appears in the internment records at the National Archives; by contrast, there is an Evergisto Micheletti listed in the category of "other persons of Italian ancestry who were taken into custody during World War II" in the Department Of Justice Report of 2001.[52] This would indicate that his arrest and detention may have occurred preparatory to internment, but his parole suggests he was considered not "dangerous" enough to formally intern. Still, the exact cause and nature of his arrest remained uncertain until new documents obtained from government files indicated that Evergisto Micheletti was arrested on Feb. 27, 1942 (records show his first stop to be Galveston jail, and then Ft. Sam Houston),and paroled on Apr. 29, 1942, whence he applied for exception to Enemy Alien status (EO 9372 allowed for release from Enemy Alien status for arrestees if they could prove their innocence). At first denied, Micheletti's petition eventually resulted in his release. On the basis of these most recent documents, then, it appears that Micheletti was indeed arrested to be interned, but the hearing board (probably in Houston) recommended that he be paroled. The Attorney General agreed with the board's recommendation in this case, a rare event. Accordingly, Micheletti was paroled in April, and sent from Fort Sam Houston in San Antonio to Galveston on or about May 5, 1942. This explains the fact that he appeared, to his family, to have been interned, but, in fact, was never formally interned by an order from the Attorney General.)

John Perata of Campbell CA, was also arrested for as yet unconfirmed reasons—he was a prune rancher, originally from Castroville, and also ran an appliance store in San Jose. His daughter, Marilyn Perata Berg, remembers her father's ordeal this way:

"As far as I know, my Dad was detained at Sharp Park (south of San Francisco) because he belonged to an Italian Club in Oakland which was considered subversive during that time. I don't know the name of the club, possibly the Sons of Italy. Of course, he was not a citizen then but received his citizenship when he left the camp. My uncle, Felix Bersano, was also a member of the club and possibly an officer. I don't know if there was a short-wave radio in the [appliance] store. My dad worked there a short time as far as I know. Dad did serve in the Italian Army during WWI and received a gold medal from the Italian Ministry of Defense, but was not a member of any veterans group.

"Prior to my Dad being arrested, the FBI came to our door one night around 7:00PM. I remember them asking for my Dad, and my Mom said he was already in bed because he had gotten up at around 3:00AM and worked hard on the ranch all day. They thought he had left, or was faking sleep. "How come you're in bed so early," they asked my mother. "If you worked as hard as we do, you'd be in bed too," she answered. Dad did not violate curfew. They searched the house for weapons and found none, but took a camera and knives we had in the kitchen. There is a photo of him and my uncle being booked. I was about 5 years old at the time, so my memories are cloudy. I do remember visiting him at Sharp's Park with my cousin, Don, his Mom and mine. Dad cried every time we went and when he was released, he refused to be picked up by family but took the bus or streetcar home instead. It was an embarrassment to him to be detained there."

As Berg notes, her father's arrest was recorded in the *San Jose Evening News*, Feb. 23, 1942, with a photo showing John Perata, Felix (Felice) Bersano and several other men being taken to the county jail prior to booking and questioning. An October 21, 2001 article in the *San Francisco Chronicle Magazine* by Patricia Yollin adds a few more details to the story:

"The FBI picked up Anita's husband, John, at his San Jose appliance store, took him home in handcuffs to Campbell, turned mattresses over and took beds apart. He was locked up in Sharp Park, an Immigration and Naturalization Service detention center in Pacifica, for two months. Oakland-born Anita Perata visited her husband once a week. Their son, Saratoga resident Don Perata, 65, former chancellor of the Foothill–De Anza Community College District, remembered only a few things: Getting off the school bus the day of the raid and seeing several large black cars in the driveway. Chatting with his father through a detention center fence on Easter Sunday.

"Sometimes I'd take the little one with us," said Anita Perata, mother of three. "We'd kind of straighten her up when we got out of the car and he'd be up at the window watching for us. We'd get up there, and he'd been crying when he saw what we'd been doing." On the day John Perata was released, he came home on the streetcar. "He was too embarrassed to have us take him home," his wife said.[53]

Phil Patane. Brooklyn, NY. There was an application to fill out, with specific questions about my mother's birth since she was an alien without citizenship. I filled it out and sent it in. There was a photo in it. My father had taken out his citizenship papers and I had derivative citizenship, so I can't understand why my mother didn't, but that's it. My mother would communicate with neighbors, and that made her feel better because there were others doing the same thing. She didn't let it bother her much, she was a real American. I remember when she was so happy to be able to climb the Statue of Liberty stairs. She was grateful. I was working in defense at the time, at Republic Aviation in Farmingdale. I was born in Italy. Then someone in the Department of Defense said since you have only a derivative citizenship, you should take out your own. Which I did. I was about 24, 25 years old and I felt like being an Italian I really didn't have any right to be an American citizen. They can push me around, I have no rights, maybe they couldn't push other people, but me, I have none. I felt pretty bad about this. I was a citizen but I'm not a citizen. What do they think, I'm going to spy on them?

Guy Guliano. Brooklyn, NY. I was nine, ten years old. We were living on Avenue X in Gravesend, where probably 90% of the kids spoke Italian in school. In fact I tutored one of the kids in school. One day my mom said these guys came over, and they took our camera. I was insulted, I was American, why are you taking our camera? My mother was born in the United States, my father was not a citizen. She was insulted too--she was involved in church, in school, she was an air raid warden. And you're taking my camera?

Jane Bongiorno. Brooklyn, NY. I vaguely recall that during WWII my father, Antonio Davi, was taken for 3 months and held somewhere because he was an Italian American. The FBI came in the middle of the night and wouldn't even allow him to change his pajamas or put on shoes when they took him. Is there some way I can find out more details on this? I think it was because they suspected the plasterer's union of which he was a member was subversive.

In the end, the only antidote to such stories and the puzzlement they generate among families is research—doing what Barbara Viale did from Italy. After perhaps a year of inquiries, she eventually obtained a sheaf of government documents that told the full story of her uncle Ferdinando Ghibaudo's arrest and detention, revealing that the primary cause of his troubles was his illegal entry into the United States. The details about Gloria Sylvernale's father have also come to light with the release of government documents. But many others, whose stories are recounted above, remain in the dark to this day.

———————————————

1. *Report to the Congress of the United States: A Review of the Restrictions on Persons of Italian Ancestry During World War II,* U.S. Department of Justice, November 2001, Proclamation 2527, Appendix L.5.

2. Ibid., Appendix L.3.

3. Mitchel Yockelson (http://net.lib.byu.edu/~rdh7/wwi/comment/yockel.htm)

4. Francis Biddle, *In Brief Authority*, p. 151.

5. *San Francisco Examiner*, Dec. 10, 1941, p. 1. There is, of course, no such thing as a "person of enemy alien citizenship."

6. *San Francisco Chronicle*, Dec. 11, 1941.

7. *San Francisco Chronicle*, Dec. 15, 1941.

8. *San Francisco Chronicle*, Dec. 28, 1941.

9. *L'Italia*, Dec. 29, 1941.

10. *San Francisco Chronicle*, Dec. 29, 1941.

11. *Oakland Tribune*, Dec. 30, 1941.

12. *Oakland Tribune*, Jan. 3, 1942.

13. Stephen Fox, *The Unknown Internment,* op. cit., p. 152.

14. *Oakland Tribune*, Jan. 3, 1942, p. 1.

15. Travel permit courtesy of Sando Bologna, personal communication.

16. Travel permit courtesy of Caterina Cardinale, personal communication.

17. "By February 16, 1942, the Department of Justice held 2,192 Japanese; 1,393 Germans; and 264 Italians and arrests continued even after that date." PJD, p. 55.

18. Peter Irons, *Justice at War: The Story of the Japanese American Internment Cases*, Oxford U Press: 1983, p. 27.

19. Irons, p. 35.

20. Irons, p. 27 (also cited in Stetson Conn, p. 117).

21. Irons, p. 28 (memo, Hoover to Tolson etc., Dec. 17, 1941).

22. *Personal Justice Denied: Report of the Commission on Wartime Relocation and Internment of Civilians (PJD),* p. 63 (Memo by Lt. Col. L.R. Forney, conversation with V. Ford Greaves, Dec. 31, 1941 [CWRIC 3164] and Letter, Greaves to DeWitt, [CWRIC 8606-07b]).

23. WDC, Final Report, pp. 23-24.

24. Stetson Conn, p. 18.

25. Irons, p. 33 (Conference in DeWitt office, Jan. 4, 1942, Box 7, RG338, NARA).

26. PJD, note 81, p. 373 (Summary, Rowe to DeWitt, Jan. 4, 1942).

27. *Alameda (CA) Times Star*, January 28, 1942, pg. 1, "Enemy Aliens Must Register at Post Office Next Week."

28. Certificate of Identification, United States Department of Justice, (Alien Registration), Form AR-AE-23.

29. It should also be noted, though reports did not mention it, that, among Italians, a drop occurred in the number of enemy aliens between the 1940 registration and the 1942 re-registration—from 694,000 in 1940, to some 600,000 in 1942. This discrepancy, apparently, was due to the nearly 100,000 who obtained their final citizenship papers between 1940 and 1942.

30. *San Francisco Chronicle*, Feb. 13, 1942.

31. *Stockton Record*, Dec. 25, 1941.

32. *Report to the Congress of the United States: A Review of the Restrictions on Persons of Italian Ancestry During World War II,* U.S. Department of Justice, November 2001.

33. Ibid, p. 24.

34. Lee Pernich, personal communication.

35. As noted previously, until 1922, derivative citizenship would have covered women like Caterina Pernich. In 1922, however, the Cable Act gave women citizenship on their own, a law which meant that henceforth, an immigrant woman could no longer count on her husband's naturalization to protect her; she had to file for citizenship on her own. Unfortunately, many Italian immigrant women remained ignorant of the new requirement and became "enemy aliens" during the war. Compounding the problem, Lee Pernich himself, born in Italy in 1928, seems to have been deemed a citizen, having derived it from his father's 1940 naturalization.

36. Joe Bentivegna, personal communication.

37. "Memorandum for the Attorney General re: Disposition of alien enemies seized with prohibited articles," April 14, 1942, *James H. Rowe Jr. collection*, Alien Enemy Control Unit, Container 33, Franklin D. Roosevelt Library, Hyde Park, NY.

38. Ibid.

39. Ibid.

40. This and subsequent 6 cases from "Abstract of Cases of Arrest on Charge of Possessing Prohibited Articles," *James H. Rowe Jr. collection*, Container 33, Franklin D. Roosevelt Library, Hyde Park, NY. Language summarized in most cases.

41. All found in National Archive and Records Administration (NARA), San Bruno, CA. RG 181.

42. NARA San Bruno, RG 181, File 1447, A8-5 (14-A-1).

43. Ibid., File A8-5/16 (14-A-1).

44. Ibid. It may be noteworthy that subject's status as an apparent anti-fascist did not sufficiently counteract the suspicion deriving from his union membership and acquaintance with the allegedly communist lawyer; accordingly, his case was not immediately dismissed.

45. Ibid., File A8-5 (14-A-1)

46. *Stockton Record*, Jan. 7, 1942, p. 1.

47. *Stockton Record*, Feb. 21, 1942.

48. *Stockton Record*, Mar. 24, 1942

49. Francis Biddle, *In Brief Authority*, p. 221.

50. All of the following accounts came to the author by personal communication.

51. Ghibaudo's story arose via an email query from his niece Barbara Viale, still in Italy. Viale had lost track of her uncle's doings in the United States, and wondered if perhaps he had been interned during World War II. After searching unsuccessfully in places she thought he had been, such as Albany and Ferndale, CA, I happened upon a document in the San Bruno archives dated Oct. 27, 1942 indicating his release from enemy alien proceedings, and noting that "alien is remaining at Sharp Park under deportation proceedings." I sent this information, which included Ghibaudo's alien registration number, to Viale, whereupon she was able to initiate a FOIA request to the Justice Deparment asking for her uncle's records. She eventually received 354 pages, including the information noted in the short description above. What seems most ironic is the fact that Ghibaudo got into trouble initially *not* by evading the enemy alien regulations, but by trying to comply with them.

52. *Report to the Congress of the United States, op. cit.*, Appendix C.2, p. 37, entry 1268.

53. Patricia Yollin, "A Secret History," *San Francisco Chronicle Magazine*, October 21 2001, p. 10.

III: INTERNMENT

When Japanese forces attacked Pearl Harbor on December 7, 1941, the American public may have been unprepared, but, as already indicated, the Federal government surely was not.[1] It had long anticipated such a conflict, and within hours of the declaration of war on Japan, the President had issued the first proclamation aimed at aliens with roots in that now-enemy nation. Presidential Proclamation 2525 stated that "an invasion has been perpetrated upon the territory of the United States by the Empire of Japan." This meant that all natives, citizens, denizens or subjects of Japan fourteen years of age or over residing in the United States and not naturalized had become "alien enemies." As such they were subject to all regulations governing such persons, including the provision in Title 50 of the U.S. Code, that they "shall be liable to be apprehended, restrained, secured, and removed." The next day, December 8, two more presidential proclamations, 2526 and 2527 were issued to cover German and Italian aliens respectively. Since Italy had *not* attacked America, Proclamation 2527 for Italians said, in part: "an invasion or predatory incursion is *threatened* upon the territory of the United States by Italy." Thus, even though Italy and the U.S. did not formally became enemies until December 11 when Italy declared war and the U.S. did the same, this proclamation made all 600,000 un-naturalized Italian immigrants—those 'natives, citizens, denizens or subjects of Italy fourteen years of age or over'—*alien enemies*, and thereby subject to all the restrictions that classification entailed, including immediate internment.

Like the President, the FBI did not wait until war was declared to begin arresting permanent resident aliens of Italian descent. It had had a kind of practice run six months earlier, when, on or about June 21, 1941, all Italian consulates in the United States were ordered closed (German consulates were ordered closed on June 16)[2]. Shortly thereafter, Italian consular personnel were taken into custody and detained at the Greenbrier Resort Hotel at White Sulphur Springs, West Virginia, to await deportation. And even before that, at the end of March in 1941, sixty-nine Italian, German, and Danish ships in American ports and Philippine waters were seized, and approximately 875 seamen (775 Italian and about 100 German) were jailed for "attempted sabotage"—attempting to disable their own ships so as to make them unusable by the United States.[3] The Italian seamen, along with orchestra members and entertainers, athletes, medical staff and a priest, were soon sent to the INS-run internment camp at Fort Missoula, Montana. They were joined by a number of World's Fair personnel who had also overstayed their visas, to make a total of somewhere around 1000 Italian nationals interned there and also called "alien enemies," even prior to the arrival of the several dozen resident enemy aliens of Italian descent who were soon to join them.[4]

After Pearl Harbor, on December 8, 1941, the FBI, initially without warrants but acting on a formal order for each individual from the Attorney General, moved against these resident enemy aliens (immigrants), many of whom had been listed, prior to Pearl Harbor, on the FBI's Custodial Detention Index (CDI). Filippo Molinari, who sold subscriptions to the Italian American newspaper *L'Italia* in the San Jose, CA area (his Basic Personnel File calls him an "agent of *The Italian Daily News*, San Francisco paper")[5], was picked up at his home on the night of December 8 and taken into custody. As he later described it in a letter, at 11 PM FBI agents surrounded his house, entered, and ordered him to accompany them by order of the President. He was not allowed to dress or to indicate to his wife where he was being taken, or how long he might be gone, which he, of course, did not know. Within days (after detention and initial questioning in San Francisco), he had been put on a train that had originated in Los Angeles on December 16; with windows darkened, the train transported Molinari and nearly 500 other civilian detainees to Fort Missoula, Montana, where it left the Italian detainees; the train then proceeded, with most German detainees, to the Fort Lincoln internment camp at Bismarck, North Dakota. Meantime, at Missoula, Molinari made his way "over the snow, still with slippers on my feet, the temperature at seventeen below and no coat or heavy clothes!"[6] It was December 19, 1941 and Molinari and hundreds of others with roots in any of the three enemy nations were beginning their long stay behind barbed wire.

BASIC PERSONNEL RECORD
(Alien Enemy or Prisoner of War)

ISN-24-4-I-129-CI
(Internment serial number)

MOLINARI, Philip
(Name of internee)

M
(Sex)

F.P.C.
Reference*

01886

Height 5 ft. 6 in.
Weight 178
Eyes brown
Skin fair
Hair grey
Age 49

Distinguishing marks or characteristics:
Mole between eyebrows;
Mole left corner of
mouth. appendicitiscar.

Fort Missoula, Montana
(Date and place where processed (Army enclosure, naval station, or other place))

INVENTORY OF PERSONAL EFFECTS TAKEN FROM INTERNEE

1.
2.
3.
4.
5.
6.
7.
8.
9.
10.

The above is correct:

Philip Molinari
(Signature of internee)

Right Hand

1. Thumb	2. Index finger	3. Middle finger	4. Ring finger	5. Little finger

Left Hand

6. Thumb	7. Index finger	8. Middle finger	9. Ring finger	10. Little finger

W. D., P. M. G. Form No. 2
December 9, 1941

Note amputations in proper space

* Do not fill in.

Filippo Molinari, Basic Personnel Record. Top, front; Bottom, back.

1. ___ (Grade and arm or service)
2. ___ (Hostile unit or vessel)
3. ___ (Hostile serial number)
4. December 22, 1892, Italy (Date and country of birth)
5. 1051 Pershing Ave. SanJose, California (Place of permanent residence)
6. Mary Molinari, wife (Name, relationship of nearest relative ‡)
7. 1051 Pershing Ave. SanJose, Calif. (Address of above)
8. Wife and two minor children (Number of dependents and relationship)
9. Same as above (Address of above)

ADDITIONAL DATA:

10. December 7, 1941 (Date of capture or arrest)
11. San Francisco, California (Place of capture or arrest)
12. Federal Bureau of Investigation (Unit or vessel making capture or arresting agency)
13. Agent of the Italian Daily News, San Francisco paper (Occupation)
14. 6 yrs. elementary school. (Education)
15. Italian, Spanish, English. (Knowledge of languages)
16. good (Physical condition at time of capture or arrest.)
17. married (Married or single)
18. ___ (Religious preferences)

Transferred from	Date depart	Transferred to	Date received	Official signature receiving officer	Personal effects not transferred *
Fort Missoula, Montana		U.S. Army, Ft. Sam Houston, Texas.	4/14/4	J. B. Bowers, Jr. Lieut., Infantry	
		Camp Forest	6/19/42	Alien Enemy Inf Bu	
		McAlester, Okla.	9/16/42	Inf Bu	
		Ft. Missoula	3/18/43	Alien Enemy Inf Bu	

REMARKS:

* If no relative, name person to be notified in case of emergency.
† If personal effects taken from individual are not transferred, note exceptions and place of storage or depot.

The FBI made similar raids upon scores of other immigrants of Italian descent, most but not all of them enemy aliens, in the early days of December 1941. None was told why he or she had been arrested; no one in their families was notified where their loved one was going or what his eventual fate would be. As Judge John Molinari of San Francisco described it years later, on the evening of December 8 he began to receive frantic phone calls from the wives of those arrested, pleading with him to help, or to at least find out where a relative had been taken, so family members could visit. It took the lawyer a while to figure out that most of those arrested in San Francisco had been taken to an Immigration and Naturalization Service (INS) holding facility on Silver Avenue, but as all were soon transported to Montana on the same train that took Filippo Molinari to that internment camp, the possibility of family visits had quickly become moot.

Arrests in other parts of the country followed a similar pattern. In New York City Louis Berizzi's family was awakened on the night of December 8 by FBI agents, who searched the apartment and then spirited Berizzi away. As his daughter Lucetta later described it:

> We were all sound asleep. My father was in his pajamas; they told him to get dressed, as they had orders to take him away. No explanation was given. They would not divulge where they were taking him. They stayed in his bedroom while he dressed, so we had no time to speak to him privately. They did not even give him time to gather personal effects or toiletries. I believe it took several days [for us] to find out that he had been taken to Ellis Island. We were pretty shaken...Several days after his arrest, we learned that my father's office at Rockefeller Plaza had been locked and sealed by the Enemy Alien Custodian, and all my father's assets were blocked. In time we learned that when my brother's tuition was due at Lehigh College, we had to petition the Enemy Alien Custodian for the money to pay for it...[7]

Filippo Fordelone, a radio broadcaster in Los Angeles, was one of forty-eight enemy aliens in that area arrested in the initial sweep. His wife, faced with caring for three young daughters without funds, kept repeating in her native dialect, "*Mi mari, mi mari, dov' è mi mari?*"[8] [My husband, my husband, where is my husband?] Others arrested in Los Angeles included another broadcaster, Giovanni Cardellini; a secretary of the *Ex Combattenti*, Spartaco Bonomi; and Giovanni Falasca, editor of the Italian American newspaper *La Parola*, along with his assistant, Zaccaria Lubrano. All were taken to detention facilities on Terminal Island to await their hearings, a few of them, lacking families in the United States, simply seeming to have disappeared without explanation.[9]

In Hawaii, at about the same time, Mario Valdastri and his son were working on the balcony to his bedroom when they saw a car drive down their country road bearing two men in suits and ties, unusual attire in the country. The suits asked if he was Mario Valdastri, and when Valdastri answered in the affirmative, they said, "Will you please come with us?" Valdastri asked if he could change, but the men ordered him to come as he was. The plaster contractor managed to slip out of his sweaty t-shirt into a sweatshirt, and was taken to a large barred room in Honolulu with several other detainees.[10] After what he described as a "perfunctory hearing," Mario Valdastri was formally ordered by the Attorney General to be interned, and shipped to the mainland "with only the Hawaiian clothes he had. He tried to keep warm by putting newspapers under his clothing."[11] Officially received and registered by the Army for internment at Camp McDowell on Angel Island in San Francisco Bay, Valdastri was then shipped to Camp McCoy, Wisconsin, his permanent place of internment 5,000 miles from his home. Valdastri was especially outraged by this treatment, for as he explained in several letters, one to President Roosevelt, he was a *naturalized citizen* who had won his citizenship by virtue of his military service to the United States in World War I. But having been caught in the internment net, Valdastri spent almost a year behind barbed wire, first at Camp McCoy, and then on Sand Island in Hawaii, before a second hearing resulted in his release.

Though the Justice Department maintained that only *non-citizens* of Italian descent were targets for internment, both Valdastri's experience and government documents suggest otherwise. For example, a December 8, 1941 memo from J. Edgar Hoover to Major Lemuel Schofield—then head of the Immigration and Naturalization Service— indicated that of the 337 Italian Americans targeted for possible arrest in the first roundup, 77 were 'enemy aliens,' 49 were American citizens said to be 'sympathetic to Italy,' and 211 were 'persons of Italian descent whose citizenship is unknown.'[12] The situation was even more pronounced with regard to German Americans: the number of American-born or naturalized citizens of German extraction targeted for arrest in the initial roundup was more than double that of the enemy aliens. In other words, in a program that derived its authority from the legal statutes applicable to non-citizens, more than half of those slated to be arrested were in fact American citizens—those to whom *the enemy alien laws did not apply*. When it came time to intern 70,000 American citizens of Japanese descent, the precedent for violating the constitutional rights of American-born citizens had already been established.[13]

Driving all of this activity were a number of factors, not the least of which was public relations. In fact, the Immigration and Naturalization Service's own administrative history notes that the arrests

> served two important purposes: [they] assured the public that our government was

taking firm steps to look after the internal safety of the nation, thereby preventing the growth of war hysteria; and it took out of circulation men and women whose loyalty to the United States was doubtful and who might therefore commit some inimical act against the nation if permitted their freedom.[14]

Thus, while government officials publicly justified depriving so-called "dangerous" Americans of their freedom as a measure "protecting the public safety," in private they seem to have been driven at least as much by the need to demonstrate that they were 'on the job.' A memo from J. Edgar Hoover in the first days after Pearl Harbor confirms this latter priority. On December 9, when Hoover realized that his years of surveillance over tens of thousands of immigrants had resulted in *only* a few hundred candidates for internment, he wrote:

> I told Mr. Shea that this morning the Attorney General decided not to issue a press statement because we had *only* taken into custody a little over 400 Germans, that if this figure were given out public opinion would be very unfavorable.[15]

Hoover's FBI set to work to improve the figures in the next days and months. By February of 1942 the number of internees had reached a more respectable total: 1,393 Germans, 2,192 Japanese, and 264 Italians. And by war's end, the arrest figures would rise by an even larger factor: almost 11,000 Germans, 3300 Italians, and 16,000 Japanese had been apprehended.[16] The publicity surrounding the arrests would also lead to increased fear and hatred of so-called aliens, to the degree that by early January 1942, the President of the United States would have to issue a public statement informing American businesses that simply being foreign-born did *not* make a person disloyal and thereby unqualified for the work place. His statement said, in part:

> I am deeply concerned over the increasing number of reports of employers discharging workers who happen to be aliens or even foreign-born citizens. This is a very serious matter. It is one thing to safeguard American industry and particularly defense industry against sabotage; but it is very much another to throw out of work honest and loyal people who, except for the accident of birth, are sincerely patriotic.
>
> Such a policy is as stupid as it is unjust…I urge all private employers to adopt a sane policy regarding aliens and foreign-born citizens…[17]

The President's statement, published in all the newspapers, reinforced a similar press release issued by the Attorney General about a week earlier, on December 26, 1941:

> To bar aliens from employment is both shortsighted and wasteful…It is the stated policy of the Federal Government that there shall be no discrimination in the employ-

ment of workers in defense industries because of race, color or national origin.[18]

Of course, this is the type of unintended effect that results from the two opposing needs of a government at war: on the one hand, to stir up patriotic fervor and hatred of the enemy sufficient to fight a war; and on the other, to maintain respect for the due processes of law on the home front. To make things even more complicated, and contradicting the need to publicize arrests, federal authorities followed a general policy of keeping the internment locations secret; even fifty years later, few Italian Americans and far fewer Americans in general knew of the many internment camps and detention facilities where enemy aliens were incarcerated.

In actual practice, it would have required a great deal of secrecy to keep the enormous number of these facilities secret. Virtually every large city had at least one INS facility where the apprehended suspects were taken to be held, questioned, recorded, and given a hearing. Where there were more permanent INS centers, such as the ones in Gloucester City, New Jersey, Sharp Park outside San Francisco, and Ellis Island in New York Harbor, the detainees were usually transported there directly—though some, like the great opera star, Ezio Pinza, was taken to the courthouse in New York's Foley Square first. In other cities, those picked up were initially taken to one of more than fifty temporary detention centers, including police stations (civilian detainees were allowed to be kept in jails for only 24 hours, in recognition of the fact that they were *not* criminals under arrest, *having committed no crime*), National Guard armories, INS centers, or several Homes of the Good Shepherd leased by the INS and converted for the job. The length of time detainees spent at these detention centers varied wildly: some were processed in a matter of days or weeks; others, like Louis Berizzi, remained on Ellis Island in a kind of limbo for more than ten months before a formal internment order sent him to the army-run internment camp at Fort George Meade, Maryland. In and around San Francisco, most seized aliens were taken first to Silver Avenue to be interrogated, thence to the INS detention center at Sharp Park (in 1941 a coastal hamlet a few miles south of San Francisco; the facility consisted of several Quonset huts surrounded by barbed wire), and, if ordered interned, turned over to the Army at Camp McDowell, located on Angel Island in the middle of San Francisco Bay. There, internees were processed and sent to one or several army-run internment camps in the South—the usual route being first to Fort Sam Houston in Texas, thence to Camp Forrest in Tennessee, with most ending up at Fort McAlester in Oklahoma.

This was not the route of the very first San Francisco internees, however, partly because coordinating the apprehension, detention and internment of resident aliens

Quonset Hut for detainees, Sharp Park, CA.

took time for the two government departments, War and Justice, to work out. The hysteria on the west coast added to the difficulty, but delays occurred elsewhere as well. In fact, according to the Immigration and Naturalization Service's administrative history, the first transfer of male internees from the INS to the custody of the U.S. Army did not take place until February 11, 1942, when

> ...69 persons were delivered of a total of 277 under orders of internment at all locations. The 69 were accepted at a temporary camp the Army had established at Camp Upton, New York [on Long Island, ed.]...However, transfers to the Army moved slowly. On May 4, 1942, of the 1276 who had been ordered interned, 1065 had been transferred to Army custody.[19]

In its panic of early December 1941, however, the Western Defense Command (WDC) was not willing to wait that long. The result was that within days of the first west coast arrests, WDC Commander Lt. General John DeWitt, incensed that "potentially dangerous" aliens remained under non-military control (which to him meant lax supervision) in his command zone, ordered the INS to move the detained but not-yet-interned alien enemies out of the Ninth Corps Area *immediately*.

This order necessitated the hasty formation of special trains to transport the detainees from west coast detention centers to the already-functioning INS internment camps in Missoula, Montana and Bismarck, North Dakota. As noted above, the first train left Los Angeles on December 16, 1941, stopping to pick up additional alien enemies in San Francisco and Seattle, and delivering 364 Japanese and 25 Italian prisoners to Fort Missoula in Montana, and 110 German prisoners to Fort Lincoln in North Dakota. A second train left Los Angeles on Christmas Day in 1941, and delivered 213 Japanese and 3 Italians to Fort Missoula, and 5 Germans to Fort Lincoln. While this did not, technically, violate the rule that formal internment would occur only *after* a hearing and a formal internment order from the Attorney General (transfer in this case being from one INS-run facility to another—i.e. both Fort Missoula and Fort Lincoln were administered by the Border Patrol, an agency of the INS), in truth those detainees who were shipped out of the Ninth Corps area to remote INS camps in the early days of the program were to all practical purposes interned *before they ever had hearings or received formal internment orders.*[20]

Hearing Boards

According to the policy established by the Justice and War Departments in November 1941, a person "under alien enemy proceedings" was not to be interned until he had been given a hearing. Policy stated that the suspect alien would be apprehended by an FBI field office, taken to an INS facility, and detained there temporarily pending a hearing by a local three-man hearing board, which would then make its recommendation. However, the INS and the Provost Marshal General both made a point of letting internees know that this hearing was given to them not "as a matter of right" (presidential proclamations 2525, 2526, & 2527 already allowed U.S. authorities to seize both the person and the property of the enemy alien without further justification), but as a matter of fairness.[21] This was because Francis Biddle, the Attorney General, was determined to avoid the abuses suffered by alien enemies in World War I, as well as the mistakes made in England earlier in 1940 when the British had rounded up German and Italian aliens almost indiscriminately (see note 21). Accordingly, Biddle instituted the hearing board policy, though his statement that "all alien enemies are subject to detention and internment for the duration of the war without hearing, which hearing has however been provided, not as a matter of right, but in order to permit them to present facts in their behalf,"[22] made clear that the policy did not imply any constitutional "rights" for enemy aliens, but was provided to demonstrate the government's fairness. Further confirmation is found in the file of Mario Valdastri. In response to a letter written by Valdastri's daughter Frances to Allen Gullion, the Provost Marshal General, asking him to reconsider her father's case, Gullion wrote, in part:

> ...your father was interned, after a hearing before a board comprising three civilians. The hearing thus accorded was not held as a matter of right but was allowed in order to avoid injustice.[23]

Gullion, to be sure, makes no mention of the obvious injustice of incarcerating a United States citizen (which Valdastri *was*) without the due process guaranteed by the Bill of Rights, but that is another matter (see below).

The hearing boards in question were made up of three prominent civilians selected from the locality where the detainee lived. Board members were charged with reading or hearing evidence presented to them by the FBI, listening to evidence or affidavits presented by the apprehended person, questioning him or her, and making one of three recommendations to the Attorney General. The Board could recommend either: 1) unconditional release; 2) release on parole; or 3) internment. The procedure was not governed by normal rules regarding evidence or legal representation, however. The detained alien could *not* have a lawyer to represent him or question witnesses (though he *could* engage a lawyer to provide legal advice); he was *not* allowed to know the charges against him (most often there were none), or examine whatever incriminating evidence the FBI had gathered; and he was *not* allowed to face his accusers.[24] Mainly, he was expected to present favorable testimony or affidavits from friends or relatives that he hoped would convince the hearing board of his good character and innocence. Hearings were often very short affairs, and turned on such things as hearsay (i.e. accusations from informants whose identity was, and still is, kept secret), the manner in which the alien responded to questions, and whether he was willing to make unequivocal declarations of his allegiance to the United States,[25] or his non-allegiance to the nation of his birth. At the end of the procedure, the hearing board was expected to make its recommendation.

The board's recommendation was then sent to the Attorney General, who was charged with making the final decision about each case. This procedure was said to "assure equal treatment in various parts of the country." Given the elaborate procedure required to find reputable civilians to serve without pay on such hearing boards, it is puzzling to note that the Attorney General was *not* required to follow the board's recommendations. In an as-yet-unknown number of cases, he did not [Stephen Fox has maintained that his examination of many German cases indicates that, in fact, it was Justice Department policy to simply dismiss all affidavits supplied by internees, ed.][26] Thus, the record of Cesare Pasqua contains his order for internment, dated January 6, 1943 (Pasqua was apprehended September 16, 1942 in Trenton, New Jersey, less than a month before all restrictions on Italian enemy aliens were canceled), which says in part:

> WHEREAS, the Alien Enemy Hearing Board has recommended that said alien enemy be paroled; and it appearing from the evidence before me that said alien enemy should be interned; NOW, THEREFORE, IT IS ORDERED that said alien enemy

be interned.[27]

The order is signed by Francis Biddle, Attorney General, with no comment on the apparent contradiction between the board's recommendation for parole and *his* decision to intern Pasqua, other than the subdued hint that the Attorney General had access to information that the hearing board lacked. But if this were the case, what sense would it make for the Attorney General to withhold information from the board charged with making so important a decision? And if, on the contrary, both hearing board and Attorney General had the same information, would not the hearing board, listening to the person before it, reading intonation and body language, have a better sense of a given individual's probity than someone simply reading a report?

We do not know. All we know is that in some unspecified number of cases, the Attorney General did, in fact, ignore or overrule his hearing board. Indeed, in the case of Federico Dellagatta, a bootblack who worked in Union Station in Providence, RI, and who was arrested apparently because informants had reported him for "making statements about the greatness of the Italian people," the reversal of the hearing board's recommendation stands as a stunning testimony to both the board's irrelevance and the intransigent opinion of government officials. Here, from Dellagatta's file, is a quote from a memo dated Oct. 8, 1942, for the chief of the review section, Alien Enemy Control Unit (part of the Department of Justice):

> ...his (Dellagatta's) chief offence has been that he has indulged in irresponsible talk about the greatness of the Italian people and the Italian army and his sympathy is doubtless with the aims and purposes of Italy.....continuing, the Board says that it does not consider subject dangerous to the people and safety of this country and recommends that he be paroled.

The DOJ reviewer of Dellagatta's case, however, disagreed with the Board's recommendation:

> In the opinion of this reviewer, subject's persistent talk in praising and boasting of the greatness of the Italian people and of the Italian army while employed in a shoe shining shop *constitutes downright subversive activity* [Emphasis added]....in view of the foregoing, unless it can be made sure that subject, if paroled, will close his mouth and desist completely from talking about and boasting of the greatness of Italy and the Italian army, without question, subject should be interned.[28]

In addition to Dellagatta's "subversive" talk (one might infer that such talk was construed as sedition, save for the fact that there is nowhere even a hint of urging the overthrow of the U.S. government), other considerations were adduced in the memo, i.e., "the effect upon the people of Italian descent in Rhode Island who constitute about one-sixth of the population there." Indeed, it appears to have been these latter considerations that tipped the balance toward internment, for, in spite of the Hearing Board's opinion that "such action [i.e. parole] will have an excellent effect on the people of Italian descent in Rhode Island," a handwritten note by yet another Department of Justice official (J.P.R., probably Asst. Attorney General James Rowe) says: "I guess intern—the Board is persuasive, but I am inclined to think that a single man with this record will be a better influence on R.I. Italians if we intern."[29] In other words, that locking up someone for "loose talk" would influence, i.e. *frighten,* more Italian immigrants than a fair judgment of the "danger" he posed to the public safety, was a sentiment with which the Attorney General's office apparently concurred. Federico Dellagatta, therefore, was interned.

Yet another internee from Rhode Island, Amleto Cafaro, a barber, received very similar treatment. An order for Cafaro's arrest was issued by Edward Ennis, Director of the Alien Enemy Control Unit on September 11, 1942 (actually, an FBI report asserts that "Subject arrested by Bureau Agent and Providence P.D. 9/10/42 at Providence, R.I.," while a note at the bottom of the same report states that Cafaro "had been rejected for service with the U.S. Army because he was an Italian alien having a brother in the Italian Army," and also that the case was "based on information received from Confidential Informant T-1 who stated Cafaro was one of the individuals who volunteered and was accepted for service with the Italian Army during the Ethiopian campaign.")[30] Cafaro was then given notice of a hearing, to take place on September 16, 1942 in Room 222 in the Federal Building in Providence. A note at the bottom of his notice says: "In the said hearing a relative, friend, or other adviser of yours may be present, but such person will not be permitted to act for you in the capacity of attorney." The report and recommendation from the hearing board includes the following:

> Ever since Pearl Harbor he has been strong in his expressions of sympathy with the cause of Italy and stated before the Board that while he would be willing to fight in the American Army, he would not want to fight against any Italians as he has a nephew and a brother serving in the Italian Army.
>
> The impression that he made upon the Board was that he was an Italian prone to indulge in loose talk and imbued with a real love for his native land...
>
> We do not consider him a man who on his own initiative would indulge in subversive activities and the only question that arises about him is to his past record as a member of the Italian Army....*In our opinion, the best disposition to make of this case would be to place him on parole....*in the custody of an American citizen of Italian

descent who is engaged in social service work in this community...We believe that this action will have an excellent effect on the community of Italian descent in Rhode Island which numbers about one-sixth of our population (Emphasis added).[31]

In Cafaro's case, the FBI weighed in with its disagreement. Citing from its interviews with confidential informants, its Memorandum for the Attorney General on October 6 said in part:

> The above entitled alien was afforded a hearing on September 16, 1942 at Providence Rhode Island, and the Alien Enemy Hearing Board has recommended that he be paroled. The facts in this case indicate that he should be interned and the following information regarding Cafera (sic) is being furnished you with the suggestion that his internment be ordered for the duration of the war...He fought in the Italian Army against Ethiopia from October, 1935 until January 1937...The subject has continually expressed himself in a pro-Axis attitude since the declaration of war and has stated that he would go to a concentration camp rather than fight for the United States. He has stated that the United States entered the war only to enrich the capitalists.[32]

As in the Dellagatta case, the Attorney General seems to have been persuaded not by the Hearing Board, but by the subsequent recommendation presented by the FBI. On October 16, 1942, therefore, Francis Biddle issued an internment order:

> WHEREAS, Amleto Cafaro, of Providence, Rhode Island, a subject of Italy, over the age of fourteen years, is within the United States and not a naturalized citizen thereof and has heretofore been apprehended as being potentially dangerous to the public peace and safety of the United States; and,
> WHEREAS, the Alien Enemy Hearing Board has recommended that said alien enemy be paroled; and it appearing from the evidence before me that said alien enemy should be interned; NOW, THEREFORE,
> IT IS ORDERED that said alien enemy be interned.[33]

An October 24 Memo for the Enemy Alien Information Bureau in the Office of the Provost Marshal General then informed the latter of the change in the Enemy Alien's status. Previously detained at the East Boston INS facility, Cafaro had been shipped to Ellis Island, NY (also run by the INS) on October 23. Another Memo on Oct. 29 then notes Cafaro's transfer from Ellis Island to the army's jurisdiction at Mt. Royal Station, Baltimore, Md, for internment at Fort Meade, MD.[34]

It is perhaps worth noting that at Cafaro's rehearing at Fort Missoula, MT on September 21, 1943, the hearing board wrote this:

> The chief impression created by this Alien at his rehearing is that he is a perfectly

honest barber who has talked too much.[35]

The authorities were still suspicious, however, and Cafaro was not released outright, but paroled on November 5, 1943. The "loose talker" would not be fully released until April 1944, several months after he had been inducted into the United States Army (Cafaro reported for U.S. military service at Fort Devens, MA on February 9, 1944).

As noted in the Cafaro case above, a second hearing board often reversed the decision of the first, resulting in the parole of the enemy alien who had earlier been interned. News that this could happen clearly gave hope to many of the interned Italians, for almost all tried to request a rehearing when word spread that it was possible. Many of those who were paroled at this second hearing must have wondered what had made them "dangerous enemies" one day and loyal Americans the next—especially those, like Cafaro (apparently considered suitable for Army service even though he'd been interned as a "dangerous" enemy alien), and Carmelo Ilacqua of San Francisco, who, upon his release from internment in 1943, was asked to teach the Italian language at Stanford University to future members of the U.S. Army Intelligence Service.

Internment Procedure

After the hearing and the issuing by the Attorney General of a formal internment order, the male internee was formally turned over to the requisite Army authority.[36] This transfer was signified by a processing or re-processing procedure that took place sometimes at an Immigration Station but usually at a nearby Army base to which all internees were sent. Processing included being photographed (front and profile views), fingerprinted, assigned an internment serial number, and examined for identifying marks. This information, plus the record of where and when the internee had been arrested and by whom, with other information about residence, birthplace, family members, occupation and education, was placed in the Basic Personnel Record (PMG Form 2, for Alien Enemy or Prisoner of War) issued by the Provost Marshal General's Office. Thus, Cesare Pasqua, arrested September 16, 1942 in Trenton, NJ, was first detained at the INS facility at Gloucester City, NJ. After he was ordered interned on January 6, 1943, he was processed at Gloucester City on January 19: his height, weight, eye and hair color, and age were recorded, as well as an "operation scar on stomach." On the back side of the form were recorded the date and place of his birth (April 18, 1913, Perugia, Italy), his occupation (clerk), education (Gymnasium 3 yrs, Commercial School, 2 years), languages (Italian and some English), physical condition at time of capture (Fair), marital state (Married), religious preference (Catholic), home address, address of nearest relatives, and number of dependents (one son, aged 21 months).

Transfer of custody to the Army followed (if necessary), with internees usually being sent in groups to the nearest Army base. In Pasqua's case, he was sent from Gloucester City (INS) to the U.S. Army facility in Philadelphia on February 12, 1943 where he was "joined to party destined to Fort Meade via the B&O Railroad," which arrived the same day at the civilian internment facility at Fort George Meade in Maryland. Many internees picked up in or around New York City were processed first at Ellis Island and then sent to nearby Camp Upton on Long Island for a brief stay before being transferred to Fort Meade. Those to the north (for example, Ubaldo Guidi-Buttrini, of Winthrop, Massachusetts) were processed at the INS station in East Boston, Massachusetts, and likewise sent to Fort Meade. At Fort Meade, and at other army bases housing civilian internees, a special section of the base was set aside for the internment of civilians.

In San Francisco, the route was slightly different. The first internees, as already noted, were kept at the INS facility at Silver Avenue for several days, but, when ordered out of the western defense command by a hysterical General DeWitt, were dispatched to Fort Missoula, Montana for continued detention. In apparent violation of protocol, they received hearings *not* in their own communities as prescribed, but in front of a hearing board of San Francisco civilians brought to their barbed-wire enclosure in Montana especially to hear these cases. Carmelo Ilacqua, for example, was arrested on December 17, 1941 in San Francisco, sent by train to Missoula, MT on Christmas Day, and given his hearing in Missoula on February 10, 1942. Formally ordered to be interned following that hearing, he and the other San Francisco internees were then processed at Ft. Missoula, with PMG Form 2s issued. It then took two more months, until April of 1942, before they were transferred, most of them, to Army custody, initially at Fort Sam Houston in Texas.

San Francisco Italians arrested in the second wave of arrests, around February 21, 1942, followed a still different route, perhaps because things had calmed down by then (or General DeWitt had). As per protocol, following arrest they were given hearings in San Francisco, and after receiving the formal internment order from the Attorney General, were sent to the Army base on Angel Island in San Francisco Bay, Camp McDowell, and held in the Prisoner of War Enclosure. There they were reprocessed (PMG Form 2s) and sent south to another Army base already outfitted with civilian internment facilities, usually Fort Sam Houston in Texas. Thus, Felice Bersano was arrested on February 21, 1942 in San Jose, California. He was detained at the Immigration Station in San Francisco until April 17, when he received his formal internment order and was sent to

Angel Island for processing (PMG Form 2). About a month later, on May 20, he was sent to Fort Sam Houston where he joined other Italian internees who had arrived from Fort Missoula.

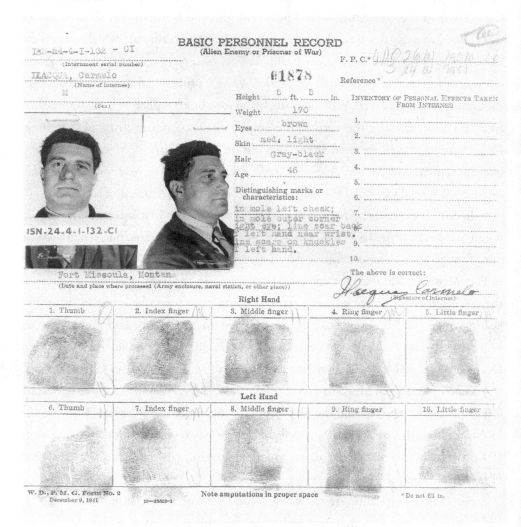

Carmelo Ilacqua Basic Personnel Record

Military Internment Camps

As noted for Camp Upton and Fort Meade, the Army had set aside, with barbed wire, specific areas of existing Army bases for the civilian internees. Once they arrived, the internees were sometimes issued POW uniforms, though some were allowed to remain in civilian clothes (civilian clothes were the rule at INS-run camps like Fort Missoula.) They were most often housed in 16'x16' pyramidal tents with wooden floors and boarded sides, accommodations which most internees described as fairly comfortable. Carmelo

Ilacqua notes in a letter that he occupied a tent with three other San Francisco internees.[37] Prospero Cecconi's diary (strictly illegal for him to have, and so, kept secretly) contains even more details about this, as well as about his travels from camp to camp, and is worth quoting at some length.

After being arrested on February 21, 1942, Cecconi notes that he was *tok* [sic] *to the Immigration Station, 108 Silver Avenue*, in San Francisco, that he was questioned and given his hearing on March 10, and that he spent thirty-six days at Silver Avenue before being transferred to the *Detention Camp, Sharp Park Cal* (Cecconi could not know about a formal order of internment, so his first intimation of his changed status appears

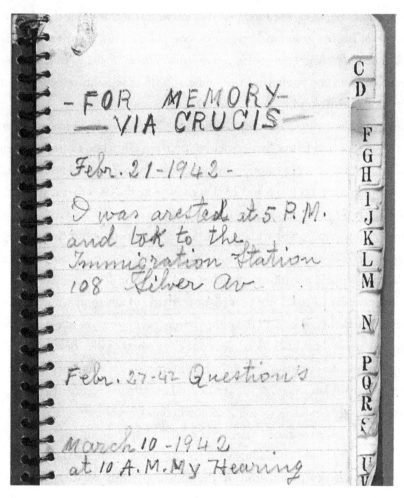

Cecconi's Diary, which he named Via Crucis (way of the cross)

to have come when he was physically transferred). On April 21, some two months after being arrested, he notes that he *left Sharp Park for Ft. McDowell; we arrived at 7 o'clock and truth was quietly fear; pitcher* [sic], *finger print, and searching our clothes.* This would seem to signify his formal internment under Army custody, as noted by the procedures for data needed to complete the PMG Form 2. After what he says was another twenty-nine days, on May 20 he *left Ft. McDowell and after 3 days trip I reach Texas at Ft. Sam Houston Internment Camp—and we was received with courtesy... We found there fine tend* [tents] *and plenty innabitant* [inhabitants]. On May 28 Cecconi records: *I received prisoner clothing,* no doubt the shirts with POW on the back described by several other internees. Several days of rain are noted until June 17, when, after twenty-six days at Ft. Sam Houston, Cecconi says he left *Ft. S. Houston San Antonio, Texas, and have 32 hours on the train and arrived here in Camp Forrest, Tenn.* It is at this point that Cecconi gives vent to one of his few emotional responses, couching his anger in ironic Italian: *June 19—ed accolti dal publico e dai soldati (col massimo rispeto) fischi, ed insulti d'aqui genere* [and received from the public and the soldiers (with maximum respect) whistles and insults typical of their kind.]

Following these moves, Cecconi records the most poignant of his entries on July 7, when his friend and fellow San Francisco internee, Giuseppe Protto, suddenly dies: *Morto il camerata Protto.* No emotion, no comment; indeed, nothing is recorded on the page, other than notes on July 8 and 13 that there were floods, and on August 1 that he *received first pay $4.30 for 43 days at 10¢ a day.* On September 16, Cecconi records his departure from Camp Forrest with another ironic comment about the journey: *27 ore di viaggio splendido—carri magnifici e cibo squisito, carni in scatola e pane secco* [27 hours of a splendid journey, magnificent coaches and exquisite food, tinned meat and dry bread.] The next day Cecconi arrives at Fort McAlester in Oklahoma, and meets what he describes as the best people of all the camps, *molto gentili con noi, ma poco da mangiare* [very polite with us, but little to eat]. It is not clear whether the "best people" refers to the camp commander and guards, or the other internees—for it appears that most Italian internees eventually landed at McAlester. Several months are recorded as being spent at McAlester with little incident (it is not clear whether Cecconi knew about the death of yet another Italian internee at McAlester, Giobatta Gasparini, also of San Francisco, on January 17, 1943[38]). Then, coinciding with the Army's decision in May 1943 to turn its civilian internees back to the custody of the INS, apparently because of its burgeoning responsibilities for Japanese internment and the great number of Italian and German POWs held at U.S. bases, Cecconi records his move from McAlester, Oklahoma, his third internment camp (not counting Fort McDowell, Sharp Park, or Silver Avenue), to Fort Missoula in Montana, his fourth. He arrives on May 23, and the next day notes that he enters the hospital because of his stomach ulcers. After a rehearing at Missoula, and more communications from Washington DC, Prospero Cecconi finally records his release: he departs from Fort Missoula on October 7, 1943, and arrives in San Francisco on October 9, where he must present himself at the INS Station on Silver Avenue once again for his formal release on parole.

Cecconi's diary thus confirms what is less vividly recorded in government documents, and in comments from other internees. First, most internees moved from camp to camp for reasons unknown to them, or to us even today. All that can be inferred is that the first Italian internees were kept wherever facilities were available, and that the authorities tried to keep internees from the three enemy nations more or less separate— though this was not always possible (clearly there were numerous Japanese internees at both Fort Missoula, the camp most associated with Italians, and at Fort Lincoln in Bismarck, North Dakota, the camp mainly occupied by Germans, a situation possibly attributable to the fact that more Japanese were interned than the INS could handle at the camp originally intended for them at Santa Fe, New Mexico.) It also seems clear that McAlester was the camp the Army had in mind for containing most civilian internees, and that most Italians ended up there (as did some Germans), though why they made stops at Fort Sam Houston, TX, Camp Forrest, TN, Fort Bliss, TX, Stringtown, OK, and elsewhere, is not. Cecconi's diary also confirms the movement of Italian internees back to Missoula in May 1943 for the reasons noted above, as well as the fact that while in Army custody, internees lived in tents, received POW uniforms, earned a stipend of 10 cents a day and were treated fairly reasonably, if sometimes rudely.

Internee Life

What neither Prospero Cecconi nor most other Italian internees from the west coast testify to are the rules and regulations governing visits and other matters of discipline. The major reason must be that Missoula, Montana and, later, internment camps in the south, were simply too distant for most California families to reach for a visit. This was not the case for east coast internees, however, and testimony and documents provide ample evidence for most of these matters.

To begin with, shortly after they were detained on Ellis Island, which was controlled by the INS, detainees were allowed to have visitors. As Lucetta Berizzi Drypolcher remembers it, "we could visit every week. We were allowed to bring him changes of clothes and food...Visitation was in a very large room with tables and benches—no privacy whatsoever."[39] Once interned under Army jurisdiction (most at Fort Meade in

Maryland), however, the rules for visitation became more detailed and restrictive. Rather than weekly visits, the internees could have only two visits per month from a total of five visitors who had to be designated ahead of time on a list. Requests for visits had to be submitted, in writing, for "Sundays only during the hours of 1:00 PM to 4:00 PM. Internees are limited to two visitors per month not on consecutive Sundays."[40] Apparently these visits took place in a kind of recreation room. Children under twelve were allowed to accompany an adult on the same pass, provided the request was made in advance; children over twelve had the same status as an adult. Though it is not noted in the formal regulations, visits were not to exceed twenty-five minutes in length. This is indicated by correspondence in the file of internee Ubaldo Guidi-Buttrini, whose daughter, Velleda Guidi, tried to request more time as follows:

> You probably are aware of the fact that to visit Camp George Meade from Boston, Mass., it takes quite a number of hours, and is very expensive. Also, on arrival there, we, his children, are so tired, that before we even get our breaths, the 25 minutes allotted us are up, and we have had very little, if any, of that satisfaction of being with our father. We know well that according to regulations, each internee is allowed two visits a month, of a 25-minute duration. We are wondering if, in our case, we couldn't be allowed but one visit a month, and allowed to be with him a little longer...[41]

The Commanding Officer of internees at Fort Meade, Colonel Ralph Hutchins, responded in the negative by writing at the top of Velleda Guidi's letter: "write sending regulations and advise that internees may have two visitors per month. Regulations the same for each internee, 25 min."

Rules governing visits to Camp Meade were equally strict concerning the conduct of internees and those visiting them. The regulations stipulated that "All conversations must be in English." To make sure this rule was observed, all visits were monitored and recorded by an army observer who spoke the requisite foreign language, in this case, Italian. Any lapses into the forbidden enemy language, or into sensitive matters such as planned movements of internees, were stopped by a signal; the entire visit could be terminated if this rule was not observed. Several recorded conversations indicate that the monitors took their jobs quite seriously. For example, on August 30, 1942, Temi Guidi visited her father and violated the rules. Here is what the monitor, Sergeant Caton Marconi, recorded:

> The undersigned was unable to prevent Miss Guidi from saying "how are you" to her father in Italian. Miss Guidi said that she was sorry, said that it would not happen again. The undersigned felt justified in allowing her to proceed, in view of the fact

that she had only uttered two words, which he understood, being conversant in that language (*Come stai*) [how are you? ed.] and felt that the rebuke that she had received was severe enough so that it would never happen again.[42]

If an internee could not get along in English at all, it was possible to get special permission to speak in the forbidden language, but that had to be arranged ahead of time. The conversation would, of course, be monitored. Other restrictions, not specifically stated in a document, but observable in monitored conversations, included the restriction on certain types of contact with other internees. At one point in a visit to internee Guidi-Buttrini by his son Mal Guidi, then a U.S. Army private in uniform, the monitor notes that several other internees entered the "recreation hall" where the visit was taking place and shook hands with Private Guidi, assuring him they would take care of his father. Then, yielding to emotion, one of the internees tried to embrace him. The monitor records his response: "When one attempted to embrace Pvt. Guidi they were all ordered to leave." In this same record another related prohibition was recorded, for when Private Guidi tried to wave goodbye to the internees he had just met, "this was stopped." Why shaking hands was allowed, but not embracing or even waving, is never explained.

Regulations concerning letters were equally detailed. In a document sent to internee families, dated October 1, 1942 from Headquarters, 1343rd Service Unit, Fort George G. Meade, MD, the rules state, in part:

MAIL – Each internee is allowed to name five (5) persons with whom he desires to correspond.

Two letters, not to exceed 24 lines each, and one post card weekly may be written by internee, on approved stationery.

All incoming and outgoing mail is censored before delivery.

RULES GOVERNING CORRESPONDENCE – In order to avoid delay in delivery, letters addressed to internees should:-

1. Not to be [sic] of inordinate length.
2. Be written on one side of paper only.
3. Be legibly written.
4. Be clear in meaning.
5. Have no writing on margin.
6. Show the full name and address of the sender.
7. Show return address envelope.
8. Show internee's name, serial number, company or group identification, name of Internment Camp.
9. Contain no deletions, erasures, strike overs.

Mail for internees that does not conform to the above regulations will be returned to the sender...

Books may be sent subject to censorship and delayed delivery.

NEWSPAPERS AND MAGAZINES – Authorized newspapers and magazines are supplied by subscription through the Internment Camp Exchange only. Unauthorized newspapers and magazines are destroyed upon receipt.

TELEPHONE CALLS – Internees will not be permitted to make or receive any telephone calls.

RALPH HUTCHINS
Colonel, QMC.,
Commanding[43]

The PMGO files of internees contain numerous examples of materials censored from letters to internees. Among them are *all* drawings, including whimsical cartoons of a pet dog sent to internee Alessandro Fabbri from his wife Mariam,[44] and an encouraging

Censored cartoon from Miriam Fabbri to her husband

poem which the Army censor feared might contain "hidden meanings." A reference in one letter of Mariam Fabbri's to the terrible living conditions in Italy was also cut by the censors. Most puzzling of all, a Catholic nun sent to internee Tullio Verrando a little paragraph meant to comfort him, which said, "Try to unite your sufferings with those of Jesus Christ. Remember, he suffered unjustly just to save your soul and mine and all other children. Therefore, give Him your Heart." The censor deleted the passage because, he noted, "it is a false analogy"[45] [meaning that Verrando's suffering was not 'unjust'? or that comparing Verrando with Jesus was a falsehood? ed.]

As to letters *from* internees, they too were subject to strict rules and regulations, though these varied from camp to camp—particularly from INS-run camps to Army-run camps. First of all, internee letters from Army-run camps had to be written on a special form letter the army provided, which folded into an envelope. Prominently displayed on the outside were the words INTERNEE OF WAR...

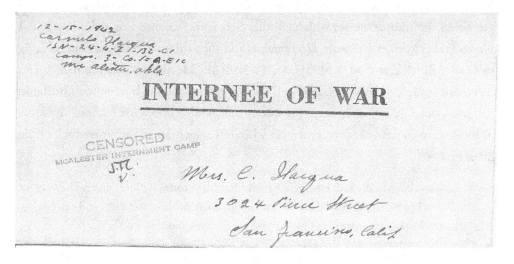

Postage was free, as noted in the place for the stamp. The delivered letter also displayed a stamp that said CENSORED, WAR DEPARTMENT, and the name of the camp, for example, CAMP FORREST INTERNMENT CAMP. One internee, Pasquale DeCicco, wrote to Col. Louis Ledbetter, commander of the McAlester Internment Camp, requesting that the humiliating "stigma of our unfortunate position," i.e. the prominent INTERNEE OF WAR label, visible on the outside of the envelope, be somehow covered. DeCicco was especially concerned about such letters being delivered to his children: "when they receive a letter from their father, that humiliating stigma of being an enemy of his adopted Country has to be stabbed into their feelings, nerves, eyes, it has to be broadcast continually by an envelope passing many hands and the scrutiny of many eyes."[46] DeCicco's request was denied. The inside of the envelope was lined in blue for writing, and contained 24 lines—the maximum an internee could write in a letter. As regulations stated, two such letters, and one postcard, could be written each week.

When internee Carmelo Ilacqua arrived at Fort Sam Houston, where he had to comply with Army rules for correspondence, he complained in a letter to his wife Bruna about the length limitation, comparing it to the rules at Missoula which were apparently more lenient, and which did not require the form letter. He also complained that "the magazine pictures I used to send Gioia from Missoula are now being removed from my letters by the censor even though I asked the censor to let them pass."[47] His wife urged him to write the longer letters in the form of a diary that he could show her when he returned, but he declined (probably because diaries were not allowed). Nonetheless, the Ilacqua letters, saved by his daughter, contain a great deal of information about his life during internment. In them he describes the activities of other internees from San Francisco; the fact that one internee, Ghirardi, had a radio; details about a show put on in the auditorium for which another San Francisco internee, radio broadcaster Nereo Francesconi, was *maestro di ceremonie*; and such things as the hours internees had to keep: "Reveille at 6:30 A.M., silence 10:30 P.M." He also tells us the name of the merchant seaman at Missoula, Egidio Dordoni, who made the boat models his family still possesses. On July 10, he urges his wife Bruna, who has been left without any source of income, to go to the Federal Emergency Board for assistance. She writes back on July 20 to report:

> I have been to the Fed. Emergency Board but they won't give me a thing. They suggest that I could work. I told them C. is too small to be left here and there and since my brother and sister are living with us, they want their money's worth.[48]

In September, Bruna writes in response to her husband's information about his new barracks, with twenty-four internees, at Fort McAlester: "But Daddy, I didn't know you had no sheets. You had them in Montana...Don't you think I better send you some? And how about some blankets? Let me know and I shall send what you need.." Whether she sent them is not clear. What is clear is that the new procedure instituted by the Army, for routing all internee mail through a central Post Office Box in New York, delayed the mails considerably: "There's a long delay between your letters as they now go through the censor in New York," Ilacqua wrote to his wife.

Given such hardship, the main interest of most internees involved measures for getting released. Most wrote letter after letter to Edward Ennis and others in the Alien Enemy Control section of the Justice Department, outlining the history of their lives in the attempt to prove that they were innocent and deserved a rehearing. For example, Louis Sdraulig of Santa Clara, CA was interned February 21, 1942. In December of that year, he wrote the following letter:

McAlester Inter Camp
McAlester, Oklahoma

December 8, 1942
Edward Ennis
Department of Justice
Alien Enemy Control
Washington, DC

Sir: It is almost ten months that I was arrested. According to radio reports and news papers I was accused of being potentialy [sic] dangerous alien treated and regarded as such after my arrest. After all this time in the enclosure I do not know yet why all this, must be some reason for, some evil I do not know, something wrong some where, except I am not citizen of this Country but with sincere intention and resolution to become soon as possible, all necessary steps already made toward, and to establish my permanent home here in this Country with one born here as companion I worked on that plan. My past record is spotless clean I always obeyed all laws of this Country. I lived to the best of my ability to the laws of God and teaching of the Catholic Church. I do not know how I am considered as potentialy [sic] dangerous. What evil I made? Please let me know where I fell short in my loyalty to this Country I wish to know my weaked [sic] points to strengthen them to perfection to please better God Country and neighbors. Investigation by honest person from honest people should proof [sic] my sincerity and truth. The space is to [sic] small to explain more and better. I do the best. Hoping in your kindness. I'll be waiting for your answer.

Sincerely yours,
Louis Joseph Sdraulig

Ralph Averga, arrested January 27, 1942 in San Pedro, CA, was likewise mystified about the cause of his arrest, and wrote the following, also from McAlester:

U. S. Attorney General
Department of Justice
Hon. Edward J. Ennis
Director Alien Control Unit
Washington, DC

Dear Sir:

The undersigned, Ralph Averga, ISN-20-4-I-51-CI, resident in San Pedro, California, 467 – 11ᵗʰ St., detained since January 27, 1942, begs your Honor to grant him a new hearing so he can clear up himself of any accusations and show his loyalty to the United States of America.

The following is a brief history of his life:

Born in Naples, Italy, October 4, 1893, at the age of 2 years came to this Country with his parents and since then never went back to his native country and frequented the American schools always feeling as a native born American.

In his childhood he lost his father never being able to find out if the same was naturalized citizen or not. In 1921, doubting his legal status as Citizen of the great republic, he applied for his First Paper, but his relatives advised him to stop the procedure because they were sure that he was a Citizen on account of his father being naturalized: following the said consel and advise [sic], the undersigned neglected to take the Second Paper, always feeling, as he feels now, American. In October 1940 he did not register as an Alien because he never considered himself such. When arrested by the Immigration Department, he asked for an attorney who is still working to find out if his father was or not a naturalized Citizen.

Being practically born in this Country and educated in the American School, the undersigned has always been loyal to this Country not knowing allegiance to any other country. The undersigned has no relatives in Italy and never had any contact with said country. All his relatives are in the United States and all are American Citizens.

Here is a list of his relatives who can show beyond doubt his loyalty and sentiments toward the American Flag, the only Flag that the undersigned ever knew:

Mrs. Enrico R., mother of 5 children all born in the U.S., of which John L, born of her first husband, is in the U.S. Navy; and Miss Theresa L at present in the W.A.A.C. Mrs. R is his sister and lives in West Haven, Conn.

Mrs. Ralph B., mother of three sons: Joseph B., at present in the U.S. Army, whose address is: Btry "A" 24 Sep. Bn.; John B., at present in the U.S. Army, M.P. stationed at Fort Dix; Ralph B., actually working for the National Defense and living with his parents at Bridgeport, Conn.

Mrs. Peter P., mother of Michael G. by her first husband: said nephew of his is working for the National Defense in Milford, Conn. Mrs. P. address is Auburn, NY.

The above mentioned are all sisters of the undersigned.

Hon. Sir, in the name of Justice, the undersigned appeals to you that a new hearing be granted to him to show his loyalty to his beloved Country, the United States of

America.

As soon as possible, the undersigned or his relatives, will send to Your office affidavits to show beyond doubt his sincerity and loyalty to the United States of America.

Respectfully yours,

Ralph Averga

The Question of Repatriation

Many of those who wrote such letters were indeed granted re-hearings, especially after September of 1943 when Mussolini's government was deposed and Italy formally joined the Allies. Even before this, however, the arrested resident aliens were faced with other major decisions. The first, and perhaps most important, was the repatriation decision. Every internee seems to have been presented with the choice to repatriate to Italy, many being faced with the question even before they were interned. In fact, the INS repatriation form, after requiring the basic information about date of birth, place of birth, and number of dependents, gave the respondent two options about repatriation:

> I, _____, a national of _____who was born at
>
> _____
>
> on _____having been arrested in the United States of America as an Alien Enemy, respectfully petition that I be repatriated:
>
> In the event of my internment.
>
> Whether or not I am ordered interned.
>
> (Delete line which does not apply)[49]

In other words, those who were arrested, and not yet judged 'dangerous' enough to be formally interned, were given a form that not only allowed them to repatriate, but offered them a kind of incentive to do so. The form said, in effect: *Wouldn't you prefer to go back to Italy rather than spend an unknown amount of time interned?* Indeed, a number of those arrested, when presented with this choice, did, in fact, choose repatriation over internment, and may have been repatriated on these grounds alone.

Most, however, seem to have declined repatriation (thus indicating their commitment to the United States) and ended up in internment camps anyway, only to have the same questions put to them again. That is, the Provost Marshal General's Office also issued a repatriation form, this one lacking the internment choice found on the INS-issued form—since the option was no longer an issue. Instead, on the PMGO -REPATRIATION DATA form, the internee had to write or type his choice at the bottom of the form under "Remarks." This would seem to indicate that the form itself was used as an indication of a preference to repatriate unless the internee, like Augusto Mauro of New York, said: "Don't wish to be repatriated."[50] Repatriation, it therefore seems, was *not* the choice of most internees, who for the most part preferred to remain in the United States. In fact, some internees who had initially expressed the desire to repatriate reversed it later on. One such internee was Luigi Vinci, arrested February 16, 1942, in San Francisco. Vinci later wrote a letter from the Fort McAlester Internment Camp to the Commanding Officer, Col. Seidel, explaining his change of heart:

> Dear Sir:
>
> Towards the end of June 1942, still under the strains of my recent internment, I applied for repatriation through the representative of the Swiss Legation when he visited Camp Forrest Internment Camp, at Camp Forrest, Tennessee.
>
> A special form which I filed at the request of Camp Forrest Headquarters, relative to my application for repatriation, was forward by such Headquarters to the War Department.
>
> I now wish to withdraw my application for repatriation, as it is my desire to stay in the United States, my country of adoption.[51]

Vinci's request was apparently respected, for he is recorded as being transferred to Fort Missoula on May 18, 1943. On the other hand, it may simply have been the case that the State Department's Special Division, which was in charge of prisoner exchanges during the war, by then had no further need of Italian enemy aliens to exchange for American civilians caught in Italy. For this is what the repatriation program seems to have derived from: the anticipated need to have bodies available to exchange for Americans caught in enemy countries.[52] This would explain why the INS first, and then the Army again, both in the early days of the war, solicited a repatriation decision from the civilian internees.

The case of Domenico Rosati provides yet another angle on how repatriation could be used. Rosati was a physician who had emigrated to the United States in 1924, after having completed his medical training in Naples, Italy. He was licensed to practice medicine in Pennsylvania in 1926, and settled in Pittsburgh PA. In 1930, according to a memo he wrote, he took part in the activities of the Italian colony there, including medical work at the Italian consulate, which work required him to join the "Italian Legion" or *Ex-Combattenti* (Rosati had served Italy as a lieutenant in World War I, and was wounded, gassed and permanently disabled). After 1937, he says, he "withdrew from these colonial activities almost completely." Having married an American citizen, he filed a petition for citizenship with the Immigration Office in April of 1941, but war broke out before Rosati could complete the process, and he was arrested on December 11, 1941 as a "dangerous" enemy alien—possibly because of his *Ex-Combattenti* membership. A hearing before his local hearing board exonerated him, however, and he was released *unconditionally* on January 27, 1942, and in May of that year filed another Petition of Naturalization.

Then his real troubles began. According to Rosati in a letter explaining his case, on May 27, 1942, he received a letter from the State Department informing him

> ..that he could be repatriated on June 2nd if he so wished. This letter was mailed at the address of another man who had been interned with him. He answered the State Department, stating his case and expressing his desire to stay, if the precedent of his detention would have no further consequences upon his status as a loyal and law-abiding citizen. This answer was not motivated by any mental reservation on his part, but simply by a natural desire to be reassured that he could stay and serve with a calm mind, a necessity for his profession, and an urgent necessity in his case because the detention had been such a mental shock that he felt dejected to the point to be unable to carry on his professional duties. The State Department never answered this inquiry...[53]

This did not end the matter, however. On July 27, the U.S. District Attorney of Pittsburgh summoned Rosati and asked about his repatriation request. Rosati explained what he thought was a mix up, but the DA then informed him that orders had come to reopen his case, "and the verdict would be internment—*unless he requested to be repatriated*" [note how this resembles the first repatriation choice offered to all internees, ed.]. Rosati resisted, asking if he could be allowed to join the U.S. Armed Forces to serve as a doctor, and be naturalized thereby. The DA told him he could not do this. Rosati still resisted signing a request for repatriation, "as it would place him in the position of returning to an enemy country and, even disabled, perhaps place him in a position where he would have to fight against America." But, according to Rosati's account, the DA assured him that "at war's end, he could return to America and the fact of his repatriation would have no bearing upon his return." Rosati, believing he had no other alternative, reluctantly consented. On October 27, he was called once more to appear before the Enemy Alien Hearing Board, "questioned about this repatriation business" and on December 18, 1942, was "again taken into custody and interned."

It thus appears that Domenico Rosati was, for some reason, solicited by the State Department as a candidate for repatriation [perhaps due to his disability, for the British Government had vehemently protested American plans to exchange able-bodied "enemy" males for American civilians; thus, in this regard, the disabled Rosati would have qualified as a 'good' exchange candidate, ed.]. It also appears that he was subsequently *pressured to repatriate* by the U.S. District Attorney in Pittsburgh, only to have his reluctant agreement used as an indication of disloyalty, and hence as a reason to re-intern him.

Interned for the second time, Rosati continued to petition for permission to put his medical training to good use, ministering either to internees or anyone else in the camp, but he was always refused. A note in his file testifies to this, along with the comment of Colonel Hutchins, the Commanding Officer at Fort Meade, MD: "Advise that under existing regulations the offer cannot be accepted." Rosati was eventually paroled in late October of 1943, after Italy had surrendered. But so fearful was he of involvement with the authorities that he ordered his family never to refer to his internment in any way, even after his death.[54]

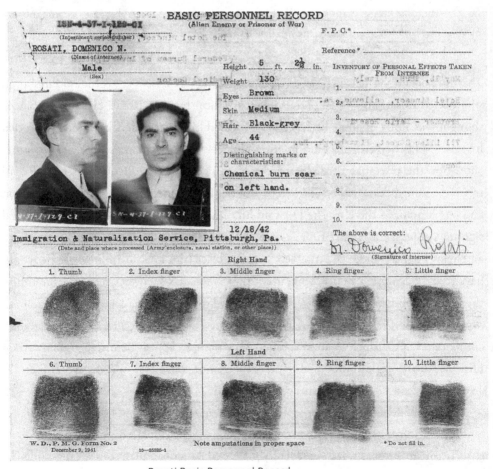

Rosati Basic Personnel Record

The Basis for Internment

The grounds for placing thousands of Americans of Italian birth on the Custodial Detention Index have already been alluded to. A person, either a permanent resident alien or a naturalized citizen, could become a candidate for the list simply by being prominent in his community, especially by being an officer of an Italian American organization. He could also qualify because of testimony against him from an informant. Authorities then presumably winnowed down the CDI, focusing on the most "potentially dangerous" or influential positions from which to cull for internees. For example, working for or publishing an Italian-language newspaper was an almost certain route to internment, as was working as a radio broadcaster on an Italian-language program. A leadership position in the *Ex-Combattenti,* or Italian War Veterans, considered a "dangerous" organization by the FBI, was an even more certain ticket to internment, as was simple membership. Teaching in an Italian language school qualified as a suspect activity, but so did any position of responsibility in such large ethnic organizations as the Italian Catholic Federation, the Order Sons of Italy in America, and the Dante Alighieri Society, or smaller ones like the Tito Minitti Club of New York. Pietro DeLuca, for example, was arrested and detained for several months on Ellis Island for having founded the latter—mainly a social club— and was released on parole only after his American-born wife wrote to Eleanor Roosevelt, among others, to plead her husband's case.[55]

Yet though alleged 'community leaders' made up a large proportion of the first internees, large numbers of laborers with no apparent role or influence in either suspect organizations, the media or their communities were subsequently interned. It would thus appear that the other major route to internment involved informants. No one yet knows how many resident aliens were apprehended because a neighbor overheard them making a laudatory remark about Mussolini, or an ex-wife decided to get even with her estranged spouse. What is certain is that all such information was taken very seriously by the FBI, and that files on internees vividly attest to the damage such information could cause. The case of Federico Dellagatta, who was arrested because someone overheard him praising Italy and the Italian army ("loose talk" also weighed heavily against Amleto Cafaro), has been referred to above. Similarly, John Galeotti, a fisherman from Anchorage, Alaska, was taken into custody for ranting drunkenly about Hitler and Mussolini. His landlord testified to this when he informed on Galeotti. But even though the hearing board recommended that he be released because, it noted, "there is considerable suspicion that John Galeotti was turned in to the Army authorities as an enemy alien to satisfy a personal grudge rather than because of any subversive activity," the DOJ review board overruled the hearing board (once again) and ordered Galeotti interned at Fort Lewis, Washington. When he was finally paroled in March of 1943, his parole was conditioned on the fact that he could not return to Anchorage.[56]

For many others who were interned, the cause of government suspicion remains a mystery. As the war continued, the ranks of those interned were swollen by longshoremen, waiters, drifters, fishermen and farm laborers. In most cases, it is difficult to see why the government would find such people suspect. They would have had little or no influence in the Italian American communities of which they were a part, and so could hardly be suspected of spreading propaganda.[57] Some may have violated immigration or registration laws, and some may have returned to Italy to visit relatives (visiting Italy was definitely considered a cause for suspicion), but it often appears that little more than their Italian-ness led a neighbor to suspect them, and to alert local or federal officials about their presence. When it came time to convince a hearing board of their innocence, they lacked both the language and the skills to marshal a cogent defense. When they were interned, some ended up so befuddled that the government sent them to insane asylums.

Fred Stella is one of the most disturbing examples. Arrested in Cleveland, Ohio in June of 1942, Stella ended up in the internment compound at Fort McAlester, Oklahoma for reasons that are unclear, but may have had to do with his having served as a soldier in World War I. This is because most Italian immigrants who fought for Italy in that war became members of the *Ex-Combattenti,* a suspect organization. The catch was, Stella had fought *not* on the side of Italy, but *for his adopted country, the United States of America,* as he explained in a letter to the Provost Marshal General, Allen Gullion:

> Dear Sir:
> My name and address are the above ones. I am a veteran of the last war, when I enlisted voluntarily to fight on the Allied side in the American army.
> At present I am, as you can judge by the address, an alien enemy in a camp for intern-ees. The reason for this has not been made clear to me, and in consideration of my past record of loyalty to this country, I consider the treatment given to me hardly fair.
> For about five years and a half I was laid up in a hospital of Denville, Illinois. When, in 1940, all aliens were supposed to register, according to a new law, I was not only un-aware of this fact, but would also have been unable to comply with the regulation, had I known about it, for the very reason of my illness. I think, therefore, that in all justice, I cannot be held responsible for my failing to comply, in view of the reasons just told. Could you be so good as to send me a copy of my record, as held in your care, to the above address. I shall be looking forward to your reply and remain in the meantime,
> Yours very truly
> Fred Stella[58]

Stella added that he hoped the army would assist him in returning to his brother's home in Clinton, Indiana so he could help that brother in his infirmity. But the response from Colonel Bryan, chief of the Aliens Division of the PMGO, was bureaucratic: it said that since Stella had been interned at the direction of the attorney general, any change in status fell under the jurisdiction of the Alien Enemy Control Unit in the Justice Department, to whom he had to write. Still ill, Stella seemed to find this bureaucratic tangle beyond him: on April 6, 1943, he was remanded to Borden General Hospital, Chickasha, Oklahoma—a hospital for the insane.

Thus, a man who had fought for his adopted country in one world war, was interned by that same country as a "potentially dangerous" enemy in the second. Nor was Stella alone in enduring this ironic fate. Mario Valdastri, mentioned above, told a similar tale, with the added irony that after fighting in World War I for the United States, Valdastri had been granted American citizenship. Thus, as a citizen and a veteran of combat service for his adopted country, he should have been immune from internment. Valdastri found out very quickly that, as an Italian American, he was anything but immune. He was arrested at his Hawaiian home on December 8, 1941 (apparently because of the complaint of a neighbor testifying that Valdastri had *talked* about "blowing up" a makeshift dam in dispute between them), and, after what he called a perfunctory hearing, sent to the mainland to be interned at Camp McCoy in Wisconsin. He complained bitterly about this, writing to the ACLU, the President of the United States, and, like Stella, to the Provost Marshal General, Allen Gullion, with whom he seemed to be acquainted. It did no good. As noted above, both Valdastri's letter and the one his daughter wrote on his behalf were handled *by the book* by the unbending Gullion. All this came to a tragic conclusion shortly afterwards. Returned to Hawaii, but still interned on Sand Island pending his imminent release on parole, Valdastri was refused the permission he requested to attend the wedding of his daughter, Frances. Shortly afterwards, Frances was attending a party for a friend's engagement, which was taking place during a blackout. Unable to see in the dark that a landing had no railing, she accidentally fell to her death. Mario Valdastri, still not released from internment on Sand Island, was allowed to view his daughter's body once, but only after he agreed to be escorted to the funeral home by armed guards.[59]

Nor was Valdastri the only American *citizen* of Italian descent to be interned. Pasquale DeCicco endured a similar fate. Even though he had been one of the first Italian immigrants to New Haven, Connecticut to become an American citizen, in 1909, and even though he had persuaded all seven of his brothers and sisters to do likewise, he nonetheless found himself, on April 24, 1942, under arrest by order of the President of the United States. He was taken to the INS detention center in Hartford, Connecticut, sent thereafter to the detention center in East Boston, and, after his hearing, to the internment facility at Fort George Meade, Maryland. The question that would not let DeCicco rest, was *why*. For, unlike many of his internee companions, Pasquale DeCicco knew the score. As the acting vice-consul in the Italian consular offices in New Haven CT, DeCicco had worked primarily to help Italian immigrants in his state adapt to the American legal system, such as when they had to liquidate estates or deal with damages from deaths or injuries due to work-related accidents. As he says in a January 16, 1943 letter to Attorney General Biddle:

> My concern had always been the maintenance of cordial relations and friendship between the United States and Italy, and to this task I earnestly devoted my modest efforts, by continually and consistently explaining to Americans and Italians the life, the customs, the habits and traditions of the two Countries, their long traditional and uninterrupted friendship, their almost similar struggle for their independence and freedom, their lofty ideals.[60]

Given all this service, both to his co-immigrants and to his adopted country, which he described as "practically preaching Americanism," Pasquale DeCicco felt both informed, entitled, and, more keenly than most, stung by the injustice of his arrest. The result was that he never accepted it, but rather kept up a string of letters and protests with demands to know why he had been interned, and explanations to counter whatever elements of his behavior the government might have found suspect.

Yes, he admitted, he *had* gone back to Italy to serve the nation of his birth in World War I, but maintained at all times, and even carried with him, his "certificate of American citizenship." Moreover, even as a soldier he had refused to take an oath of allegiance to the Italian government, but instead returned after the war to America to resume his duties at the consular agency in New Haven. There he had remained until the day his office was "closed by order of the president on June 28, 1941" [sic], this time because of Italy's role in the century's second world war. And yes, he admitted, he did believe that Fascism "had been a salvation for Italy...considering the unhappy circumstances in which the century [sic; 'country'?] was at the time" but "I did not think that we had any use here for its philosophy or principles." DeCicco's behavior at that time seems consistent with this attitude, for when asked by his superior, the Italian consul general in New York, if he intended to return to Italy with other repatriated consular personnel, he said he did not because, as an American citizen, he "had no business in Italy." As to why he had remained working at the Italian consular offices for so long, DeCicco attributed this to economic factors, specifically the Italian law which promised him a substantial bonus—equal to one half of his monthly salary for each year of service—for his thirty-six years on the job, all of which he would have forfeited if he had quit. As it turned out, however, he never did receive his bonus from the war-devastated Italian government.

DeCicco's decision to remain in America thus cost him dearly, he complained. Not only had he lost his pension, but his arrest as a "dangerous alien" cost him his life savings and "eliminated all chances of redeeming my home, and I lost it." Now, at 63 years of age, he wrote, "broken in health by the humiliating life of this camp—have already lost 32 pounds of my weight—burdened by an undeserved and unjust stigma, I am afraid I am heading for a nervous breakdown."

Neither this nor his other letters—explaining in detail why his Italian army service in 1915 had *not* nullified his American citizenship, nor had his consular service "because these positions abroad were, by law, open also to non-Italians," and besides he had voted unchallenged in every American election for twenty-five years and had three American-born children—none of this seemed to matter. Pasquale DeCicco was not released from internment until December 10, 1943 (long after Italy had surrendered and joined the Allies in September of that year), having been paroled somewhat earlier. This meant he had been forced to spend at least a year behind barbed wire. For a man who had become a U.S. citizen in 1909, this must have seemed hard time indeed. What is equally notable, here, is that in DeCicco's case especially, we see how arrest and internment without due process can affect those who are trapped in its web. Pasquale DeCicco was never told what had caused the government to suspect him as "dangerous." In the absence of formal charges, in the absence of an attorney to question witnesses or documents or government officials, and in the absence of any need for the government to provide evidence for its allegations—whatever they consisted of—a man like DeCicco could only seize upon hints, patterns of questioning, and examinations of his own behavior in order to figure out what to defend himself against. In DeCicco's case, he assumed, from the very fact of his arrest (only enemy aliens were supposed to be arrested) and questions at his hearing, that his 'crime' must have had something to do with nullified citizenship. As he wrote,

> The Hartford Immigration Office attempted to put on trial some intentions that they claim were into my head some twenty-five years ago, when I went back to Italy in 1915, basing its allegations on an arbitrary interpretation of an old Italian law, of which I did not even know the existence.[61]

Accordingly, he kept hammering at that point. But the fact is, neither DeCicco in 1943 nor we many years later are really sure what got him arrested and interned.

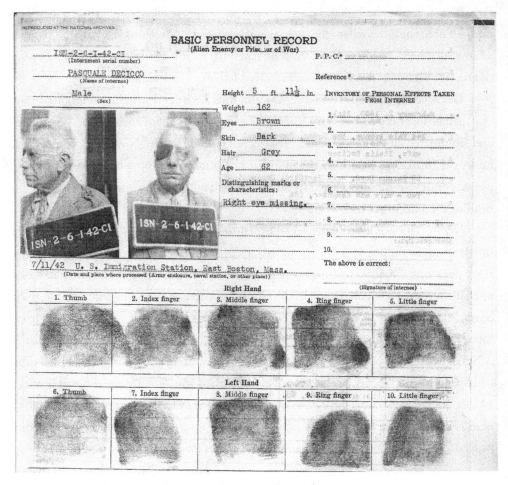

DeCicco Basic Personnel Record

This reminds us of many other cases. Louis Sdraulig, whose letter is quoted above, said:

> After all this time in the enclosure I do not know yet why all this, must be some reason
> for, some evil I do not know, something wrong some where...I do not know how I
> am considered as potentially dangerous. What evil I made? Please let me know where
> I fell short in my loyalty to this Country I wish to know my weaked [sic] points to
> strengthen them to perfection to please better God Country and neighbors.

The case of Ezio Pinza, mentioned earlier, is even more specific. Pinza in his autobiography noted that, at his hearing, the enemy alien is "presumed guilty until he can prove his innocence"—the complete reversal of the cardinal law of American jurisprudence that every suspect is to be considered "innocent until proven guilty." He also made clear that without any notion of the charges against him, the enemy alien is at a loss to know how to defend himself. Indeed, at his first hearing, Pinza failed so miserably in his own defense that the Attorney General ordered him interned. Only his wife's persistence in persuading the Attorney General's office to grant Pinza a second hearing saved him, for in preparing for that new hearing, Pinza was able, with the help of his attorney, to ferret out what he was suspected of by closely examining the pattern of questions he had been asked at his first hearing. Armed with this information, Pinza at his rehearing was able to mount a cogent defense, defuse or counter the charges, and win his release on parole. Sadly, most internees were unable to take advantage of their first hearing until they were already behind barbed wire. From within that guilt-producing enclosure, without lawyers or others to help, they were subject to self-examination and, all too often, the kind of self-blame and shame displayed by Louis Sdraulig. Thus, in addition to being deprived of their freedom, those subject to such arbitrary procedures are often deprived of their inner freedom as well.

Aftermath

As may be obvious by now, internment for long periods during World War II was not without its consequences, both for the internee himself, and for his family. Though some internees emerged virtually unscathed to resume their lives almost as before, the damage to many others varied from emotional to psychological to physical to material, up to and including collateral damage to family members.

To begin with, a large number of internees complained of stomach ailments. Whether these were the physical manifestation of what is known as "barbed wire sickness" or not [writer John Christgau[62] explains the German term, *gitter krankheit*, as the inner conviction that since one is behind barbed wire, one *must* have done something wrong, ed.], the complaints ranged from simple digestive problems to more serious complications that required hospitalization. Illidio DiBugnara, for example, spent two months in the hospital shortly after arriving at the McAlester Internment Camp with an ailment he described as some form of stomach trouble. Giobatta Gasparini did worse: interned at Fort McAlester, he died of complications related to ulcers. Prospero Cecconi also landed in the hospital due to stomach ulcers, first at the internment camp in Missoula, Montana, and then upon his release in San Francisco. According to his daughter, he nearly died from peritonitis during the latter illness, and, with no family in San Francisco, was coaxed back to health by Rina Bocci, who worked at the Italian Welfare Agency in North Beach. But it was Cecconi's mental state after his release that caused his real problems. As testified to by his daughter and by the same Rina Bocci,

Cecconi considered the requirements of his parole a continuing humiliation, especially since he felt he had done nothing wrong. Bocci wrote on his behalf:

> He feels grateful that he was released from internment; however, the parole is also causing a hardship in that he feels it is a stigma and his former friends now avoid him. This, as well as the fact that he cannot proceed towards naturalization, thereby hindering the return of his wife and children to the U.S., is causing a mental strain which, he feels, will in a short time cause a physical and mental breakdown.[63]

This was one of the side effects: those arrested suffered the inevitable stigma that all enemy aliens felt was aimed at them to one degree or another—that is, would the U.S. government have targeted such people if they had done nothing wrong?

Eventually, Cecconi did secure his U.S. citizenship, and was reunited with his wife and children. However, what he had endured seemed to have unsettled him permanently regarding life in the United States, and in time he returned to live out his life in his native village in Italy. Similar problems were felt by Mario Valdastri, who returned to Italy at the end of his life as well; journalist Giovanni Falasca, who never wrote for a newspaper or in any other form again; and Lucetta Berizzi Drypolcher, who lost her job at Saks 5th Ave. because of her father's internment.

Conclusions

There is much still to be learned about the internment program. One thing is clear, however. Large numbers of people born in Italy were targeted for flimsy reasons, mainly having to do with sympathy for their country of origin. The Department of Justice's own report on the Individual Exclusion Program—a program that targeted naturalized citizens, who were then exiled from their communities from October of 1942 to late 1943 and early 1944—makes this clear (see Chapter 5, for details on this program). This 1943 study's conclusions—that the Army's exclusion program was both unnecessary and unconstitutional—can, in this writer's opinion, be applied as well to the program of internment under discussion here. As in the exclusion program, many interned individuals were targeted for reasons having to do in large part with their pre-war ethnic sympathies, which were often taken as signs of disloyalty to the United States. Moreover, the use of the concept "potentially dangerous" as applied to those arrested and interned was found to be particularly noxious to the Department of Justice reviewers. As they wrote in their report:

> Practically, the use of phrases such as this [potentially dangerous] suggests that those

who use them hold the view that a subject of an exclusion case must be excluded unless it is clear that there is no reason to exclude him. This is analogous to saying that the burden of proof is on the excludee, although the excludee, of course, cannot meet the burden, since he is not advised of the charges against him.[64]

Nor did such concerns occur only to DOJ officials. Olga Bruschera Trento, of San Francisco, wrote letters to the Department of Justice pleading the case of her interned husband, the actor Guido Trento. Born in the United States, Mrs. Trento had a strong enough sense of her entitlement as a U.S. citizen to raise questions about why her Italian-born husband had been interned. Her April 29, 1942 letter to Assistant Attorney General Earl Harrison (the very man who had written, in 1940, that the "American alien" was *never* an "enemy alien") said in part:

> My husband, Guido Trento, is now interned by the United States Government at Fort Sam Houston. He was taken into custody on December 8, 1941, first taken to Missoula, Montana, and a few weeks ago sent from there to Texas.
>
> I have never clearly understood with what subversive activities against the United States my husband was charged—at least, only in the most general way. Of course, I do not believe my husband guilty of the charges. Is there any way by which I may have more precise information in this regard; and is there any authority to which I may, perhaps, present testimony in favor of my husband?[65]

On June 4, Mrs. Trento received a reply from Edward Ennis, Director of the Alien Enemy Control Unit in the Justice Department. It said, in part:

> (Name blanked out) was apprehended as a potentially dangerous alien enemy. He was afforded the opportunity of a hearing before an Alien Enemy Hearing Board which determined and recommended that in view of the past expressions of loyalty by Mr. Trento [why the name is used here, and not previously, is not known, ed.] to a country now at war with the United States he should be interned for the duration of the war.
>
> The power of internment of aliens of Italian nationality...is exercised whenever it is believed that such person, through allegiance to the country of his birth or citizenship, may possibly be disloyal to the United States. It is not necessary that he be guilty of any specific acts of a subversive nature, but that he may or, because of his indicated loyalty to a foreign power, could be deemed potentially dangerous to the safety of the United States.[66]

Ennis then advised Mrs. Trento that she could "submit facts or proof of such loyalty" and that such data would be added to Trento's file in "consideration of a rehearing or reconsideration." Mrs. Trento then wrote another letter on July 3, 1942, to both Ennis and the Attorney General, questioning the "past expressions" of loyalty alleged, and pleading for some information about specific charges:

> I have never been able to ascertain what these past expressions could possibly have
> been, nor when they were made, that would have him considered potentially danger-
> ous. I can assure you that my husband is harmless. He is absolutely committed to the
> principles of the Constitution and the laws of the United States and would not and
> could not because of his sincerity of purpose do anything of any kind against this
> country, of whom I, his wife, am a citizen. I have never been able to ascertain what the
> charges were at this hearing you speak of before the Alien Enemy Hearing Board so
> as to be able to combat these allegations...Is there some way that I can be advised as to
> who testified against him and of what this testimony consisted so that I may present
> evidence, which I am sure I can, to prove the injustice of any charge or decision that
> my husband is potentially or otherwise dangerous to this country?[67]

Mrs. Trento's letter, indeed, could have been used as a textbook case of precisely the
argument that Justice Department reviewers and the Attorney General himself employed
against the Individual Exclusion Program: "the burden of proof is on the excludee," but
"the excludee cannot meet the burden since he is not advised of the charges against him."
If one replaces the word "excludee" with "internee," it is easy to see that the very same
conditions and strictures were applied to all enemy aliens in the internment program.
That is, they were interned not for anything "subversive" they had *done*, as Ennis admits
in his letter, but for the *possibility* that they *might* do something—in short that they
"could be deemed potentially dangerous." This double and triple concept of possibility
(the idea that someone could possibly be considered possibly dangerous is a net that
would leave virtually no one innocent) made the entire hearing procedure a catch-22. If
you are required to prove your innocence, but cannot learn what you are accused of (other
than past loyalty to the country of your birth), it is impossible to defend yourself. This
is precisely the reason that the United States Constitution contains the Amendments
known as the Bill of Rights. Amendments V & XIV guarantee that *"No persons shall be...
deprived of life, liberty or property without the due process of law."* Amendment VI expands
on due process, guaranteeing an accused person the right *"to be informed of the nature
and cause of the accusation; to be confronted with the witnesses against him...to have the
assistance of counsel for his defence."* During World War II, the "persons" known as enemy
aliens were deprived of each and every one of these due process rights. Many people
considered and still consider this denial of rights permissible because enemy aliens are
not U.S. citizens, but it is notable that renowned legal scholar David Cole has specifically
emphasized the error in this point:

First, properly understood, the Constitution imposes substantial limits on sacrificing immigrants' liberties for citizens' purported security. The basic rights at stake—political freedom, due process, and equal protection of the laws—are not limited to citizens, but apply to all "persons" subject to our laws. These rights are best understood not as special privileges stemming from a specific social contract, but from what it means to be a person with free and equal dignity. They are human rights, not privileges of citizenship, and ought to apply whenever we seek to impose legal obligations on persons.[68]

In short, those classified as "enemy aliens," though often considered to be undeserving of the rights thought to be reserved for citizens, do in fact deserve to be equally protected. This is, quite simply, because they are "persons," human beings who are permanent residents of the United States and, therefore, as deserving of constitutional guarantees and protections and civil rights as anyone else. As Cole points out, the language of the Constitution emphasizes this, reserving such rights not for citizens alone, but for "all persons" resident in the United States.

Most fundamentally of all, if you are targeted because of what you *might* do, which is to say because of *who you are*—it is not only impossible to defend yourself, it is more or less guaranteed that *who you are becomes the problem*. There is more to say about this below. For now, it is enough to emphasize that targeting people not for anything they have done, but for *who they are*, is not only unconstitutional—it is unAmerican and perhaps un-human as well.

---

1. The most vivid evidence of American preparedness for a Japanese attack came with the Office of Naval Intelligence break-in at the Japanese consulate in Los Angeles, in the spring of 1941. The ONI photographed everything in the consulate safe, including the names and locations of some 450 Japanese agents in southern California, all of whom were immediately arrested on December 7, as well as hard evidence that Japan considered most American Japanese (Nisei) not potential allies but untrustworthy in their loyalty. *Personal Justice Denied*, pp. 52-54.

2. June 17 *New York Times*, "US Orders All Nazi Consulates Closed," by Frank L. Kluckhohn, pg. 1, http://www.freerepublic.com/focus/f-chat/2735999/posts (accessed July 11, 2011). This article also notes that "Today's action, moreover, followed closely upon the heels of President Roosevelt's freezing on Saturday [July 14, ed.] of German and Italian assets in the United States..."

3. From website, http://www.grolier.com/wwii/wwii_14.html. See also photocopy of *New York Times*, April 1, 1941, "Axis Protests Seizure of Ships," on www.freerepublic.com/focus/f-chat/2698088/posts (accessed 7/15/11). This article along with another titled "The International Situation" notes that 28 Italian and two German vessels were seized, along with 36 Danish vessels. (NB: differing estimates of the numbers continue to prevail: oocities.org says 65; it also says that on June 6 FDR seized 40 foreign ships in US ports and used them for Lend-Lease convoys; and that on June 14 FDR freezes axis funds in US.)

4. The confusion between these Italian nationals, mostly merchant seamen, and the resident aliens of Italian descent, who were immigrants, has continued to the present day. The *Una Storia Segreta* project has tried to always distinguish between these Italian citizens in the U.S by chance and always temporarily, and the permanent resident aliens living in the United States by choice, and who were interned as a matter of domestic policy emanating from the Justice Department. What is discussed and examined here concerns the latter, i.e. immigrants of Italian descent who were branded as enemy aliens by Proclamation 2527.

5. Molinari file, RG 389, Entry 4661, NARA II, PMG Form No. 2, p 2.

6. Molinari letter cited in Rose Scherini, "When Italian Americans Were 'Enemy Aliens,'" in *Una Storia Segreta: The Secret History of Italian American Evacuation and Internment During World War II*, ed. Lawrence DiStasi, (Heyday Books: 2001) p. 13.

7. From "Orders to Take Him Away," by Lucetta Berizzi Drypolcher, in *Una Storia Segreta*, op. cit., p. 217.

8. Gloria Ricci Lothrop, "Unwelcome in Freedom's Land," in *Una Storia Segreta*, op cit, p. 168.

9. Ibid.

10. Historian Arnold Krammer asserts that the FBI arrested, for a few days, the entire German and Italian communities in Hawaii: Krammer, *Undue Process*, p. 33.

11. From "Two Men in Suits," by Mario Valdastri, Jr., in *Una Storia Segreta*, op cit, p. 153.

12. Memo, J. Edgar Hoover to Lemuel Schofield, December 8, 1941, cited in Krammer, op cit, p. 32. Another Hoover dispatch cited by Krammer, dated Dec. 17, 1942, asked all FBI offices, to "furnish the Bureau... the names concerning persons of American citizenship, either by birth or naturalization, who you believe should be considered for custodial detention..."

13. David Cole, in "Enemy Aliens" (*Stanford Law Review* 54: 953ff), makes a major point of this spill-over effect. One reason, he argues, for diligently protecting the rights of aliens in periods of crisis, is that abrogating the rights of aliens paves the way for the same violations to be imposed, sooner or later. on American citizens.

14. *Administrative History of the Immigration and Naturalization Service during World War II*, Prepared by the General Research Unit, Hugh Carter, Supervisor, August 19, 1946, p. 278.

15. Krammer, op cit, p. 33.

16. Willard Kelly (Asst. Commissioner, INS) letter to A. Vulliet of YMCA, Aug. 9, 1948

17. Press Release, The White House, Statement of the President (Jan. 2, 1941), as cited in *Report to the Congress of the United States*, p. 39.

18. Press Release, U.S. Department of Justice, Dec. 26, 1941, cited in Report to the Congress of the United States, pp. 38-39.

19. *Administrative History*, op cit, p. 283.

20. This distinction between "detention" and "internment" derives from the fact that not all those who were arrested and detained were ordered to be interned. Only after a formal hearing board recommended internment and the attorney general issued an official internment order did the enemy alien become an *internee*. Because of this, confusion still exists over numbers interned: in the Italian case, for example, official figures state that 3284 enemy aliens were arrested and detained for varying periods at INS stations; of that number, PMGO files indicating internment have been located for some 260 individuals. Even this number is not definitive, however, since the PMGO gave up custody of civilian internees in May of 1943 and arrests of Italian resident aliens continued after that date; therefore, the total is no doubt higher.

21. In his autobiography, Francis Biddle makes clear that it was the mass internment and persecution of aliens in WWI, as well as the recent experience in England, that he was determined to avoid: "We had been watching the British experiment. At the outbreak of war there were in Great Britain a good many Germans and Austrians, chiefly Jewish refugees. In the beginning the policy was selective and discriminating and only 568 were interned. But by August of 1940, when it was realized what fifth columnists had done in France and the Low Countries, caution gave way to panic. The government yielded to popular pressure, about 74,000, mostly German and Austrian Jews, and all aliens, were taken into custody and thrown into hastily laid out camps." (See Francis Biddle, *In Brief Authority*, op. cit., p. 207. For internment in England, see Peter and Leni Gillman, *Collar the Lot: How Britain Interned and Expelled its Wartime Refugees,* Quartet Books: 1980. For Canada, see Franco Iacovetta et. al., *Enemies Within: Italian and Other Internees in Canada and Abroad*, Univ. of Toronto Press: 2010. For Australia, see Ilma Martinuzzi O'Brien et. al, *Enemy Aliens: The Internment of Italian Migrants in Australia During the Second World War*, Connor Court Publishing: 2005. Martinuzzi O'Brien's father, Alfio Martinuzzi, though born in Australia, was considered guilty-by-association with Italian immigrants, and hence was interned with the "20 percent of the Italian-born population of Australia" interned during WWII.)

22. Instructions to Alien Enemy Hearing Board, Supplement #1. Jan. 7, 1942. RG 85, General files 1942-45, Ft. Missoula, Montana, WWII Internment files, INS, NARA I.

23. Letter, Allen Gullion to Frances Valdastri, July 18, 1942, Valdastri File, RG 389, Entry 4661, NARA II.

24. Amendment 5: No person shall be...deprived of life, liberty, or property, without due process of law. Amendment 6: The accused shall enjoy the right...to be informed of the nature and cause of the accusation; to be confronted with the witnesses against him.

25. As an example of the importance attached to such declarations, Illidio Di Bugnara, already serving in the U.S. Army when war broke out, was asked if he would be willing to fight in Italy and kill Italian soldiers. Knowing he had two brothers serving in the Italian army, DiBugnara replied that he would not. He would serve in the Pacific or anywhere else, he vowed, but he would not kill his own brothers. The board hearing his case considered this evidence of disloyalty to the U.S., and DiBugnara was interned. (Letter to J. Sexton Daniel, U.S. District Attorney, January 30, 1943, DiBugnara file, RG 389, Entry 4661, NARA II.)

26. Personal communication. Fox's book on German Americans in WWII is titled *America's*

Invisible Gulag: A Biography of German American Internment & Exclusion in World War II, (Peter Lang: 2000).

27. Internment Order, Jan. 6, 1943, Pasqua File, RG 389, NARA II.

28. Memo for Chief of Review Section, October 8, 1942, Federico Dellagatta DOJ file, #146-13-66-24.

29. This note indicates that in addition to "protecting the public safety," and "assuring the public" that the government was taking steps to prevent sabotage, the internment program also constituted a demonstration project to the Italian communities warning them that "dangerous" elements could suddenly disappear. Ibid.

30. FBI case file, Amleto Cafaro, 100-1741.

31. DOJ case file, Amleto Cafaro, #146-13-2-66-27.

32. Ibid.

33. Ibid.

34. Ibid.

35. DOJ case file, Amleto Cafaro, Memo from Hearing Board to Attorney General, #146-13-2-66-27.

36. Most female internees were sent to a special facility run by the INS at Seagoville, Texas.

37. "Letters to 3024 Pierce," in *Una Storia Segreta*, op cit., p. 228.

38. Giobatta Gasparini file, RG 389, Entry 4661—Records Relating to Italian Civilian Internees During WWII, Box 10, NARA II.

39. From "Orders to Take Him Away," in *Una Storia Segreta: The Secret History of Italian American Evacuation and Internment during World War II*, ed. Lawrence DiStasi, (Heyday Books: 2001), p. 219.

40. Copy of Camp Meade regulations, sent to author by Lucetta Berizzi Drypolcher.

41. From "Let's Keep Smiling: Conditions of Internment," in *Una Storia Segreta*, op cit. p. 208.

42. Ibid., p. 205.

43. Camp Meade regulations, op. cit.

44. See "Let's Keep Smiling," op. cit., p. 212.

45. Ibid., p. 210.

46. Letter to Col. Louis Ledbetter, November 6, 1942, DeCicco file, RG 389, NARA II.

47. "Letters to 3024 Pierce," op cit., p. 230.

48. Ibid., p. 231. This would seem to contradict the Justice Department's assurances that relief agencies had been instructed to aid the families of internees deprived of their breadwinner.

49. Rosati file, RG 389, Entry 4661, NARA II.

50. Mauro file, RG 389, Entry 4661, NARA II.

51. Vinci letter, January 9, 1943, Vinci file, RG 389, Entry 4661, NARA II.

52. Several books have been written about repatriation and prisoner exchanges, most notably, Scott Corbett's *Quiet Passages: The Exchange of Civilians Between the United States and Japan During the Second World War* (Kent State Univ. Press, 1987) and Harvey C. Gardiner's *Pawns in a Triangle of Hate* (Seattle: 1981).

53. This, and all subsequent quotes, from Rosati letter and memo, Jan. 14, 1943, Rosati file, RG 389, Entry 4661, NARA II.

54. Private communication from Anthony Ghezzo, Rosati's in-law. Recently, however, Rosati's son has agreed to release more information about his father.

55. Personal interview, Joseph DeLuca. A fuller version of DeLuca's story can be found in his account, "Pippo l'Americano," in *Una Storia Segreta*, op. cit., pp. 255-265.

56. John Galeotti file, RG 389, Entry 4661, NARA II.

57. Propaganda, not coincidentally, ranked as one of the major offenses attributed to influential Italians, allegedly trying to keep America out of the war. But it has been well-documented that on the eve of Pearl Harbor, more than 85% of Americans opposed entry into the war anyway.

58. Stella letter, September 25, 1942, Stella file, RG 389, Entry 4661, NARA II.

59. For the full story of Valdastri's internment, see my "A Tale of Two Citizens," and Mario Valdastri Jr.'s "Two Men in Suits," both in *Una Storia Segreta*, op. cit., pp. 137-155.

60. Pasquale DeCicco file, RG 389, Entry 4661, NARA II.

61. DeCicco, Ibid.

62. John Christgau, *Enemies*, Iowa State U Press: 1985.

63. Document in possession of Doris Giuliotti, Cecconi file, USDOJ.

64. Alien Enemy Control Unit, *Preliminary Report on Study of Individual Exclusion Order Cases*, August 1943, p. 28.

65. Letter, Olga Trento to Earl Harrison, April 29, 1942, Guido Trento file, Department of Justice-INS, Italian Enemy Aliens, CO 2.12-C.

66. Ibid, Edward Ennis letter to Olga Trento, June 4, 1942.

67. Ibid, Olga Trento to Edward Ennis, July 3, 1942.

68. David Cole, "Enemy Aliens," *Stanford Law Review*, V 54, p. 957.

IV: Evacuation and Curfew

W hile all of the various phases of the wartime measures imposed on enemy aliens
    of Italian descent have been distorted, minimized or outright denied, perhaps
none has been less well understood than their forced evacuation from West Coast prohibited zones in early 1942. Even the Justice Department, perhaps as confused as everyone else, claimed until 2001 that no mass action had been implemented against persons
of Italian descent during the war. In response to a 1992 resolution and letter from Richard Armento of the Order Sons of Italy in America asking for a "full public disclosure of
the injustices suffered by Italo-Americans during WWII," including the evacuation from
prohibited zones, the Justice Department wrote that "only a relatively small number of
ethnic Germans and Italians received individual exclusion orders in contrast to the mass
detention of Japanese Americans."[1]

The fact is, a mass evacuation of Italian immigrants *did* take place in California,
and while it was not nearly as complete, nor as violative of civil rights as the relocation
and internment of over 120,000 Americans of Japanese descent, it deserves no less to be
known, acknowledged, and understood.

The story actually commences well before the war. On August 21, 1940, Allen Gullion, then the Adjutant General, and soon to be appointed Provost Marshal General
of the United States with jurisdiction over everything of a military nature within the
nation, sent a memo to the Chief of Staff, Liaison Branch, of the Adjutant General's
office, posing legal questions about possible military control over civilians within the

continental United States in the event of war. The memo asks: "Can the Military in the zone of the interior participate in the arrest and temporary holding of civilians who are not alien enemies but citizens of the United States?" This means, as Guido Tintori points out in an essay which referred for the first time to this document,[2] that the U.S. military from at least 1940 had been contemplating the possible arrest, detention and removal of American civilians, *including citizens,* from areas it judged critical to defense. As most people now know, the military proceeded to act on just such a plan with respect to Japanese Americans, in what was to become the major violation of civil rights during World War II, and one of the worst civil liberties violations in American history.

Less well-known is the fact that Lt. General John L. DeWitt, commander of the huge Western Defense Command (WDC), at first disagreed substantially with General Gullion about what was needed to defend his area. DeWitt's plan to protect the West Coast had initially focused not on citizens so much as on aliens with roots in the three enemy nations, the so-called "enemy aliens" (aka "alien enemies"). Numerous accounts and documents testify to the General's preoccupation with the enemy aliens.[3] As one example, DeWitt sent a message just twelve days after Pearl Harbor, on December 19, to the War Department in Washington DC recommending that "action be initiated at the earliest practicable date to collect all alien subjects fourteen years of age and over, of enemy nations and remove them to the Zone of the Interior."[4] This had been preceded by an even earlier initiative by the General's staff to designate a wide strip of the west coast as a "combat zone" from which all undesirable persons should be removed.[5] Thus, though Morton Grodzins[6] was the first to observe that before early January of 1942, General DeWitt had shown no interest in the "mass evacuation" of civilians from the West Coast, what Grodzins was referring to was what would become the massive evacuation of all Japanese on the West Coast. Nothing in the term, however, dictates that it cannot be used more generically. That is, a *mass evacuation* can simply be employed to mean the compulsory eviction or exclusion of large numbers of people from a given area on the basis of race or nationality, without any attempt to ascertain individual guilt or innocence. And what General DeWitt's thinking had long involved was, in fact, a mass evacuation of *all enemy aliens*—those immigrants who had been born in Germany, Italy, or Japan and were not yet naturalized—from his area of jurisdiction.

The area DeWitt's plan had targeted was the Pacific Slope, an enormous sweep of land which extends from the Pacific ocean to the foothills of the Sierras, ranging from thirty to one hundred-fifty miles in width and extending from the Canadian border to southern Arizona. What General DeWitt had been demanding for that area, from almost the first days of the war, was a thorough cleansing—that is, the removal from it of *all non-citizens* born in any of the three enemy nations. Notwithstanding the fact that, with Executive Order 9066, he was eventually given the green light to clear this area of *all* the Japanese, the General never stopped arguing and planning for a similar removal of the other two suspect groups, the Italian and German enemy aliens, who lived there.[7] And evidence of this enduring military intention to expand the removal beyond the Japanese can be found in what Tom Clark—the Department of Justice's liaison with the Western Defense Command—publicly stated in April of 1942:

> Anyone who has the idea that General DeWitt is going to delay the evacuation of German and Italian aliens is in error. He has consistently said publicly and otherwise that he intends to evacuate these groups as soon as his program with reference to the Japanese is completed.[8]

Clark knew whereof he spoke. General DeWitt seems never to have given up on his original plan. The problem, in terms of the received standard history of this time, is that in the end he *did not succeed*. I term this a 'problem' because it is the *failure* of DeWitt's plan to remove *all* the aliens from the Pacific Slope that historians have emphasized. Again and again it has been pointed out in the literature that everyone from the President on down distinguished between the Japanese on the one hand, and German and Italian enemy aliens on the other. And indeed they did. To cite just one example, Attorney General Biddle, in a memo to the President regarding a later proposal to remove enemy aliens from the East Coast, wrote: "The Executive Order [i.e. EO 9066, ed.] was couched in general terms to avoid the charge that it was directed solely to the Japanese, but it was not intended to be used elsewhere.."[9] Again, historians have interpreted this to mean that German and Italian aliens were *never* forced to evacuate from large areas, that they were always treated *as individuals*. But as historian Stephen Fox was the first to emphasize,[10] the scuttling of the plan to totally remove all enemy aliens from both coasts was not instant, nor was it automatic. The planning to remove *all* enemy aliens proceeded very far indeed, and long after February 19, 1942 when Executive Order 9066 was first announced. It proceeded long after early March of 1942 when EO 9066 was implemented and the Japanese relocation commenced. It proceeded long after the Tolan Committee had held its hearings into the matter (February 21-23, 1942) and made its report recommending that "any such proposal [i.e. to move massive numbers of Italian and German aliens] is out of the question if we intend to win this war."[11] In fact, it was only in May and June of 1942, when President Roosevelt personally intervened—mainly based on his fear and the fear of many others, that if such an evacuation plan were extended to the eastern and southern coasts, it would involve moving millions of individuals at great political and economic cost—that General DeWitt's plan for a Pacific Slope cleared of *all* enemy aliens was put to rest.

What this has meant is that the discussion about the wartime violations of Italian Americans, even where it is mentioned, has virtually always ended here, with the failure of General DeWitt's enemy alien plan. In fact, it has usually ended with the decision of the Justice Department in mid-February of 1942 to go along with the more drastic, but numerically (and politically and economically) more limited plan—the plan to target only those of Japanese descent (both aliens and citizens) and remove them en masse to WRA camps. This has come to mean, in effect, that the "other evacuation" never took place.

But the fact is, *a West Coast evacuation of Italian resident aliens—from California cities like Richmond, Pittsburg, San Francisco, Santa Cruz, Stockton, Monterey, Alameda and Los Angeles and including the coastal areas in between--did take place.* Even a cursory glance at any newspaper of early February 1942 will demonstrate that.

Front page of *Richmond Independent*, February 2, 1942.

Perhaps more important, this general evacuation had been ordered even before the discussions relevant to Executive Order 9066 took place, and certainly before EO 9066 was promulgated on February 19, 1942. And it took place on the basis of the earliest contestation between the War and Justice departments, mainly in December of 1941 and January of 1942, a struggle which is best comprehended by following the plans, fears, and discussions emanating from the Western Defense Command, with Lieutenant General John L. DeWitt commanding.

Western Defense Command

To begin with, it should be noted that the proclamations issued by the President immediately following Pearl Harbor already contained the authority to remove enemy aliens from various areas identified as critical. Proclamation 2525, for example, stated:

> (9) Whenever the Attorney General...or the Secretary of War...deems it to be neces-
> sary, for the public safety and protection, to exclude alien enemies from a designated
> area, surrounding any fort, camp, arsenal, airport, landing field, aircraft station, electric
> or other power plant, hydroelectric dam, government naval vessel, navy yard, pier,
> dock, dry dock, or any factory, foundry, plant, workshop, storage yard, or warehouse
> for the manufacture of munitions or implements of war or any thing of any kind...or
> from any locality in which residence by an alien enemy shall be found to constitute a
> danger to the public peace and safety of the United States...then no alien enemy shall
> be found within such area or the immediate vicinity thereof. Any alien enemy found
> within any such area or the immediate vicinity thereof prescribed by the Attorney
> General or the Secretary of War, as the case may be, pursuant to these regulations, shall
> be subject to summary apprehension...[12]

Either the Secretary of War or the Attorney General, under this authority alone, could designate a given area *critical to the public peace and safety*, and exclude or eject from it *all alien enemies*.

This was clearly what General DeWitt had in mind ten days after Pearl Harbor when he first mentioned this issue by phone to the San Francisco head of the FBI, Nat Pieper—who then relayed it to FBI chief J. Edgar Hoover. Pieper, as noted above, learned that the General and his staff had designated a 100-mile strip along the West Coast a 'combat zone,' from which they wanted to remove *all undesirable persons*. When Director Hoover heard this, he responded skeptically and even contemptuously, noting that the Western Defense Command, bedeviled and beguiled by amateurish intelligence, was reacting hysterically to such things as cows brushing their backs against power lines near the Bonneville Dam, and interpreting it as sabotage.[13]

With the first attack by a Japanese submarine on an American merchant ship, also on December 17, and subsequent attacks resulting in the sinking of two American tankers, however, General DeWitt stepped up his demands for clearing his 'combat zone.' This time he wrote a memo to the War Department, demanding action (see above), specifically, the collection of all enemy aliens and their *removal to the Interior.* Indeed, in this December 19 memo, according to Peter Irons in *Justice at War*[14], DeWitt made no distinction among the alien groups, any or all of whom he was certain were signaling the Japanese Navy with crucial targeting information. War Department officials in Washington, however, understanding that hundreds of thousands of enemy aliens on the West Coast would have to be moved to comply with such an order, chose to politely ignore the General's memo. This does not mean, however, that General DeWitt was alone in his determination to clear his area of suspect persons. On January 8, for example, General DeWitt learned that he had military company, in that "Admiral C.S. Freeman, Commandant 13th Naval District, recommended that all enemy aliens be evacuated from the states of Washington and Oregon."[15]

Washington's non-responsiveness to these military demands seemed only to energize General DeWitt, and in the last weeks of 1941 he switched his demands slightly, firing a withering barrage of memos and phone calls to Washington, complaining repeatedly about the failure of the Justice Department to implement the regulations needed to enforce the terms of Presidential Proclamation 2525. The terms in question were mainly those prohibiting enemy aliens from possessing 'contraband'—especially weapons and short-wave radios—which the General was sure aliens were using to signal Japanese submarines. He noted that even though FBI agents were ready to seize contraband, they could not move until the Attorney General issued specific regulations. DeWitt therefore called for blanket authority to raid the homes of anyone with a link to the enemy nations, so the military itself could seize such items. And if the Department of Justice kept resisting his entreaties, he made clear, he was determined to push the President to transfer *all* control over enemy aliens to the Army. When this request was relayed to J. Edgar Hoover, the FBI chief again opposed it, noting that with some 200,000 homes occupied by enemy aliens, mass raids would have a "very bad effect," especially on law-abiding people.[16]

General DeWitt's unyielding focus on the danger presented by enemy aliens ("I have little confidence that the enemy aliens are law abiding or loyal in any sense of the word")[17] needs to be contrasted with his initial, and very different position regarding the treatment of American citizens. This contrast is revealed in a crucial telephone conversation the WDC General had with Allen Gullion, the Provost Marshal General, on December 26, 1941. In that conversation, where Gullion approvingly cited a Los Angeles Chamber of Commerce report urging the evacuation of *all* Japanese residents, including American-born citizens, DeWitt expressed serious reservations about such a removal. First, he said, if we arrest all 93,000 Japanese, both native- and foreign-born, "we will have an awful job on our hands and are very liable to alienate the loyal Japanese..." Next, he maintained that state and local authorities, aided by the FBI and military intelligence, could adequately handle espionage and sabotage. Third, in response to Gullion's enthusiasm for the wholesale internment of *all* Japanese, including the American citizens among them, General DeWitt expressed confidence in the Army's ability to "weed the disloyal out of the loyal and lock them up if necessary." Finally, sounding almost like a Justice Department lawyer, the General capped his argument with the words,

"An American citizen, after all, is an American citizen."[18]

These December discussions merit consideration for several reasons. They make plain that it was the Provost Marshal General, Allen Gullion—the man in charge of all domestic military affairs—who had early contemplated, and now pushed for the extreme measures against *both* aliens and citizens of Japanese descent. It seems that he was the one who understood—from his post in Washington, DC—the politics of military control over civilians. Where General DeWitt was driven mainly by fear—of sabotage, espionage and invasion—and the related desire to secure his area against actions by those he primarily distrusted, *i.e. those he considered foreigners, and hence, most likely to be disloyal: the enemy aliens*, General Gullion seems to have been just as driven to find a measure against civilians that would at once play well in public (i.e. show that the military had taken a visible step to secure the Pacific coast against a repeat attack) and not alienate large numbers of potential voters. On both counts, the Japanese, easily blamed for Pearl Harbor and not very numerous as voters, fit the bill better than the far more numerous Italians or Germans.

The steps that were soon taken reinforce this view. Based on the disagreement between the Justice and War Departments, particularly General DeWitt, over how best to handle the enemy aliens, Assistant Attorney General James Rowe visited San Francisco on January 4, 1942 to see if he could work out a compromise with the Army. As noted earlier (see Chapter 2, War and General Restrictions), his mistake was to arrive without a plan of his own. The result was that he was overwhelmed by a detailed plan prepared by General DeWitt and his liaison from the Provost Marshal General's office, Major Karl Bendetsen. What emerged from these meetings, therefore, was a nearly complete capitulation by the Justice Department to the military's demands: first, a re-registration of all enemy aliens, who would be required to carry, at all times, pink booklets with photo I.D. and fingerprints [initial order issued January 14]; second, the issuance of search warrants based only in the fact that an enemy alien resided in a given premises—a clear violation of the "probable cause" stipulation of the 4th Amendment; and third, *the establishment of prohibited zones from which all enemy aliens were to be removed.* This latter measure also included the establishment of a larger "restricted zone" where the activities of enemy aliens would be severely curtailed, most visibly by a 9 PM to 6 AM curfew.

In the ensuing two months, each of these measures was ordered by the Justice Department, and their implementation formed the backbone of the mass violations against Italian Americans, primarily in California and the West Coast, but also nationwide (see Chapter 2: War and General Restrictions). What concerns us here, however, are the last two recommendations: 1) the establishment of prohibited zones from which all enemy aliens had to move, and 2) the designation of a larger more general restricted zone where a 9PM to 6AM curfew was put into effect. The first meant that every enemy alien of Italian descent living or working in a prohibited zone would have to move, or face arrest and internment. Since upwards of 10,000 such resident aliens would have to move, without regard for individual identity or any judgment as to any individual's "dangerousness," this qualifies as a mass evacuation. And, as we shall see, it took place *well before* the more egregious and well-known relocation and internment of 120,000 Japanese, both aliens and citizens alike, made possible by Executive Order 9066.

The Evacuation Orders

Despite his vigorous complaints about Justice Department delays in issuing orders to restrict the enemy aliens (i.e., seize contraband, limit their travel, and so on), General DeWitt took considerable time providing the Attorney General with the specific zones he was so zealous to clear. It was not until January 21, 1942 that he provided the DOJ with his first list of restricted zones (the confusion over what was meant by the term "restricted" as opposed to "prohibited" seems to have lasted for some time, with the terms often used interchangeably; in the end, a "prohibited" zone was one in which no enemy alien could remain, or even enter; the much larger "restricted" zone was one in which enemy aliens could live and work, but in which their movements were sharply curtailed, mainly by a dusk-to-dawn curfew). Be that as it may, DeWitt in January 1942 designated some eighty-six areas as Category A zones, meaning that all enemy aliens would have to leave them. Eight additional zones were designated as Category B zones, meaning that access to such zones would be limited to individuals carrying some form of pass or permit (docks and waterfront areas were already limited to those persons, like fishermen, with a special identification card, though the recurring idea to limit re-entry into larger zones to persons with special passes never came to fruition). An additional complication arose when the Navy insisted that *its* areas, such as Bainbridge Island near Seattle, should be cleared of even American citizens of Japanese extraction who could not prove that they had cut off their alleged ties to Japan.[19]

Still, the Attorney General continued to insist that he had no problem acceding to the military's demands for ordering enemy aliens out of *specific, limited* areas. Accordingly, in late January, the Justice Department issued a series of press releases setting up the *initial* West Coast prohibited zones that General DeWitt had specified. Those orders came in two segments: the first, on January 29, called for *all* enemy aliens—German, Japanese, and Italian—to vacate two areas: the San Francisco waterfront and parts of Los Angeles; the second order, on January 31, called for vacating some 69 coastal zones— essentially the California coast west of Highway 1 (though in the far north near Eureka, the boundary was Highway 101), from the Oregon border to Santa Barbara—as well as additional prohibited zones near vital industries throughout the West. The latter zones included areas near power grids, military installations, and along waterfronts and inland waterways like San Francisco Bay and the Sacramento Delta. By February 7, additional orders had raised the number of prohibited zones to 84 in California, 7 in Washington, 24 in Oregon, and 18 in Arizona[20]—a number that would continue to shift, depending on who was doing the counting. For example, a draft by the Justice Department six days earlier, on February 1, said "The Army has surveyed and recommended 88 prohibited areas in California,"[21] while a Memo for the President on "West Coast Prohibited Areas" drafted by the Attorney General on February 6 stated that "I have already designated about 110 specific areas of this character in California, Washington and Oregon."[22]

Even this was modest compared to what was to come. For at about this same time, it became clear that the military, and especially General DeWitt, had in mind far more ambitious evacuation plans, to cover many more areas. Although these plans did not become public until February 9 and 10 of 1942, they reached the Attorney General by February 6, as indicated by the above-mentioned Memorandum for the President, "West Coast Prohibited Areas," found in his papers. In it, the Attorney General first reviewed his cooperation with all previous demands of the military for clearing limited areas of alien enemies, but balked at what he now gathered would be the latest one:

I have been informally advised that the Secretary of War and General DeWitt, Commanding General of the 4th Army, plan to recommend to me that *the entire cities of Los Angeles, Seattle, Portland and Tacoma be declared prohibited areas* from which all alien enemies, Japanese, German and Italian, must be evacuated [Emphasis added.]

He then reviewed the authority, under Presidential Proclamations 2525, -26, & -27, to exclude said alien enemies from any designated area, and the fact that he had already announced "about 110 specific areas of this character in California, Washington and Oregon." With his cooperation established, he outlined his objections to the proposed Army expansion:

> I have assumed, until yesterday, that these areas were recommended by the Army to me for strictly military reasons. For that reason alone I have accepted them automatically.
>
> I am amazed, therefore, to find that the Army now plans to recommend the evacuation of alien enemies from four of the largest cities on the West Coast, including the fourth largest city in the United States. Here *40,000 persons are involved* [Emphasis added.]
>
> If I continue to have the primary responsibility for designating these areas I must in this case seriously question the Army's recommendation. The Army 10 days ago recommended quite small areas in Los Angeles. For minor additional reasons it now recommends the entire city of Los Angeles. ...Either the military situation has radically changed from its first recommendation of several small areas 10 days ago—and I have not so been informed—or the Army is accepting the pressure of public opinion....
>
> In any event, it is clear that the Department of Justice, certainly, and probably all other civil agencies of the Government, are unable to handle a mass evacuation of 40,000 aliens (not including the thousands of citizens who are members of the families of these aliens and will move with them).[23]

As it turned out, the Attorney General's information about the upcoming demands was quite accurate, for three days later, on February 9, 1942, General DeWitt returned to his original obsession with the Pacific Slope: he formally recommended to the Department of Justice that the entire western half of Oregon and Washington, as well as part of Arizona, be transformed from a "restricted zone" (curfew only) to a "prohibited zone" (full evacuation). That is, the Western Defense Command now wanted *all enemy aliens* evicted from the northern part of the Pacific Slope—a mass removal that would have added well over 10,000 people to the thousands already slated to move. More ominously, the sweep of the order and the above-mentioned rumors about already-drafted plans for similar orders for Los Angeles County made it plain that this was only the first step in clearing the entire Pacific Slope, including California, of the nearly 200,000 enemy aliens living there.[24]

One day later, on February 10, Naval authorities on Bainbridge Island in Puget Sound asked the Department of Justice to order the removal from that island of *not only* enemy aliens of all three groups, *but also* American citizens of Japanese ancestry. The Attorney General saw the implications clearly, and formally *refused both recommendations.* Although it gets somewhat ahead of our story, it is worth noting here that it is these refusals by the Justice Department, and the way they were expressed, that would lead not only to Executive Order 9066 and the internment of 70,000 American citizens of Japanese descent, but also to the full takeover of enemy alien control on the West Coast by the military. For what the Attorney General said in response to these early-February demands was simply that his department *could not*, and therefore *would not* carry them out; the military would have to do the job itself:

> If therefore it is your opinion that Bainbridge Island should be declared a military area, then the Department of Justice cannot carry out the assignment...
> *and*
> The evacuation of all alien enemies from this area would, of course, present a problem of very great magnitude. The Department of Justice is not physically equipped to carry out any mass evacuations. It would mean that only the War Department has the equipment and personnel to manage the task.[25]

Still, all this would come a bit later. In January and early February of 1942, the Attorney General clearly thought he could forestall the Army's more ambitious plans, partly by proceeding to carry out the evacuation of enemy aliens from the limited areas General DeWitt had first designated, and then objecting to the rest as they came up. This meant that the Department of Justice continued to announce in several press releases that two dates would become evacuation days for thousands of west coast enemy aliens. First, on *February 15*, a few areas, mainly around defense plants, hydroelectric plants, and oil fields, but also including prohibited zones in Washington and Oregon, would have to be evacuated. Second, *February 24* would be designated as the major evacuation deadline, when all other prohibited zones, including the entire coastal zone in California from the Oregon border to Santa Barbara, had to be cleared of all enemy aliens. For the Italian community, this meant that thousands of the resident aliens of Italian descent living in areas suddenly prohibited to them (including ports and docks where many hundreds fished for a living), were forced to make plans to leave their homes and/or businesses and find other places to live. And again, it is important to note that these Justice Department orders *required no additional authority at all*—because, recall, those branded as enemy aliens had already lost their constitutional protections and so, based on the Executive orders of December 7 and 8, could be ordered to do virtually anything.

Accordingly, on January 30, 1942, the *Stockton Record* headlined the first order for removal of enemy aliens: **186,000 Enemy Aliens to Be Moved on Coast.**[26] Ascribing the move to a plan to "prevent espionage and fifth column activity similar to that preceding Pearl Harbor," [note that the reporter takes as fact that fifth column activity had taken place at Pearl Harbor; no such espionage or sabotage was ever substantiated, ed.] the article noted that the Attorney General "has ordered Japanese, German and Italian aliens out of two areas in San Francisco [Prohibited Area No. 19, ed.] and Los Angeles [Prohibited Area No. 33, ed.] by February 24," with 27 additional areas to be designated today, and several more to come" [69 additional areas in California were announced the next day, ed.]. Nor, as we have seen above, would the orders be limited to California alone. On Feb. 4, Department of Justice Press Release No. 9 ordered seven areas in Washington and 24 areas in Oregon cleared of enemy aliens, all to be vacated by February 15.[27] And on Feb. 7, Press Release No. 11 announced 18 prohibited zones in Arizona from which all enemy aliens were to be evacuated after Feb. 24.[28]

Absent specific government instructions, however, confusion reigned among Italian enemy aliens about *if and when* they had to go, *where* they had to go, and *how* they were allowed to go. Virtually the only source of information was newspapers, many of which carried conflicting reports as well as rumors. For example, the February 4, 1942 *San Francisco Chronicle* carried an article headlined, **Aliens in California: U.S. to Move Thousands Inland to Undisclosed Farm Colonies**. It quoted Tom Clark, alien coordinator for the Western Defense Command, to the effect that the Federal Government would be moving thousands of enemy aliens out of defense zones to ominous-sounding "inland farm colonies." But the article added the disquieting news that the "single indication that many of them would be moved to inland farm colonies provided little help. The alien co-ordinator did not reveal where these colonies would be established, whether in inland California or on the other side of the Rocky mountains." Worse, the article noted, "waiting for detailed instructions from anybody, the aliens facing evacuation were left completely in the dark for another day." The paper did note that four areas heavily populated by Italian immigrants would be hit hard by the evacuation orders—the cities of Pittsburg, Monterey, Alameda, and Santa Cruz: "Surveys showed the enforced evacuation will involve approximately 2000 in Pittsburg—approximately one-third of the city's population; 3,000 in Monterey, and 1600 in Alameda" while another section, "Artichoke Crop Is Threatened," stated that "In Santa Cruz county, the $500,000 artichoke and sprout crop was periled by the impending evacuation of Italian farmers." To add to the panic, the article quoted California Governor Olson:

> Governor Olson asked State Guardsmen, Sheriffs and Police Chiefs to be on "special alert" against sabotage in areas to be cleared of aliens between now and February 24. "I am advised by Lieutenant General John L. DeWitt, commanding, Western Defense Command, that the military personnel is especially alerted and ordered to take extra precautions against sabotage during this period," he declared, "and I hereby request that similar precautions be taken and special alertness exercised by the State Guard forces and all civilian police authorities."[29]

The clear implication was that California citizens should assume that enemy aliens would be attempting to take advantage of the twenty days left to them in critical military areas by trying to implement plots of sabotage or espionage, or both.

Though most local newspapers indicated that the enemy aliens would be forbidden to remain in prohibited zones, which were described in general, no specific instructions were ever given about where to go. This led to confusion among individual aliens, many of whom could not read English, especially regarding how far they had to move to get clear of the areas prohibited to them. Some moved only a few blocks; others moved nearly a hundred miles. As to those who might experience difficulty finding living quarters, the February 9 *Stockton Record* assured them (or frightened them further) with these words:

> For those who are unable to find other residence outside of the forbidden area, it was indicated by wire service reports that CCC camps, vacated because of the war emergency, may be used to house the evacuees.[30]

For those who could read, the Feb. 9 article provided additional useful and/or alarming information. It quoted Tom Clark's warning that "'restricted martial law' may be required in some sections to clear aliens from restricted and forbidden areas." The article also reported that the California Personnel Board was meeting to implement its decision to "drop from civil service lists naturalized citizens born in enemy nations and their first generation descendants," even though this move was opposed on legal grounds by California's attorney general, Earl Warren. Finally, it noted that "Aliens affected will receive only public notice to vacate the areas...No individual warnings will be sent out."[31]

But as was typical early on, a February 7 article in the *San Francisco Chronicle*, **Aliens: The Government Starts to Clear 10,000 from California Homes**, directly contradicted the *Record's* information about individual warnings. Its second paragraph said:

On Monday, first written notices will be delivered by registered mail to between 200 and 300 Japanese, German and Italian nationals who must be out by February 15.

In many cases, local police will give personal notice.

Later in the week the notices will be sent to others who must be evacuated by February 24....

The evacuation orders will instruct each alien to report to a U.S. employment office in his district. There he will receive all information and any legal aid he may require.

He will receive financial aid if he has no funds to pay for his move.

Before he moves, however, he must obtain permission from a U.S. Attorney covering the date of the move and the location of the new home. Permission will be given after suitable investigation.[32]

Though it would be highly unusual for a single enemy alien to read both newspapers (or to read a newspaper at all, though their American-born children might), it is easy to see how conflicting rumors would be flying and a level of panic taking hold in immigrant communities in early February of 1942.[33] The February 12 *San Francisco Chronicle* only heightened these emotions with its headline, **Martial Law Moves Closer to California.** For not only did the article report that "legislators and defense officials [had] buckled down to the problem of potentially dangerous citizens," the solution to which, it appeared, "was martial law;" it also displayed the notices being posted, in four languages, warning aliens away from prohibited zones:

NOTICE: ENEMY ALIEN PROHIBITED AREA NO. 19.

The United States Government requires all aliens of German, Italian, or Japanese nationality to vacate this area by midnight, February 24. Go to the nearest local public employment office of the United States Employment Service for details.

United States Department of Justice

NOTICE
ENEMY ALIEN
PROHIBITED AREA NO. 19

The United States Government requires all aliens of German, Italian, or Japanese nationality to vacate this area by midnight, February 24

• Go to the nearest local public employment office of the United States Employment Service for details.

AVVISO
AGLI STRANIERI DI NAZIONI
NEMICHE È PROIBITA LA ZONA NO. 19

Il Governo degli Stati Uniti richiede che gli stranieri di nazionalità tedesca, italiana, o giapponese sgombrino questa zona, non più tardi della mezzanotte del 24 Febbraio

Rivolgetevi per dettagli all'ufficio di collocamento pubblico più vicino del UNITED STATES EMPLOYMENT SERVICE

所有 敵性 ── **BEKANNTMACHUNG**

Beneath the notice was printed the newspaper's threatening explanation:

> **A Sign for Aliens---Keep Out!**
> This sign, written in four languages, means Keep Out in every language. It is directed to enemy aliens, barring them from forbidden zones by orders of the Government. Two hundred of these warnings were posted yesterday at boundaries of the four forbidden zones in San Francisco. The posting was done by the motor transport division of the American Women's Voluntary Services.

With so many differing instructions, warnings and speculations (in its report of February 13, the *Stockton Record* included a photo of the notice being posted with the added threat, "In any language, Scram!"), it is also easy to see how confusion, fear, and even cynicism would take hold. Some must also have thought it ironic that the government was forcing people to move out of their homes and communities, but then requiring them to apply for travel permits to comply with its own orders.

As to the specifics of those prohibited zones—that is, where exactly the boundaries of each zone lay—that was again left to local newspapers. Most did a fairly creditable job of describing the local prohibited area, though, again, it would be of little help to an Italian immigrant who could not read English. On February 2, for example, under its headline, **Entire Port Area Barred to 'Enemy' Nationals,** the *Stockton Record* described the boundaries of the forbidden area there as "the Stockton Channel from the San Joaquin River to Lincoln Street; Lincoln Street from the Channel to Charter Way, and along Charter Way to the Santa Fe railroad crossing and thence to the San Joaquin River and finally to the channel." The *Richmond Independent*, on the same date, ran a banner headline, **AXIS ALIENS IN RICHMOND MUST LEAVE** (see illustration above) with a subhead reading **U.S. Sets February 24 Deadline for Eviction.**[34] The article began alarmingly:

> Practically the entire city of Richmond and all of El Cerrito, along with all of the county's shoreline from the Alameda-Contra Costa line to a point east of Antioch, today were designated prohibited areas for Axis aliens who will be required to move out by Tuesday, February 24.
> All of the county's population centers of Richmond, El Cerrito, Pinole, Rodeo, Oleum, Crockett, Port Costa, Martinez, Pittsburg, Antioch and much of the county's rich agricultural region come under the banned areas.[35]

A sidebar, **Axis Aliens Must Leave These Areas**, provided more specific details about the banned zone:

Contra Costa and Alameda counties including part of Berkeley and commencing at the west end of Berkeley municipal fishing pier. The line then runs east along said pier to University Avenue, then east along University Avenue to Grove street, then north along Grove street to Arlington avenue to Barrett avenue to United States Highway No. 40, follows United States Highway No. 40 north to San Pablo Creek road across Sobrante ride [sic. 'ridge'?] which connects the San Pablo creek road and the Pinole Valley road and then follows east along the Pinole Valley road to Alhambra Valley road and easterly along the Alhambra Valley road to a road running north to Muir, continues along said road to Muir then east along California State Highway No. 4 to the Sacramento Northern Railway, and continues north along the Sacramento Northern Railway to Suisun Bay.

Anyone from the area would understand that the prohibited zone covered virtually the entire shoreline along the northeastern side of San Francisco Bay, and extended from there up into the Sacramento delta, east as far as Stockton (see map).

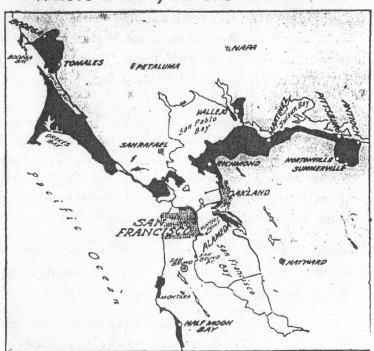

Where Enemy Aliens Are Banned

The above map shows the San Francisco Bay area zones from which all enemy aliens will be expelled in the drive to prevent sabotage and fifth column activity. Blacked-out sectors will be entirely cleared of Jap, German and Italian aliens. In the East Bay, it will be noted, all of Richmond, Martinez, Pittsburg, Antioch, Vallejo and Alameda are included, with parts of Oakland and much of the surrounding terrain. Bodega and Tomales are in the restricted coast line sectors, while down the peninsula San Bruno, Half Moon Bay and the Montara district will be cleared. The San Francisco waterfront and Hunters Point Drydock are banned sectors.

Bay Area Map in *Richmond Independent,* Feb. 5, 1942

As to Richmond itself, home of the new shipbuilding industry run by Henry Kaiser, the article noted that those affected would include "scores of Japanese in the florist business along San Pablo avenue, many Italians in the truck garden business in North Richmond and west San Pablo, many Italians in other parts of the city and a scattering of persons of German nationality." It is also notable that the term "Axis Aliens" is employed, thus joining the two loaded concepts, "axis" and "alien," to emphasize the presumptive dangerousness of those being evicted. Subsequent headlines from the same newspaper continued to use the term (Feb. 23 and 25), sometimes employing other terms such as "foreigners" (Feb. 3), "aliens" (Feb. 4), or "axis nationals" (Feb. 4). The February 5 edition included a helpful map under the headline, **Where Enemy Aliens are Banned,** with blacked-out areas indicating zones forbidden to all enemy aliens. Virtually the entire northern half of the East Bay is blacked out, as are parts of the San Francisco waterfront, most of Sausalito in Marin County, and the Pacific coastline from the Golden Gate to Bodega Bay where the map ends. Notably, in the Berkeley to Richmond area, the prohibited line, Arlington Ave., was located well into the east bay foothills, not, as one might expect, encompassing just western urban portions closest to the water.

In Alameda (also the East Bay, and site of the Alameda Naval Air Station), the *Alameda Times Star* ran a banner headline in its January 31, 1942 edition: **Enemy Aliens Barred from West End,** with the subhead, "West of Webster Restricted." The article reported:

> Effective Feb. 15, all enemy aliens will be barred from the Alameda territory west of Webster St., under penalty of internment for the duration of the war....The local area, known as Restricted Area No. 17, Alameda County, was designated as follows:
>
> **"Commencing at Neptune Beach, running north along Webster St., to Oakland Inner Harbor, and thence westerly along the shoreline of Oakland Inner Harbor to San Francisco Bay to the point of beginning."**[36]

Three days later, on Feb. 2, another banner headline, **Entire Island Hit by Latest Enemy Alien Restrictions,** announced that the prohibited zone had been expanded to include *all of the city*, with a new deadline of February 24:

> A wide extension of the local area restricted against Axis aliens today will virtually push Japanese, German and Italian aliens completely out of Alameda.
>
> In a new order from Washington this morning, Attorney General Francis Biddle extended the Alameda restricted area to include all of the city west of High St., a move which will force nearly all enemy aliens from the city proper. The only unrestricted territory in the city as the result of the order is the eastern tip, including the Fernside district, and Bay Farm Island.[37]

A similar revised extension of the prohibited zone was announced in the *Monterey Peninsula Herald* on February 14: **Alien Change Looms Here**. The subhead, "Apparent Error of Federal Authorities Would Alter Plans of Many Local 'Enemy Aliens,'" seemed to attribute the confusion to a government error. The report described the change:

> The Fremont extension of the old Castroville highway—NOT Abrego street, Del Monte avenue and Broadway in Seaside—will be the boundary of the zone "forbidden" to enemy aliens, it was indicated today.
>
> And the net result of the "last-minute" change in boundaries will upset the plans of many a Monterey Peninsula family which had planned to move into Oak Grove or residential sections of East Monterey to comply with federal restrictions on their movements and activities.[38]

Another article on the same front page, **Aliens Given Information**, indicated that the confusion in the boundary derived from the "discovery by government officials...that Fremont street had been mistaken by them for Highway No. 1." Since the area west of Highway 1 was everywhere declared off limits for enemy aliens (with most of the Italian enemy aliens, being fishermen, residing in this western, or coastside portion of many cities), the mistake made a big difference.

The city of Pittsburg, on the Sacramento Delta, evidenced no such confusion. From the very first announcement in the *Pittsburg Post Dispatch*, on February 2, the headline read: **Order All Aliens From City**[39], with a subhead declaring, **1732 Residents to Leave Feb. 24.** This was due to the fact that all of Pittsburg, a fishing village whose residents were mostly Sicilian immigrants, was off limits to all who were not American citizens. The *Post Dispatch* carried headlines virtually every day during February 1942 about the enemy aliens who had to leave: **Alien Residents Preparing to Leave Town** and, **Evacuation of 10,000 Aliens is Underway.**[40] Perhaps the most devastating bit of yellow journalism in this local newspaper involved the front page photo display of many of those who had to leave, the first on February 11, 1942.[41] The photos were all head shots and appeared to be a kind of "rogue's gallery" of enemy aliens (see photo p. 141). Most were older women who had neglected to get American citizenship or even learn English because it was so easy to carry on business and social life in Pittsburg, where virtually everyone spoke their native Sicilian dialect.

Curfew Orders

As if the month of February were not traumatic enough for West Coast enemy aliens, the announcement of a curfew for them was added on or about February 4. It should be remembered that this new restriction was announced during the very time that all of California's enemy aliens were being compelled to re-register (photograph, fingerprints, detailed questions) to obtain their pink identification booklets, the dates being February 2 through February 9, and while thousands more were frantically making plans to find new places to live. Notwithstanding all this, on February 4, 1942, most newspapers carried a headline similar to the one in the *Richmond Independent*: **U.S. BARS ALIENS FROM CALIFORNIA SHORE LINE.**[42] The subhead referred to the "New Restriction Ordered for All Axis Nationals," and the article noted that the new restrictions, like the final evacuation, would go into effect on February 24 (this date, when many older Italian immigrants had to leave their homes, was dubbed *Mala Notte* [evil night] by Celestina Loero of Santa Cruz). The article explained:

> ...aliens residing in a prescribed area about 500 miles long and varying from 30 to 150 miles in width, extending from the Oregon border along the coast line to a point about 50 miles north of Los Angeles, will be subjected to a curfew and permitted to travel only between their homes and jobs.
>
> The curfew restrictions, affecting all Japanese, German and Italian aliens in the big coastal area, including all of Contra Costa County, are:

1—Between the hours of 9 p.m. and 6 a.m. all enemy aliens shall be within
the place of residence indicated on their identification certificates.
MUST STAY HOME
2—At all other times they must be found only at the place of residence or employment indicated on their identification certificates, or going between these two
places, or within an area not more than five miles from the place of residence.

Biddle warned that an enemy alien found during the curfew hours anywhere
except at his home or place of employment, would be subject to immediate arrest and
internment.

The *Stockton Record* more clearly pinpointed the eastern boundary of the curfew
line in its February 4 edition. Its subhead read: "Drastic New Regulations Imposed on
Wide Area Extending to Mother Lode." The second paragraph described the general
boundaries:

In an area bounded on the east by Highway 99, on the north by the Oregon border, on the west by the coast and on the south by a line running 50 miles north of Los
Angeles, enemy aliens after February 24 must remain in their homes at night...

A subsequent paragraph, headlined **PROSCRIBED AREA**, provided local details:

The boundary runs along the east side of Highway 99, from the county line
through Lodi, along Cherokee Lane to Stockton; along the east side of Wilson Way
to the fairgrounds, along the north side of the Mariposa Road and the east side of the
Hogan Road to Manteca, then cuts west from Manteca through Mossdale along the
south side of the highway to the point east of Tracy where the West Side Highway in-
tersects. At that point it cuts south along the east boundary of the West Side Highway
to Los Banos, where it again swings west.

Everything west of this line is in the restricted zone....

Biddle explained that the restricted area does not extend south to the Mexican
border, because no recommendations for such action in southern sections of California had been received yet from the War Department.[43]

The next day's edition of the *Monterey Peninsula Herald* added a little twist to the
previous day's announcement of the huge restricted/curfew zone. Beneath a headline
that read **All Enemy Aliens To Be Investigated,** the AP report explained:

All enemy aliens living in restricted areas of California will be investigated, Tom
C. Clark, in charge of Alien enforcement on the Pacific coast, said today.

Machinery for conducting the investigation and for issuing passes to those who
will be permitted to remain in the area, have yet to be worked out. Only those aliens
considered potentially dangerous will be removed from restricted areas, Clark said.[44]

It is not clear precisely what Clark was referring to, because a majority of the enemy aliens judged "potentially dangerous" had already been interned (see Chapter 3). Perhaps he was referring to the upcoming series of raids by the FBI around February 21, when dozens more enemy aliens from California were apprehended, and interned.[45] Whatever its intention, the headline could not help but alarm the Italian enemy aliens already reeling under the February measures that, after February 24, would have thousands moving to new residences, and some 52,000 in California under the virtual house arrest known as the *curfew*.

The Army Takes Over

While the promulgation of Executive Order 9066, on February 19, did not directly affect most Italian enemy aliens (as noted above, the order for their removal and curfew had already been issued and many had already moved), several types of fallout from that now-infamous order did have indirect impact. Recall that early on (February 9 and 10), Attorney General Biddle had asserted that if the military persisted in its demand for a mass removal of either American citizens or very large numbers of enemy aliens, his Justice Department could not, and *would not* implement either. He would yield authority over civilians to the War Department. Though the Attorney General no doubt considered this a threat designed to rein in the more reckless ideas emanating from the military, it turned out to play directly into the hands of commanders like General John DeWitt and Provost Marshal General Allen Gullion. The military *did*, in fact, take over the relocation and internment of over 120,000 Japanese, and while it was at it, assumed jurisdiction over the enemy aliens as well. This pre-emption of authority over civilians (a jurisdiction normally left to the Department of Justice) began to be felt as early as March 3, 1942. On that date, the *Stockton Record* carried this headline: **ARMY SETS NEW ALIEN AREAS**, with a subhead, "Enemy Aliens, Citizen Japanese to Be Moved from Coast Zone." The article said, in part:

> The army today declared the western half of Washington, Oregon and California and the southern half of Arizona a military area from which enemy aliens and American-born Japanese will be ousted progressively to rid the Pacific Coast of a potential fifth-column threat.
>
> Created in the most drastic step yet taken toward alien control, the area was designed [sic] by Lt. Gen. John L. DeWitt, chief of the Western Defense Command, under authority granted by President Roosevelt and the War Department. It affected 140,000 enemy aliens and 70,000 American-born Japanese....
>
> DeWitt's proclamation split the four states into fourths. One fourth—the coast-

al areas of the three Pacific Coast states and the southern border of Arizona—was designated prohibited Zone A-1. The second fourth, except for certain prohibited zones within, was designated restricted Zone B. Together, these two fourths form Military Area No. 1. The third and fourth quarters of the four states form military area No. 2. There are to be no restrictions in area No. 2 except for certain established prohibited zones...

After defining the zones, DeWitt gave a glimpse of the procedure which would be followed in removing or restricting enemy aliens and Japanese-Americans from their boundaries.

He announced that future proclamations affecting the area would be concerned with five classes of persons, namely:

Class 1—All persons suspected of espionage, sabotage, fifth column or other subversive activity.

Class 2—Japanese aliens, of whom there are more than 50,000.

Class 3—American-born Japanese, of whom there are an estimated 70,000.

Class 4—German aliens.

Class 5—Italian aliens.

...When that work is completed [i.e., moving the Japanese, ed.], DeWitt said, German and Italian aliens would be next in line for evacuation.[46]

This and subsequent orders and statements left no doubt that General DeWitt had never given up on his plan to evict most enemy aliens from his "combat zone," notably the Pacific Slope, which had now officially been designated Military Area No. 1 (i.e. Zones 1A [prohibited] and 1B [restricted]; see map, next page). In other words, General DeWitt was not satisfied with simply controlling enemy aliens in the western half of the Pacific states with a curfew; he wanted *all of them removed*.

On March 17, General DeWitt struck again, with new orders expanding some already-existing prohibited zones, such as the ones in and around Stockton. The *Stockton Record* carried the bold headline: **NEW ALIEN BAN HITS CENTRAL CITY,** with subheads reading: "Bridges, Air Fields Under Latest Defense Orders" and "29 Areas to Be Closed Near City When Army Further Details Restrictions." The article described the new military orders affecting enemy aliens in Stockton and the Central Valley:

Twenty-nine areas in this vicinity, including a major portion of down-town Stockton itself and Stockton Field, were included in **934 new prohibited zones** announced by Lt. Gen. John L. DeWitt today to be banned to enemy aliens...The Stockton city area to be declared "out of bounds" for suspicious persons, including enemy aliens and Japanese descendants of aliens, is designated as **"Zone A-206."** [Emphases added, ed.] It is

Military Zones, West Coast, *San Francisco Chronicle*, Mar. 4, 1942, p. 10.

described as bounded on the north by East Park St., on the east by North American St., on the south by East Weber Avenue and on the west by North Center Street. It includes a large portion of the city's business district, the County Jail, City Hall, Emergency Hospital and Post office.

Bridge Zones

Stockton Field and all land within a mile of it in all directions, is resignated [sic] as Zone A-192. Twenty Western Pacific railroad bridges and the area within a mile of each of them also are included in prohibited zones. Four of these are near Lathrop, eight near Stockton, two near Kingdon, north of here, and six near Thornton.

The half-dozen bridge zones between here and Lathrop, plus the one-mile area around each, make virtually a two-mile belt of prohibited territory between here and Mossdale.

The Merced Municipal Airport, the army air base near Merced and a section of the city itself were included among the prohibited zones....

The office of alien control in San Francisco told the *Record* that "probably all enemy aliens will be moved from Stockton..."[47]

With his Military Areas and the restrictions therein established, General DeWitt, on March 24, then extended the evening curfew for enemy aliens from its original 9 p.m. to 8 p.m. The *Stockton Record* carried the banner headline: **New 8 P.M. Axis Alien Curfew**. The article reported that

Strict and extensive new curfew regulations affecting all Japanese, Italian and German nationals, and all Japanese-Americans in vital defense areas, which include this and surrounding counties, were announced today in San Francisco by Lt. Gen. John L. DeWitt, head of the western defense command.

Effective Friday at 6 a.m., alien nationals and American citizens of Japanese extraction must remain within their homes between 8 p.m. and 6 a.m...

DeWitt wrote the regulations in Proclamation 3, which applies specifically to Military Area 1—embracing the western half of California, Oregon and Washington and the southern half of Arizona—and to hundreds of smaller prohibited zones in other parts of those states and in Nevada, Utah, Idaho and Montana.

Previously announced curfew regulations, which did not include Japanese-Americans, affected Stockton only west of Wilson Way. Enemy aliens living east of Wilson Way were not affected. Military Area No. 1, however, takes in all of Central California west of the Mother Lode Highway. All of Stockton, all of San Joaquin County, all of Stanislaus County and the western section of the Mother Lode counties are included in the area.

Lt. Col. W.A. Boekel, assistant provost marshal of the western defense command, announced emphatically that the new order revokes all previous exemptions permitted enemy aliens who work at nights or have been granted special privileges because of other reasons. Cooks, night watchmen, porters and others who previously were given exemptions must be in their homes after dark.[48]

What seems quite clear from these actions is that General DeWitt and the military had been fretting about the previous regulations and restrictions governing enemy aliens—i.e. that they were too "soft" and inadequate to the putative danger presented by alien enemies. With the Army takeover, the enemy aliens could be assured, if they needed assurance, that the Justice Department's excessive concern with legal niceties and civil liberties no longer applied. The Army had both the authority and the manpower needed to get tough, and it was now indicating that it would have no qualms about doing so. Though this would not end the conflict between the two departments (see below), the signs were ominous for many of the Italian enemy aliens who seemed to have escaped the worst restrictions: everything indicated that though, at the moment, the military was fully occupied in moving the Japanese, the Italians and Germans, once the Japanese removal was complete, would be the next to go.

❊

PART II: Evacuation's Effect on Individuals

The stories of individuals affected by the evacuation from prohibited zones have comprised a major part of the *Una Storia Segreta* project's effort to correct the historical record. Initially, most information concerned two communities, Pittsburg and Monterey, California, both of them mainly fishing communities. In Pittsburg, a community on the Sacramento River whose rich salmon fishery had attracted hundreds of Sicilian immigrants from as early as the 1850s, nearly 2,000 individuals, including the American-born such as Rose Scudero (as a 13-year-old minor, she had to move with her mother), were forced to leave town. The majority of evacuees were elderly women who spoke no English (see photo, p. 141). While some found living accommodations without much trouble, others had far more difficulty: many families of women and their minor children were reduced to living in migrant worker housing in the nearby farming community of Oakley, and even there, four families were unable to find any accommodations and so resorted to cramming themselves into the Oakley railroad station. Pittsburg resident Bettina Troia had an even harder time: unable to find a dwelling, she ended up living in a chicken coop. Most disturbing of all, 97-year-old Placido Abono, with over 100 American-born children, grandchildren and great-grandchildren, was so frail he had to be moved out of the home he had occupied for fifty years on a stretcher. All four of local historian John Buffo's grandparents were forced to move, and were among those whose photos were displayed in the local newspaper. Angelina Bruno expressed her frustration about all this:

What burned me up was this: I came here at age ten, went to school here. I had three children, my husband was an American citizen. But when the war came, they said I wasn't....Why should I be taken out of my home when I hadn't done anything wrong? It was mostly women who were shipped out, and old men, the ones who weren't fishing any more....My husband's grandmother moved to Oakland, looking over the shipyards. What good was that?[49]

Frances Cardinale, whose parents, Caterina and Vincenzo, moved from Pittsburg to Centerville with Vincenzo's sister and sister-in-law, while she remained in Pittsburg with her brother to take care of the family's house, spoke about the pain of separation:

My father was a fisherman, but he couldn't fish. He paced all day long. What could he do? And the curfew—inside at eight o'clock. After, whenever my father heard the eight o'clock factory whistle, he would get scared and go to bed. I remember the day we moved out, it looked like a funeral. We were all dead. We couldn't part. We never were separated before.[50]

In Monterey, it was just as bad. The family of former white house chief of staff, CIA director and Secretary of Defense, Leon Panetta, were forced to leave their Monterey home and move to San Jose. As in Pittsburg, many fishermen's families had to split up, with the citizen father remaining to fish, and the enemy alien mother and her children forced to move outside the prohibited zone, or vice versa. Vitina Spadaro related how she and her parents looked for housing:

When orders came for my mother to leave Monterey, I went with my parents to look for a house in Salinas. When we would ask for a place to live, they would ask why we had to move. We told them, and they said, "Italians from Monterey? You're aliens. We're not renting to you." I felt devastated. I would say, "I'm an American citizen, my father is an American citizen." My father would say, "Keep quiet." But how could they hurt my mother like this? She was crying all the time. When we were getting ready to move to Salinas, there were moving vans all over the neighborhood, and all the women were crying. After we found a place, my father would go back and forth to Monterey, check the house there."[51]

Perhaps the most poignant story of evacuation from Monterey involves Rosina Trovato. A widow, Trovato learned on one fatal day that her son, in the Navy, had gone down with the *Arizona* at Pearl Harbor. The next day, another son joined the same Navy, and shortly thereafter, Trovato learned that she, a Gold Star mother, would have to remove herself from her Monterey home.

The Tolan Committee Hearings

Rosina Trovato's story, along with the stories of many other evacuees, was presented in evidence at the hearings of the Tolan Committee Investigating National Defense Migration, chaired by U.S. Representative John Tolan, of Oakland.[52] The initial hearings, focusing directly on the problems anticipated in removing so many thousands of enemy aliens, took place in San Francisco on February 21 and 23, 1942, just days before the final evacuation date of February 24. Here is what Ottorino Ronchi, a former Professor of Italian at UC Berkeley and one-time editor of the San Francisco Italian newspaper, *La Voce del Popolo*, said about interviews he had recently completed in Monterey:

> Among them I interviewed a woman about 60 years old. She was a widow. Her son was killed at Pearl Harbor and the next day the other son enlisted. Now she is alone. She is not an American citizen. So I asked her about how she felt. "Well," she said, "I wish I had a couple of more children. I will send them to fight. My interest is in America."[53]

Ronchi described another Monterey case, "a young woman, about 25 or 26, I think, married to a soldier. She has two children. They have to move. And those people, they have no money, they have no place to go."

Also testifying at the Tolan Committee hearings were San Francisco Attorney Chauncey Tramutolo, and Milano Rispoli, Executive Secretary of the Italian Welfare Agency in San Francisco. Attorney Tramutolo described one family from San Francisco, with a mother married to an American citizen, who, "upon attempting to prove it...was unable to do so. This family has two children and they must vacate under the existing military order of evacuation and they do not know where to go." Another family forced to move had a father—"a member of the carpenters' union for twenty-odd years"—supporting a wife and eight children all born in the United States, one of whom "is now in the Navy and is one of Commander Tunney's right hand men." The father is "unable to become a citizen because he cannot read or write in the English language." Yet another family, he said, had a mother born here, but she would have to move because she "lost her citizenship by reason of her marriage to this man prior to 1922. The husband thereafter acquired his citizenship, but this fact did not automatically restore his wife to citizenship."[54] Citing another hardship case in the same situation, Tramutolo referred to a "widow born in the United States" who

> ..lost her citizenship by reason of the fact that she married a noncitizen prior to 1922. As you are undoubtedly aware, anyone who married an alien prior to 1922 lost her citizenship even though born here. This widow [her name was given later as Margue-

rite Valdez Vezzolo, born in San Ardo, CA in 1898, then living in Salinas, CA with her eight children, ed.] has never been out of the United States and her only means of livelihood is the dairy farm of which she owns a half interest and the other half is owned by her brother-in-law, who must vacate because he is an alien. I am sure you can readily appreciate that it would be a tremendous hardship to ask this woman and her children to remove from the dairy farm, which is in a prohibited area.[55]

This situation—of American-born women losing their citizenship when they married Italian men prior to the 1922 law which ended this practice—came up again and again in both the Tolan Committee testimony, and elsewhere.[56] Hope Cardinalli of Monterey, for example, said that though she was born in the United States, she had lost her citizenship and thus become an "enemy alien" because she had married an Italian. She was ordered to leave Monterey, but refused and hired a lawyer, who managed to persuade authorities to allow her to stay. Elaine Null, a postal employee in Pittsburg, wondered why she had to fingerprint her American-born mother as an enemy alien; only much later did she learn the reason: her mother's pre-1922 marriage to an Italian-born immigrant. The *Stockton Record* under the headline "Local Aliens Tell Tales of Woe," related another story of a woman "born in California" and thus an American citizen until

> in 1908 she married a man of Italian nativity. It was in that period that a woman lost her citizenship if she married a citizen of another country. Several years ago her husband applied for his papers and later became a citizen of the United States. Recently his wife learned that although she lost her citizenship by marriage, she did not regain it when her husband became naturalized....Consequently, her husband, born in Italy, is now a full-fledged citizen of this country while she, born in California, is an Italian subject, cannot vote and must register as an enemy alien.[57]

Apparently, the grim irony of such cases came to the attention of Immigration authorities, because the *Stockton Record*, on February 18, 1942, carried an article, "Some Alien Problems Cleared by Lions Club Speaker Here." Paul Armstrong, San Francisco assistant district director of the Immigration and Naturalization Service, was reported to have testified that "much confusion" has existed, and that many American-born women have been registered unnecessarily under the blanket alien registration orders of 1940 and the enemy alien registration of February 1942:

> He explained that women who have married aliens and who have never left this country fall under neither classification and are not affected by any alien restrictions. This includes the orders banning certain areas to enemy aliens.
> Under the Repatriation Act of June 25, 1936, women who lost citizenship

through marriage to aliens are deemed generally as citizens, it was explained. They cannot avail themselves of certain rights, such as voting, until they follow either of two courses. If they have left the United States, they must follow regular repatriation procedure. If they have not left the United States, they must simply take an oath of allegiance. Therefore, the Immigration Department has adopted the stand the latter group is not affected by restrictions aimed at enemy aliens.[58]

Though it appears that Hope Cardinalli of Monterey, with the help of a lawyer, availed herself of her actual rights and managed to remain in her home, many others, including my Aunt Ruth in Bridgeport, Connecticut, who lost her citizenship by marrying my immigrant uncle in 1921, did not.[59] Again, the problem of those who could not or did not read daily newspapers (and the *Stockton Record* is one of few, if not the only paper to have noted the resolution to this problem), or have the means to hire lawyers, proved critical. It should also be noted that though some rights of citizenship (it is not clear what "deemed generally as citizens" actually means; the chief right of citizenship is, in fact, the right to vote; all other rights, such as those enumerated in the Bill of Rights, pertain to "all persons") were said to be restored to those who had never left the country, the crucial right to vote was not—not, that is, until the proper procedures were followed, one of which, for those who had "left the country" (apparently a suspect act), was "repatriation."

Rispoli, of the Welfare Agency, testified to the Tolan Committee about several other hardship cases. Rodolpho Manciardini, for example, was a single man, aged 43, employed by the Ghirardelli Chocolate factory in San Francisco for twenty years: "He was required to give up his job and home because both were located in a prohibited area. He speaks no English at all and although entitled to employment benefits will have difficulty in reestablishing himself in another industry since he is not known in other sectors of the State where he may be required to move." Vittoria Santo, of Castroville, was an "alien mother whose husband is a citizen. She has three sons in the United States Army in the Philippines, while another son is with the Navy in this country."[60] Nevertheless, she would have to move, according to Rispoli. Santo's case brings up the other type of casualty resulting from insufficient knowledge of new laws—immigrant women whose husbands became naturalized U.S. citizens *after 1922*. Many such women thought they still qualified for derivative citizenship through their husbands. But following the 1922 Cable Act, women had to apply for citizenship on their own; derivative citizenship no longer applied. Since many failed to understand this, they thought, like Angelina Bruno above, that they were American citizens when they were not, and hence became "enemy aliens" subject to all the restrictions pertaining to that fearsome designation.[61]

Tolan Committee testimony by some of the actual enemy aliens provided even more dramatic evidence of the difficulties facing those who had to leave their homes. Mrs. John D'Amato testified on behalf of her mother, Mrs. Francesca Crivello, living at 2751 Hyde St.—a prohibited area of San Francisco. Mrs. Crivello had eight children, all American citizens. Among them were Nicholas, a San Francisco police officer, Vincent, in the U.S. Navy, and yet another brother in the Navy at Pearl Harbor. Committee member Rep. Sparkman of Alabama queried Mrs. Damato as follows:

> SPARKMAN. Will it be necessary for your mother to move tomorrow?
>
> DAMATO. Yes. She will be the only member in the family who has to move and she owns her own home here. The family owns the home.
>
> SPARKMAN. The family owns the home?
>
> DAMATO. The family owns the home, yes. She is the only one who has to leave home. She has to leave and she feels badly about leaving the rest of the family. She is the only one who has to go....
>
> SPARKMAN. How long has she lived in the United States.
>
> DAMATO. Forty years...
>
> SPARKMAN. How does it happen that she never became an American citizen?
>
> DAMATO. She was illiterate. She didn't know how to read or write Italian either, and then when she came here she started to raise this large family and she didn't have time for anything. She just worked night and day and it never entered her mind in any way that she should become a citizen for any reason, because she always felt loyal to the United States...
>
> SPARKMAN. Your father was not an American citizen?
>
> DAMATO. No. He was illiterate also and it never entered his mind either to become a citizen because he didn't know how to read or write and it is difficult for anyone who doesn't know a language....
>
> SPARKMAN. Do you have anything further to say...
>
> DAMATO. She can't speak very good English, though, but she does feel as if she shouldn't be treated as an enemy alien—a dangerous alien. She thinks she ought to have a little more consideration because she has two sons in the service and she has been here for years, most of her life. As far as she is concerned she feels as much a citizen as we American-born citizens...[62]

Nor did the troubles of the Crivello family end with evacuation. In August 2000, Tony D'Amato, grandson of Francesca and Giuseppe Crivello, revealed in an interview that by 1941 his family, fishermen on both sides, owned four fishing boats: the *Anna B* (owned by his uncle Sal), the *Virginia* (his grandfather's crab boat), the *Rose* (owned by his Uncle Joe), and the *Josephine*, owned by his father. The Navy then informed the Crivellos that both the *Virginia* and the *Anna B* were required for conversion to patrol and anti-mine work, this at a time when the elder Crivellos were being forced to leave their home. (see more details of this story in Chapter 6, The Plight of Fishermen).

The testimony of Mrs. Luciano Maniscalco, (48 years of age, living at 1846 Powell Street, in San Francisco's North Beach, with 12 children) involved both elements above: the hardship for California fishermen, and wives who lost their citizenship. She was questioned by Committee member Rep. Laurence Arnold, of Illinois:

ARNOLD. Are some of the children in the armed services?

MANISCALCO. One is in the United States Navy; he has been there 7 years. One is on a United States transport; he has been there a couple of months. One is in the Army; he is in Tacoma, Wash. My daughter is in the ambulance corps and the other was reclassified for the Army. ...

ARNOLD. What occupation has your husband practiced for the last 20 years?

MANISCALCO. Well, at first he used to work at the Union Iron Works and he went to Alaska. Then he got his boat and he has been a fisherman for 20 years...

ARNOLD. Has your husband been able to obtain any work since the 7th of December?

MANISCALCO. No, sir.

ARNOLD. He was barred from fishing after December 7?

MANICSCALCO. That's right....

ARNOLD. Are you a citizen and is your husband a citizen?

MANISCALCO. My husband is not a citizen, but I am a citizen. I lost my rights, but I took my citizenship. I lost my rights when I married him, and then in 1934 I got my papers out....

ARNOLD. You say you were married in Pensacola?

MANISCALCO. Yes. I was born there....

ARNOLD. Has your husband made any effort to become a citizen?

MANISCALCO. Oh, yes; many times. He went in 1932. He was examined and he passed a hundred percent, him and his two witnesses. But he don't know how to write his name, and I have tried since and he can't learn yet.

ARNOLD. He can't learn it?

MANISCALCO. No. Sometimes he even cried. He tries to write and he can't do it....

ARNOLD. Is that the only thing that prevents him from being a citizen?

MANISCALCO. That is all.

ARNOLD. And, in fact, he has severed all connections with Italy? I mean, with anyone in Italy? He hasn't written back there for 17 years?

MANISCALCO. No; for 40 years. He hasn't been to Italy in 40 years....

ARNOLD. Your husband has never been arrested?

MANISCALCO. No. He brought me two crabs one time. He brought me two crabs home one time. He got arrested for bringing some crabs home one day, but I don't call that arrested...

ARNOLD. Does he have any membership in any Italian organizations?

MANISCALCO. No....

ARNOLD. You don't have to move tomorrow?

MANISCALCO. No. He used to own his own boat and then he gave it to me.[63]

The last reference—that Luciano Maniscalco, noncitizen, gave his boat to his wife, a U.S. citizen—alludes to the fact that during the war it became hazardous, virtually illegal, for enemy aliens to own fishing boats.

The testimony of Victor diSuvero, of San Francisco, added yet another element to the hardship being borne by Italian "enemy aliens." DiSuvero noted that he had been born in Venice, Italy in 1888 of Jewish parentage, gone to the Naval academy, and served as a commander in charge of submarines in the Italian Navy during World War I and beyond. In 1931, he left Italy to work in China as agent for the Italian Shipbuilding Corporation. When the Italian Fascists put anti-Semitic laws into effect, diSuvero, as a Jew, lost all his rights and rank in the naval reserve and was put under surveillance as an Italian "enemy alien." Struggling to survive, he finally managed to get his wife and four children out of China and into San Francisco, arriving on February 27, 1941. He tried to find employment in local shipyards, but "already in the spring last year there were no defense jobs for aliens." After working four months in a cold-storage plant as a janitor, he finally thought he had a job at the Pacific Bridge Co. in Alameda, but with the outbreak of war on December 7, 1941, lost that opportunity as well, and became an enemy alien in a second country. His attempt to volunteer to put his expertise to work for his new country, in the naval reserve, was rejected. DiSuvero concluded by saying that

> "I resent to be labeled as an enemy alien. I am here not only as a loyal future citizen, but as an allied alien in time of war. I have exhausted my resources and, under the present circumstances, I am unable to make a living for my family. My four children, ages from 6 to 15, all speak English as their own language and are doing well at school."[64]

DiSuvero did not mention it, but the eldest of those children, Victor, age 15, would also be classified as an enemy alien, and needed to obtain a travel permit from Western Defense Command headquarters each week to travel from his San Francisco home to Santa Clara College. Victor further reported that his father did, finally, obtain clearance to work at Marinship in Sausalito shortly after the Tolan hearings, and was employed there as a shipfitter throughout the war—with his eldest son doing duty as a welder's clean-up assistant for a short time.[65]

Another bit of personal testimony, this time from the Tolan Committee Hearings held in Seattle, Washington on February 28, 1942, gives some sense of the situation north of California. The witness was a Mrs. LaSalle of Seattle, herself a naturalized citizen of Italian descent, who worked in a social center serving Italian immigrants. She was questioned by Committee member Rep. Carl T. Curtis of Nebraska:

> MR. CURTIS. Mrs. LaSalle, we understand that you know a large number of people who will be affected by evacuation orders. Can you give us a brief description of a few of these cases?
>
> MRS. LASALLE. Yes; I can.
>
> MR. CURTIS. All right; will you do so?
>
> MRS. LASALLE. There are several that are old people, very old people. There is a couple, and he is 84 and she is 87. They have got a little home. They have no children. And as I am in the store there, they came in, both crying about the article that came out of the paper. They can't read. "Did you read? Are they going to make us lose our home? Where are we going?" The poor souls, you know, it is pitiful.
>
> There is another one, and she is 84, and she is blind; she is living with her daughter. The daughter has children of her own. They are American-born. The daughter says, "What am I going to do? Shall I let my mother go alone? Shall I leave my mother with the family?" And there is another big problem there. The old lady is blind; they have got to lead her around.
>
> There is another man, 87 years old. He is a lone man. He is a single man. And he shakes—he is just a nervous wreck. He just shakes. Sometimes he can't pick up the nickel from the counter that he has coming. He hears these things, and I asked Mr. Danney, I said, "What are you going to do?" "Well," he says, "I don't know, but Lake Washington is awful close. That is the best I can do. I can't go any other where or any other place." So that isn't all. There are several, but mostly in the old people. The young folks are mostly all American citizens. It is pitiful for the very old people.
>
> MR. CURTIS: And you feel that in working out the details, something should be done?...
>
> MRS. LASALLE: The old, they have no place to go; they can't earn anything, and they can't do no harm, because they don't get out of the house.
>
> I went to see a lady yesterday and she hasn't been out of the house for 6 months—from the bathroom to the kitchen and then back to the bed. Now, she can't read, she can't write, and she can't use the telephone. She doesn't understand a radio. So what harm could she give, even if she was left? She couldn't do no harm to anybody. To evacuate anybody like that would be—well, it is pitiful; that is all....
>
> There is another example. Now, there is a lady, she has two boys in the Army, already there, and her husband and her—of course, they are not too old. They are people of about 56; something like that; well, they both got to go. Now, when the boys come

back and they leave for home, and they don't find mother and father there, well, that don't look so good, either. You see, those boys, it kind of breaks their morale, too. They are going out to fight to save them, and they come back and don't find them there. That is just something that I think you should think about...[66].

Unfortunately, Mrs. LaSalle's admonition to the Committee to "think about it," did not affect those whose minds were already made up. At the February 26 hearings in Portland, Oregon, for example, the Mayor of Portland, Earl Riley, testified, in response to questions from Committee Chairman Tolan:

> CHAIRMAN. How about loyal Italians and Germans, mothers and fathers, say 60 or 75 or 80 or 100?
>
> RILEY. I can't see that age would make any difference. We know that there are people more alert and with keener minds at 60, 75, and 80, than a lot of people that are 25 and 30.
>
> CHAIRMAN. What about invalids and cripples?
>
> RILEY. I don't know as that would make any difference. They still would have contacts, if they wanted to use them.
>
> CHAIRMAN. We are not like England...not like Italy. Here, we have a country of all nationalities, and some of these days...this war is going to be over, and we will still have to live with them. At the same time, there is a war...and your thought is that there is only one thing to do, and that is to evacuate them, whether they are Japanese aliens, Germans, or Italians.[67]

Letters to California Attorney General Earl Warren that the Committee entered into the record generally reinforced this rigid position. Here is one from Elmer W. Heald, District Attorney of Imperial County (the southernmost part of California) and R.W. Ware, Sheriff of that county. First the letter admits that "...aside from Japanese aliens we do not have more than six or seven enemy aliens of Germany and Italy combined in this county...." Then, in response to questions that Warren had posed to all his District Attorneys, "Do you believe that danger can be adequately controlled by treating all enemy aliens alike regardless of nationality...?" Heald and Ware replied:

> All of our alien enemies are joined together in a very closely-knit alliance commonly known as the Axis Powers and they should all be treated in the same manner. They are all dominated and controlled by the same ideals and principles, namely, to overthrow and destroy the democracies and subjugate the free peoples of this world; consequently, all alien enemies should be treated alike regardless of their nationality.

In response to a third question--"What measures do you believe should be taken with reference to each nationality or enemy aliens as a whole in order to eliminate danger of sabotage and fifth column activities?"—the two replied:

> It is our belief that immediate evacuation of all enemy aliens is the only solution of the problem. It is absolutely impossible with the small force of police officers available in any county of the State of California to provide adequate protection against the depredations of sabotage which will be committed in the future...Criminal prosecutions under peacetime conditions are wholly inadequate to meet the urgency of the present situation. Any criminal prosecution is subject to long delays...What we must have is immediate, swift, and certain action. This can only be provided by the Federal Government itself through evacuation of all alien enemies and their concentration in internment centers provided by the United States Government.[68]

The District Attorney of Madera County added this in his letter:

> If we are not to run the risk of disaster we must forget such things as the writ of habeas corpus, and the prohibition against unreasonable searches and seizures. The right of self-defense, self-preservation, on behalf of the people, is higher than the bill of rights. Martial law should be declared all over California.[69]

As for Earl Warren himself, the then-Attorney General of California and future Chief Justice of the United States Supreme Court, his direct testimony before the Tolan Committee sounded an ominous warning for those who believed in the fundamental principle of civilian control over the military, or civil rights:

> ...the solution of our alien enemy problem with all its ramifications, which include the descendants of aliens, is not only a Federal problem but is a military problem. We believe that all of the decisions in that regard must be made by the military command that is charged with the security of this area....there is no way that civil government can cope with the situation.
>
> On the other hand, we believe that in an area, such as in California, which has been designated as a combat zone, when things have happened such as have happened here on the coast, something should be done and done immediately. We believe that any delay in the adoption of the necessary protective measures is to invite disaster. It means that we, too, will have in California a Pearl Harbor incident.
>
> I believe that up to the present and perhaps for a long time to come the greatest danger to continental United States is that from well-organized sabotage and fifth-column activity...
>
> To assume that the enemy has not planned fifth column activities for us in a wave of sabotage is simply to live in a fool's paradise.[70]

Warren further stated that the fact that no sabotage or fifth column actions had yet taken place was the "most ominous sign" yet, for it indicated that the deadly actions sure to come were timed to take maximum advantage of an attack or invasion. With this kind of logic, based on no evidence whatsoever, there appeared to be little hope for anyone to stop and "think about" the full implications of forced evacuations.

Accordingly, those who lived in the prohibited zones simply bowed to the inevitable, and moved, while the stories of hardship heard by the Tolan Committee were replicated in dozens of cities affected by the evacuation. In Richmond, Teresa Bottini's extended family moved en masse from their home in north Richmond to a house on Carleton Street in Berkeley because her mother and grandmother, enemy aliens, were obliged to move. Several related families lived there: the Scalises, the Brunos (Bottini's maiden name), and the Corteses, including Bottini's citizen father who worked for the Pullman Company in Richmond, and Dominic Scalise who was attending UC Berkeley. The Rampoldis moved only a short distance out of their home in Richmond's prohibited zone, to the nearby Alvarado Park area to the east. As Jimmy Rampoldi, about to be drafted into the army at the time, told it years later:

> There was a lady, a family there, they had about an acre and a half of land, they told my mother and father to, somebody told them to buy a trailer, not a, not a mobile trailer, you know one of these fifteen-sixteen foot trailers that you could tow behind your car. For the four of us, my mother and father, my brother and I....that's a heck of a thing, you know? Here's your son fighting overseas and you're kicking them out of the, the parents, kicking them out of their house.[71]

Angie Accornero's father was a citizen who worked at the American Radiator Co. in Richmond, but her mother, Enrica Mapelli, was not. So Mrs. Mapelli moved in with a friend, Mrs. Merlo, who, fortunately, lived in Alvarado Park. As Angie remembered it, "to be referred to as 'enemy aliens' was the worst. Mom felt terrible about it." Angie, thirteen at the time, remembers "really missing Mom. We'd go almost every night" to visit her. Angie's aunt, Giovanna Traverso, also had to move, to North Beach in San Francisco, while another aunt who had to leave Alameda also moved to San Francisco. Angie's husband, Henry Accornero, was living at the time in nearby Albany, and remembers not only that his mother had to move south to Oakland, but also that he was called into the principal's office (he was in high school at the time), and questioned about his mother—a procedure that he came to view as a kind of government spying on enemy aliens. The Pericolis, like many of the Italians in Richmond at that time, owned a truck farm of about 25 acres. Though Sergio and his citizen father were able to remain at the farm, his mother, a non-citizen, and younger brother moved to Berkeley, along with two non-citizen uncles. Sergio remembers visiting his mother each night, as well as the difficulty he and his father had trying to keep the farm going. They managed for about eight months, but finally gave it up and joined many others from Richmond working on Liberty ships at the Kaiser shipyards. John Bruzzoni of Richmond had a similar story, differing only in that both his parents, being non-citizens, had to move to Oakland. John and an older brother kept the farm going until their father was able to return. Margaret Baker (nee Traverso) remembers that her father, a non-citizen at the time, moved from Richmond all the way to Calistoga in the north. This pattern—of enemy aliens moving to both distant and nearby places—was especially noticeable in Richmond: Emma Nuti, Giovanna Traverso and several others moved across the bay to San Francisco; the Brunos and Pericolis moved south to Berkeley; the Siris and Bruzzonis moved farther south to Oakland; the Mapellis and Rampoldis moved to nearby Alvarado Park in Richmond; the Colombos and Siris moved inland to Oakdale; the Forners moved north as far as Petaluma.

The above-noted pattern speaks to a major peculiarity of the Italian American experience on the WWII home front: because of the wide geographical distribution of those affected, and the various levels of restrictions on different enemy aliens, each family had to cope with the relevant restrictions pretty much on its own. The result was a pattern of isolation: fathers separated from mothers, mothers from their families, and families from each other and neighbors—all with widely different notions of what they had to do, where they had to move (if they had to), how far they had to go, and with little information, aside from rumors, about the fate of others both in their own communities and beyond. The result was the kind of desperation felt by Pearl Piziali's father: distraught over his separation from his wife and family (he had no car to drive from Richmond to Oakland where she had moved), and with no idea, aside from rumors, about how long the separation would last, he seriously considered giving up his Richmond job, selling his home, and moving to Oakland to join his wife. He was only dissuaded from doing so by his local representative who advised him to hold on a bit longer, since confidential information indicated that the restrictions would be lifted soon.[72]

Nor was Piziali the only Italian enemy alien to despair. Many lost their businesses or their ability to work because of the restricted zones, or the curfew, or both. Al Bronzini's father was an owner and mainstay of a fruit and vegetable stand in Oakland that was doing very well. With the imposition of the prohibited zone, the elder Bronzini could no longer go to his market since it was located on the west side of East 12th Street in Oakland, off limits to enemy aliens (had it been on the *east* side of 12th Street, it would have been legal). Without his father's input, the market soon closed. The loss of his business and his resulting depression had a devastating effect on Bronzini's wife, who suffered a nervous breakdown and ended in a sanatorium until her husband personally took her home.[73]   Health problems affected several others subject to evacuation. Frances Cardinale, noted above, came down with appendicitis while separated from her parents, and was taken for an operation from Pittsburg to St. Francis Hospital in San Francisco. Her mother and father, enemy aliens who had moved to Centerville, were unable to travel the more than five miles to the hospital until they applied for permits. The delay kept them from visiting until well after the operation. Nancy Billeci, of Pittsburg, suffered a sterner fate: she was taken to the County Hospital to deliver her baby, but her alien husband, under restriction, was allowed to see his new baby for only a few minutes under guard, and in handcuffs.[74] And Aniceto Vannucci, of San Francisco, a concrete finisher living with relatives, blacked all his windows in fear of being caught not observing blackouts and the curfew, stopped visiting friends, and ended in the hospital with pneumonia. He died within two weeks, partly, his niece Vera was sure, because he had lost all desire to live.[75]

Most tragic of all, no less than five of those classified as 'enemy aliens' were so shamed, discouraged, or overwhelmed by their fate that they took their own lives. Martini Battistessa, of Richmond, was a locksmith with a shop on Macdonald Avenue who feared the overturning of his life and work portended by his forced move. The February 17 *Richmond Independent* reported his end as follows:

> Shortly after 7 o'clock last evening he [Battistessa] took his own life by flinging himself under the wheels of The Owl, a speeding Southern Pacific passenger train, near the Espee avenue and Twenty-third street crossing....
>
> Acquaintances of the man reported to police that for several days he had been despondent and threatening to take his own life....
>
> Battistessa was unmarried and had no known relatives in this country. Because he was an Italian alien he had been notified to move from the Richmond defense area.[76]

Stockton was rocked by not one but two similar incidents. The February 9 *Stockton Record* carried the headline, **Alien Hangs Self over War Worry**. The paper reported:

> Believed to have been deeply despondent because of his new status as an "enemy alien," Giovanni "John" Tassano, 69, landscape gardener here for 20 years, hanged himself late yesterday in the basement of a house at 3647 North Hunter Street.[77]

The paper further reported that Tassano had been found hanging from a beam in the basement by his landlady, Mrs. Molinari, after she missed him. A little more than a week later, the *Stockton Record* reported a second suicide: **Despondency Said Cause of**

Suicide. The report again attributed the suicide to worry over enemy alien status:

> Worry over his status as an enemy alien was the cause of Giovanni Sanguinetti's despondency and death...Sanguinetti undressed himself before he took his life with a light rope, hanging himself from a rafter in the basement of one of the farm buildings where he had been working for 27 years. A resident of the United States since 1899, Sanguinetti spent most of his time working on the Solari Ranch. Friends described him as patriotic.[78]

A kind of grim confirmation of Sanguinetti's death came many years later when this writer interviewed Joseph Solari about his experiences in cherry farming in Stockton. It turned out that Sanguinetti was an Italian-born cousin who had immigrated to California before the turn of the century, always worked with the Solari family, always kept to himself, but feared that he would be imprisoned as an enemy alien.

At least two other California suicides were reported in local newspapers. On February 12, 1942, the *San Francisco Chronicle* ran an article on page 9: **An Alien's Life Wasn't Worth Living.** The paper reported that when Joseph Mecheli was told that he couldn't live in his Vallejo, California home after February 24, he decided not to wait till then:

> The 57-year-old fisherman didn't wait for February 24. Yesterday he cut his throat with a butcher knife. He died in the Vallejo Hospital, where he fought off an attempted life-saving blood transfusion.[79]

Five days later, the Chronicle attributed yet another death, this time in San Francisco, to the same mental state: **Restrictions Too Much, an Alien Leaps to Death.** The report said:

> A three-story plunge yesterday ended the brooding of Stefano Terranova, 65, Italian alien jewelry salesman living at 510 Columbus avenue. Police said he had been despondent over restrictions faced in the alien control order. He plunged from the roof of a building adjoining his hotel residence.
>
> An incoherent note found in his room by Coroner's deputies said in part:
>
> "I believe myself to be good, but find myself deceived. I don't know why...It is my fault for blaming others...My brain is no good."[80]

Though the report seemed to dismiss the suicide note as "incoherent," its import today seems quite clear. In the face of U.S. government measures which appeared to blame Italian-born immigrants for who they were rather than for what they had done ("I believe myself to be good"), the most isolated and pessimistic of those so targeted descended into a spiral of self-blame, self-disparagement ("My brain is no good") and self-destruction. Such attitudes might be compared to those evinced by Italian internee

Louis Sdraulig (see Chapter 3, Internment), in his letter to Alien Enemy Control when he sought a second hearing:

> After all this time in the enclosure I do not know yet why all this, must be some reason for, some evil I do not know, something wrong some where, except I am not citizen of this Country but with sincere intention and resolution to become soon as possible...What evil I made? Please let me know where I fell short in my loyalty to this Country I wish to know my weaked (sic) points to strengthen them to perfection to please better God Country and neighbors.[81]

That is, in the absence of specific actions and specific charges, those who are arrested, imprisoned, or simply branded as both "alien" to and "enemies" of their country, can begin to feel that they have, in fact, committed some infraction of which they are unaware, or simply that they have been born defective. John Christgau, as noted above, was told that for German internees, this affliction had a name, *gitter krankheit* or "barbed wire sickness"—the feeling that since one has been accused and imprisoned, one *must* be guilty of something. For those disposed to pessimism or despair, that conviction of guilt and the prospect of more severe measures to come led them to the ultimate act of self-punishment.

❦

PART III: Arrests for Violations & Expanding the Evacuation

The *Report to the Congress of the United States* prepared by the Justice Department in 2001 indicates that its "review of thousands of pages of documents revealed 354 arrests for curfew violations, over 85 percent of which occurred in California."[82] The report does not cite a comparable figure for violating the rule against entering or remaining in prohibited zones, so our only source for those violations derives from either anecdotes from those affected, or raw FBI reports found at the National Archives at San Bruno. An examination of the latter indicates that arrests of Italian enemy aliens for both offenses took place regularly in the northern Pacific region.

Concetta Maroni Servante lived in Vallejo, California, in a prohibited zone until she had to evacuate from her home. Her FBI report states that

> On June 11, 1942, the subject was brought to the Vallejo Police Department by two Vallejo policemen from her apartment at 40 Main Street, Vallejo, California.

She advised that she was born on May 10, 1876, at Tuscany, Italy, and had been in the United States since 1906. In February, 1942, she moved to San Francisco, residing with her daughter, Mrs. C.R. Goodenough, 147 Maddux Avenue, in view of the fact that Italian aliens are no longer permitted to reside in Vallejo...Mrs. Servante's daughter, Mrs. Goodenough, recently removed to 1890 Lucerne Street, Stockton, California, and at that new home does not have room for her mother. Mrs. Servante has been ill for several years, she advised, and she owns a small rooming house at 40 Main Street, Vallejo, and that is her only source of income. She believed that inasmuch as she had made application for her final citizenship papers and had appeared with two witnesses at Fairfield, it would be permissible for her to return to her home in Vallejo, in view of the fact that she was ill and had no one to take care of her rooming house in order that she might receive income for her subsistence.[83]

The report notes that given the above facts, Assistant U.S. Attorney Zirpoli "declined to authorize subject's apprehension and prosecution...He advised that Mrs. Servante should be released and instructed not to return to Vallejo until she had received written instructions from the United States Army."

The case of Joe Lupo (Giovanni Battista Lupo) bore some resemblance to Mrs. Servante's. Lupo, according to his FBI report, dutifully moved from his home in the prohibited zone at 935 Evelyn Street, Albany, California, in early 1942, as required. The report then details how Lupo returned to his Albany home around May 9, 1942, but failed to notify authorities of his move:

This investigation is predicated upon information received from the Richmond Police Department that the subject had changed his address from 1735 Evers Street, Oakland, to 935 Evelyn Avenue, Albany. The alien registration file on the subject in this office failed to reflect any notification of the return of the alien to 935 Evelyn.... Subject was interviewed at his residence on September 16, 1942 by the writer and Sergeant John J. Viarengo of the Albany Police Department. Sergeant Viarengo advised that he had known the subject and his wife for a number of years, and that no information indicating disloyalty had come to him concerning the Lupos....Subject advised that upon exclusion of enemy aliens from coastal areas in the early part of this year, he and his wife and child moved to Oakland, California, and when the restriction was terminated, he and the family returned to their home at 935 Evelyn Street, Albany. He stated that the date of their return was about May 9, 1942. Subject stated he had not been advised of the need to notify the FBI of a change of address or employment.... Subject was in possession of a temporary certificate of exemption from the curfew and exclusion dated April 6, 1942 at San Jose, California. The certificate is signed by R.R. Wilson, Captain, Infantry, Northern California Sector, and authorizes the subject to reside in Oakland California. The exemption authorizes the subject to travel and work free from the curfew...Subject stated that he is presently employed at the Ford Motor Company in Richmond, California; that he worked there previously and had gone back to work there about a month ago. Subject advised he worked for the Albany Concrete Company, 1936 Ashby Street, Berkeley, California, prior to being re-employed at the Ford Company....At a later date, Assistant United States Attorney A.J. Zirpolo, San Francisco, advised that no willful violation was involved, and therefore he would decline any action.[84]

Given the many confusions regarding prohibited zones, it seems reasonable to suppose that many more Italian enemy aliens entered, remained in, or returned to prohibited areas in violation of the law, though, absent the specifics, this is difficult to verify. But then, so is the date when authorities believed the order keeping Italian enemy aliens out of prohibited zones was lifted. Anecdotal evidence suggests that late June or early July of 1942 was the end date, and the *Report to the Congress of the United States* confirms this, citing June 27, 1942 as the date when "Lt. General DeWitt lifted the exclusion-zone regulations of the Western Defense Command."[85] Giovanni Lupo, however, seemed to have believed that the prohibition ended in early May—and the U.S. Attorney seemed to share this view since he did not penalize Lupo for his premature return (though later, on June 11, he *did* forbid Concetta Servante to remain in Vallejo's prohibited zone!) Whether by reason of this confusion, or by dint of the fact that aliens considered prohibited zone violations more serious and so avoided them, or for other reasons, the violations of curfew, which affected far more people and which lasted longer, show up more often in FBI reports. Some of the latter are narrated below.

Aristide Bertolini was a truck farmer living in Santa Rosa. Restricted by the curfew from working after 8 p.m., he nonetheless had an important order of tomatoes to deliver, and so risked completing his day's orders with a final trip after the curfew hour. He was spotted (or reported) and arrested by local police, taken to the Sharp Park Detention facility as a curfew violator, and detained for several weeks behind barbed wire.[86] The result was that his son, Larry, then 16 years old, had to leave high school to run the family's farm operation. The Sichi family of Arcata owned a chicken ranch, but since it was within the prohibited zone, the elder Sichi had to sell nearly 5,000 chickens at a loss when he moved his family. Living virtually across the street from their old home, the Sichis could look at it, but could not and did not enter it. Marino Sichi, 21 years old and an enemy alien, was courting his wife-to-be at the time and though he obeyed the prohibited zone law, he decided to risk violating the curfew law. He spoke about his curfew arrest years later:

...we weren't allowed out after eight o'clock at night. We had to be inside, but I figured, "Oh, to hell with it." I'd go where I'd want. Went all my life, so why not now? Well, somebody turned me in. Called the FBI. A so-called friend....And next thing I know, I had a real sharp-looking young man knocking on my door. He was looking for my dad, then found out he had the wrong guy and wanted me. He says, "I understand you were out after eight o'clock?" What could I say? I said yes. So he arrested me for violation of the curfew; I forget what else he called it. This time they caught me. I was on the right side of the line, but I was out after eight...They confiscated all of our guns. I had a .22 and a .410 and my dad had a .22....The guy who arrested me was nobody local. Even the police chief said afterwards, "Heck, I've known you all my life. I never knew you weren't born here." "No, I've been living here since I was two years old." I didn't know any other country, really.

So they locked me up in the county jail for five days, waiting for transportation, I guess. And from there they took me, two marshals, and another prisoner in a car—a Chevy, I remember. They said, "We can be tough on you, or be easy. Whatever you want. If you want to cooperate we won't put handcuffs on you, but if you want to get smart, we'll cuff you." I said I wouldn't do anything. What could I do?...

They brought us to what I think was FBI headquarters on Silver Avenue in San Francisco, a big mansion up on the hill with a big wall around it. When they turned us over to the manager, he said, "Well, what am I going to do with them? We have no facilities to keep these people." So he locked us in a big closet. We sat there for quite a while, just sat on the floor. Pretty soon they opened the door and let us out and loaded us into a paddy wagon. We didn't know where we were going. It turned out they took us to Sharp Park, near Pacifica. They had quite a concentration camp there, a holding camp I guess you'd call it. [Sharp Park was a detention facility run by the INS, ed.]

I remember the camp was divided in half. The Japanese were on the left side as you went in, and we were on the right. I don't know, it seemed like there were thousands of people; it was quite a large gathering. There were Germans, English, French, Italians, every nationality you could think of...

There were guard towers at every corner and all around the perimeter. Those guards were armed; I found out the hard way. We were playing baseball one day, and I was out in the field. Somebody hit a ball and it got past me. I ran after it and everybody was shouting to hurry up and throw the ball in. All at once I heard a sound that made the blood kind of stop. Heard a "click-click," and when I looked up, I'm looking down the barrel of a .30-caliber machine gun aimed right at my head. I wasn't more than five or six feet from the fence and he was right above me, just motioning me off. He says, "You aren't supposed to be near this fence. Back off." I tried to explain that I was just after the baseball, but he said, "I don't care what you were after. The next time we're going to shoot." There was no next time.[87]

Ugo Giuntini, also of Arcata, adds another observation to Sichi's story, describing his visit to see Sichi at the Sharp Park Detention Center:

> The very first time my brother and I got to this wire compound, we saw him.
> It does something to you. It's just like looking at animals caged in a pen. We'd visit
> with him, and then come back and report on his condition to his folks. When I left,
> there he was on the other side of that wire. You could just read his thoughts: "Why?
> Why?"[88]

Mary Tolomei, of nearby Eureka, adds another observation about the effects of the
curfew on her Italian neighbors:

> I remember there was a curfew—eight o'clock, and everybody had to be in.
> Sometimes a lot of the Italians would be five minutes or so late. The rule caused an
> awful lot of hubbub in this town. All the young ones were citizens because they were
> born here. And all the older ones, they liked to go down to Second Street. There were
> two or three saloons down there run by Italians. They'd go down there and have a
> game of cards or something like that, and sit and talk by the hour. And they couldn't
> do that anymore. I tell you it hit them pretty hard. The ones that didn't go out stayed
> in all the time, and they would tell on the ones that were out. There was one man, he
> was scared to go out anywhere, so he wouldn't go. Even if he could be back by eight
> o'clock, he still wouldn't go. And then somebody would be out late. Oh boy, there was
> an awful uproar. There was a lot of jealousy...It made a lot of hostility; that's why it was
> such a bad law...It made enemies; it really made enemies. Anything like that would.
> Whoever thought up that law had screws loose somewhere.[89]

FBI reports are replete with cases of those arrested for curfew violations. Sam Tri-
dente, of Oakland, was arrested as a curfew violator and sent to Sharp Park to join Sichi.
The Attorney General ordered his release on September 18, 1942. Enrico Sorelli, also of
Oakland, worked for the Oakland Scavenger Co. Sorelli had to walk two blocks from
his home to work each morning, and left at 5:55 a.m. to be at work on time by 6:00 a.m.
This made him a 5-minute violator of the curfew, and he was arrested. In San Francisco,
Barbara Lena Linda of 209 Charter Oak Avenue was arrested for a curfew violation in
August of 1942. She was visiting her sister when San Francisco police called at her home
to check on her. When her stepfather, Ignacio Audino, told them she was at her sister's
house, they arrested her for being out after hours and booked her at the City Jail. She
was released on August 21. Arturo Pecchia, of 1934 Powell St., in San Francisco ran into
trouble because his job at New Joe's Restaurant at 536 Broadway required him to be out
past the curfew deadline of 8 p.m. He dutifully changed jobs to the New Lucca Lunch
Restaurant, but having changed both his job and residence without notifying authorities,
he was arrested. His case was dismissed as involving "no willful failure." Pia Mary Parenti,

of Stockton, was arrested in October for extending her visit to a friend and fellow worker at the Flotil Cannery, Elvira Sonni, after curfew hours. The mother of four children was remanded to the San Joaquin County Jail, and then to the custody of a U.S. Marshal, her case listed as "pending." Jack Copello was part owner of the Copello Market, 617 San Mateo Street, San Bruno, California. Remaining one night in his market until 9 p.m. to check over the day's receipts, he was arrested and ordered to the custody of the U.S. Marshal. Luigi Rosso, owner of a shoe repair business in San Francisco, was apprehended one night at 10 p.m. taking his son home from the movies. His wife, a U.S. citizen, said she didn't even know he was not a citizen. Rosso explained that this was why it was hard for him to abide by the curfew: he couldn't explain to his wife why he wanted to stay in the house when she wanted to go out at night.[90]

FBI Reports also reveal that authorities made "spot check" curfew raids to check up on possible violations by known enemy aliens. Pasquale Magni (alias Peter Magni) was found in one such raid, on September 16, 1942, when the FBI were attempting to locate Adolph Muselman, a German alien living at 16-Mile House, El Camino Real Drive, in Millbrae, California. Though Muselman was not there, Magni was found to be living at that address and, when he arrived home at about 8:30 or 8:45 p.m., was arrested for a curfew violation. Magni explained that he had been

> ..eating and drinking wine at a nearby eating place; and he also stated that he had been about ten minutes late at least one evening within the past thirty days, and that he had gone to Redwood City, California, by automobile September 16, 1942, even though he did not have a permit to so travel. It is noted that the distance from subject's residence to Redwood City is about fourteen miles. Magni further stated that he has never served in any army; has never been affiliated with any un-American groups; that he realized he should not have violated the curfew and travel restrictions; and that he did not have any permit or exemption although he was waiting for one, for which he applied about September 11, 1942, on the grounds that his son, Alexandra (sic) Magni, was presently in the United States Army.[91]

On some occasions, the FBI would make multiple arrests for curfew violations. One such case occurred in San Jose, California on July 10, 1942 and involved one John Maiolo, as well as several others arrested and mentioned in his file: Louis Longinetti, Celestino Andresano, and George Pio. The FBI Report cites the information it derived from the San Jose police:

> ...on July 10, 1942, at 9:30 p.m. John Maiolo had been arrested at the Liberty Tavern where he was employed as a chef for violation of the curfew regulation. The

Police Department advised that Maiolo was a flagrant violator of the curfew regulations inasmuch as he was out every night after 8 p.m. The Police Department advised that Maiolo had made the statement that he was as good an American as anyone, and "To Hell with the curfew." Maiolo...resided at the Gunn Hotel, 210 West Santa Clara Street, San Jose, California....The above facts [including Maiolo's entry date into the U.S., April 11, 1910] were telephonically presented to the Assistant U.S. Attorney A.J. Zirpoli on July 11, 1942, and he authorized that the subject be held and booked en route to Immigration and Naturalization Service for a preliminary hearing before the United States Attorney.[92]

Other documents in the file indicate that a Presidential Warrant for John Maiolo's arrest was received on August 5, 1942, that Maiolo was thereupon placed in custody at the detention center at Sharp Park, California. He was subsequently released from Sharp Park on August 28, 1942 and paroled on September 5. The FBI report on Maiolo goes on to describe a larger "problem" police were having with the curfew in the Santa Clara Valley:

Special Agent L.D. Wine, San Jose, California, telephonically contacted this office on July 11, 1942, and explained that the Police Department at San Jose had referred a local problem to him. This problem which exists is that the Santa Clara Valley is being flooded with an influx of itinerant farm labor engaged in picking fruit. Among these farm laborers are a number of alien enemies all of whom have an utter disregard for the Presidential Proclamation and the Commanding General of the Western Defense Command Proclamation regulating curfew in restricted areas. The Police Department advised that on a tour of the town on the night of July 10, 1942, the Police Department conservatively estimated that at least 75 potential curfew violators could have been picked up. The Police Department added that pending an opinion from the United States Attorney as to how to handle this problem, four individuals were arrested and booked at the San Jose City Prison on investigation. The names of these individuals were Louis Longinetti, Celestino Andresano, George Pio, and the subject John Maiolo. These facts as well as the general problem related by the Police Department were telephonically transmitted to the Assistant U.S. Attorney A.J. Zirpoli on July 11, 1942, who ordered that the subjects be booked en route to the Immigration and Naturalization Service, and as to the larger problem, he recommended that the Police Department endeavor through the *Mercury Herald*, San Jose, to give these arrests wide publicity in the hope that other potential violators might curtail their illegal activities.[93]

Maiolo's interview with the FBI conflicts in several respects with the San Jose Police report: he stated that his "most recent employment" was at the Cerittes Café as a chef, and that the cause of his arrest was due to

...late customers who came into Cerittes Café and ordered steaks just as he was closing up and leaving for home. Cerittes, his employer, had requested that he stay and cook these steaks for these late customers, and in order to hold his job he had done so, and when he had finished cooking these orders it was past the curfew hour and he started home at the time he was apprehended.[94]

Since he spent about a month in confinement, it appears that this explanation did not suffice to excuse Maiolo.

Another case with multiple arrests occurred in Asti, California at the famed Italian Swiss Colony Winery there, with reports made at the Sheriff's office at Cloverdale and the FBI office at Santa Rosa. The case involved no less than eight enemy aliens working after the 8 p.m. curfew at the Winery, under the direction of Enrico Prati, vice-president of the Winery. Prati had notified Police Chief Ledford, of Cloverdale, that he needed to work the men after hours [it was harvest time, ed.], whereupon Chief Ledford simply advised Prati of the regulations for permits authorizing temporary exemptions from curfew. The relevant regulations stated:

> "'Where the alien in traveling to or from his actual place of employment to his residence is accompanied by a peace officer,' exemption from curfew restrictions may be granted."
>
> "Peace officer may be a policeman, deputy sheriff, constable, special policeman, deputized special guard. Permits will be granted only for a thirty-day period, subject to renewal. A letter from the employer stating that he understands the limitations of such permit is required."

The FBI Report notes that when the aliens were apprehended, Mr. Prati had the above-referred-to rules in his possession. The problem was that registering for permits could only be done at the Cloverdale police station from 10:00 a.m. to 1:00 p.m. daily. Mr. Prati complained that his men could not drive the six miles to Cloverdale during those work hours, but he received no response other than a review of the penalties for curfew violations. On October 1, 1942, he wrote a letter to Chief Ledford:

> This is to confirm phone conversation of this moment in reference to aliens living in Cloverdale, Asti, and vicinity coming to work from 7:00 pm to 1:00 am at our Asti plant. We assume the responsibility of those men to be escorted home by an officer as per section 4-A, item 5, of the Western Defense Command, and Fourth Army Wartime Civil Control Administration.

FEDERAL BUREAU OF INVESTIGATION

Case originated at: SAN FRANCISCO, CALIFORNIA   SFile No: 100-14416

Report made at:	Date made:	Period made for:	Report made by:
SAN FRANCISCO, CALIFORNIA	10-21-42	10-8,9-42	G. EDWARD GOODWIN emb

Title:	Character of case:
GIUSEPPE PAVAN wa Giuseppe Pajan	INTERNAL SECURITY-I ALIEN ENEMY CONTROL CURFEW VIOLATOR

CONFIDENTIAL

SYNOPSIS: Subject, with 7 other Italian aliens, arrested 10:00 pm while at work for curfew violation. Subject admits violation but advised employer stated he had permit for him to work. Employer states was attempting get permits and expected do so in few days. Subject booked Sonoma Co. Jail enroute USM on authority of USA. Subject resided in U.S. since 1923; served in Italian Army in last war.

- P -

DETAILS: AT SANTA ROSA, CALIFORNIA

This investigation is predicated upon information received from Deputy Sheriff WILLIAM BARNETT, Sonoma County Sheriff's Office, to the effect that he had been advised by Chief of Police JAMES LEDFORD of Cloverdale, California, that several Italian aliens were working after curfew hours at the Italian-Swiss Colony Winery, Asti, California, without curfew permits.

Deputy BARNETT further advised that Chief LEDFORD had informed him that he had had considerable trouble with Mr. ENRICO

Approved & Forwarded	Special Agent in Charge	Do not write in this space
2-Bureau 3-USA, S.F. 1-G-2, S.F. 2-ONI, S.F. 1-INS, S.F. 2-San Francisco		A8-5 (14-A-1)

Prati subsequently informed FBI agent Bresnahan that the men had been escorted not by a peace officer but by a winery foreman who was an American citizen. Prati also tried to get Chief Ledford to send Miss Simis [in charge of registering aliens for exemptions, ed.] to Asti so that she could do the registering all at once without each man having to go to Cloverdale during working hours. Chief Ledford informed Prati that he (Ledford) would have to take the matter up with the District Attorney and head of civilian defense for Sonoma County. A note in Prati's possession when arrested said: "Jim Ledford said he talked with the District Attorney's office and the lady in town is not permitted to come down here." The raid then followed:

> The writer, accompanied by Special Agent J.J. Bresnahan, Jr., and Deputy Sheriffs Fred Barnes and Lester Sheeley of the Sonoma County Sheriff's Office, arrived at the Asti Winery at approximately 8:55 pm on October 8, 1942 and contacted Mr. Prati. The latter advised that there were aliens working in the plant after 8:00 pm without permits but that he had planned to have these aliens apply for permits within the next few days. Mr. Prati explained that he had discussed the situation with Deputy Sheriff Sheeley on the afternoon of October 8, 1942 and that Sheeley had given him a period of three days in which to have the aliens register. According to Mr. Prati, Sheeley further stated that the aliens could work after 8:00 pm during this three-day period. Deputy Sheriff Sheeley, in the presence of Prati, denied ever having made this statement. However, on October 9, 1942 the writer and Agent Bresnahan interviewed Lewis Pellegrini, Office Manager, and Deputy Sheriff Lyman H. Cash, both employees at the winery who were present during the discussion between Mr. Prati and Sheeley, and they advised that Sheeley had given Prati a three-day period in which to comply with the curfew regulations....
>
> An examination of the premises at approximately 10:00 pm by the writer and special agent J.J. Bresnahan, Jr., and the above-referred-to deputies revealed that the following enemy aliens were working: John Faccini, Mario Cretier, Diego Petruzzi, Giovanni Petri, Giuseppe Pavan, Joe Capella, Ugo Martinelli, and Vincenzo Fanesi. It is here noted that none of these men other than Giovanni Petri had applied for curfew permits and Petri had been refused a permit because of the fact that no arrangements had been made to have him accompanied from work after curfew hours by a peace officer. Separate cases have been opened on all the above-named individuals by the San Francisco Field Division....
>
> Mr. Prati insisted on telephonically contacting Mr. A.J. Zirpoli at San Francisco, and after this had been done and both Agent Bresnahan and Mr. Prati had explained the facts of the case, Mr. Zirpoli advised that the above-named alien enemies should all be apprehended and booked at the Sonoma County Jail enroute to the United States Marshal. In accordance with Mr. Zirpoli's instructions, subjects were booked at the Sonoma County Jail at 12:15 am October 9, 1942.[95]

The irony of this case (aside from the refusal of those enforcing the curfew to give any consideration to the critical and well-known needs of wineries at harvest time) inheres in the fact that a mere *three days* after the eight men were arrested, on October 12, 1942, Columbus Day, the Attorney General of the United States, Francis Biddle, made an announcement in Carnegie Hall freeing all 600,000 enemy aliens of Italian descent from the restrictions that had been imposed on them. A week later, on October 19, the curfew they were arrested for violating during the grape harvest was also lifted by the WDC, and the violations had become moot.

Expanding the Evacuation

As has been emphasized repeatedly, the original intention of Lt. General John De-Witt of the Western Defense Command had been to clear the entire Pacific Slope of all three enemy alien groups—Japanese, German and Italian. As stated in the WDC's own report, "Individual Exclusion Program of Non-Japanese,"

> WDC believed it was going to be necessary to remove all enemy aliens from certain vital sections of the Pacific Coast, regardless of their country of origin. At the time Executive Order 9066 was drawn up early in February 1942, it was still the intent that not only the Japanese *but also the German and Italian aliens would have to be excluded.*[96] [Emphasis added.]

Newspaper reports of the time also made clear that though their main effort, after the promulgation of Executive Order 9066, had devolved to excluding all the Japanese from Military Zone No. 1 and interning them in WRA camps, the General and his staff never lost sight of the remaining two enemy alien groups. The March 3, 1942 *Stockton Record* (cited above), for example, carried this information:

> After defining the zones, DeWitt gave a glimpse of the procedure which would be followed in removing or restricting enemy aliens and Japanese-Americans from their boundaries.
>
> He announced that future proclamations affecting the area would be concerned with five classes of persons, namely:
>
> Class 1—All persons suspected of espionage, sabotage, fifth column or other subversive activity.
>
> Class 2—Japanese aliens, of whom there are more than 50,000.
>
> Class 3—American-born Japanese, of whom there are an estimated 70,000.
>
> Class 4—German aliens.
>
> Class 5—Italian aliens.
>
> ...When that work is completed [i.e., moving the Japanese, ed.], DeWitt said, German and Italian aliens would be next in line for evacuation.[97]

This message was reiterated and re-emphasized in several different ways, and in various forums. In a March 2, 1942 article in the *San Francisco Chronicle* on the Tolan Committee Hearing, "Inland Western States Will Fight Alien Influx," journalist Floyd Healey reported that inland states were vehemently rejecting any idea that they could become "dumping grounds" for aliens evacuated from the Pacific Coast:

> Not one of the Governors offered a welcome mat for the aliens which a majority
> of witnesses in California, Oregon and Washington have said should be removed from
> the Pacific Coast. Those who said they would take the evacuees if the army so decreed
> insisted they should be concentrated and guarded, and this applied to Germans and
> Italians as well as Japanese.[98]

The states mentioned were located between the Mississippi River and the Pacific Coast
and included Arizona, Wyoming, Nevada, Montana, Oklahoma, Arkansas, Colorado,
and South Dakota. On March 4, 1942, the same paper on page one (**Army Rules Coast,
Orders All Japs Out**) described the huge size of the proposed military operation, attributing it, as always, to an allegedly growing "fifth-column menace":

> The U.S. Army last night took over nearly 250,000 square miles in the Western
> United States to wipe out a *growing fifth-column menace.* That zone, stretching 2000
> miles from the Canadian border, all the way to the Arizona-NewMexico-Mexican bor-
> der, was transformed into military territory where army law will be supreme.
>
> Every Japanese, alien or American-born, must leave that area—nearly 120,000
> of them. *Thousands of German and Italian aliens will follow soon afterwards.* That new
> strip of forbidden territory, now known as Military Zone 1—includes two-thirds of
> California, from the ocean almost to the slopes of the Sierra Nevada, and swinging
> eastward into Death Valley. It covers two-fifths of Oregon, two-thirds of Washington
> and one third of Arizona.
>
> The boundaries of this area, bigger than all New England—nearly twice as big as
> Japan—were announced here yesterday by Lieutenant General John L. DeWitt, head
> of the Western Defense Command. His orders brought to an end nearly two weeks of
> waiting marked by rumors, vitriolic denunciations, outbreaks of vigilantism, and the
> fears of the 210,000 aliens and their children who may be affected...
>
> There will be no "mass-evacuation." General DeWitt claimed immediate com-
> pulsory evacuation is impracticable. Instead, evacuation will be conducted slowly and
> regularly until all unwanted aliens and citizens are out.
>
> Exemptions will be made for Italian and German aliens who are 70 or older, and
> who are not suspected of disloyalty, and for the parents, brothers, sisters, wives and
> children of men in U.S. Armed Forces...
>
> German and Italian aliens will probably not be affected until after the Japanese
> have been removed. General DeWitt asserted, however, that any aliens or citizens sus-
> pected of sabotage, espionage or disloyalty would not wait their turn, but be picked up
> immediately by the FBI and other enforcement agencies.[99] [Emphases added.]

The article is also notable for its report that, for the first time, General DeWitt seemed to be moderating his position somewhat. He claimed there would be no "mass evacuation" (though how the forced movement of 120,000 Japanese and the subsequent evacuation of thousands more Italian and German aliens could be otherwise described is not explained), and also that Italian and German aliens over 70, as well as those with relatives in the Armed Forces, would be exempted. According to Stephen Fox, these concessions, and others to come, can be attributed to the hearings still being held by Representative Tolan of Oakland (see testimony above), three of whose central issues were hardship, exemption, and whether all three enemy alien groups should be treated alike.[100]

The partial softening of his position notwithstanding, General DeWitt remained committed to two courses of action: 1) evacuating the remainder of the enemy aliens from the Pacific Slope, and, by example, 2) spreading the virus of mass evacuation to other military areas, especially the Eastern and Southern Defense Commands. At this very time, in fact, The Senate Committee on Military Affairs was holding hearings on S. 2352, a bill "Providing Penalty for Violation of Restrictions or Orders with Respect to Persons Entering, Remaining in, or Leaving Military Areas or Zones." In the course of the hearings, witnesses offered testimony on the possible evacuation of large numbers of enemy aliens from military zones *other than those on the West Coast*. Some of the testimony from Colonel B. M. Bryan, head of the Provost Marshal General's alien division, as questioned by Senator Johnson, addressed the numbers the army might have to remove, how such people would be controlled, and the overall effect this would have on the nation as a whole:

> **Sen. Johnson:** The Bill we have, S. 2352, makes it a violation of law for any person to enter, remain in, or leave a military area. The military area, as I understand it, will be designated by the authorized Commander of any specific area, or could be designated by the Secretary of War.
>
> **Colonel Bryan:** Yes, sir. Under executive order.
>
> **Sen. Johnson:** Now, the law we have before us for enactment will cover everything in the United States?
>
> **Colonel Bryan:** That is correct, sir.
>
> **Sen Johnson:** However, at this moment we have before us a map that portrays to the members of this committee, by way of drawing, all of that territory on the West Coast from the Canadian border to the Mexican border.
>
> Now, the census reports reveal that under the registration of those called upon to register, it designated places, and there were designated, during the latter part of the registration date, approximately six million aliens in the United States.
>
> **Colonel Bryan:** Yes, sir.

Sen. Johnson: Now, of those six million that were registered and finger-printed, how many were of enemy nations? That is to say, of Germany, Italy, and Japan.

Colonel Bryan: I think I can go directly to the point in this way: I believe we are contemplating here on the West Coast—the best figure at this time on the move from the West Coast is over 100,000 persons. That is this area affected here (indicating)....

Sen. Johnson: But is that the answer to my question?

Colonel Bryan: No, sir, and I can not give you specifically that information throughout the whole country.

Sen. Johnson: All I know in reference to the census is that there were approximately 6 million aliens of all kinds registered and finger-printed in the United States. I was trying to ascertain how many aliens there are and from how many countries, in order that we might get in mind initially information in connection with that, in order that we could formulate some idea as to plans that you might have in mind now, and formulate in our minds plans about the handling of this situation throughout the United States, *because the same thing is going to have to be done on the East Coast.* [Emphasis added.]

At least, you are going to have to take charge of enemy aliens whether you move them or not—the Army is going to have to take charge of enemy aliens. Isn't that right?

Colonel Bryan: Let me go back just a moment. Enemy aliens ordered interned that the Federal Bureau of Investigation turns over to the Army, we put those people in internment camps, under guard, and we intend to be humane about that.

Sen. Johnson: Right there, I have some letters in regard to this thing. When you gather these enemy aliens through the offices of the F.B.I. you put them in concentration camps, is that correct?

Colonel Bryan: Internment camps. We intern them in internment camps....[101]

Clearly, in his last comments Colonel Bryan was talking about a related but quite different procedure—the internment program referred to in Chapter 3 (see above), wherein resident enemy aliens classified as "potentially dangerous" were arrested *individually* by the FBI, given a hearing by a hearing board, and, if ordered interned by the Attorney General, sent to Army-run internment camps located on Army bases. The program under discussion, by contrast, would have involved (and in the case of the Japanese, *did* involve) not individual internment but *mass evacuation* of civilians from huge military zones such as Military Zone No. 1 on the West Coast (i.e. the "restricted" rather than the already-cleared "prohibited" zones). In subsequent testimony, the Chairman of the Committee asked Colonel Bryan more about the numbers this mass movement might involve:

> **The Chairman:** Now, you stated a moment ago to the committee that you approximated that there would be 100,000 enemy aliens for incarceration in these concentration camps.
>
> **Colonel Bryan:** That is the figure I was given for planning purposes.
>
> **The Chairman:** Now, how is that proportioned: the number of Italian, Japanese, and Germans.
>
> **Colonel Bryan:** Roughly speaking I should imagine that that would be approximately 60 percent Japanese, sir.
>
> **The Chairman:** 60 percent?
>
> **Colonel Bryan:** Pretty close.
>
> **The Chairman:** What percentage of Germans?
>
> **Colonel Bryan:** Approximately an even split in the Germans and Italians.
>
> **The Chairman:** 20-20?
>
> **Colonel Bryan:** Yes, sir.
>
> **The Chairman:** 60 percent of Japanese, 20 percent of German, 20 percent of Italian....[102]

Ignoring for the moment the fact that these were figures only for the West Coast (and that many of the Japanese were already removed), the Chairman then asked how the enemy alien prisoners would be used during their "incarceration" to take advantage of such a large pool of manpower:

> **Colonel Bryan:** Under the Geneva Conference we can't use them in making munitions of war.
>
> **The Chairman:** We don't want to.
>
> **Colonel Bryan:** And the United States intends to live up to that. We have agreed to that...we will use these people in work that is of value to this country.
>
> **The Chairman:** Could we use these people in the construction of the extension of the pan-American highway from Seattle to Fairbanks?
>
> **Colonel Bryan:** Provided we can guard them. Every time we have a group out we have to increase our guard force. If my present plan is approved—I want to make these people grow as much as they can grow. I want to use them wherever it is possible. I intend to use these people to help recondition shoes.
>
> **The Chairman:** Of course you find cobblers among them?
>
> **Colonel Bryan:** Yes, sir. I would concentrate those people and put them into certain camps so that they can do that work...[103].

It almost goes without saying that the "cobblers" envisioned as repairing shoes would be largely Italian, thus confirming the fact that a great many Italian enemy aliens were among those slated to be excluded from military zones on the East Coast, and placed in "concentration" camps administered and guarded by the United States Army. As to the numbers, Colonel Bryan's figure of 100,000 aliens to be removed applied, again, only to the West Coast—and according to his percentages, that would have involved about 20,000 Italians from that sector. On the other hand, according to Stetson Conn, the figures would have been higher:

> As for the number of people to be involved, General DeWitt's memorandum [of February 13, 1942] contained an estimate that 133,000 people would have to be evacuated either voluntarily or by compulsion. A breakdown of this figure (based on his previous Category A recommendations) discloses that his plan would have involved about 69,000 Japanese (25,000 aliens and 44,000 American citizens), about 44,000 Italians, and about 20,000 Germans.[104]

As to the East Coast, Colonel Bryan was unable to come up with a figure, but other estimates ranged as high as *10 million people* to be removed. As the Senate Committee report then concluded:

> The numbers involved in the Japanese evacuation are large, but they are by no means as large, for the whole country, as those who will be involved if we generalize the current treatment of the Japanese to apply to all Axis aliens and their immediate families...[105]

With regard to these axis aliens on the West Coast, Tom Clark, the Department of Justice's liaison with the Western Defense Command, continued to insist that no amount of hearings or civilian hand-wringing would affect the Western Defense Command's thinking about clearing its territory. As late as April 27, for example, Clark wrote to James Rowe, Assistant Attorney General, that General DeWitt had no intention of abandoning his original removal plan:

> ..anyone who had the idea that General DeWitt is going to delay the evacuation of German and Italian aliens is in error. He has consistently said publicly and otherwise that he intends to evacuate these groups as soon as his program with reference to the Japanese is completed.[106]

And even into late May of 1942, the *San Francisco Chronicle*, in buttressing its support for the hearings then being conducted in San Francisco by the Tenney Committee investigating the alleged fascist influence still at work among that city's Italian immigrants (see Chapter Five, "Exclusion"), ran a cartoon that graphically encapsulated the sentiment in favor of ridding the city of the allegedly subversive groups:

Cartoon, *San Francisco Chronicle*, May 27, 1942.

These indications of military rigidity set off alarms both in the Justice Department, and in the War Department itself, for it was clear that General DeWitt and his colleagues in the military, especially Provost Marshall General Allen Gullion, were serious about extending the evacuation *to both German and Italian enemy aliens,* not just in California, *but in all areas of the nation.* As Stetson Conn notes,

> The Washington opposition to German and Italian evacuation developed in part as a consequence of the Provost Marshal's February proposal to extend the military area scheme to the entire continental United States. On 13 February the War Department had asked eight of the corps area commanders to submit recommendations for areas within which the Army should control the residence or presence of civilians to a greater or lesser degree. Each of them responded with recommendations, which, if adopted, would have required a fairly sizable alien exclusion program throughout the nation. For example, the Second Corps Area commander recommended a prohibited zone ten miles wide along the seacoast from the Delaware-Maryland state line northward to the eastern tip of Long Island (and including all of Suffolk County, N.Y.) from which all enemy alien residents were to be evacuated. Within this area he thought that

it would probably be necessary to regulate the residence and movement of all other civilians by a permit and pass system. He also recommended a prohibition against enemy aliens approaching or being found within one hundred yards of any waterfront installation in the New York-New Jersey metropolitan area.[107]

On April 9, 1942, Attorney General Biddle responded to these plans with a memo to the President calling his attention to the "situation" developing on the West Coast and elsewhere, and the enormous numbers involved:

> In terms of national morale, any extension of military areas becomes, in my opinion, a matter of high national policy to be determined by the President.
>
> For instance, among Germans and Italians alone, there are *ten million persons*, counting aliens or naturalized citizens, or American born citizens, one of whose parents was born in Germany or Italy. These figures are from the latest census. A rough guess would indicate that at least one grandparent of at least seven million more was born in Germany or Italy. There is the possibility of disaffecting *seventeen million persons* through thoughtfulness [sic; Biddle no doubt meant to write "thoughtlessness," ed.]. My mail already indicates some disaffection among loyal Germans and Italians because of the West Coast exclusion order. I have reason to believe that the War Department is seriously considering reversing itself with regard to German and Italian aliens on the West Coast. [Emphases added.]
>
> This entire alien problem is causing more and more agencies of the Government concern. The Office of Facts and Figures, for example, believes a serious morale problem has already been created. The entire approach is being reexamined. Hitler himself could not have achieved a result so desirable to him in years of hard work...I am informed that Lieutenant General Drum has held numerous conversations preparatory to designating military areas along the East Coast. Any area so designated in New York City, for example, would create the problem of another mass evacuation much larger than is occurring on the West Coast. The answer of General Drum may be that these areas will be very small in extent. My experience on the West Coast indicates that they expand very rapidly and sooner or later encompass the entire coast line.[108]

On April 29, Biddle fired off a similar letter to the Secretary of War, raising even more alarm about General Hugh A. Drum, head of the Eastern Defense Command, and his April 26, 1942 statement to the press indicating that all states along the Atlantic Coast were to be designated a restricted military area similar to Military Area No. 1 on the West Coast. The General's announcement, potentially affecting sixteen states and over *50 million people*, followed by four days a general War Department order authorizing domestic military commanders to designate such military areas in all parts of the country. Referring to his April 9 memo to the President, Biddle wrote that the military's plans now appeared to be progressing far beyond even his worst fears:

> General Drum's press statement, however, and the press comments accompanying it were the first I heard of the proposed East Coast plan. Even though specific orders of evacuation have not been made within the framework of the announced plan, the very large part of the entire population of that area with alien enemies in their family will be greatly disturbed by the statements about evacuation. It was precisely this result of a local military announcement not cleared as a matter of policy in Washington that it was the purpose of my memorandum to the President to avoid.
>
> I still think it very important from the point of view of public morale and social and economic dislocation that fears of evacuation be not needlessly aroused. It is time enough to speak of evacuation when specific areas or persons to be evacuated are determined. It seems clear from the West Coast experience that a great deal of confusion was created by impressing upon the Germans and Italians that they should evacuate voluntarily because they would be evacuated immediately after the Japanese.[109]

One day earlier, Assistant Attorney General James Rowe raised the same concern—i.e. the expanding use of the extraordinary powers of Executive Order 9066 to deal with ordinary situations—with John McCloy, the Assistant Secretary of War:

> The power to declare a whole state a military area was not needed to dim lights along the shore. Express power for that purpose could be easily obtained if it does not already exist. Moreover, the military order of April 22 designating all Defense Commanders did not appear to have the dimming of shore lights as a principal purpose because it does not mention the subject and is addressed also to the Central Defense Command where the problem has not arisen so far as I know...The military order does, however, expressly apply to "Segregation and evacuation of enemy aliens...."
>
> As I understand it from our conversation yesterday, General Drum's announcement, which this Department learned about from the press, that all states along the Atlantic Coast are to be designated as a military area, did not and has not received the prior approval of the War Department contemplated by the order. I have not yet read of any similar announcement by the Commanding Generals of the Central and Southern Defense Commands who also have been authorized to designate military areas by the military order of April 22. In view of the public uncertainty caused by General Drum's premature announcement it might be well to advise the Commanding Generals that there shall be no publicity of prospective military areas to be designated before the War Department approves recommendations, which it might not do.[110]

But it was not just the military that was jumping on the evacuation bandwagon. Even the Tolan Committee, most of whose members, like Chairman John Tolan of Oakland, were sympathetic to the plight of the Italian and German aliens (though decidedly *not* to the plight of the Japanese), faced testimony like that of C. R. Schwannenberg, Alameda's city manager: "I would rather see 50,000 people put in a camp and be sure that we were protected than to have one person stay out of an interment camp who was a danger to the protection of this coast."[111]

Resistance Mounts

Still, though the military fought fiercely to preserve its prerogative for absolute control over its command areas, the work of at least four influential sectors eventually brought the specter of a truly massive evacuation of enemy aliens from *both* coasts to an end: first, the continuing objections of the Justice Department to mass rather than individual action; second, the appointment of New York lawyer Alfred Jaretzki as a special consultant to Assistant Secretary of War John McCloy (mainly to rein in the Western Defense Command); third, the actions of Italian Americans working in the Office of Facts and Figures under Archibald MacLeish; and fourth, the continuing reports and pressures brought to bear on both the Executive Branch and the military by Representative John Tolan's Committee on National Defense Migration. Their combined efforts began to focus on one primary problem: the actual damage to the overall war effort if massive evacuations of foreign-born Americans from designated military zones were to spread nationwide.[112]

We have already seen how the Attorney General had long opposed the War Department's approach to the enemy alien problem. From the very beginning, the nation's chief law enforcement officer and his assistants had stressed the importance of considering enemy aliens as individuals.[113] Though they did not always succeed—witness the evacuation from prohibited zones, and the West Coast curfew to which they had already yielded—Justice Department officials continued to argue for distinguishing among individuals, especially with respect to Italian and German aliens. As we have seen above, Attorney General Biddle also argued that the numbers involved in a mass evacuation of all three enemy alien groups were simply too large to contemplate—not just with regard to the government forces needed to control them, but also regarding the potential loss of manpower in critical defense industries where many aliens worked. Finally, as noted above, Biddle wrote the President and other government officials several times about the morale problem (and the resultant disaffection of voters from the Democratic President) he saw stemming from a massive removal of German and Italian aliens from huge military zones on both the West and East Coasts.

The hearings and reports of the Tolan Committee hammered away at these same themes. In its Preliminary Report, for example, released on March 19, 1942, the Tolan Committee, referring to the 300,000 German and 675,000 Italian enemy aliens in the country, wrote:

> It is doubtful whether our war effort could bear the consequences of shifting them all from their present residences to new settlements, even on a voluntary basis. Their incarceration for the duration of the war is unthinkable to this committee.[114]

The Preliminary Report also concluded that even the contemplation of evacuating such large numbers of these aliens from military zones throughout the country was "out of the question if we intend to win this war."[115] Nor did Chairman Tolan rest with issuing reports. In early March, Tolan and members of his committee met with Tom Clark in Los Angeles at the latter's request, and agreed to advise Clark and the Western Defense Command on matters relating to enemy aliens. Clark was quoted as saying that Tolan's committee had "saved us lots of headaches and made it possible to avoid a lot of pitfalls."[116] But though Tolan's committee and the military issued a joint statement the next day about being in agreement about policy, in late April and early May Representative Tolan again complained to both Attorney General Biddle and Assistant Secretary of War McCloy, this time about the press statements issued by General Drum for extending the evacuation zones to the East Coast, and Drum's attempted reassurance that only limited evacuations mediated by "selective processes" would be allowed. Still concerned about the reliability of such assurances from the military, the Congressman recommended that a new presidential order be issued shutting off the possibility of any additional exclusion orders.[117] These activities and the publicity from Tolan's Committee Hearings exerted a noticeable effect on the War Department. According to Stephen Fox, the War Department's conferences on May 15, 1942 included

> the Tolan Committee's latest report, which continued to hammer home the logic of its earlier paper: [that] the size of the Italian and German communities—more diverse and ten times larger than the Japanese—presented "problems more vast and far reaching than the Japanese. Emergency measures must not be permitted to alter permanently those fundamental principles upon which this Nation was built."[118]

Even before early May, moreover, the warnings from Tolan's Committee and elsewhere, added to the obtuseness and obduracy of the Western Defense Command, began to exhaust the patience of civilian officials in the War Department. The most obvious sign of this was the appointment, by Assistant Secretary of War John McCloy, of New York lawyer Alfred Jaretzki as a special consultant. Jaretzki's main task was to be an outside and independent conduit of information regarding developments on the West

Coast. Within days of his appointment, Jaretzki was already warning McCloy that the 80,000 Italian and German enemy aliens being considered for evacuation were not only *not* disloyal, but also that evacuating them would likely arouse "public apprehension" and a resultant "public clamor for protection."[119] In other words, declaring that so many more individuals had been deemed too dangerous to remain at large could have ignited domestic fears of enemy activity so extreme that they might well impede the war effort. When he got to the West Coast, Jaretzki warned Major Bendetsen by phone that a mass removal of German and Italian aliens would require relocation camps for them since they would not be accepted in inland states,[120] adding yet another warning about the inflammatory effect of such a move on public opinion. Bendetsen apparently got the message for, in a later memo to Assistant Secretary McCloy, on May 11, he recommended that Italians not be moved or interned en masse, but only as individuals in the program already being implemented by the Justice Department.[121]

Finally, even prior to these initiatives, there was a group of Italian Americans working in and through the Office of Facts and Figures (on June 13, 1942, OFF was incorporated into the Office of War Information, or OWI, under Archibald MacLeish) to change the government's treatment of Italian Americans as "enemies." According to Italian historian Guido Tintori, the key figure in this effort was Joseph Facci, an anti-fascist immigrant from Milan who had worked with the Special Defense Unit in the Justice Department before being appointed as an adviser to OFF. Facci's task was to find ways to "win maximum support of Italian Americans for the war effort."[122] As early as January 1942 Facci had submitted a memo to his sponsor, Alan Cranston, entitled "Italian Americans and 'Morale,'" which criticized the "super-legalistic approach" employed in dealing with Italian immigrants. Facci argued that such an approach left at large (because of naturalization and/or political influence)

> ..some of the people most responsible for the Fascist propaganda of the last seventeen years, while at the same time burdening with largely unnecessary regulations, which hurt economically and morally, thousands of innocent and loyal aliens.[123]

Facci's analysis, as well as the analyses of those whom he commissioned and championed, focused not on legal or military concerns, but rather on psychological ones: morale, a mass sense of not belonging, and what he envisioned for the future as a "powerful psychological offensive" to be applied both to Italian American assimilation and to the victory of democracy in a liberated Italy. At Facci's request, one of his associates in OFF, Renzo Sereno, wrote about it this way:

The Italians suffer from mass guilt. The anxiety aroused by this guilt is cultivated by their leaders and increased by the impact of discrimination. The enemy registration card is *per se* a stigma; it means that the bearers, through events beyond their control, lost their civil rights and that they are now on probation...A prolongation of the discriminatory system may well transform these people from potential fifth columnists, potential saboteurs, into actual fifth columnists, actual saboteurs. A revocation of their alien enemy status would produce such release of tension as to simplify enormously the security problem presented by these people.[124]

In short, what Facci and Sereno were proposing was that rather than evacuating additional thousands or even millions of Italian immigrants from their East Coast homes, thereby *increasing* the likelihood of the danger they presented, the government should consider moving in precisely the opposite direction: ease up on them by freeing them from the humiliation of being "enemy aliens." As Tintori explains, Facci was able to prevail because of his own logic, as well as because of his two powerful allies: Eleanor Roosevelt and Max Ascoli. Ascoli, an anti-fascist refugee who had been a chairman of the American anti-fascist organization, the Mazzini Society, was then working for the government. In early February of 1942 in response to a suggestion by the First Lady, he wrote a 10-page booklet entitled "On the Italian Americans." It attempted to encapsulate the assimilation process of Italian immigrants and their confusion, with the war, over the conflict they were experiencing between two allegiances—to their homeland, and to their adopted country. Ascoli described this as an important historical crossroads for the immigrants:

In the abnormal conditions created by the war, this process of assimilation may be arrested and the bulk of the Italian Americans, which means five to seven million people, transformed into an alien body or into a national minority. If we realize the gravity of the problem and deal with it realistically, we can render a great service to the United States and to Italy...

What Ascoli had in mind was, by an act of calculated political generosity, making these immigrants "Americans before ever having become Italians." This was because the primary loyalty felt by most of them had always been to a village, not to a nation called "Italy"—until, that is, they arrived in an America which saw them, first, as "wops," and then, with the outbreak of war, as "Italian nationals" or "Axis aliens" loyal to a nation ruled by a fascist dictator. Extending the evacuation of millions of such people and their families on both coasts would risk making them even more confused, more marginalized and far more alienated than they already were. Instead, Ascoli wanted to incorporate them into the war effort, not simply in the United States, but, by virtue of their still-strong ties to relatives and friends in Italy, in the coming battle for the soul of the Italian nation: "Gradually the Italian Americans can be led to realize that America's victory in the war will mean the liberation of Italy."[125]

Eleanor Roosevelt found Ascoli's thesis compelling enough to send it to Earl Harrison, now a special assistant to the Attorney General. Harrison quickly informed Mrs. Roosevelt that the plan for an advisory board on Italian American affairs was being implemented under Archibald MacLeish in OFF. Ascoli's thesis became the central text for most of OFF's work regarding Italian Americans in the next few months. Facci used it as the basis for his strategy to mount a psychological offensive among Italian Americans to have them persuade their relatives in Italy to see the benefits, for them and all Italians, in an American victory. As ILGWU leader Luigi Antonini, now working in conjunction with OFF and OWI, phrased it:

"America's victory is Italy's Freedom."[126]

Among the first weapons in its campaign on behalf of Italian Americans was OFF's April 21, 1942 report, "Distinction Among Alien Groups," explaining the results of a public opinion poll conducted by its Bureau of Intelligence. The poll reported that, when asked about the relative dangerousness of the three enemy alien groups, 46% of U.S. citizens were concerned about Germans, 35% were concerned about the Japanese, while only 2% were concerned about Italians. The report explained:

> Although this comparative ranking cannot be regarded as an indication that the American public is unconcerned about Italians, it does show plainly that it distinguishes them sharply from the Germans and Japanese. A similar distinction may be valid in government handling of the three alien groups...Separation of them from the other enemy alien groups in this country may prove a useful first step in separating Italy itself from the other members of the Axis.[127]

Whether by chance or by design, this preference for separating Italians from the other two enemy alien groups dovetailed almost perfectly with one of the main themes in the Tolan Committee Hearings, even up to and including the idea of aiding the American war effort by reducing the chance that millions of enemy aliens and their families would be forcibly moved. It also fed into a growing disposition in the Justice Department and in the military itself to reduce the problems it began to increasingly anticipate if evacuation was extended beyond the Japanese on the West Coast to massive numbers of German and Italian aliens there, and even greater numbers on the East Coast. President Roosevelt himself was growing daily more concerned about the effects of the possible East Coast evacuation on millions of Italian and German voters in the upcoming election.

Accordingly, on May 5, 1942, the President sent a memo to Secretary of War Stimson stating that alien control was "primarily a civilian matter," except for the evacuation of the Japanese on the West Coast. Therefore, the War Department should not take any action against East Coast Germans and Italians without first consulting the President himself.[128] By this order, the President took a huge step in reversing the military's assumption of control over civilians that Generals DeWitt and Gullion had engineered in February. Of course, this still left General DeWitt on the West Coast chomping at the bit to remove enemy aliens there, and as late as May 10 he was still threatening to dispatch thousands of Italian and German enemy aliens to relocation camps similar to those already established for the Japanese.[129] But by this time even his closest aides were distancing themselves from the General's mania for a mass evacuation. Thus it was that in mid-May, now-Colonel Bendetsen, in a memo to Assistant Secretary of War McCloy, recommended that Italians *not* be moved or interned en masse, but only as individuals in the internment program still being implemented by the Justice Department (i.e. since December 8, 1941; see Chapter 3, Internment). McCloy agreed, and persuaded his boss, Secretary of War Stimson, to approve a plan restricting area commanders from removing more than a very few individuals from military areas, with weekly reports of the removals to be sent to the assistant Secretary. This effectively cut the legs out from under General DeWitt. He had no choice but to submit to this reduction of his authority, that is, to a much-curtailed exclusion program over only certain "dangerous" individuals, rather than whole groups. At the Cabinet Meeting on May 15, Secretary Stimson made this decision official by recommending to the President a plan to prevent military area commanders from evacuating whole groups of Germans or Italians, but to allow them to exclude specific individuals.[130] The President readily agreed, expressing his relief that the domestic war over a mass evacuation of enemy aliens was now effectively over.

In short order, McCloy ordered General DeWitt to end the curfew on Italians and Germans as soon as the Japanese were fully removed, and to clear all his future public announcements with Washington. Still, the General, like an aircraft carrier, was not easily turned, and though the Japanese had all been transported from his military area by May, and he abolished the prohibited zone regulations (evacuation) for Italians on June 27, he refused to abolish the curfew and other restrictions on Italian enemy aliens until October 19, 1942. This was a week after all other restrictions on them had been publicly lifted by Attorney General Biddle in his Carnegie Hall speech on Columbus Day, October 12, 1942.[131]

In short, though the President, the Attorney General and the civilian leaders in the War Department had been persuaded by Joseph Facci and his colleagues in OWI that ending the restrictions on Italian enemy aliens made good political and military sense, General DeWitt apparently never did. He bowed to the pressure from Washington, as he had to, but not without kicking, screaming and clinging to at least some vestige of his control over the foreign-born "enemies" in his midst to the bitter end. That last vestige, when implemented, became known as the Individual Exclusion Program.

---

1. Richard Armento to President George H.W. Bush, 10 April 1992; "External Resolution" of Sons of Italy in California, 26 June 1992; John Dunne, Department of Justice, to Richard Armento, 25 June 1992. (Correspondence in files of Social Justice Commission, Sons of Italy, San Francisco, CA)

2. Guido Tintori, "New Discoveries, Old Prejudices: The Internment of Italian Americans during World War II," in Lawrence DiStasi, ed., *Una Storia Segreta: The Secret History of Italian American Evacuation and Internment,* (Heyday Books: 2001), p. 237.

3. Stetson Conn, in *Guarding the U.S. and its Outposts* (see full citation in note 16), writes as follows: "The central objective of the DeWitt plan was to move all enemy aliens and American-born Japanese out of all Category A areas in California, Oregon, and Washington that the general had recommended through 12 February. Although General DeWitt had repeatedly described the Japanese as the most dangerous element of the west coast population, he also made it clear as late as 17 February that he was "opposed to any preferential treatment to any alien irrespective of race," and therefore that he wanted German and Italian aliens as well as all Japanese evacuated from Category A areas.73 His plan assumed that all enemy aliens would be interned under guard outside the Western Defense Command, at least until arrangements could be made for their resettlement. Citizen evacuees would either accept internment voluntarily or relocate themselves with such assistance as state and federal agencies might offer. As for the number of people to be involved, General DeWitt's memorandum contained an estimate that 133,000 people would have to be evacuated either voluntarily or by compulsion. A breakdown of this figure (based on his previous Category A recommendations) discloses that his plan would have involved about 69,000 Japanese (25,000 aliens and 44,000 American citizens), about 44,000 Italians, and about 20,000 Germans." pp. 135-6.

4. Peter Irons, *Justice at War: The Story of the Japanese American Internment Cases*, (New York: Oxford University Press, 1983) p. 27.

5. Ibid.

6. Morton Grodzins, *Americans Betrayed: Politics and the Japanese Evacuation*, (Chicago: 1949), p. 279.

7. Indeed, it is important to note that the removal of all those born in the enemy nations, including naturalized American citizens, was allowed by the fact that EO 9066 nowhere refers

to the Japanese per se, but to *all persons*, thus allowing the military to remove any person or any group it chose. See also note 3 above.

8. Tom Clark to James Rowe, April 27, 1942, CWRIC 25:573 (referenced in Fox, see note 10 below)

9. "Draft letter, Attorney General Francis Biddle to Secretary of War Stimson," April 29, 1942, *James H. Rowe, Jr. collection*, Alien Enemy Control Unit, Container 33, FDR Library, Hyde Park, NY.

10. Stephen Fox, "General John DeWitt and the Proposed Internment of German and Italian Aliens during World War II," *Pacific Historical Review*, 1988.

11. Preliminary Report, *The House of Representatives Select Committee Investigating National Defense Migration*, 77th Congress, 2d Session, Pursuant to H. Res. 113, p 24, (cited in Fox, *Unknown Internment, p. 129.)

12. Presidential Proclamation No. 2525, 6 Fed. Reg. 6321, 55 Stat. 1700 (December 7, 1941), in *Report to the Congress of the United States: A Review of the Restrictions on Persons of Italian Ancestry During World War II*, Nov. 2001, U.S. Department of Justice, Appendix L.3.

13. Irons, op. cit., p. 28.

14. Irons, op. cit., p. 27.

15. *Personal Justice Denied: Report of the Commission on Wartime Relocation and Internment of Civilians,* (Washington DC: 1982), p. 63. (Hereafter cited as PJD).

16. Irons, p. 29.

17. PJD, p. 65.

18.   Phone conversation, Gen De Witt with General Gullion, 26 Dec 41, WDC-CAD 311.3, as quoted in Stetson Conn, *Guarding the U.S. and its Outposts,* Center of Military History, United States Army, Washington DC, 2000 (1st printed1964). accessed online at http://www.history.army.mil/books/wwii/Guard-US/index.htm#contents.

19. Irons, p. 37. How such a thing as a "cutoff of ties to Japan" could be "proved" is something else again.

20. PJD, p. 72.

21. PJD, p. 73.

22. Feb. 6, 1942 Draft Memorandum for the President from Attorney General Biddle, "West Coast Prohibited Areas," FDR Library, James H. Rowe Collection, Container 33, file Alien Enemy Control Unit. 1940 Census figures reported in the Feb. 16 *Stockton Record* "Foe Aliens Cleared from 111 Key Areas," gave these numbers: California 52,000 Italians; Washington 3911 Italians; Oregon 1960 Italians; Arizona 290 Italians.

23. Ibid.

24. See Morton Grodzins, *Americans Betrayed,* op. cit, pp 258-262. See also *Stockton Record*, Jan. 30,1942: "186,000 Enemy Aliens to Be Moved on Coast." Stetson Conn (op. cit., p. 129) confirms this as follows: "General DeWitt on 4 February was considering putting the whole Los Angeles area into Category A, because his Air commander had recommended Category A zones around 220 different installations that, when plotted on the map, almost blanketed the area anyway. For the same reason, General DeWitt believed he might have to put all of San Diego in Category A also. He finally recommended the blanket Category A coverage of these two cities on 7 February, and five days later he recommended that almost all of the San Francisco Bay area be put in Category A. If all of General DeWitt's recommendations for Category A areas through 12 February had been accepted, it would have made necessary the evacuation of nearly 89,000 enemy aliens from areas along the Pacific coast--only 25,000 of whom would have been Japanese."

25. Grodzins, p. 261.

26. As this and other headlines and news reports indicate, the reading public must have been fully aware of the evacuation of enemy aliens due to banner headlines and lengthy articles about the movement of thousands. Any literate person who claims ignorance, therefore, must be either forgetful, or engaged in denial for personal or political reasons.

27. Press Release No. 9, U.S. Dept of Justice, Feb. 4, 1942, cited in *Report to the Congress of the United States: A Review of the Restrictions on Persons of Italian Ancestry During World War II* , November 2001, Dept. of Justice, p. 19

28. Press Release No. 11, *Report to the Congress*, p. 20.

29. Aliens in California," *San Francisco Chronicle*, February 4, 1942, page 6.

30. "Move to Shift Local Aliens is Started," *Stockton Record*, Feb. 9, 1942, p. 1 (cont. p. 2).

31. Here again, the conflicting information sowed confusion. A *San Francisco Chronicle* article on February 7, 1942, "Aliens: The Government Starts to Clear 10,000 from California Homes," p. 1, reported: "On Monday, first written notices will be delivered by registered mail to between 200 and 300 Japanese, German and Italian nationals who must be out by February 15. In many cases, local police will give personal notice. Later in the week, the notices will be sent to others who must be evacuated by February 24."

32. Ibid. p. 1, cont. p. 4.

33. Of course, if an immigrant had been able to read the *Alameda Times Star* for February 9, with a headline reading "Martial Law' May Hit Aliens," and a subhead reading 'Advisors to Aid Aliens,' he might have got the clarification he needed. The UP article explained the contradictory orders: "An earlier program to give personal removal notices to those affected was dropped today and the Department of Justice said public notice would be given instead." 'Public notice' apparently signified the signs, in four languages, posted around prohibited zones. It is interesting to note that in his study of the evacuation in *The Unknown Internment*, Stephen Fox declares "None of the interviewees remembers learning about the relocation order from these signs, however." Curious, Fox asked Lily Boemker of Arcata how she first learned she had to move? Her answer: "Well the Italians in these days would visit. People would meet in one house and just visit. This one evening our friend down the street came and said, 'The news is on the radio that the aliens have to move.' Then I went to the post office and found out for sure." Stephen Fox, *The Unknown Internment*, (Twayne: 1990), pp. 75-76.

34. *Richmond Independent*, Feb. 2, 1941, p. 1.

35. Ibid.

36. *Alameda Times Star*, January 31, 1942, p. 1.

37. *Alameda Times Star*, February 2, 1942, p. 1.

38. *Monterey Peninsula Herald*, February 14, 1942, p. 1.

39. *Pittsburg Post Dispatch*, February 2, 1942, p. 1.

40. *Pittsburg Post Dispatch*, February 3 and February 9, respectively.

41. *Pittsburg Post Dispatch*, February 11, 1942, p. 1. The caption read: "Among the aliens photographed for registration this week at the Pittsburg post office were (first row, left to right)" followed by the names. Thus was the humiliation completed.

42. *Richmond Independent*, February 4, 1942, p. 1.

43. *Stockton Record*, February 4, 1942, p. 1.

44. *Monterey Peninsula Herald*, February 5, 1942, p. 1.

45. See *Monterey Peninsula Herald*, Feb. 21, 1942: "Alien Raids Launched on 550 Mile Coast Front," p. 1. See also Chapter 3: Internment, pp. 15 & 16.

46. *Stockton Record*, March 3, 1942, p. 1.

47. *Stockton Record*, March 17, 1942, p. 1.

48. *Stockton Record*, March 24, 1942, p. 1.

49. Angelina Bruno, personal interview, "Pittsburg Stories," in *Una Storia Segreta*, op. cit., p. 57. Bruno's story raises another issue, related to derivative citizenship (see notes 52 and 54 below). That is, many Italian-born women thought that they derived American citizenship when their husbands became naturalized. They would have if the naturalization took place before 1922, when the Cable Act made women's citizenship independent of their husband's. But after 1922, a husband's naturalization *applied only to himself*; women had to apply independently. This was no doubt the case with New Mexico Senator Pete Domenici's mother, Alda Vichi. She was apparently advised by a lawyer that Cherubino Domenici's naturalized citizenship conferred citizenship on her when she married him. But since the marriage took place in 1926, after the 1922 Cable Act, she remained an alien. Like many others, she found this out to her dismay, in 1942, when she was arrested as an "enemy alien."

50. Caterina Cardinale, personal interview, "Pittsburg Stories," in *Una Storia Segreta*, op. cit., p. 58.

51. Vitina Spadaro, personal interview, Oct. 2, 1999, "Fish Story," in *Una Storia Segreta:* op.cit., p. 82.

52. *The House of Representatives Select Committee Investigating National Defense Migration*, 77th Congress, 2d Session, Pursuant to H. Res. 113, held hearings known as the Tolan Committee Hearings, from February 21, 1942 through March 12, 1942. Hearings were held in San Francisco (Feb. 21 & 23), Portland, Seattle, and Los Angeles.

53. This woman, whose son was killed on the *Arizona*, sunk at Pearl Harbor, was later identified as Rosina Trovato.

54. Tolan Committee, transcript, p. 11126.

55. Tolan Committee, transcript, pp. 11126 & 11131. The Vezzolo dairy farm was located about a mile from the eastern boundary of Fort Ord. So though it was not on the coast, it was designated a prohibited zone from which enemy aliens had to remove themselves. According to relatives, however, Marguerite Vezzolo—perhaps because of the testimony about her at the Tolan Committee Hearings—was granted an exemption and did not have to move.

56. The law which deprived American women of their citizenship for marrying an alien was the Expatriation Act of 1907. Section 3 of that law states that "Any American who married a foreigner shall take the nationality of her husband. At the termination of the marital relation she may resume her American citizenship, if abroad, by registering as an American citizen within one year with a consul of the United States, or if residing in the United States at the termination of the marital relation, by continuing to reside therein." This is known as derivative citizenship, but it was not always applied to women in this way; as Ann Marie Nicolosi points out, women were earlier assumed to have independent citizenship. In the 1830 Supreme Court case, Shanks v. Dupont (3 U.S. 242-9), Supreme Court Justice Joseph Story held that the marriage of a South Carolina woman to a British officer during the American Revolution did NOT make her an alien: "because marriage with an alien, whether friend or enemy, produces no dissolution of the native allegiance of the wife. It may change her civil rights, but it does not affect her political rights or privileges." (Ann Marie Nicolosi, "'We Do Not Want Our Girls to Marry Foreigners'": Gender, Race, and American Citizenship," *NWSA Journal*, Volume 13, No. 3.) The 1907 law changed all this until it was repealed by the Married Women's Act of 1922, aka the Cable Act, after which women who married foreign men no longer lost their citizenship. The problem for many was that they no longer could gain it when their husbands naturalized either.

57. *Stockton Record*, Feb. 9, 1942, p. 5.

58. *Stockton Record*, Feb. 18, 1942, p. 13. Apparently, what neither the *Stockton Record* nor the INS official nor any of the women involved seemed to know is that derivative citizenship should have worked the other way: when an alien man became naturalized (before 1922), his wife regained her citizenship as well (a proviso stemming from the 1855 Immigration law). The other apparent problem with the INS official's statement is that the 1936 law restoring citizenship to those who lost it applied *only to those who were widowed or divorced.* Those who remained married to their foreign-born husbands had to wait until 1940, when Congress allowed all women who had lost their citizenship via the 1907 law to regain it, regardless of their marital status. Nonetheless, by 1942, all such women should have been considered American citizens, and hence, immune to rules or restrictions affecting "enemy aliens." Sadly, as the cases cited above demonstrate, many were left ignorant of their rights, and suffered accordingly. (see Ann Marie Nicolosi, op. cit., and Marian L. Smith, "Any woman who is now or may hereafter be married..." *Prologue Magazine,* National Archives, Summer 1998, Vol. 30, No. 2).

59. My cousin related this story when the *Una Storia Segreta* exhibit visited New Haven, CT, not far from Bridgeport where I grew up. My father's older brother, my Uncle Hector, had never become an American citizen. When restrictions on enemy aliens were imposed on December 8, he became an enemy alien. More surprising was the fact that his American-born wife, with forebears who had fought in the American Revolution, also became (at least her family believed she did) an enemy alien. Their home was raided by the FBI and the short-wave radio removed.

60. Tolan Committee, transcript, p. 11134.

61. See Lawrence DiStasi, "Derived Aliens: Derivative Citizenship and Italian American Women During WWII," *Italian Americana,* Winter 2010.

62. Tolan Committee transcript, p. 11117-11120.

63. Tolan Committee, transcript, pp. 11121 ff.

64. Tolan Committee, transcript, pp. 11135-36.

65. Personal interview with Victor diSuvero, September 2009.

66. Tolan Committee, transcript, pp. 11575-76.

67. Tolan Committee, transcript, pp. 11304-05.

68. Tolan Committee, transcript, pp. 10996-97.

69. Tolan Committee, transcript, p. 10997.

70. Tolan Committee, transcript, pp. 11010-11.

71. Rampoldi interview, in *Not at Home on the Home Front,* ed. Donna Graves, 2004.

72. Most of the Richmond stories came from personal interviews. Many are gathered in *Not at Home on the Home Front,* ed. Donna Graves, 2004.

73. Velio Al Bronzini, "A Market Off Limits," in *Una Storia Segreta,* op. cit., pp. 33-4.

74. Billeci's story recounted in the catalogue to *Una Storia Segreta: When Italian Americans Were 'Enemy Aliens,'* (American Italian Historical Association, Western Regional Chapter: 1994), p. 4.

75. Personal interview, Vera Vannucci Fasso, July 2000.

76. *Richmond Independent,* February 17, 1942, p. 1.

77. *Stockton Record,* February 9, 1942, p. 9.

78. *Stockton Record,* February 21, 1942, p. 13.

79. *San Francisco Chronicle,* February 12, 1942, p. 9.

80. *San Francisco Chronicle,* February 17, 1942, p. 6.

81. Louis Sdraulig, Letter to Edward Ennis, Dec. 8, 1942, Sdraulig file, RG 389, NARA II.

82. *Report to the Congress of the United States,* op. cit., p. 22.

83. FBI file of Concetta Servante, NARA San Bruno, RG 181, Italian FBI Reports, Volume

1447: A8-5.

84. FBI file of Joe Lupo, NARA San Bruno, RG 181, Italian FBI Reports, V 1447: A8-5.

85. *Report to the Congress of the United States*, op. cit., Appendix B, p. 6.

86. Personal interview, Rita Bertolini, 1993.

87. Marino Sichi, quoted in Stephen Fox, *The Unknown Internment*, (Twayne: 1990), pp. 94-96.

88. Ugo Giuntini, in Fox, op. cit., p. 98.

89. Mary Tolomei, in Fox, op. cit., pp. 98-99.

90. All from FBI files, NARA San Bruno, RG 181, Italian FBI Reports, Vol 1447: A8-5.

91. FBI Report, Pasquala (sic) Magni, NARA San Bruno, RG 181, Italian FBI Reports, Vol 1447: A8-5 (14-A-1).

92. FBI Report, John Maiolo, NARA San Bruno, RG 181, Italian FBI Reports, Volume 1447: A8-5 (14-A-1).

93. Ibid., p. 3.

94. Ibid., p. 4.

95. FBI Report Giuseppe Pavan, RG 181, Italian FBI Reports, Vol 1447: A8-5 (14-A-1).

96. *INDIVIDUAL EXCLUSION PROGRAM OF NON-JAPANESE*, Part III, Chapter I, WDC Supplemental Report, RG 338, Access 290, Box 9, NARA, p. 836.

97. *Stockton Record*, March 3, 1942, op. cit.

98. *San Francisco Chronicle*, March 2, 1942, "Inland Western States Will Fight Alien Influx," p. 4.

99. *San Francisco Chronicle*, March 4, 1942, "Army Rules Coast," p. 1.

100. Stephen Fox, "The Relocation of Italian Americans in California during World War II," in *Una Storia Segreta*, op. cit., p. 45.

101. U.S. Senate, Report of the Proceedings, Hearing held before Committee on Military Affairs S.2352, March 13, 1942, Ward & Paul, official reporters: Washington, DC, pp. 10-12.

102. Ibid, p. 18.

103. Ibid, p. 26.

104. Stetson Conn, op cit, p. 136.

105. Quoted in Fox, op.cit., p. 47.

106. Clark to Rowe, April 27, 1942, CWRIC 25:573.

107. Stetson Conn, op cit, p. 136.

108. April 9, 1942 Draft Memorandum, Francis Biddle to Franklin Roosevelt, FDR Library, Hyde Park, NY, James H. Rowe Collection, Container 33, file Alien Enemy Control Unit.

109. April 29, 1942 Letter, Francis Biddle to Secretary of War, FDR Library, op. cit. General Drum's statement appeared in the *New York Times* on April 27, 1942. Quoted as an appendix in the Tolan Committee's *Fourth Interim Report* (U.S. Govt Printing Office, May 22, 1942), it said in part: "The Secretary of War has designated Lt. Gen. Hugh A. Drum, commanding the Eastern Defense Command and First Army, who is charged with the defense of the eastern seaboard, to designate military areas. General Drum will designate the entire Eastern Defense Command as a military area, called the Eastern Military Area. The Eastern Military Area includes the New England States and the Middle and South Atlantic States and Florida west of the Apalachicola River, and the District of Columbia...The plan embodied in the administration of the Eastern Military Area contemplates the control of conduct within the area on the part of enemy aliens, as well as of all other persons...Enforcement of restrictions, and consequently control of the area, will be accomplished by the application of penalties provided by law for violations of the restrictions and orders of the commanding general. Those include exclusion from the area, internment of aliens,

prosecutions under Public Law No. 503 of March 21, 1942, and evacuations."

110. April 28, 1942 Letter, James Rowe to John McCloy, Asst Secretary of War, FDR Library, op. cit.

111. Tolan Committee, transcript, p. 11115-17. cited in Fox, op cit, p. 124.

112. Again, it is worth noting that though there can be no doubt that racism was a major factor in the internment of Japanese American citizens, the fact that the overwhelming majority of them were concentrated on the West Coast, and not, as in the case of German and Italian aliens, spread throughout the country in very large numbers, cannot but have contributed to the differences in the way the groups were treated. As is evident from the concerns registered by the Attorney General and others, the huge numbers of Italian and German enemy aliens on the East Coast posed a serious potential problem, both politically and logistically, for any mass evacuation from those areas.

113. Stephen Fox, *Unknown Internment*, p. 126.

114. Tolan Committee, *Preliminary Report*, p. 25. Cited also in Tolan Committee, *Fourth Interim Report*, May 22, 1942, p. 31 (viewable online at: http://babel.hathitrust.org/.) The statement in full reads: "If the Japanese evacuation creates serious questions, it is because an entire group out of our population is being bodily removed, family by family. This is in the nature of an exodus of a people. The numbers involved are large, but they are by no means as large, for the whole country, as those who will be involved if we generalize the current treatment of the Japanese to apply to all Axis aliens and their immediate families. Indeed, this committee is prepared to say that any such proposal is out of the question if we intend to win this war."

115. Ibid., p. 24.

116. *San Francisco Chronicle*, "Members of Tolan Group in S.F. Today," Mar. 9, 1942, p. 8.

117. Tolan to Biddle, May 1, 1942, cited Tolan Committee, *Fourth Interim Report*, p. 23.

118. Fox, *Unknown Internment*, p. 133, citing Tolan Committee, *Fourth Interim Report*, pp. 11, 25.

119. Jaretzki to Stimson, March 31, 1942, CWRIC 1:58-69, cited in *PJD*, p. 286.

120. Telephone transcript, Jartetzki to Bendetsen, April 27, 1942, CWRIC 5226-32, cited in *PJD*, p. 286.

121. Bendetsen to McCloy, May 11, 1942. CWRIC, 287-89, cited in PJD, p. 286.

122. Guido Tintori, "New Discoveries, Old Prejudices: The Internment of Italian Americans during World War II," in *Una Storia Segreta*, ed. Lawrence DiStasi, op. cit., pp 236-254.

123. Joseph Facci, "Italian Americans and Morale," cited in Guido Tintori, op. cit., pp 245-46.

124. Renzo Sereno, "Enemy Aliens," cited in Guido Tintori, op. cit., p. 246.

125. Max Ascoli, "On the Italian Americans," cited in Tintori, op. cit., pp. 247-48.

126. Tintori, op. cit., p. 249.

127. OFF Bureau of Intelligence, Intelligence Report #9, April 21, 1942, cited in Tintori, op.cit., p. 250.

128. Memo, Roosevelt to Stimson, May 5, 1942, CWRIC: 196, cited in *PJD*, p. 287.

129. Fox, *Unknown Internment*, p. 133.

130. Memo, Stimson to Roosevelt, May 14, 1942, CWRIC: 197, cited in PJD, p. 288. This became the Individual Exclusion Program, which will be treated in the following chapter.

131. *New York Times*, June 29, 1942, p. 4. and *San Francisco Chronicle*, October 19, 1942, p. 1, "Friendly Aliens: DeWitt Lifts all Curfew Travel Restrictions Against Italian Nationals on Coast."

V: INDIVIDUAL EXCLUSION

As we have seen repeatedly, though WDC commander Lt. General John DeWitt tabled his original plan to remove *all* enemy aliens from the Pacific Slope in order to concentrate on removing everyone of Japanese descent, including the American-born, he never abandoned it. The Western Defense Command in its report, "Individual Exclusion Program of Non-Japanese," specifically admits this:

> Immediately after Pearl Harbor and for the first sixty days of 1942, the CG, WDC believed it was going to be necessary to remove all enemy aliens from certain vital sections of the Pacific Coast, regardless of their country of origin. At the time Executive Order 9066 was drawn up early in February 1942, it was still the intent that not only the Japanese but also the German and Italian aliens would have to be excluded.[1]

Accordingly, General DeWitt and, within a very short time, General Drum of the Eastern Defense Command, clearly intended to implement a mass removal of non-citizens of the two European groups—German and Italian enemy aliens—from 'sensitive' areas of their command as soon as the removal of the Japanese was completed. Though the Justice Department was alarmed by such plans, and tried to undermine them as unnecessary, the Army's preparations proceeded to the point that, in response to a query from the War Department, General Drum of the Eastern Defense Command designated a ten-mile-wide prohibited zone along the east coast that would extend from the Delaware-

Maryland state line north and east to the tip of Long Island, and from which millions of enemy aliens of the two European groups would have to be removed.[2] Eventually, as we have seen above, the President himself put a stop to these plans, but to placate the Army and its area commanders, a substitute plan was proposed by the War Department and agreed to by the Justice Department. As the WDC report puts it,

> By April 1942, the CG, WDC had agreed with the War Department not to hold
> a mass evacuation of the Germans and Italians *provided he be granted the power to*
> *individually exclude members of these groups* or members of any other groups, whether
> citizen or alien, from the critical area upon finding the individual was potentially
> dangerous.[3] [Emphasis added.]

Though this puts a better face on it than was warranted (General DeWitt had been stopped cold by his superiors and actually retained very little bargaining power), the expedient known as the Individual Exclusion Plan can be said to have been created as a bargaining chip in an interdepartmental dispute over the proposed mass removal of foreign-born civilians.[4]

This interdepartmental dispute, moreover, did not end with the apparent agreement between the War and Justice departments over the individual exclusion program. Infighting continued over both the theory on which the program was based, and on its implementation. In theory, that is, both the Western Defense Command and the War Department as a whole maintained that there were allegedly dangerous persons, mainly *naturalized citizens* with roots in Italy and Germany, whose continued presence in critical zones near the U.S. coastline constituted an unacceptable risk of sabotage or espionage. Notwithstanding the fact that the Justice Department, through its Alien Enemy Control Program, had already interned the non-citizen residents from both nations who had been designated as "dangerous," the War Department never stopped insisting that the enemy alien internment program had left coastal defenses incomplete. It maintained that there still remained in Military Areas on both coasts "potentially dangerous" naturalized *American citizens* who were beyond the reach of the Alien Enemy Control Program, as well as some enemy aliens who had been released early by the Justice Department, but about whose loyalty the Army still had doubts. These were the persons against whom the Individual Exclusion Program was eventually directed.[5]

As to how to reach such citizens, the Army claimed the right to move against them via the same legal documents that gave it the authority to remove the Japanese: Executive Order 9066 and Public Law 503, the latter being the Act of Congress which provided the penalties to enforce compliance with EO 9066. The Executive Order, promulgated on February 19, 1942, "authorize(d) and direct(ed) the secretary of war, and the military commanders whom he may from time to time designate," to "prescribe military areas in such places and of such extent as he or the appropriate military commanders may determine, from which *any or all persons* may be excluded..."[6] As we have seen, General DeWitt of the Western Defense Command did in fact issue Public Proclamation No. 1 on March 2, 1942, which designated as Military Area No. 1 a broad coastal swath of land that encompassed the western halves of California, Oregon, and Washington and the southern half of Arizona. Soon, all persons of Japanese origin would be removed from that ocean-to-mountain-zone. Eventually, under the Individual Exclusion Program, naturalized American citizens of Italian birth who were individually targeted would likewise be forced to vacate that zone, as well as others.

As to enforcement, Congress had swiftly passed a bill, Public Law 503, which the President signed on March 21, 1942, providing penalties for anyone violating the military orders to be issued. Though the Western Defense Command initially proposed that the penalty for such violations be classified as a felony, with mandatory prison sentences of up to five years, Assistant Secretary of War John McCloy softened these provisions so that the violation of a military order became a misdemeanor, with a maximum penalty of one year in prison.[7] The bill passed Congress almost without debate on assurances that it related mainly to enemy aliens[8]--though in fact it was applied mainly to American citizens, first 70,000 American-born children of Japanese immigrants, and later those naturalized citizens of Italian and German descent who were individually excluded. The bill's problems were not noted at the time, however, except by a few congressmen such as Senator Robert Taft of Ohio, who criticized the law's sloppiness and vagueness, and even its constitutionality:

> I have no doubt that in peacetime no man could ever be convicted under it, because the court would find that it was so indefinite and so uncertain that it could not be enforced under the Constitution.[9]

Taft nonetheless supported the bill, and President Roosevelt signed it into Public Law 503 immediately. The machinery for individual exclusion was now fully in place: the Army would issue proclamations for excluding specific persons from areas it declared 'sensitive,' and the Justice Department would enforce those proclamations through the courts.

While maneuvering between the War Department and the Justice Department over enforcement continued through the summer of 1942, and the Japanese were being removed from their homes to internment camps, one more crucial element added to the mix critically shaped the exclusion of naturalized citizens of Italian descent. Beginning in May of 1942 (technically, the hearings had started in early December 1941 in San Francisco before being interrupted by Pearl Harbor, and so *resumed* in late May 1942), the Assembly Fact-Finding Committee on Un-American Activities in California held hearings in San Francisco to investigate what it called the "Fascist influence in California."[10] The committee, chaired by California Assemblyman Jack Tenney of Inglewood, and thus commonly known as the Tenney Committee, held its hearings at the St. Francis Hotel on May 25, 26 and 27, 1942. Though not overtly coordinated with the Western Defense Command, the Tenney Committee summoned to its hearings most of those in San Francisco's Italian American community who, it had been informed, were the "dangerous" leaders in the community, and who, still at large because they were citizens, would later be targeted by the WDC. Prominent among them were Sylvester Andriano, Renzo Turco and Ettore Patrizi, three Italian-born, naturalized residents of San Francisco whom the committee identified as the leaders of what it called the Fascist movement in California.[11] The committee also subpoenaed the then-mayor of San Francisco, Angelo Rossi, whom its star witness accused of Fascist sympathies and more.

That witness, Carmelo Zito, was a noted anti-fascist who had published in his San Francisco newspaper, *Il Corriere del Popolo*, ringing denunciations of Mussolini and all those who allegedly supported him in the United States. His chief target was Ettore Patrizi, the publisher of the rival newspapers *L'Italia* and *La Voce del Popolo*, in whose pages the activities of Mussolini and his government had received continuing support in the pre-war period. The Italian-born Zito denounced the Italian-born Patrizi in detailed testimony before the committee, having evidently directed the committee to materials with which it could question and expose his rival. The committee did just that, grilling the aging publisher of *L'Italia* in two days of testimony that were covered by all the San Franicsco newspapers. It did the same with noted San Francisco attorney Sylvester Andriano—one of Mayor Rossi's close associates, head of a local draft board, and a former Police Commissioner—and Renzo Turco, also a lawyer and prominent leader in San Francisco's Italian American community. In all, more than fifty San Francisco Italian Americans were called to the hearings and grilled about their activities over the three days of hearings.

San Francisco's daily newspapers featured the hearings in blaring headlines. On May 26, 1942, for example, the *San Francisco Chronicle* carried this banner headline in bold capitals: S.F. FASCIST LINK CHARGED, with subheads filling in the sensational details.

The first sentence by reporter Floyd Healey set the tone with this startling lead:

San Francisco's Italian colony—one of the largest in the United States—is shot through with Fascists who have been propagandizing the philosophy of the dictators with Axis knowledge and Rome's financial aid for 20 years.

This broad accusation, accompanied by names of individuals and organizations—and followed by prompt denials—was painted in words and exclamation points in the St. Francis Hotel yesterday for the benefit of the Tenney committee on subversive and un-American activities.[12]

San Francisco Chronicle, May 26, 1942, p. 1.

The article, like similar headlined stories in the other San Francisco dailies, the *Examiner*, the *Call-Bulletin*, and the *News*, then went on to describe highlights of the testimony—first the fervent denunciations by Carmelo Zito, especially foregrounding his sworn statement that he had "seen Mayor Rossi give the Fascist salute at Dreamland

Auditorium," (the *San Francisco News*, an afternoon paper, featured this as its headline: FASCIST SALUTE CHARGED TO ROSSI[13]); then the responses and testimony of those he accused. In answer to committee counsel R.E. Combs' question whether there was a pro-Fascist element in San Francisco, Zito is quoted as replying: "There is. There has been ever since 1922 when Mussolini came in power." When asked, "has it continued to exist?" Zito answered: "To the extent that it has drawn public opinion until it is not capable any more of understanding the blessings of democracy." Zito went on to allege that there were five pro-Fascist newspapers in the city: *L'Italia, La Voce del Popolo, Il Leone, L'Unione* (the latter two were publications of well-known organizations, the first, *Il Leone,* of the Sons of Italy, and the second, *L'Unione,* of the Italian Catholic Federation), and *La Rassegna Commerciale* (published by the Italian Chamber of Commerce, it had been discontinued according to Zito). Zito charged Ettore Patrizi, editor of *L'Italia,* with being the "brains of all this," meaning not just the newspapers but also, as the sponsor of the allegedly pro-fascist *La Voce dell'Italia,* a radio program on station KROW, of an entire fascist network in California. Zito included the San Francisco scavengers (mostly Italian) in his diatribe, accusing them of shipping scrap iron to Italy free, while charging America $9 per ton. Nor did he leave out the Catholic Church, charging that "the Church of SS Peter & Paul was predominantly pro-Fascist, and the children in it give the Fascist salute, and are instructed with Fascist books written in Italian." Zito's accusations concerning what he called "the Fascistic school" because "they aim to teach no language whatsoever—they have the aim to teach that Mussolini is God"—were equally damning, though somewhat redundant (the Italian *dopo scuole,* or after-school classes in San Francisco, had closed days after the first sessions of the Tenney Committee on December 4, 5, and 6, 1941 led to accusations, again by Zito, that they were agents of fascist propaganda).

When he was asked for his recommendations to combat all this, Zito waxed vindictive, if not poetic:

> Without infringing on any bill of rights, take away the citizenship from all leaders, ring leaders, who took the oath of allegiance to the United States with mental reservations...They took this oath, and they violated the oath, so strip them out from the citizenship and treat them as enemy aliens. Once they are no longer citizens of the United States, use towards them the same yardstick you use towards those who are in the concentration in Montana [i.e. the interned enemy aliens, ed.]. That is No. 1.[14]

Zito then went on to recommend that authorities use the radio stations to promote American values, disband all the associations that foster "fascist propaganda," and generally "clean house" of any groups allegedly trying to "plant foreign ideals."

Responses from those accused were reported as immediate and vehement. Mayor Rossi issued a statement saying of Zito's accusation about the Fascist salute: "It's an unqualified lie!" adding that he did not know, and had never met Carmelo Zito. Sylvester Andriano was quoted as saying that Zito's accusations about him were a "pack of lies." A spokesman at the office of Archbishop Mitty of San Francisco, said "That's the first we ever heard of such things [fascist books in Catholic schools; the Italian flag on the altar, ed.]. If it were true, the archbishop would have closed the church in a minute."[15]

The *San Francisco News* of May 26, covering the previous day's hearings, carried another banner headline on its front page: ROSSI WEEPS DENIAL. The first paragraph set the scene:

> Tears streaming and voice choking at times, Angelo J. Rossi, mayor of San Francisco for nearly 12 years, today testified under oath that he never had given the Fascist salute, that he always has been and always will be "perfect in my loyalty to this country," and that "I have no sympathy for fascism—I am only for the American form of government."[16]

He added his own accusation that the testimony given against him by previous witnesses was "inspired by a cowardly attempt at political assassination." As an ironic way of responding to the accusations about the fascist salute, Rossi is described as asking, as he was about to be sworn in, "that he be permitted to do so without raising his right hand when pictures were being taken. He explained he did not want the pictures to be misinterpreted as showing him saluting."[17] When questioned about a picture of Mussolini allegedly hanging in his office, the American-born mayor said he "took the picture down 'along with photos of other Axis leaders,' prior to declarations of war." Not unaware of the effect of his appearance and the headlines it was even then generating, Rossi protested its unfairness:

> People don't read the entire article, they read only the headlines...You know how it is for a public official to be attacked like this. Because I have an Italian name the headlines spread all over the country.[18]

Though he would be politically damaged precisely as he predicted, the San Francisco mayor, a Republican, was able to find support in two places, albeit after the hearings ended. On May 28, the *San Francisco News* reported that one of Rossi's opponents, City Supervisor Chester MacPhee, was introducing a confidence vote on the mayor's Americanism: "'I've differed with Mayor Rossi on policies and political issues,' said

Supervisor MacPhee, 'but I've certainly no reason to doubt his Americanism.'" The same issue carried yet another level of support, this from the mayor of Los Angeles, Fletcher Bowron. In a letter, Bowron charged

> ...that the efforts of the Tenney Committee "have been directed to smearing public officials, particularly those connected with the Civil Defense, for purely political purposes, rather than to establish any facts."...(and) that the hearings were used largely to further Mr. Tenney's career.[19]

Sylvester Andriano testified as the final witness on the first day of hearings. The head of Draft Board No. 100 had nearly as rough a time on the witness stand as did his friend, the Mayor, but employed his skill as a lawyer to deflect or dismiss many of the committee's questions and deny its allegations. Concerning the Italian school (which he had closed in December), he insisted that he knew nothing of the curriculum, or the certificates given, but, as president, mainly solicited funds and signed checks. At one point, he noted that the recent reign of the Italian Consul named Renzetti encountered resistance in the community because of the Consul's "aggressiveness:"

> ...he certainly had a lot to say at that time. He's the only man I know that exercised that power—no one else used it in the same way. For instance, in the Italian community, on the Columbus Day celebration—we have had that celebration for 25 years in San Francisco, and we always invited the Italian Consul as a guest of honor, but it was only during Rensetti's (sic) time that he sought to inject himself, to intrude in the celebration and control the appointment of committees. Well, we were not aware of his plans, and when we became aware, why, we simply took the thing out of his hands. I take it it was the same way with regard to the schools, although I must say I never had any personal part in the conduct of the schools except to collect moneys and to appoint the board of directors from those who contributed to the support of the school.[20]

A final colloquy on the Italian schools came shortly after. The line of questioning attempted to induce Andriano to admit that he, and by implication, Fascist Italy, placed greater emphasis on Italian American children learning the Italian language than their own American language and culture:

> Q. You consider it just as important to know as much about a foreign country as their parents should know about the country of the children of which they are parents?
> A. My experience has been a child who knows something about the language of his parents makes a better American citizen.
> CHAIRMAN TENNEY: That is the same statement made by the Japanese.[21]

This exchange, especially the interjection by Chairman Tenney, was highlighted by the

San Francisco Examiner in its May 26 report as follows:

"Asked why children were urged to attend Italian language schools, Andriano asserted:

> "We thought they should know the language of their parents; we felt it would make them better Americans."

"That," dryly commented Tenney, "is exactly what the Japanese said."[22]

It took little to figure out that the Tenney committee, as well as the press, had already concluded that Sylvester Andriano, as a "proven" Fascist leader, should be dealt with as harshly as his now-interned counterparts in the Japanese community.

Though he was able to maintain his calm throughout this exchange, several other moments seemed, according to press reports, to take Andriano by surprise.[23] These were highlighted and foregrounded by both the major newspapers, the *Examiner* and the *Chronicle*. Following up on its headline, **Andriano Accused As Fascist Leader,** the *Examiner* boldfaced another subhead to focus its coverage of Andriano's testimony: **Confronted by Record.** Asserting that Andriano had "contradicted himself, other witnesses, and the mute testimony of documents and records," the report described the lawyer as "obviously flustered" when he "flushed and shouted, 'That's a damnable lie.'" This was in response to a copy of the minutes to a 1929 meeting at Fugazi Hall in North Beach, Andriano presiding, which the article described as the meeting place of

> many organizations considered actively pro-Fascist, specifically, the Ex-Combattenti, an Italian war veterans' organization; the secret Fascist society, Dante Alighieri, and a group simply known as the Fascio.
>
> "That's a damnable lie," the witness shouted. "This is the first time I ever heard of a Fascist club in San Francisco."
>
> Asked if he considered the record a forgery, he stammered:
> "Well...yes; so far as it concerns my participation in such a meeting."[24]

The transcript of the hearings indicates that this colloquy continued for several minutes, with Andriano continuing to deny that he had ever seen the document, or heard of any such organizations at such a meeting. Shortly after this denial, Andriano was confronted with another document, alleging another contradiction (the *Examiner* wrote that "Andriano was again at loggerheads with his own testimony"), this time his own earlier statement that he was not connected with any organization, other than the Chamber of Commerce, that received a subsidy from the Italian government. The document, a financial statement of the Fugazi Building Association from December 1937, showed one entry indicating that 15,000 lire, or $770, had been received from the Italian government. Andriano again denied any knowledge of such payment, and admitted that if it had been made, the Fugazi Building Association, of which he was a board member, would have had to register with the State Department as an agency of a foreign government. Again, Andriano denied ever having seen the document, or knowing about the payment.

Sylvester Andriano, 2d from left, serving on the S.F. Police Commission

Finally, Andriano was shown, and required to read aloud yet another document, this time an article in the newspaper, *L'Italia*, which purported to quote his views on his return from a trip to Italy in a July 21, 1938 issue. The committee called it an "interview," but Andriano insisted it was the result of a "luncheon" he had had with the editor, Ettore Patrizi, in which the two discussed his recent trip. He insisted that the article had been constructed of impressions taken from that luncheon by the editor, who used words, in Italian, that Andriano never used—words such as *Il Duce* [the Italian words meaning "the leader" referring to Mussolini, ed.], and the word "regime," which Andriano insisted was "not in my vocabulary." The transcript shows that as he read the article for the committee, Andriano inserted his explanations and objections:

> "There are complaints and some objections and some reservations in so far as the men--" in the government are concerned—they use the word "regime," but I said there are complaints and reservations about the people in the government.... (Continuing to read:) "But invariably as soon as the name of Mussolini is mentioned a smile comes

on the faces of those whom you speak to with words of admiration"—and, now, there again I must make the reservation—I said, as far as I could note the people were for Mussolini. I think that was a little rhetorical edition of the editor when it speaks about admiration. I don't think I used that expression.

(Continuing to read:) "—and I may say admiration for Il Duce."

Now that I am pretty sure I did not say; I am sure I did not use the word Il Duce, I don't use it in my conversation; when I mean Mussolini I use his name; I never use the word Il Duce.

(Continuing to read:) "Nobody can deny or place this fact in doubt, for Mussolini all the Italians are disposed to everything." I don't know what that means. "For Mussolini all the Italians are disposed to do anything, and spontaneously, and you hear this added all for him because he is Italy." Again I say that is a rhetorical embellishment of the editor. I certainly don't use that expression.[25]

Though the newspaper account does not say so, the above phrasing does sound very much like someone, presumably the writer or whoever translated the article, who lacks the precise command of the English language that Andriano everywhere displays.

Notwithstanding his attempts to defend himself and deny the committee's charges, Andriano left the hearings seriously damaged. The *San Francisco Examiner*, on May 28, headlined the formal request of the Tenney Committee, to President Roosevelt, to remove the lawyer from his position as head of Draft Board No. 100, and quoted from its telegram:

> In the public interest and to guarantee unquestioned unity of purpose of this Nation's fight for existence, we respectfully and most earnestly urge upon you the immediate necessity of removing forthwith the aforesaid Sylvester Andriano from the chairmanship of San Francisco Draft Board 100.[26]

According to the report, the request to the President contained "a brief resume of testimony against Andriano." The same issue noted that Andriano was refusing to resign his position. In the end, it did him no good. On October 12, 1942, an INS report quoted Lt. Colonel Kenneth Leitch, state director of selective service, to the effect that Sylvester Andriano had been suspended from his Draft Board post by the national director of selective service.[27] The paper did not note that the suspension appeared moot since Sylvester Andriano, complying with his exclusion order, had by that time already departed from San Francisco.

The committee then turned to Ettore Patrizi, whom it had already examined in its December hearings. This time the editor, accused of being the "brains" of west coast fascism, was grilled even more pointedly, with samples of his writings. The first was printed in a July 1940 edition of *La Rassegna Commerciale*, the now-discontinued publication of the Italian Chamber of Commerce. Titled, "What About Italians in the United States if Italy enters the war," and written by Patrizi, it wonders "how they will behave" if Italy enters the war. One sentence, about the early years of Fascism and the sympathy for it in American cities like San Francisco, states: "Numerous Fascist organizations were formed called Fasci, and were active." The witness was faced with the contradiction between this written statement and his earlier testimony that he was *not* aware of any pro-Fascist activities in San Francisco. In response, Patrizi tried to parse his earlier meaning:

> No, I said before I had no knowledge of real—allow me to say this word—real Fascist activity. There have been some sentimental demonstrations shown among the society, but never no activity injurious to the United States was ever took place (sic) in San Francisco.[28]

This idea of "sentiment" became Ettore Patrizi's essential defense. In response to allegations concerning an October 27, 1941 interview with a reporter for the *San Francisco News*, concerning, again, how Italians would behave in case America and Italy went to war, Patrizi paraphrased his answer:

> I remember I said: 'No matter how they loved their mother country, they will do their duty....They are American citizens—they will obey;' I said, 'I am sure the American authorities will not commit the error, if there be an expedition into Europe, I am sure the authorities would never send those of Italian origin to fight against their mother country, at least.'...Let me explain—the mother country, I use that to express the kind of feeling the Italians have to fight against their brothers; that doesn't mean they shouldn't go to war, but to shoot their own brothers—that is the meaning of that article, with a sentimental and humanitarian feeling.[29]

Ettore Patrizi in his *L'Italia* office.

Finally, the editor was presented with a letter he wrote directly to Mussolini when he left Italy following a visit there in 1924 (Patrizi made clear that he had already been a U.S. citizen for twenty years at that time). Comitttee counsel R.E. Combs confronted the witness with a phrase with which he ended the letter:

> Q. Did you state when you left Italy on that occasion to come back to your own coun-
> try, the United States, did you state you were going abroad?
> A. I go back to my home, my office.
> Q. You didn't state you were going abroad?
> A. No expression to that effect.[30]

But when asked to read the passage, Patrizi read as follows:

> "With Italian feeling to the marrow of my bones, to the thrills of my soul for over 25 years I was the defender in America of the good name and the glories of the prestige of my native country over the ocean. Going back in the foreign land abroad to take again my place in my newspaper, I put myself at your disposal, if I can help you in any mission, any work bound for the welfare of the mother country."

The implication was clear, and clearly the editor knew it was coming, for he had earlier tried to defuse it with a long preface on the chaotic condition of Italy prior to Mussolini's rise, and another plea about his sentiment for his native land:

> I had in Italy my mother, my sister, all my family—all my family is there; I am unat-
> tached here in America except for my good wife, I have no relatives whatever, so my soul, my heart was for my mother—I don't want to move you, but I speak frankly, and I speak sincerely.[31]

But the appeal did no good. A letter by the alleged "brains" of west coast Fascism, addressed to the dictator with whom the U.S. was not then but was now at war, offering whatever would advance the cause of the "mother country," and using words which, in the context of the hearings then underway, suggested that that enemy nation was his "home," could not help but appear to be evidence of divided loyalty, at the least.

And this was the point. The hearings had aimed to establish that San Francisco's Italian colony in North Beach was a poisonous hotbed of 5th-column activity on behalf of Italy. The witness who had testified prior to Ettore Patrizi perhaps put this more starkly than anyone else. His name was Gilbert Tuoni, and he claimed to be a filmmaker (though Ettore Patrizi accused him of being not just "an enemy of mine," but "one of the bitterest and most active Fascist; he belonged to the so-called squadron of punishment...I know he was also working for the Italian Consul as agent to spread and exhibit Italian propaganda films"[32]). Not yet an American citizen, and undisturbed by the accusations against him, Tuoni started out with a rapid-fire approach that included the Bank of America:

> Well, first of all I shall recommend you to close all the radio stations of California, to stop printing Fascist newspapers of the type that Mr. Patrizi prints. I would even close some of the branches of the Bank of America..[33]

When asked about the "Fascist flavor of the papers" (i.e. Patrizi's), Tuoni, with the help of his interrogator, shifted into saturation-bomb mode:

> A. As I was saying to you before, gentlemen of this Committee, the best thing is to close the papers, close the Italian broadcasting, reorganize or close the Italian organizations, they are poison—this is the time that the Italians should come into the American family and to breathe finally the free atmosphere of this country. If you do not do that they will still persist in a campaign which finally the result will be you will have the Italians away from the American family, and maybe tomorrow the situation will be as to the war effort right here in San Francisco.
> DR. KELLEMS: Q. It is your opinion—or, rather, I should say conviction—that there are a special group of people whose culture and background is so different from ours and I think we do admit it is radically different—
> A. (Interrupting) Yes.
> Q. (Continuing)—and it will only be possible for them to forget that only if they will enter into the American way of life—
> A. (Interrupting) They will.
> Q. (Continuing)—and I believe they will. Is it not your feeling that instead of persisting generation after generation teaching these things, creating a little Italy here, that they will only find their own happiness and strength by forgetting—
> A. (Interrupting) In that particular way you still have an Italy in America. I am speaking for the majority of Italians in California.[34]

Aside from the questionable nature of Dr. Kellems' (California Assemblyman Jesse Kellems, of Los Angeles) overt leading of the witness, the specific exhortation to Italian immigrants to "forget" their "radically different culture and background" would be found astonishing, if not un-American, today.

Still, in 1942 the Tenney Committee was virtually unopposed, save for one comment in the *San Francisco Examiner's* report on the final day of hearings. At that time, the Australian-born head of San Francisco's longshoreman's union, Harry Bridges, was called to testify against Mayor Rossi. *The Examiner*, in its report, commented:

> With [the] appearance of Bridges as a witness, the committee took off on an obvi-
> ous fishing expedition and even went to the fantastic lengths of asking the longshore

leader—himself the object of numerous "subversive activities" investigations—for his opinion of Mayor Rossi.

Bridges smiled. He was permitted to put this unsupported statement on record: "I always thought Rossi was a Fascist. I was always sure of it, in my own mind—politics aside. I am glad people are waking up to it."[35]

The trouble with such "fishing expeditions" is that they have real consequences for real people. Thus, in the end, the incendiary allegations and recommendations of several committee witnesses that Ettore Patrizi, Sylvester Andriano, Renzo Turco and others should be either de-naturalized, or excluded from the war zone, or both, were splashed across newspaper pages far and wide. If they did not directly influence the Western Defense Command when it began to exclude from Military Area No. 1 the Italian-born civilians it considered "dangerous," they certainly predisposed the general public to approve of those exclusions.

The Exclusions Begin

The actual exclusions commenced on or about September 1, 1942.[36] The program, as outlined by the WDC in its Supplemental Report, proceeded as follows: The intelligence division of the military command, in this case the Western Defense Command, would consult the FBI and the Office of Naval Intelligence to help it determine who should be recommended for exclusion. A summary of the intelligence information available would then be provided to the *Individual Exclusion Board* to use at its hearing. This board was made up of three Army officers of field grade, and they would set the case for a hearing. The suspect individual was served with a notice by mail, giving the time and place of the hearing, usually to be held in major cities such as, on the west coast, Seattle, Portland, San Francisco, Los Angeles, and San Diego. At the hearing the subject was, after filling out a lengthy questionnaire, sworn in, and instructed as to his rights. According to the Army itself, the subject (and his attorney if he had one), "was informed in general of the evidence being considered in his case. All confidential sources were, of course, not disclosed nor were the names of informants or informers given to the subject."[37] The words "in general" are key here, for in a later critique of the entire procedure and its basis, the Department of Justice insisted that the excludee was "not advised of the charges against him."[38] Be that as it may, the subject was then questioned at considerable length about matters already known to the board from the intelligence reports.[39] After the hearing, the board made its recommendation—to exclude or not to exclude—sent it for approval to the Civil Affairs Division (CAD) for review, and then to the United

States Attorney in the subject's area of residence for his recommendation.

The entire file, with recommendations, was sent next to the Commanding General of the (in this case) Western Defense Command for his final decision. The CG could either agree or not agree with his exclusion board (or with the U.S. Attorney—see Andriano case, below), but if he decided to exclude the individual, he or she was "served with notice in the form of an exclusion order and notified where to appear for the necessary processing." This processing included being photographed and fingerprinted so that these documents could be sent to the FBI. The excludee was then advised "on matters relating to his property and his transportation from the exclusion area," and given help, if he needed it, to remove himself by the target date. He was then "placed under surveillance until his departure from the exclusion area."[40]

Two additional clarifications should be added. As noted above, the Western Defense Command's Supplemental Report states that the subject and his attorney were "informed in general of the evidence being considered." We have seen that the Department of Justice disagreed with this claim that constitutional guarantees were more or less observed. But even more telling, the letter which San Francisco excludee Nino Guttadauro received from the Western Defense Command ordering his appearance before the Individual Exclusion Board stated specifically that "material in the hands of the Board will not be made available for your inspection."[41] That is, according to this letter, and according to Guttadauro's son, Angelo, his father was *not* allowed to see evidence used against him, nor to know what he was being charged with, or who was accusing him (all Bill of Rights violations). Second, though the WDC report appears to indicate that excludees were allowed, as in a civilian court, to be represented by a lawyer, Nino Guttadauro's notification letter makes it clear that the subject's lawyer was rendered virtually mute by the conditions imposed: "You may be accompanied by counsel to act only as your personal advisor. He will not be heard by the Board nor be permitted to examine witnesses."[42] The chief functions of an attorney in a court of law—to cross-examine witnesses and to examine and attempt to refute charges against his client—were denied to those called to these military hearing boards. It should be noted that this condition closely resembled the one imposed on enemy aliens at *their* hearings: lawyers were allowed into the hearing room to give their clients advice, but *could not see evidence or examine witnesses*—if, indeed, witnesses were ever present.

In Nino Guttadauro's case, such restrictions left him on his own before the military hearing board, which convened, according to his son Angelo's account, in "Room 483 of San Francisco's Whitcomb Hotel at 9:30 A.M. on Tuesday, 8 September 1942."[43]

With FBI accounts of his activities in San Francisco—Guttadauro was an accountant who worked often for the Italian consulate, and was also, as a World War I veteran, the president of the San Francisco branch of the Federation of Italian World War Veterans, or *Ex-Combattenti*—as evidence against him, Guttadauro was unable to provide the board with enough "mitigating factors" to counter the apparent charge that his presence in California constituted a danger to the public safety. At 10:18 A.M. on 29 September 1942, he was served with Individual Exclusion Order F-1, dated September 23, 1942, demanding that he remove himself not just from Military Area No. 1, but from several other military areas as well, including some twenty-nine states from Connecticut to North Carolina, from Vermont to Virginia and parts of Alabama, New Mexico, Mississippi and Texas.[44] To implement his departure, Guttadauro was ordered to report two days later at 10:00 A.M. to Major Ray Ashworth for processing, and to inform the WDC "in writing the time of your departure, initial and ultimate destinations, route to be followed, and means of travel; upon arrival at ultimate destination, you will report in person the fact of your arrival and your address at such destination to the Special Agent in Charge of the nearest office of the Federal Bureau of Investigation, Department of Justice."[45] These notification and reporting requirements remained in effect whenever Guttadauro traveled more than five miles or changed his place of residence.

Nino Guttadauro with daughter Josephine and son Angelo

Guttadauro's travel and changes of residence would be frequent in the next two years. Like many other excludees from San Francisco, Guttadauro traveled first to Reno,

Nevada, which was the nearest large city beyond the excluded zone. According to his son's account, Guttadauro found it impossible to find work in his field of accounting because he had to let potential employers know of his exclusion. The result was that "the first job he was able to find following the exclusion was as a grocery clerk in Salt Lake City, Utah. This economic disruption and hardship, as well as the psychological scars, remained with my father for the rest of his life."[46] Nor was Guttadauro alone in this. In the attempt to keep the family together, Guttadauro's wife and two children followed him to Reno and beyond, renting housing at exorbitant costs because of their transient status. As his son Angelo, a retired Colonel and thirty-year veteran of the U.S. Army, put it, "We had become, by military fiat, a family of involuntary gypsies."[47]

Nino Guttadauro's ordeal lasted until March 13, 1944, at which time he received a letter from the Western Defense Command rescinding the original Exclusion order, and allowing him to return to San Francisco. Then on March 14, 1944, one day after receiving the notification of his release, Nino Guttadauro, as Commander of the Italian American Legion in San Francisco (the allegedly fascist *Ex-Combattenti*), received a letter from the U.S. Department of Justice, Immigration and Naturalization Service, inviting him to take part in an upcoming celebration. It began:

> Dear Sir: More than ever we should be anxious to make this year's observance of 'I Am An American Day' an auspicious event.[48]

Thus, the man whose leadership position in the *Ex-Combattenti* caused him to be considered so dangerous he had to be removed from twenty-nine states and almost stripped of his citizenship (denaturalization proceedings were inaugurated against Guttadauro, as they were against virtually all excludees who were naturalized citizens, but neither Guttadauro nor any others of Italian descent were ultimately denaturalized—except Domenico Trombetta, editor of *Il Grido della Stirpe*, an openly anti-semitic publication) is, upon his release, invited in that formerly dangerous capacity to celebrate the very thing he had been suspected of subverting.

According to its Supplemental Report, the Western Defense Command heard some 335 exclusion cases between September 1942 and April 1943. These resulted in the exclusion of 174 persons, some two dozen of whom were of Italian descent (the rest being German).[49] Most of these were from the northern district of California, with a few cases from Los Angeles and San Diego. Nationwide, according to a report on Individual Exclusion prepared by the Department of Justice, there were, as of August 7, 1943, some 263 exclusion orders issued by the Commanding Generals of the Eastern, Western and Southern Military Commands. With some 154 additional cases pending, this brought the total exclusion cases to 427.[50] Figures compiled by other researchers vary, but generally agree with those above. Historian Arnold Krammer concludes that as of July 1943, 268 people had been excluded, though another report he cites, from January 1944, gives the breakdown as follows: 173 in the Western Defense Command, 69 in the Eastern Defense Command, and 16 in the Southern Defense Command.[51] Despite the disparity in totals, the figures indicate that the Western Defense Command excluded by far the largest number, both as a total, and as a percentage of its alien population.

In that command, as noted above, some two dozen Italian Americans were ordered to remove themselves by order of the Commanding General. Most went to Reno, where a small community of excludees gathered. Among them was the former publisher of San Francisco's Italian newspaper, Ettore Patrizi. A major figure in San Francisco's Italian community for nearly fifty years, and a U.S. citizen for thirty of those years, Patrizi was seventy-two years old and in the Dante Hospital when he received his exclusion order dated September 28, 1942.[52] Though many notable citizens tried to intercede for him on grounds of age and illness, the WDC insisted that he leave, either by midnight October 21, 1942, or within twenty-four hours after his discharge from the hospital. On October 5, 1942 the editor was processed by the Army at the hospital,[53] where he was photographed, fingerprinted, and asked numerous questions about his plans; because of his illness, he was unable to give the time he would be able to move. On October 14, 1942, he notified the War Relocation Authority at the Whitcomb Hotel that he had sufficient funds to move, and shortly thereafter moved to Reno, Nevada.[54] Because of failing health he was allowed to return to San Francisco in October 1943, but he never resumed his duties at his newspaper, and died within a year.[55]

Renzo Turco also complied without protest to his exclusion order: he closed his San Francisco law office and with his wife moved to Chicago. Like Guttadauro, he had difficulty finding employment—again, because the requirement for each excludee to report weekly to the FBI as a "potentially dangerous" person made it difficult to convince employers of one's trustworthiness—until, through friends, he was able to land a job as an auditor for the Internal Revenue Service. In November of 1943 he tried, through Senator Hiram Johnson, to get his exclusion order modified so that he could work in Washington, DC; his request was denied and the exclusion order continued.[56] Years later, Turco told a San Francisco reporter that his exclusion "was obviously political, just to stir up the American people. It amounted to nothing, a handful of dead flies."[57]

Other Italian American excludees included the architect Pietro Canali of San Francisco, electrical repairman Edgar Castellini of San Francisco, clerk at the Italian

Consulate in Baltimore James Arena, restaurateur and acting consular agent in Tijuana Carlo Boccaccio of Coronado California, hotel manager Alberto Campione also of Coronado, bookkeeper Umberto Giovacchini of San Francisco, fisherman Vincenzo Abramo of San Francisco, housewife and Italian American activist Carolina Angeli of San Francisco, odd-jobber Giovacchino Anguzza of San Francisco, *L'Italia* editor and amateur pilot Remo Bosia of San Francisco, Lea Traina, Enrico Morelli and Giulia Morelli, all of San Francisco, and attorney Sylvester Andriano of San Francisco.

The Andriano Case

The case of Sylvester Andriano merits more detailed attention because much of his case played out publicly in San Francisco newspapers, while another, perhaps more important portion played out behind the scenes in the long-simmering conflict between General DeWitt of the Western Defense Command and Attorney General Francis Biddle of the Department of Justice. Andriano, as noted above, was a prominent San Francisco attorney who had emigrated to the United States in 1901 at age 11 to live with his married brother, worked his way through high school and St. Mary's College from which he graduated with high honors, taught elementary law at St. Mary's while attending Hastings College of Law in San Francisco, became a U.S. citizen in 1914, and began his law practice in 1917. He quickly became active in the Catholic Church, helping to found the Italian Catholic Union and its weekly paper, as well as a local chapter of Catholic Action. At the same time he was active in the Italian American community, serving as director of the Italian language school in North Beach, lawyer for the Italian consulate, and board member of the Italian Chamber of Commerce. The latter positions, as well as his local prominence as a former Police Commissioner, elected city Supervisor, and wartime head of Draft Board #100 in North Beach, brought him to the attention of the FBI, the Tenney Committee, and later the Western Defense Command, by whom he was ordered excluded from Military Area No. 1 on September 28, 1942. After considering various forms of resistance, he decided to comply with the military order, removed himself to Chicago and, aside from a few short trips, spent his exile there until relocating, in Spring 1943, to Denver, Colorado where he remained until his exclusion order was lifted.

His prominence alone would have made Andriano's exclusion stand out, but two other factors added to its importance. First was his decision, in early 1943, to defy his exclusion order by returning secretly to Military Area No. 1, once to stay for a time at his home in Los Altos, California, and shortly thereafter to attend in San Francisco a memorial mass for his mother, who had died in Italy. This set off a singular conflict between the Western Defense Command and Attorney General Francis Biddle, one which brought the entire Individual Exclusion Program into question and reignited the longstanding conflict between the two cabinet-level departments, Justice and War, responsible for control of civilians on the home front. The War Department made no secret of its anger and frustration with the Justice Department. According to the WDC Supplemental Report cited earlier,

> Early in 1943, the Attorney General, Mr. Biddle, began to show signs of an unwillingness to prosecute for violations of the orders [i.e. the individual exclusion orders, ed]. He took the attitude that he alone was the one to judge whether or not a violation should be prosecuted, and further, went so far as to state that he considered the procedure unconstitutional and, as such, refused to test the matter in the courts."[58]

The Andriano case thereupon became a prime citation in the WDC Report's accusations against the Attorney General, to wit, that the Attorney General had refused to prosecute an excludee, Sylvester Andriano, who had violated its orders. Moreover, the Commanding General of the WDC, John L. DeWitt, claimed to have information that Andriano had not only violated his order by entering Washington, DC, but

> ...in fact, had held conferences with the Attorney General on that trip. Andriano repeatedly violated the order and came into the exclusion area. In each instance the CG, through the War Department, requested the Attorney General to prosecute for violation of the order. In each instance, the Attorney General refused and took the position that he knew best as to the potential dangerousness of Andriano, which was in conflict with the recommendations of the FBI."[59]

The WDC report does not, of course, refer to Biddle's reasons for refusing, i.e., the due process provisions of the U.S. Constitution which rendered the exclusion program of doubtful legality, but rather states that his refusal was due to arrogance—the fact that "he knew best." The report then goes further to suggest that Andriano was being tipped off by someone in government—presumably the Attorney General—whenever the Army was about to forcibly eject him from the area, and "had already made arrangements for transportation out of the area."[60]

These suspicions and accusations take on enormous importance in retrospect, because the Andriano correspondence, especially the numerous letters the lawyer wrote from exile to his longtime personal friend and colleague in Catholic Action, Professor James Hagerty of St. Mary's College, make plain how agonized was the decision of the excludee regarding whether or not to contest his exclusion, and how easily he could have prevailed if he had refused to comply immediately and directly. Clearly, the lawyer in Andriano sensed some of this, but was conflicted about not just *whether*, but also *how* to fight what he considered an injustice. This is evident from his very first letters, where Andriano seeks to justify his decision *not* to fight, but to *obey*. On October 21, 1942, not long after his departure from San Francisco on September 28, he writes from Chicago:

> I am more convinced than ever that *the course that I have followed was the right one.* Without going into the question of the real origin of this iniquitous order, and in the light of subsequent events—the lifting of the curfew law against the Italians and reliev-ing them of the stigma of Alien enemies [i.e. on October 12, 1942, ed.], the strange coincidence of the sudden emergence of Count Sforza in S.F. with my departure, the triumph of the Mazzini program after nearly two years of fruitless efforts...the fact remains that in time of war in a key military zone like S.F. the authority of the army is supreme...[61] [Emphasis added.]

What is noteworthy in this letter, and in the rest of the correspondence, is that Andriano and his friend differed vehemently about how to respond to what both con-sidered an injustice. Hagerty consistently argued for a direct approach and a straightfor-ward defense:

> I still believe that you should write a straightforward account of your career and activi-ties in San Francisco—the which might have disproved the insidious charges against you in the F.B.I. and the Army Board....all this fustian against you could be dissipated on legal grounds, and you could defend yourself in open court.[62]

In the Oct. 28 letter cited above, however, Andriano gives voice to his preferred method of resistance:

> In those points wherein I thought the requirements of the army, (as distinguished from the order) *violated my rights and dignity as a person and a citizen, such as being fingerprinted and photographed* against my will, without being charged with a crime and not in conformity with some regulation that applied to all citizens of a class equally, such as your St. Mary's case, I refused to comply...[Emphasis added.]

In short, Andriano opted to demonstrate his resistance in small particulars that per-tained to his "dignity as a person," but in ways which did not constitute a direct refusal of the military order; indeed, he often referred to his need to demonstrate his "obedience" to authority, as if outright rebellion or refusal were a crime he could not bear to contem-plate. The correspondence between these two devoted friends returns repeatedly to this difference. On November 15, 1942, for example, Hagerty writes:

> Now that the election is passed it may be opportune to consider it simply as the case of Sylvester Andriano vs. the Western Army Command. There have been several cases where the exclusion order has not been put into effect, and I believe at least one where it has been rescinded...

Five days later, Hagerty repeats his exhortation, with more evidence:

> The case in Oregon is but the confirmation of my non-professional opinion that you had grounds in the civil courts to defend your rights. As it turns out, had you decided to remain, you would still be with us, your friends and your wife. I do not think the legal principles involved have anything to do with the place, unless we say that those who advised you in San Francisco in legal matters were unaware of the rights that Americans can claim by law...in the light of subsequent events, it seems to me incontrovertible that you were badly advised.[63]

For the Italian-born Andriano, however, nothing was ever straightforward or simple (he was apparently persuaded by his law partner, John Doran, that the *real* cause of his exclusion was the upcoming political battle for the governorship between incumbent Governor Olson, a Democrat like Andriano, and his Republican challenger, Earl Warren—with the Warren forces in the San Francisco newspapers eager to get rid of Andriano, especially in light of his influence among Italians and Catholics.[64]) Though intimately familiar with the law, he remains convinced that clever and clandestine moves, along with influence by friends in high places, will serve him better than a head-on, and in his mind, fruitless confrontation with military or governmental authority:

> Knowing that Warren's supporters were in a large measure responsible for the attacks against me and knowing too that they were not satisfied with my exclusion but that they aimed to destroy me completely, make an outcast of me, so to speak, whom everybody would forever shun, and rob me of any possible influence either now or in the future, I said I would be willing...provided it was agreeable to Olson's manager (Olson having nominated me on the Draft Board of which I am still a member) to go on record as in favor of giving full support to the President..[65]

Again, on November 17, Andriano writes to Hagerty about the results of San Francisco Mayor Angelo Rossi's attempts to intervene on his behalf with General DeWitt, and then agrees to an even higher-level intervention by the president of the Bank of America, Louis Ferrari:

> I have learned that the visit of my friend at the City Hall [i.e. Mayor Rossi, ed.] to the Gen'l was wholly negative. The latter was curt and uncooperative ...nothing to

be expected from that source....Louis Ferrari of the Bank wrote me that if I approve, he would like to write a letter to the President, confident that through close personal friends the same will at least be read by him...I had no objection...[66]

The culmination of these "inside" efforts[67] came with the visit of San Francisco Archbishop Mitty to Washington DC. The archbishop stopped in Chicago on his way east but Andriano was in Santa Fe, New Mexico at the time; as Andriano notes in his November 25 letter, the two met on the prelate's return trip. Here is Andriano's summary of the intervention by the A.B. [archbishop]:

> The A.B. called on me last Monday at 5:30 P.M. and we were together until 8:35... While in Washington, he went to see Biddle [Attorney General Francis Biddle, ed.]; Biddle turned him over to one of his assistants, Mr. Fahey, a Catholic who was familiar with my case. Mr. Fahey admitted confidentially that the evidence against me was very weak and that the U.S. Atty's office had serious misgivings about the procedure that was followed, but there was nothing that his office could do since the matter was in the hands of the Army. He suggested that the A.B. go to the War Dept to see a Mr. McCloyne [sic—John McCloy, Asst. Secretary of War, ed.]...McCloy (said) that the only man who could do anything was DeWitt and suggested that the A.B. go and see him upon his return to S.F. The A.B. said he didn't care to see DeWitt since he had heard that he had not shown proper courtesy to the Mayor of S.F. when he went to see him about my case, but after McCloy had assured the A.B. that he would be shown the proper courtesy by DeWitt and had promised to write to him to arrange for the visit, the A.B. agreed to go to see him upon his return, and that's where the matter stands at present..[68]

As might have been expected, this intervention by a powerful friend, like all the others, turned out to be useless. (Actually, the Archbishop's intervention was worse than useless, for, as we have seen above, General DeWitt was convinced, and noted in his report, that Andriano *himself* had gone to Washington to see the Attorney General, and more, that the Attorney General was tipping off the excludee about imminent moves to arrest him by the WDC forces—see below.)

It was after the failure of every intervention by supposedly influential friends that Sylvester Andriano decided to resist, but *not* as his friend Hagerty counseled, by contesting the order's legality directly and openly in court (as one might expect a lawyer to do), but rather to *surreptitiously* enter the military zone prohibited to him. He had, in fact, planned to do this earlier:

> I propose to wend my way back quietly to Calif., Los Angeles, to be exact, and there await developments. In the event I am arrested I will have legal counsel ready to take

up the case, not as a challenge to or even for the purpose of contesting the Army Authority but merely for the purpose of having my legal rights judicially determined.[69]

But the plan to enter Los Angeles was based on the idea that there he could 'determine his rights' in court unobserved by the vicious press he had been subjected to in San Francisco. Since Hagerty argued strenuously against this move, Andriano put aside the trip for the time being. By February of 1943, however, he decided to try again. Nor was this second attempt predicated on a key decision in Portland, Oregon in which a Federal judge had "flatly declared that DeWitt was without authority to issue exclusion orders as regards citizens without a prior declaration of Martial Law."[70] Rather, Andriano seemed to have been impelled to make his move by a new FBI investigation which, he was sure, would result in his being stripped of his American citizenship, i.e. de-naturalized and interned and/or deported. Figuring that he now had little to lose by defying his exclusion order, Andriano decided once again to try to slip into California unnoticed, this time to his Los Altos home. His reasons are laid out in a long, typed letter he wrote to Hagerty on March 10, on his San Francisco Office stationery. Though he later asked Hagerty to destroy this letter, the latter kept it, perhaps knowing its historical value. In any case, Andriano answered Hagerty's question, "Why did I return home?" (first noting his now-familiar reasons for not contesting the exclusion order earlier, i.e. so as not to "stir up controversy or bring about a division among the people that would be detrimental to the national effort or to imperil the legal structures for Army exclusions and with due regard to the prestige of the military authority"):

> Shortly after my arrival in Chicago I received a copy of the October 15 issue of the "Corriere del Popolo" whose editor, Carmelo Zito, had been one of the two chief witnesses against me before the Tenney Committee hearings...ending with this paragraph: "When he (Gen. DeWitt) will have finished, you may rest assured, there will be no more fascist henchmen around. In order that the work of redemption may be completed the Department of Justice will have to intervene to deprive Mussolini's agents of citizenship. They are not worthy of it. They must be sent to a concentration camp and compelled to work for the entire duration of the war and at the end shipped to Italy by parcel post."
>
> On October 26, 1942 "The [San Francisco] Examiner" came out with a two-column article entitled: "Andriano Facing Citizenship Ban."....
>
> I should still be living at the Hotel La Salle in Chicago...but for a new investigation, the fifth or sixth of its kind, to which I was subjected by the F.B.I. in Chicago. From the tenor of the questions put to me by the F.B.I. examiner, I was forced to conclude that I was wrong in refusing to believe the stories that appeared in the "Corriere

del Popolo" and in other San Francisco newspapers about impending denaturalization proceedings against me and that this latest investigation was precisely for the purpose of laying a foundation for such proceedings. Moreover, I had good reason to suspect that I was under constant surveillance while in Chicago.

As I reflected on these latest developments, it became more and more apparent to me that even though I was willing to make a sacrifice and stay away from restricted areas for the duration of the war, seemingly that was not enough and I was to have no respite until I was deprived of citizenship, thrown into a concentration camp and ultimately deported. Under the circumstances I thought that if I must live under constant surveillance and if I must defend myself against further proceedings and particularly against attempts to deprive me of citizenship, I might as well be under surveillance in my home and defend myself in the City where I have lived and labored for more than forty years even if that involved a technical violation of the order of exclusion.[71]

Accordingly, when Andriano's wife, Leonora, was to depart from Chicago after a visit, he decided to accompany her to their Los Altos home. It was sometime around mid-February, 1943, and he would stay until mid-May.

Andriano's presence did not go unnoticed for long. Another letter to Hagerty from Los Altos on April 10 reports that "two F.B.I. men" had called at Andriano's San Francisco office on or about March 28 and were told that Andriano was in Los Altos (a residential community about forty-two miles south of San Francisco). They called upon him the same day, whereupon he talked with them for about twenty minutes, but writes that he had not heard from them since. Whether this indicated that denaturalization was not, in fact, proceeding, or that he was now to be allowed to remain, is not mentioned. Nonetheless, after two side trips to Los Angeles, and one to San Jose, Andriano remained in Los Altos only until about May 20, when he decided once again to exit the forbidden area, stop at Albuquerque, NM for a couple of days, and then settle himself a little closer, this time at the Sears Hotel in Denver, CO, which he reached on May 23.

All these travels are recounted in a long letter Andriano wrote to Hagerty from the Sears Hotel on June 24, recounting his peregrinations not only on this trip, but also a subsequent one on June 1, when he violated his exclusion order for the second time, to attend the San Francisco memorial service for his mother. First, Andriano gives his reason for leaving Los Altos the first time:

> I left Los Altos because I learned that my friend Bill Hennessey, the U.S. District Attorney is a permanent resident of Los Altos, and I didn't want to see the newspapers put him on the spot, particularly as just at that time there appeared an ominous editorial in the Chronicle entitled "Tenney Committee" which contained a sinister reference to me.

Thus, once again we see Andriano attributing his departure *not* to the F.B.I. interrogation or the dreaded denaturalization, but to his reluctance to discomfit a friend, the U.S. Attorney, with negative publicity. As further justification, he claims that "the main object for my return to California, viz. to refute the charge that I was a potentially dangerous citizen or that they had anything of an incriminating nature against me, had been attained," though he does not explain exactly how his innocence had been demonstrated. He simply writes, without elaboration, that "I became convinced that it would be better if I did not stand on my civil rights, but complied with the order even if I knew it to be wrong." Andriano then relates how news of his mother's death came to him shortly thereafter in Denver, including news of a memorial service to be held for her in San Francisco, and his determination to attend.

It is at this point that Sylvester Andriano narrates the almost Keystone-cop-like adventures he had with government agents, who followed him into St. Brigid's Church when he attended mass, remained parked outside his wife's San Francisco apartment, and tracked his every move up to and including his attendance at the memorial service. Here is his ruefully humorous account:

> In the meantime I had Leonora get me a ticket and pullman reservation to Denver for Saturday evening. Every morning I went to St. Bridgid's and every morning they followed me in Church…I have no doubt that the purpose of the F.B.I.'s was to terrorize me into departing forthwith. Saturday morning as I was backing the car from the garage to go to Fr. Hunt with my wife, sister and brother-in-law, six men swooped down upon us from three directions and formed a cordon around me at the wheel of the car. One of them said that he was Lieutenant___ from the 4th Army Command Headquarters and that he had a letter from [sic: 'for'] me from General DeWitt. I took the letter, thanked him and put [it] in my pocket. When he saw that I wasn't reading it, he said that the letter stated that I was given until the following Tuesday at 4 o'clock to withdraw from the prohibited Area otherwise steps would be taken to enforce the order. I pulled out of my pocket the envelope containing the railroad ticket and reservation and showed it to him, at the same time advising him of the reasons for my presence in S.F. Another man asked me if I planned to remain in Denver. I replied that as far as I knew at that time I did, but that I still considered myself a free American citizen, whereupon they very courteously took their leave. Needless to say they followed us to Church and also to the Ferry in the evening and one of them boarded the same train. I am enclosing a copy of the General's letter for your information.[72]

In addition to quoting from his mother's last letter, Andriano in this same June 24, 1943 letter wrote that, due to revelations from two priest friends who said they knew of his mother's death in early 1942 but kept it from him "out of charity," he was now

> ...convinced she died right after the declaration of war between Italy & America. That was more than her stout heart could endure and no doubt she pleaded with God to take her as the first victim of what was for her a most cruel and unnatural conflict wherein her grandsons would be fighting against one another.[73]

It seems quite clear that Sylvester Andriano was speaking not only for his mother, but for himself, as well as many other Italian Americans, who often gave voice to this same painful dilemma—relatives fighting each other from opposite sides of a major war.

It is immediately after this that Andriano makes his first reference to "some kind of skin trouble." In his very next letter, he informs Hagerty that he's actually been hospitalized for this skin problem—"my arms and hands and legs began to swell up from the inflammation and I was a sight to behold." A skin specialist pronounced it "a very bad case of neuro dermatisis" [sic: "dermatitis," perhaps eczema, ed.] which "is caused by suppressed nervous or emotional strains and is most severe in those who exhibit no outward manifestation of the strain."[74] Clearly, Sylvester Andriano, conflicted over how to comport himself in the face of public attacks, government persecution, and exile from everything he knew and loved, would seem a prime candidate for such a condition. It haunted him for most of his remaining time in Denver, and accords with similar psychosomatic ailments suffered by many others who were targeted on the homefront during World War II.

Why Not Fight?

What remains puzzling is the reason, or reasons this brilliant lawyer and public figure refused, to the very end, to fight his case directly, in open court. On November 12, 1943, for example, he wrote to Hagerty that he was remaining in Denver

> a few weeks longer in order to allow still more time to the powers that be to take action if they intend to do so. If no action is taken by the Feast of the Immaculate Conception [December 8, ed.] I intend, God willing, to return home to face the music or the freeze-out silence or whatever else may come to pass.

He writes this even as he notes that "most of those Italians who were excluded as well as most of those who were sent to concentration camps [interned enemy aliens, ed.] are back in San Francisco" and, moreover, that "more than three months have passed since peace was made with Italy" [Italy formally joined the Allied effort against Germany in September of 1943, ed.]. The question remains, why did Sylvester Andriano, even after

all this, bow his head and continue to obey military orders that he considered illegiti-
mate? For that matter, why did no other Italians, naturalized American citizens all, fight
their exclusion orders either?

While human actions are notoriously difficult to fully comprehend, Andriano's letters point to at least four related factors which contributed to his decision: 1) his deep
religious faith, especially concerning his ideas about obedience to constituted authority;
2) his related sense that suffering and/or submission to God's will is the way to salvation;
3) his tendency, common in Italian culture, not to confront authority directly; 4) his
exaggerated response to shame and public humiliation (to which Andriano was exposed
in newspapers, and to which he refers constantly). Taken together, these factors may
help us understand why Andriano, a trained and experienced lawyer, never challenged
his exclusion order in the courts—especially given the U.S. Army's apparent helplessness
in the face of the flat-out refusal to comply with its orders by several other individual
excludees (see below).

To begin with, Sylvester Andriano's letters are brimming with references to his religious faith, his felt necessity to abide by its edicts, and the comfort he felt such faith
gave him in his hours of need. In his October 21, 1942 letter, for example, he begins by
saying to Hagerty,

> Thank you particularly for your prayers because I am positive that they and those of
> others have made it possible for me to go through these days of trial with a serenity,
> an equanimity and a joy, even, which, conscious of my weakness, I could not have
> believed possible.[75]

The very next paragraph continues this theme and expands on it with particulars about
his "banishment" to the "Land of Egypt" and his linking of it to an indebtedness to di-
vine providence for its goodness and bounty to him:

> Our dear Lord in the Blessed Sacrament and she whom we poor banished children of
> Eve address daily, and not always appreciating what we say, as Holy Queen, mother of
> Mercy, Our Life, Our Sweetness and Our Hope have been ineffably good to me and
> with their continued help I hope to [be] able to treasure this bountifulness to one so
> unworthy, all the days of my life. The Catholic Action ritual too has taken on a new
> and hitherto unsuspected beauty and luster in what you are pleased to call the Land of
> Egypt.

This reference to Mary, Mother of God, returns, later in this same letter, with a key reference to Andriano's own mother, and her favorite teaching to him:

> My dear old mother has a favorite word which she has said all through life and even

now repeats quite frequently, it is: *Fiat...fiat...fiat...*and conscious of the profound wisdom in her homely philosophy, I say "Amen."[76]

The word, *fiat*, means, in Latin, "let it be done." Repeated three times, it constitutes a deep expression of Catholic faith in God's will—God's will, that is, over what mere humans, with their limited understanding, would prefer or will for themselves. It is not too much to add that the Italian context conveys its own flavor, a kind of resignation to the world, especially the world of authority, not as we would like it to be, but as it is; as in *che sara sara*: what will be, will be.

Andriano returns to these themes again and again, so often, indeed, that they convey the second flavor noted above: that suffering and submission to God's will is, in fact, to be welcomed as the way to salvation for Roman Catholics. This patience, and indeed, near-exultation in and exaltation of his suffering (in his March 10, 1943 letter quoted above, he refers to his willingness to "make a sacrifice by staying away"), is especially notable in Andriano's later letters, as, for instance, in this passage from his April 10, 1943 letter from Los Altos:

> Little did I dream when we set up those stations [of the Cross, ed.] along Holy Rood Road that I was so soon to have occasion to make the Stations daily and still less that I would sooner still be *privileged to carry a tiny little cross of my own* along a much longer road and far from home. Believe me, Jim, I wouldn't trade that experience for anything in the world; no, not for any possible vindication either [Emphasis added].[77]

This entire complex of ideas about suffering is concretized even more vividly when Andriano describes his travails from his skin condition, the dermatitis that landed him in hospital. On August 26, 1943, for example, he compares himself with Job:

> The Vesuvius did erupt again and for a while threatened to send me scurrying back to the hospital for protection, but having become somewhat of an expert myself in the handling, not of potsherds, like Job, thank God, but of cotton, gauze, bandages and safety-pins, I managed with the aid of solutions, lotions, salves, balms, and ointments if not completely to repel the attacks of the enemy, at least to hold him in check.[78]

And earlier, on July 19, 1943, he repairs for relief from his skin condition to his mother's favorite exhortation, "Fiat," this time elevating it to an affliction he deserves:

> Once again I had the opportunity of repeating my mother's favorite word, "Fiat," with this notable difference, however, that with her it was a free-will offering, whereas with me it isn't even an infinitesimal payment on account of the debt that I owe.[79]

Oddly enough, Andriano has just finished referring to the doctor's diagnosis "which according to him is most severe in those who exhibit no outward manifestation of the strain." Yet he maintains, shortly afterward in this letter, an outward front of acceptance and even welcome to his sufferings—precisely the attitudes that have contributed to their severity. Such a view—that his exclusion was a kind of "via crucis" required of him to pay for the debt he has incurred, presumably for having been given a "bountiful life" in America—could help explain why Sylvester Andriano was inclined *not* to fight his exile.

Moreover, two related factors might be added to those suggested above: Andriano's tendency, as an Italian, not to confront authority directly; and his hyper-sensitivity to the shame and public ridicule to which the San Francisco newspapers exposed him. He refers to the latter constantly and consistently, not only as goads to his pride and self-respect, but also as determinants of his strategy. Recall, for example, that he tried to justify his planned trip to Los Angeles as logical because "There I won't have to contend with a poisonous press."[80] Indeed, even before he was excluded, though after he had been pilloried in the San Francisco newspapers during the Tenney Committee Hearings in late May, 1942, Andriano wrote to Hagerty on June 22 about "the politicians, Masons and Mazzinians and their confederates in the papers [who] have ceased their clamor for my scalp for the time being, but it's just a lull." He was right; on July 29 he again refers to "the ever more vicious onslaughts of those who are seeking my poor scalp."[81] On October 21, 1942, now in exile in Chicago, he writes even more poignantly:

> My wife, valiant woman that she is, knows something of how heartless and tormenting newspaper-men can be when they are after someone. Thanks to them, the 24 hours that preceded my departure left a searing in my soul that I don't think will ever be effaced.[82]

Finally, the precipitating event for Andriano in his decision to move back to his home in Los Altos, was a newspaper report, indeed, two of them, which are cited above: the October 15, 1942 issue of *Corriere del Popolo*, in which Andriano's main antagonist, Carmelo Zito, called for his denaturalization; and the subsequent article in the *San Francisco Examiner* which reported on October 26, 1942 that such a process was imminent: "Andriano Facing Citizenship Ban." He refers to both articles in his letter explaining his return, as well as the new F.B.I. investigation that convinced him that the newspaper "calls for his scalp" were serious. It bears noting, in this regard, that the Italian culture in which Andriano was born places great store by reputation—which Andriano always refers to as his "self-respect"—and takes seriously any public shaming which results in the diminishing or destruction of that reputation. The constant news stories that battered him for months and years could not have been other than what he describes above, a "searing in my soul," and could not have done other than figure in his decision to submit to the exclusion without a public fight that would have been sure to generate more shameful headlines.

The related inhibition against publicly confronting governmental authority was an equally Italian tendency. As we have seen, Andriano, when he did choose to resist, was always inclined to do so quietly, avoiding a direct or noisy or public confrontation wherever possible. He did this when he chose to go to Los Angeles. He did it when he chose to return to his Los Altos home, without a fuss. And when it appeared that a fuss might be made—because his friend U.S. Attorney William Hennessey lived in Los Altos, and might be drawn into a public scandal in the newspapers—Andriano chose to withdraw rather than risk such a possibly messy confrontation. Indeed, even when shielded by the human right to grieve for his departed mother at her memorial service in San Francisco, Andriano eschewed any public insistence on his right. He claimed to have acted with dignity when the six officers "swooped" down upon him in his car, but even shielded by his grief and his return trip ticket to Denver, he simply responded quietly and with due deference to authority. This is because it always seemed far wiser and more natural to him not to fight publicly, but rather to engage several powerful figures to intercede for him with the authorities, *behind the scenes*. These, as we have seen above, included several attempts by Archbishop Mitty of San Francisco, one by the Bank of America president Louis Ferrari, one by Mayor Rossi of San Francisco, and several others by influential friends.[83] None succeeded in the least. Nonetheless, even when his fellow-excludees were being allowed to return home, after Italy was no longer a belligerent, when other excludees were defying their orders with impunity, and when it was clear that the Department of Justice was not enforcing the military's orders, Andriano was loathe to take a public stand in defiance of his order. The most he would do, throughout his ordeal, was to refuse to be photographed and fingerprinted, and then to quietly flout his exclusion order by slipping quietly and unnoticed into California.[84]

Thus, though Sylvester Andriano's strategy did nothing to help others, or to advance the case against the legitimacy of exclusion in general, or even rebut the public charges against him, it did provide a galling episode to General DeWitt and his minions outraged to see their authority dismissed. It also, in retrospect, brought the long-simmering dispute between the military and the Department of Justice over the exclusion of American citizens, at least those of European extraction, into sharp focus.

We know this because of the already-cited Western Defense Command report on the exclusion of Non-Japanese. The WDC report not only accused the chief law enforcement officer of the United States of reneging on his agreement to enforce military orders, thereby undermining military authority; it also suggested that the Attorney General was aiding a known violator to evade the attempts of the Western Defense Command to enforce its own orders. To understand why this was so, it is now necessary to look more deeply into the dispute between these departments, and the cases and documents to that dispute.

Military Problems with Enforcement

To begin with, it was not Sylvester Andriano alone who flouted the individual exclusion orders imposed by the military. Numerous other citizen excludees, nearly all of German extraction, simply *refused to obey* their exclusion orders. Mrs. Olga Schueller, an American citizen living in Philadelphia, refused the Eastern Defense Command's order to leave her area. She admitted that she was an officer in several German-American societies, including one that was once the Central Bund—the German-American organization classified by the FBI as 'highly dangerous'—but claimed there was nothing wrong with that. The army was alarmed to find that a federal judge agreed with Mrs. Schueller, and she was allowed to stay in Philadelphia.[85] Several other citizens who received exclusion orders not only refused to comply with them, but actually sued the government for loss of income and deprivation of rights. Kenneth Alexander, of Oregon, took this approach, suing General John DeWitt of the Western Defense Command for $50,000, arguing that since he (Alexander) was not a member of the U.S. military, he couldn't be ordered by the military to leave the area. Though Alexander's case never came to trial, his counterattack seemed to work, for he was allowed to remain in Military Area No. 1. This situation became such an affront to the military that Lt. General Hugh Drum, the commanding general of the Eastern Defense Command, petitioned the War Department in May 1943 for more authority to enforce exclusion orders on his own. Drum asked that he "be given authority to convene military commissions for the trial of violators of military orders and regulations."[86]

The problem for Drum, as well as for the War Department, lay with the Department of Justice and its head, Attorney General Francis Biddle. From the very outset, the Attorney General had expressed grave doubts about both the necessity and the legality of the individual exclusion program demanded by the military. Therefore, he refused, as General DeWitt had charged with respect to Andriano, to prosecute the cases of violators. In a memo to President Roosevelt on April 17, 1943, the Attorney General made his deep reservations about the entire program clear:

> We [the Justice Department, ed.] have not approved the Army procedure, which does not permit the persons excluded—American citizens—to confront witnesses before the Military Tribunal. This is against a fundamental conception of constitutional rights. Prosecution would have little practical effect. Bail would be granted and the individuals would go on living where they chose until the cases were ultimately decided by the Supreme Court. If the Army believes that they are dangerous they have the express power to exclude them under the Executive Order.[87]

What the Attorney General was saying is that the exclusion procedure could not be upheld in a civil court of law; if the army thought it could be sustained by military means, and under the authority of Executive Order 9066, then let it do the enforcing itself.

This put the military in a position where it could either allow civilians to thumb their noses at its orders, or take it upon itself to enforce its orders by military means. In some cases (as with Andriano), it did exactly this, tracking down some of those who refused to leave its Military Areas and escorting them out under threat of force. But it had to rely on the fact that most people were easily intimidated by armed military police. Where citizens were not intimidated, and initiated legal proceedings as Kenneth Alexander did, the army itself backed down and let the cases wither. Only in the case of excludee Remo Bosia was the army on firmer ground. That was because Bosia had joined the army just before he received his exclusion order, and was therefore *legally subject to military control*. When the Western Defense Command learned he was at Fort Ord in Monterey, California for basic training, it ordered him court-martialed for failing to obey a military order, i.e. his exclusion—blithely ignoring the fact that for Bosia to comply with the exclusion order, he would have had to violate his military orders, i.e. not to desert his military post! Though Bosia was found innocent at his court martial, and eventually discharged from the army for health reasons, he continued to be doggedly and maliciously pursued by General DeWitt: shortly after his return to California as a civilian, Bosia was served with a new exclusion order at his home in San Carlos, and forced once again to leave Military Area No. 1.[88]

The DOJ Report on Exclusion

In November of 1943, the long-simmering dispute between the army and the Justice Department over the Individual Exclusion Program reached its boiling point. At that time, the director of Alien Enemy Control, Edward Ennis, sent a preliminary report his department had prepared on exclusion to Captain John Hall in Assistant Secretary of War John J. McCloy's office. Ostensibly meant to aid Hall and McCloy in their discussions with the Eastern Defense Command about modifying the exclusion program there, the report amounts to a devastating condemnation of the entire individual exclusion procedure. It accords, in fact, with the Attorney General's memo the previous April to the President: "Exclusion is based on MILITARY danger. This element is entirely lacking from these cases."[89]

Titled "Preliminary Report on Study of Individual Exclusion Order Cases," and dated August 1943, the report analyzes some 100 cases of exclusion, with digests of all the cases included. The cases are separated into ten categories, with German and Italian cases grouped separately. The categories proceed, in order of 'dangerousness,' from Category I, active leaders of German organizations, to four lesser categories such as members of those organizations, and people who are simply pro-Nazi or pro-German without being linked to dangerous organizations, and so on. While German excludees are assembled into five categories, Italian excludees are treated in only two: Category VI, which includes those with "fairly strong pro-Italian and probably pro-Fascist sentiments, at least prior to Pearl Harbor" and Category VII, which includes those with "weak evidence of pro-Italian or pro-Fascist sympathy." As explanation for the fewer Italian categories, the report notes that "the Italian cases present an entirely different security problem, and whereas it is reasonable to set up a special category for members of the Bund, there is no Italian organization of comparable subversiveness."[90] There is one additional category in which Italian excludees appear, Category IX, set up for cases in which there is "no basis for exclusion whatever."

The report provides examples of the various categories. For Category VI, the "strong" evidence category, we find the case of Domenico deGregoris:

> This man was born in Italy and was naturalized here. He has four children, one of whom, at the time of the proceedings, was employed in Italy by the Italian Government. The subject was active in Fascist circles in Philadelphia, and was Treasurer of the American Friends of Italy, which collected some money for the Italian Red Cross during the Ethiopian War. Subject admitted that before the United States entered the war he hoped to see Italy defeat England. He also admitted that he had received medals from the Italian Government.[91]

Medals from the Italian government and an admission that 'before the United States entered the war,' he hoped to see Italy defeat *not* the United States but England, are here said to constitute 'strong' evidence of "dangerousness." For 'weak' evidence in Category VII, the report cites the case of Edgar Castellini of San Francisco:

This man was a naturalized citizen of Italian birth, who owned an electrical repair shop. A police Department report indicated that the subject had a good reputation, was a Republican, and was opposed to the Administration. It also appears that an informant states that the subject stopped her on the street and pointed to *Time Magazine* and told her that she 'should not read that stuff.' Subject also made derogatory remarks concerning General MacArthur, whose picture was on the cover. There is other information that the subject said that Japan was a rich country which would take Singapore and would go on to win the war.[92]

Category IX, for cases with essentially no basis for exclusion, includes the case of an excludee named Angelini:

This man, who was recommended for exclusion from Richmond, Virginia, was hired by a *Life* photographer to go with him to act as interpreter when he photographed some Italian vessels tied up at Norfolk. Subsequently the vessels were sabotaged by their crews[93] and photographs of the subject on board the vessels were published in the Richmond papers. The *Life* photographer, however, stated that at the time he went to the ships, and presumably took the published photographs, the subject was unacquainted with the crew members. In addition to this, an informant stated that he had seen a picture of Mussolini on a calendar in subject's home. Another informant stated that the subject's son had obtained his discharge from the Navy by asserting that he had flat feet.[94]

The nature of the alleged evidence of "dangerousness," supplied mostly by informants and used against Angelini, needs no comment.

The exclusion report then goes on to analyze the one hundred cases from a number of different perspectives. The first is geographic. To begin with, the report says, the "number of cases arising in the various Judicial Districts bears no relation to the population of those Districts, and, similarly, bears no relation to the alien enemy population."[95] Since it is reasonable to assume that the size of the alien enemy population in any state is a fair indication of the number of people who would be likely to sympathize with the enemy nations, the report calls this 'surprising.' There were, for example, no cases in Connecticut or New Jersey, states with very large Italian American populations, but twenty seven cases in Pennsylvania, with twenty of those in the eastern part of the state. With only one case in Massachusetts, and only nine in all of New York state (the state with the highest population of Italian Americans), the data, says the report, suggest that "factors other than the sensitivity of the area and the dangerousness of its inhabitants govern the institution of these cases."[96]

The next geographical conclusion concerns the relationship of the exclusion cases to the location of essential defense or war-related facilities. The report makes this assumption about the exclusion program:

> Theoretically, the principal usefulness of the program is that it removes potentially
> dangerous persons from areas in which there are many vital defense plants and other
> installations to areas in which there are fewer of such installations. In the testimony
> which has been offered in the three cases which have been litigated so far, officers on
> the staffs of General Drum and General DeWitt, in attempting to show the desir-
> ability of the program, have relied heavily on the concentration of defense plants and
> the amount of defense production in the two areas. Table B shows conclusively that by
> far the most important concentrations of defense plants are in the 5th and 6th Service
> Commands, which embrace the states of Ohio, West Virginia, Indiana, Kentucky,
> and Illinois, Michigan and Wisconsin....the 3rd command, in which approximately
> one-third of all the exclusion cases arise, has less than one-half the number of listed
> facilities which the 6th command has.......[97]

This part of the report ends with a conclusion which, if accepted, would appear to invalidate the entire rationale for the exclusion program:

> ...the exclusion program is, to a considerable extent, moving persons out of areas where
> there are relatively *fewer* defense facilities and permitting them to go into areas in
> which there are *more* facilities [Emphases added].[98]

That is, not only is excluding civilians from designated military areas *not* reducing the risk of sabotage or espionage, in fact, it is *increasing that risk* because it shifts allegedly dangerous people into areas where they would have *more opportunities to endanger the war effort* than if they had been left at home!

The report then goes on to analyze the one hundred cases under discussion with regard to the standards used to select people for exclusion. It attacks the key concept of "potential dangerousness" used to exclude people, because, in its words, "the concept of dangerousness itself contains the element of possibility."[99] Saying someone is "potentially dangerous," that is, is equivalent to saying that someone *might possibly be a possible threat.* The conclusion warns against this extreme case of "guilty unless proven innocent" with these words:

> Practically, the use of phrases such as this [i.e. 'potentially dangerous', ed.] suggests that
> those who use them hold the view that a subject of an exclusion case must be excluded
> unless it is clear that there is no reason to exclude him. This is analogous to saying that
> the burden of proof is on the excludee, although the excludee, of course, cannot meet
> the burden, since he is not advised of the charges against him.[100]

This conclusion dovetails almost completely with the Attorney General's July 1943 memo to J. Edgar Hoover, in which he orders the FBI director to dispense completely with the concept of "dangerousness" as employed in the Custodial Detention Index. In Francis Biddle's words in that memo, "it is now clear to me that this classification system is inherently unreliable."[101]

One of the reasons the Attorney General came to this conclusion had to do with the basis upon which innumerable "dangerous" classifications were made—the statements of informants. The Preliminary Report addresses this issue as it applies to excludees, pointing out that "many of the cases based on alleged pro-Hitler or pro-Mussolini statements spring, to a considerable extent, from baiting by friends, neighbors, customers or fellow workers, and the like."[102] Relying on such provoked hearsay evidence, as large numbers of exclusion cases do, shows "the extreme danger involved in taking rigorous security measures against persons on the basis of their remarks to informants."[103] The reason this is so has to do with a further conclusion of the report regarding the types of people who end up being excluded:

> The principal category of person being excluded is composed of persons as to whom there is no evidence whatsoever of any tendency toward espionage or sabotage, but who have displayed, in greater or lesser degree, a sympathy with the Nazi or Fascist forms of government, or at least with Germany or Italy.[104]

The report then wonders how expelling such people—those who have displayed "*no evidence whatsoever* of any tendency towards espionage or sabotage"—from seaboard areas can possibly contribute to the safety of the United States.

Given such observations, it is not surprising that the report's conclusions thoroughly and completely invalidate the Individual Exclusion Program. Beginning with the selection process of those to be excluded, it refers to its earlier observation that since people are *not* selected according to *real* danger (i.e. being in places where they could do damage, or where there could be high concentrations of possibly dangerous people) but rather by the large element of chance in who happens to inform on them (the Tenney Committee in San Francisco can be seen as a type case), the chief factor in selecting excludees appears to be that of *chance itself*. Because of this, the report's first major conclusion states that..

> The principal effect of the exclusion program is the *selection at random* of a minute percentage of the pre-war pro-German or pro-Italian groups, and the exclusion of this small fraction of the total group [Emphasis added].[105]

Based on the sample examined, in other words, the people selected for exclusion by the military tribunals were not dangerous at all:

> ...in no case (with the highly debatable exception of the Krause case) is there any evidence of any conduct since the outbreak of the war which would in any way hinder the prosecution of the war.[106]

The report then goes on to the second major question, which is whether, even had some excludees been correctly identified as dangerous, "there is any utility in moving them from the Military Areas into other parts of the country."[107] Its answer is an unequivocal "NO." This was a key element of the entire program as the military justified it: that there were seaboard areas so vulnerable and so vital to the nation's defense, that it was a *military necessity* to remove potentially dangerous persons from those areas. But the report's analysis of one-hundred cases indicates that no such military justification existed. There was no justification due to large concentrations of defense facilities; no correlation of excludees with large alien populations likely to harbor potential fifth columnists; and no justification that seaboard areas were any more vulnerable to spies and saboteurs than the areas to which excludees were sent. With regard to this last argument, the report is specific, and not a little ironic, with regard to the Western Defense Command and the excludees of Italian descent concentrated there:

> It is extremely hard to believe that the Italian war potential is such that it is necessary to remove Italians from California in order to make it impossible for saboteurs landed on that coast by Italian submarine to obtain assistance.[108]

Finally, since "there is no practical justification for the exclusion even of dangerous persons from the areas now designated to other parts of the country," the report concludes that "the program as it is now conducted is *substantially without utility*"[109] and should be abandoned.

In the Italian cases of exclusion, most excludees were allowed to return to their homes on the West Coast in late 1943 or early 1944, some months after Italy had surrendered and joined the Allies. None challenged the exclusion orders, either at the time they received them, or later. But as noted above, several German American excludees *did* challenge their orders, and were allowed to remain in the coastal areas. The final question that arises has to do with the army's reluctance to take such cases to court. One reason certainly had to do with what the Attorney General wrote in his memo to the President in April 1943: that the military's exclusion procedure for American citizens was *unconstitutional* because citizens have the constitutional right, in civilian courts, to be informed of the charges against them, and to confront witnesses.

Another reason for the army's reluctance to take its violators to court, however, may lie in a Supreme Court precedent that was cited by Japanese Americans who challenged their mass exclusion and internment under Executive Order 9066. That precedent is the 1866 *Ex Parte Milligan* decision. In that Civil War case, Lambdin Milligan, who sympathized with the Confederacy, had been tried by a military tribunal for conspiracy to overthrow the government, and was sentenced to hang. The tribunal had based its decision on Congress' earlier authorization for then-President Lincoln to suspend the writ of habeas corpus "whenever in his judgment, the public safety may require it," only providing that the operation of civil courts had become impossible. The case moved all the way to the Supreme Court, whose majority then ruled *against the army's jurisdiction over civilians.* In doing so, the court said that "Martial law can never exist where the courts are open, and in the proper and unobstructed exercise of their jurisdiction." The court added that military rule "cannot arise from a *threatened* invasion. The necessity must be actual and present; the *invasion real,* such as effectively closes the courts and deposes the civil administration."[110] [Emphasis added.]

It appears that this precedent would provide an additional reason for forestalling the army from prosecuting violators of its individual exclusion orders. The civil courts were certainly fully functioning in 1942. Though an invasion of the coastal areas might have been threatened, (mainly in the minds of some military commanders,) it was far from actual, thus negating any military necessity for excluding civilians from the seacoast. Thus, with no military necessity for exclusion, and civilian courts in session, the actions of military tribunals to force civilians to stay out of huge areas of the country because of their "potential dangerousness" appear to lie on extremely dubious legal grounds. The military normally has no jurisdiction over civilians.[111] Without the extreme conditions of invasion or civil unrest where courts cannot operate, American citizens have the right to the normal legal proceedings provided for in the Constitution. All this may explain why, when tested by civilian excludees who refused to comply with its individual exclusion orders, domestic military commanders during World War II most often retreated into bitter complaints about the Justice Department's refusal to cooperate, but, in the end, meekly let the cases wither.

———————————————

1. Western Defense Command, *INDIVIDUAL EXCLUSION PROGRAM OF NON-JAPANESE*, Supplemental Report on Civilian Controls Exercised by the Western Defense Command (Jan. 1947), Part III, , 319.1, RG 338, Access 290, Box 9, NARA, Washington DC, p. 836. (Hereafter WDC Supplemental Report).

2. Arnold Krammer, *Undue Process: The Untold Story of America's German Alien Internees*, Rowman & Littlefield: 1997, p. 60. also Stetson Conn, *Guarding the U.S. and its Outposts*, p. 136.

3. WDC Supplemental Report, op cit, p. 848.

4. As an aside, it is interesting to note that where General DeWitt's original plans focused on removing enemy aliens from what he considered to be vulnerable coastal areas, his eventual programs for all three groups with roots in enemy nations ended up targeting primarily American citizens.

5. The program also went after a few American fascists—citizens of American birth with no connection to the enemy nations except an ideological one.

6. Executive Order 9066, as cited in *Only What We Could Carry*, ed. Lawson Inada, (Heyday Books: 2000), p. 401.

7. Peter Irons, *Justice at War*, Oxford U Press: 1983, p. 65.

8. Ibid, p. 68.

9. Ibid, p. 68.

10. The Tenney Committee also held five days of hearings in December, when its findings were not as well publicized, though they were, apparently, used in identifying enemy aliens to be rounded up shortly after December 7, 1941.

11. Rose Scherini, "When Italian Americans Were 'Enemy Aliens,'" in *Una Storia Segreta: The Secret History of Italian American Evacuation and Internment During World War II*, (Heyday Books: 2001), p. 22.

12. *San Francisco Chronicle*, May 26, 1942, p. 1.

13. *San Francisco News*, May 25, 1942, p. 1.

14. *Assembly Fact Finding Committee on Un-American Activities in California*, Committee transcript, May 25, 1942, San Francisco CA, Vol. XII, pp. 3375-76. (hereafter cited as "Tenney transcript.")

15. Quoted material from *San Francisco Chronicle*, May 26, 1942, and *San Francisco News*, May 25, 1942.

16. *San Francisco News*, May 26, 1942, p. 1.

17. Ibid., p. 3.

18. Ibid.

19. *San Francisco News*, May 28, 1942, p. 3.

20. Tenney transcript, op. cit., p. 3402.

21. Tenney transcript, op. cit., p. 3405.

22. *San Francisco Examiner*, May 26, 1942, p. 5.

23. This is not surprising, since hearings such as this are not required to share evidence with the defense. Indeed, there is no defense, nor are witnesses allowed to question those who accuse them. As Edward L. Barrett, in his study of the Tenney Committee (*The Tenney Committee*, Ithaca: Cornell U. Press, 1951) points out, "friendly" witnesses, such as Carmelo Zito, were allowed to dominate such hearings, making unchallenged accusations against which the "unfriendly" witnesses, those like Andriano and Rossi, were forced to defend themselves in a

highly biased context.

24. *San Francisco Examiner*, May 26, 1942, pp. 1 & 5.

25. Tenney transcript, pp 3418-19.

26. *San Francisco Examiner*, May 28, 1942, p. 7.

27. *San Francisco Chronicle*, October 12, 1942, "Andriano Ousted from Draft Job, Leitch Reveals."

28. Tenney transcript, pp 3687-89.

29. Tenney transcript, p. 3690.

30. Tenney transcript, p. 3702.

31. Tenney transcript, p. 3701.

32. Tenney transcript, pp. 3678-80.

33. Tenney transcript, p. 3663.

34. Tenney transcript, pp. 3667-68.

35. *San Francisco Examiner*, May 28, 1942, p. 7.

36. The War Department created the Individual Exclusion Program on August 19, 1942. Issel, p. 153.

37. This information is redacted from the eleven steps outlined in the WDC Supplemental Report, cited above, pp. 839-841. Quoted material is from same report.

38. PRELIMINARY REPORT ON STUDY OF INDIVIDUAL EXCLUSION ORDER CASES, RG 107, Entry 183, General Correspondence of John J. McCloy, 1941-1945, Boxes 5-13, NARA II. p. 28. Hereafter cited as "DOJ Exclusion Report."

39. Reports available to the board included Andriano's FBI case file, including the first accusation on July 18, 1939 from a confidential informant that Andriano directed a school where "children of Italian parentage are taught fascist ideology," and later allegations from those like Myron B. Goldsmith, a member of the American Legion, and Antonio M. Cogliandro, a former president of the Speranza Italiana Masonic lodge, both of whom testified against Andriano before the Dies Committee Hearings on UnAmerican Activities in July/August of 1940. There, Goldsmith, who admitted his testimony came mainly from Cogliandro and Carmelo Zito, asserted that "Andriano's leadership in the Italian Chamber of Commerce and in the Italian language classes for children held after school hours constituted prima facie evidence that the lawyer served Mussolini." He added that, "This man [Andriano], is indubitably the fountain head of all Fascist activities on the Pacific Coast. He is always one of the principal speakers at all Fascist gatherings where his reiterated theme is 'Our Light Comes from Rome.'" Cogliandro joined Goldsmith in singling out both Andriano and Father Joseph Galli, the pastor of Saints Peter and Paul Church, as Fascist leaders. Galli came under attack for his sponsorship of an alleged Fascist organization, the Gruppo Giovanile Italo-Americani, a North Beach ethnic pride drill team and marching band that Andriano also supported. (see William Issel, *For Both Cross and Flag: Catholic Action, Anti Catholicism, and National Security Politics in World War II San Francicsco*, (Temple U Press: 2010), 153 & 124-127).

40. Ibid. (DOJ Exclusion report).

41. "Announcement of Individual Exclusion Hearing Board," WDC letter to Nino Guttadauro, September 1, 1942, in possession of Angelo deGuttadauro.

42. Ibid.

43. "Exclusion is a Four-Letter Word," by Angelo deGuttadauro, in *Una Storia Segreta*, op cit, p. 158.

44. Ibid, p. 159.

45. Ibid, pp. 159-60.

46. Ibid, p. 160.

47. Ibid.

48. Letter, March 14, 1944, "I am an American Day," in possession of Angelo deGuttadauro.

49. WDC Supplemental Report, op. cit., p. 842.

50. DOJ Exclusion Report, pp. 2-3.

51. Krammer, op cit, p. 61 and note 49, Chapter 5, p. 186.

52. Individual Exclusion Order A-7, to Ettore Patrizi, 2700 Pierce St., San Francisco, CA, Patrizi file, NA.

53. Memo, Processing of Exclusion Order A-7—Ettore Patrizi, to Major Ray Ashworth, Chief of Interior Security Branch, Patrizi file, NA.

54. Letter, Oct. 14, 1942, Ettore Patrizi to War Relocation Authority, and Evacuee Report by Victor Furth, Asst. Chief, Evacuee Property Division, Patrizi file, NA.

55. See Scherini, op cit, p. 23.

56. Letter to Senator Hiram Johnson, 30 November 1943, RG 107, Entry 183, General Correspondence of John J. McCloy, 1941-45, Boxes 5-13.

57. "Other 'Aliens' the U.S. Put in Camps," by Steve Magagnini, *San Francisco Chronicle*, Aug. 14, 1981, p. 24.

58. WDC Supplemental Report, op cit, p. 853.

59. Ibid, p. 854. The United States Attorney in San Francisco, it should be noted, recommended that Andriano *not* be excluded. However, according to William Issel, "Andriano's Ordeal," Mills College Faculty talk, Apr. 23, 2008, the FBI had been assembling information on Andriano since 1939, and by 1941 considered him "one of the strongest pro-Fascist sympathizers in the San Francisco Area." Based on this and other statements by informants, as well as its own surveillance of Andriano, the FBI, supported by Assistant Secretary of War John McCloy, attempted to persuade Attorney General Biddle to prosecute Andriano for violation of Public Law 503 (i.e. for violating his exclusion order). The Attorney General refused on both the grounds that the exclusion program itself was based on shaky legality and that Andriano's would be a poor case to test its validity.

60. Ibid.

61. Sylvester Andriano to James Hagerty, October 21, 1942, pp. 1-2. from Dr. James Leo Hagerty Collection, Box 215, Folder: Letters to Sylvester Andriano, St. Mary's College of California Archives.

62. James Hagerty to Sylvester Andriano, All Saints Day (Nov. 1), 1942, p. 1, Hagerty Collection, op. cit.

63. Ibid, November 15 & 20, 1942.

64. William Issel, in *For Both Cross and Flag,* op. cit., argues that Andriano was targeted in large part due to his position as a conservative Roman Catholic with a leading role in the group Catholic Action. This put him in the sights of far-left forces such as the Mazzini Society and other leftists in San Francisco (of course, part of the reason for the bitter antagonism of Mazzinians and leftists towards the Catholic Church had to do with the Church's continuous opposition to Italian unity and independence during the Risorgimento—Italy's fight for independence. In the battle for the Roman Republic in 1849, for example, the Pope, Pius IX, called on French forces to lay siege to Rome, which it did, and restore him to his temporal power, which it did. Austrian and Neapolitan forces joined in this attack on republicanism. Mazzinian opposition to organized Catholicism, therefore, stemmed from the political conflict, i.e. the Papacy siding with foreign monarchies in attacks on its own Italian people, and not the other way round). The abstract of Issel's *Pacific Historical Review* (Vol. 75, 2 (May 2006)

essay, "Still Potentially Dangerous in Some Quarters," begins as follows: "The charges that led Gen. John L. DeWitt to deport Sylvester Andriano from the Western Defense Region in 1942 were bogus, the product of an anti-Catholic campaign by Communist Party activists, Masonic anti-Catholics in the Italian community, and recent Italian anti-Fascist exiles (*fuorusciti*)." Though Issel is undoubtedly right in asserting that Andriano's San Francisco opponents had anti-Catholic biases, it is equally true that their antagonism was fiercely political as well (as Issel admits above). The fact that Andriano had well-publicized associations with conservative Catholicism (itself associated with the fascist government) played directly into the hands of Andriano's anti-fascist opponents, but it would still appear that, as already stated above, leftist opposition to Catholicism stemmed from the longstanding political antagonism between the two, not the other way round.

65. Andriano to Hagerty, October 28, 1942, op. cit.

66. Andriano to Hagerty, November 17, 1942, op.cit.

67. It might be noted that Italian culture makes a necessity of having "friends with influence." Almost no one believes that a powerful adversary can be overcome by considerations of "right" or "justice." Intervention by a powerful protector is always preferred. This cultural predilection can be seen dramatized in the iconic Italian novel, *I Promessi Sposi*, by Alessandro Manzoni. Each development in the novel involves an appeal to a higher power to counteract a similar move by the criminal elements persecuting the heroes, Lorenzo and Lucia. Roberto Saviano's book *Gomorrah* (Farrar Straus: 2007), about the criminal syndicate, the Camorra, in Naples, makes the same point: "Around here, you always need a protector, someone who can at least get your foot in the door [i.e. for a job, ed.], if not the rest of you. Presenting yourself without a protector is like showing up without arms and legs." p. 260.

68. Andriano to Hagerty, November 25, 1942, op. cit.

69. Andriano to Hagerty, November 17, 1942, op. cit.

70. Ibid., p. 3.

71. Andriano to Hagerty, March 10, 1943, pp. 12-15.

72. Andriano to Hagerty, June 24, 1943, pp. 2-3. The copy of the General's letter is dated June 5, 1943, refers to the original exclusion order, and reiterates that order. It is quite clear from this episode that the agents Andriano refers to as "F.B.I's" were military agents from the 4th Army and General DeWitt.

73.. Ibid., p. 4.

74. Andriano to Hagerty, July 19, 1943, p. 1.

75. Andriano to Hagerty, October 21, 1942, p. 1.

76. Ibid., p. 5.

77. Andriano to Hagerty, April 10, 1943, p. 3. This comparison of his ordeal to a small version of Christ's "cross" brings to mind the similar metaphor employed by Prospero Cecconi, when he titles the diary he kept during his internment "Via Crucis."

78. Andriano to Hagerty, August 26, 1943, p. 1.

79. Andriano to Hagerty, July 19, 1943, p. 1.

80. Andriano to Hagerty, November 17, 1942, p. 2.

81. Andriano to Hagerty, June 22 & July 29, 1942.

82. Andriano to Hagerty, October 21, 1942, p. 3.

83. William Issel ("Andriano's Ordeal," Mills College faculty talk, 4/23/08) notes that among the twenty-two business and political leaders who telegraphed FDR on Andriano's behalf were District Attorney and later governor Edmund G. "Pat" Brown.

84. The FBI continued its investigation of Sylvester Anddriano even after he was paroled

and returned to San Francisco. J. Edgar Hoover wanted to indict Andriano on criminal chargers, this time on the grounds that during his term as president of the Italian Chamber of Commerce, he had failed to meet some of the formal requirements of the Registration Act for foreign-sourced organizations. But finally, on April 13, 1944, Assistant Attorney General Tom Clark ordered Hoover to discontinue all investigatory proceedings against Sylvester Andriano (J. Edgar Hoover to Asst AG Tom C. Clark, Feb.12, 1944, and Tom C. Clark to the Director, April 13, 1944, FBI Files 100-32005-121 and 134), see Issel op.cit., p. 164.

85. Krammer, op cit, p. 61.

86. Krammer, op cit, p. 66.

87. Memo, Francis Biddle to FDR, 17 April 1943, as cited in Krammer, p. 67.

88. See much more on Bosia's story in his book, *The General and I*, (Phaedra Press: 1971), and in *Una Storia Segreta*, op cit, pp 286-87 and pp 290-302.

89. Ibid.

90. PRELIMINARY REPORT, op cit, p. 18.

91. Ibid., p. 19.

92. Ibid.

93. These vessels were those of the Italian merchant seamen subsequently interned at Missoula, Montana. Though they had nothing to do with Italian Americans, nor the war (they were caught in American ports in Spring of 1940), any association with them was apparently looked upon with suspicion by American authorities. Nereo Francesconi, who on his radio broadcast, advocated sending them clothing and supplies in their internment, found this appeal used against him with regard to his allegedly pro-Fascist leanings, and was interned in Missoula with them. Here, the mere presence of Angelini in a photograph with Italian sailors who had crippled their own boats is used as evidence of his "dangerousness" and helped lead to his exclusion.

94. PRELIMINARY REPORT, op cit, p. 20.

95. Ibid, p. 5.

96. Ibid.

97. Ibid, p. 6.

98. Ibid.

99. Ibid., p. 28

100. Ibid., p. 28. It might be noted that this concept of "potential danger" is precisely the one espoused by Vice President Richard Cheney in his so-called "one-hundred percent doctrine," i.e., that unless the F.B.I. (or any other enforcement agency) could say with one hundred percent certainty that suspect persons (in this case, the Lackawanna Six) were *not* planning an attack, the F.B.I. should apprehend them.

101. Memo, Francis Biddle to Hugh Cox and J. Edgar Hoover, July 16, 1943, found in file of Nino Guttadauro.

102. PRELIMINARY REPORT, op cit, p. 29.

103. Ibid.

104. Ibid., p. 10.

105. Ibid., p. 33.

106. Ibid.

107. Ibid.

108. Ibid. p. 34.

109. Ibid., p. 35.

110. All quotes from Peter Irons, *Justice at War*, op. cit., 146. Irons notes that James Purcell

argued on the basis of *Ex Parte Milligan* in defending his client, Mitsuye Endo, who was interned with the rest of the Japanese. The Supreme Court in the Endo case, however, ruled against the majority precedent of the Milligan case, and sided with the minority in Milligan, which argued that the military *did* have authority over civilians.

111. The other legal precedent forbidding military control over civilians is the Posse Comitatus Act of 1878, now Title 18 US Code, Part 1, Chapter 67. It provides penalties for military attempts to impose its rule over civilians in these words: "Whoever, except in cases and under circumstances expressly authorized by the Constitution or Act of Congress, willfully uses any part of the Army or Air Force as a posse comitatus or otherwise to execute the laws, shall be fined not more than $1,000 or imprisoned not more than two years or both." Cited from *Washington U. Law Quarterly*, Vol 75, #2, Summer 1997, online.

VI: THE PLIGHT OF FISHERMEN

On December 7, 1941, the Gloucester, Massachusetts fishing vessel, *Santa Maria*, owned and mastered by Pietro Mercurio, a naturalized United States citizen, was boarded by the Coast Guard. Upon hearing the Italian language spoken on board, the Coast Guard immediately detained the captain and his crew, releasing Mercurio later that night. The members of the crew, unnaturalized Italian aliens, were kept overnight and prohibited from reboarding the boat; they subsequently worked at fish-processing plants until they gained citizenship.[1]

For the many immigrants of Italian descent working as American fishermen, this incident was a harbinger of what was to come in the months following the Japanese attack on Pearl Harbor, and the declaration of war between the United States and Italy four days later. The crews of fishing boats operating throughout United States coastal waters, composed of Italian (mainly Sicilian) "enemy aliens," would be grounded indefinitely. Many of these same enemy aliens would be forced to move out of West Coast prohibited zones, and many others, the boat owners who were mostly naturalized U.S. citizens, would have to turn over their boats to the U.S. Navy.

None of these measures could have been implemented without months, if not years of preparation. In fact, since at least 1936 the United States Navy had been making plans for the emergency it would face in the event of what it called an ORANGE WAR—code for an expected war with Japan. The plans stemmed from two major concerns. First, the United States felt vulnerable chiefly along its 12,383 miles of seacoast,[2] a weakness which the Japanese would exploit with the attack on Pearl Harbor, and which, with war, left the

West Coast's 7,623 miles of seacoast (5,580 of them in Alaska) virtually unprotected. On the East Coast, submarine wolf packs from Germany that had long been roaming the Atlantic in the early days of the war sank hundreds of American merchant ships, while fears of sabotage rocketed even higher with the near destruction, in February 1942, of the *SS Normandie,* a passenger liner docked in New York Harbor. Second, the U.S. Navy was seriously under-funded and lacked not only personnel but equipment—the patrol boats, sub-chasers and minesweepers it knew it would need to protect its coast. Something had to be done quickly to fill that lack.

Accordingly, a major portion of American military strategy early in the war focused on protecting the American coastline, not least by instituting measures designed to safeguard the nation from the threat of sabotage from within and possible invasion from without. With regard to both measures, the presence in the American fisheries of thousands of fishermen with roots in the enemy nation of Italy led the U.S. Navy, by accident or design, to concentrate much of its early fire on them. As noted in previous chapters, the most extreme measures were implemented along the West Coast, apparently due to the fact that the Japanese attack had taken place in the Pacific Ocean. But the nation's ports and docks all along the eastern and southern coasts—Boston and Gloucester and Philadelphia, Norfolk and Charleston and Jacksonville, Pensacola and New Orleans and Galveston—were all under severe restriction as well. Across at least four of the main U.S. port entrances—San Francisco, San Diego, Seattle and Boston—steel nets were stretched below the surface to block or discourage the entry of enemy submarines. The net guarding San Francisco's Golden Gate, for example, extended for three miles, from the St. Francis Yacht Club on the south side of the Gate to Point Sausalito on the north, and ranged from 30 feet deep near the shore to a depth of 150 feet in the central channel where maximum water depth reached 392 feet. Ten-ton concrete anchors held the net in place, while a thousand-yard movable section was set up a quarter mile off the San Francisco side to allow the wartime traffic to pass. Two net tenders were moored at each end, both attached to the sea floor by huge anchors; together they controlled this gate within a gate by activating powerful winches— two to pull the huge movable section open, two to pull it closed.[3]

These and other measures had a devastating effect on fishing, and the lives of fishermen. As a Monterey, California newspaper put it in retrospect, "Anti-submarine precautions at San Francisco killed sardine fishing, for all practical purposes, on the first day of the war."[4] This was no small matter, for the Pacific fishery had become, in the days leading up to the war, one of the world's richest and most advanced. From tuna in San Diego, to squid in San Pedro, to sardines in Monterey, to crab and herring in San Francisco, to salmon from Santa Cruz north to Alaska, the Pacific fishery, much of it manned by Genoese and Sicilian immigrants, had been experiencing a boom of epic proportions before the war. The sardine industry especially—including not just the fishing, but the canning of these fish for food and the processing of them for fertilizer—had been racing to ever-new heights like a modern gold rush. Employing purse seiners—huge diesel-powered vessels eighty or ninety feet long that could store up to one hundred fifty tons of fish in their holds, and another fifty tons on deck—Sicilian-born fishermen were hauling in staggering tonnages of the sardine schools that homed in on Monterey Bay and its environs from August to February. The tuna fishing and canning industry, centered mainly in San Diego, with numerous Italians working in both ships and canneries, was booming as well.

With the attack on Pearl Harbor, all this activity came to an abrupt halt. This was because the military authorities were more than a little concerned about the national origins of so many of the nation's fishermen, and their tendency to isolate themselves from all but relatives and friends in the fishery. Due to the nature of fishing itself as a more or less ingrown, almost genetic way of life, son followed father to the sea, boat crews were related, if possible, and even the language used to impel crews into action remained Sicilian, as it had for generations. The corollary to this world and its still-Italian ways was that hundreds, if not thousands, of America's fishermen on the eve of the war still lacked American citizenship. The result was that right after Pearl Harbor, fear spread through docks and wharves and fishing boats, fear that for those without citizenship, not just one's loyalty to America was questioned, not just one's possessions and movements were proscribed, but one's entire habitat was under threat. The waterfront everywhere, the whole Pacific coast—indeed the whole U.S. coast—had become a zone of suspicion. Though in some places a fisherman without proper identification might still approach the docks to check on his boat, if he were an enemy alien he certainly could not. As Captain Stanley Parker, the senior Coast Guard officer and Captain of the Port of San Francisco, put it in a January 27, 1942 letter to Dominick Strazulo of Monterey's Market Fisherman's Corporation (Strazulo had asked if Monterey's fishermen might be given some consideration since there was no clear border, no Golden Gate marking the boundary between Monterey's bay and the open sea):

> The movement of aliens is controlled by paragraph 10 of the President's Proclamation of December 7, 1941. This forbids movement except in compliance with the regulations issued by the attorney general...The movement from the waters of a port or

bay to the high seas is across a coastal frontier and is, in my opinion, of much greater significance than movement from home to office or church. I have taken the position that alien enemies may not pass this frontier casually, but only in compliance with the attorney general's regulations. Until they are issued, I assume that such movement is not permitted.[5]

In short, if you were an alien fisherman plying offshore waters, you could pretty much forget about fishing. And if you were a fisherman in San Francisco, alien or not, you were in trouble. That port, in 1941 considered the most vital on the Pacific Coast, was closed to commercial traffic completely. This meant that no fishing or merchant or pleasure boats, no matter their size or the composition of their crews, were allowed to pass through the Golden Gate into the open Pacific Ocean. Period.[6]

Still, the sardine fishermen could not accept the idea that their whole season, not yet completed, with billions of sardines waiting to fill out a record year, could be so unceremoniously scuttled. As the Sardine Fishermen's Association wrote in another letter to Captain Parker, what about the nourishment the sardines supplied to U.S. forces? What about sardine oils, so critical as to be controlled as a national defense priority? What about the fact that the sardine fleet in San Pedro—the 11th Naval District—had been allowed to go to sea? On December 9, 1941, Captain Parker wrote a memo to the Chief of Staff, 12th Naval District, asking for his opinion about these matters:

> 1. The Captain of the Port has insisted upon keeping commercial vessels, including fishermen and also including yachts, within the harbors of the 12th Naval District until the situation clarifies itself.
> 2. Representatives of the Sardine Fishermen's Association have called twice upon the Captain of the Port to plead their case for relaxation in their favor of this restriction of operation at sea...
> 3. The operators of fifty-five of these boats are intensely anxious to take advantage of favorable conditions now existing and have reported that under an arrangement with the Captain of the Port of San Pedro similar vessels are now permitted to proceed to sea. The Association's representatives agree to eliminate from their crews all but native-born individuals and naturalized citizens other than Japanese and Italians. In other words, Japanese and Italians, even though naturalized, are to be eliminated from the crews, and the Captain of the Port would be supplied with a list of the vessels concerned, the names of the masters, and cards containing the names of the crew members of each vessel.[7]

In short, the sardine fishermen, aware of how serious was the trouble they were in, were agreeing to do just about anything to salvage their season. Unfortunately, their best wasn't going to be good enough. Though the Coast Guard commander was sympathetic, he had to get his orders from the chief of the 12th Naval District, and relief wasn't forthcoming from that quarter, at least not for a good long time.

Indeed, conditions for fishermen in the early days of the war got progressively worse. Not only were those branded "enemy aliens" not allowed to fish, they were subjected to increasingly more onerous restrictions: no movement without permission; no possession of shortwave radios, cameras, flags, or flashlights; no going anywhere near the wharf even to mend nets or play cards or sniff the sea air that was their life blood. As Benny Palazzalo, president of the Fishermen's Association of Boston put it: "Take a man off the water after he's fished thirty or forty years and give him a laborer's job ashore, and he's dead."[8] In early February, with the new regulations forcing enemy aliens to register, and carry pink ID booklets, things looked even more funereal: if you were one of those required to carry a booklet, you were already buried.

Tom Cutino's I.D. allowed him access to the port at Monterey.

Thus it was reported that not even the father of the great Joe DiMaggio could get within blocks of Fisherman's Wharf, not even to look in on his son's San Francisco restaurant. Giuseppe DiMaggio, along with his wife, were enemy aliens. The same was true of hundreds of fishermen, all of whom knew each other, many of whom were related with names like Aiello and Mercurio and Maniscalco, fishing out of ports from Seattle to San Pedro, from the Delta towns of Pittsburg and Martinez to the barranca at Santa Cruz. Go near the wharf at any of those places and you were sure to be questioned and inspected, and maybe jailed. Maybe you would even be sent to the internment camps like both Maioranas, the Sercias, one of the Billantes, an Aliotti—all of them fishermen in San Francisco until one day they and several others were gone, and no one knew where, or what for, or how many more were about to join them.

Nor was that all. Scuttlebutt was, the West Coast generals had been huddling with the admirals and the Justice Department lawyers, and they had decided that not only were enemy aliens prohibited from going onto or near the wharves, they were, in late February, going to be prohibited from being anywhere near the water at all. Which was going to be a serious problem, for where else would a fisherman live but as close to his work as possible? No matter. On February 24, everyone with a pink booklet was going to have to move away from the West Coast entirely, with no one agreeing on how far. In Eureka, it might be only a few feet, to the east side of Highway 101. In Pittsburg you had to get out of town completely. The same in Monterey, though again, no one seemed to know how far: east of Highway 1, to be sure, but while some Montereyans moved to nearby Salinas, others traveled all the way to San Jose.

For most it didn't matter much at that point, for already, in December and on into January and February, what no doubt was the worst blow of all had already struck, focused this time not just on the aliens, but on the boat owners—American citizens for the most part, owners of the most advanced and expensive boats on the coast. The navy needed their purse seiners. And there was no arguing. The deal had already been cut.

The Seizure of Boats

As noted above, the U.S. Navy had been planning for an ORANGE war with Japan since the mid-1930s. One of its main concerns involved the possibility, or even likelihood that the enemy would plant mines in American harbors. A November 1938 memo from the commandant of the 12th Naval District in San Francisco to the Chief of Naval Operations in Washington, D.C., laid out the problem, specifically mentioning the purse seiners used for sardine fishing:

> 1. The Planning section of the Twelfth Naval District has been much concerned with the problem of achieving security of San Francisco Harbor and its approaches immediately before and during the period of Fleet concentration preparatory to an ORANGE war. Only three XAMs [minesweepers, ed.] are listed for this District, and their availability or even presence at the time of a sudden emergency is problematical.
> 2. It is envisioned that the outbreak of an ORANGE war may be not only undeclared, but sudden, and disclosed by an incident on the Pacific Coasts of the United States, such as the planting of mines by submarines or a submarine campaign against merchant or naval vessels. If such an incident were to occur, instant defense measures

would be required for San Francisco Harbor, and this would require, with little or no notice, such vessels as might be available and suitable for minesweeping. Little or no time would be available for alterations. The only class of such vessels probably available in considerable numbers is the purse seiner class, discussed in references (c) and (d).[9]

Of equal or greater significance in the remainder of this memo was the reference to the navy's anticipation of using such vessels *along with their crews*—crews made up of mainly Italian fishermen:

> Personnel of the fishing boats are being investigated and it is believed that an adequate number of boats will be found available with crews already aboard suitable for this work. Future correspondence will cover the advisability of inducting an appropriate number of these men into the Naval Reserve.

Lieutenant Commander Grant Stephenson was then recommended as a consultant to investigate purse seiners and their crews, with the memo signed by W.R. Gherardi, the acting commandant.

This, then, was the impetus for what would transpire almost immediately following Pearl Harbor in the 12th and other Naval Districts: the seizure of fishing vessels, most of them owned by Italian Americans, for use by an American navy not yet equipped to defend its coasts. To prepare for this, the navy had to determine, first, how well purse seiners could serve as minesweepers, sub-chasers and other types of patrol craft: were they fast enough? powerful enough? what would have to be done to convert them into a general class fit to serve in possibly hostile conditions? To answer such questions, surveys would have to be conducted, and negotiations with owners and with the Maritime Commission would have to be engaged in to decide how the commission, acting for the navy, would compensate the boat owners—by either buying the vessels outright, or by chartering them for a monthly fee—and what compulsions to use if the owners proved reluctant.

Naval memos reveal much discussion about these matters. The experience of England and Canada, both of which had already, by 1940, drafted fishing boats along with their crews, into a naval reserve, proved invaluable. So did experiments, begun in Boston's 1st Naval District, to convert the large east coast fishing trawlers into mine sweepers. A memo, "Arrangement of Vessels Converted to Naval Auxiliaries (XAM) Mine Sweepers," was sent to the commandants of all sixteen naval districts on July 6, 1940, and included the following attachment regarding specifications for the conversion of purse seiners:

> Install two 50 cal. A.A. machine guns in the following locations: (1) on top of the After Deck House, the gun to be located on the centerline of ship about 12" aft of frame #6;

(2) on the Forecastle Deck, the gun to be located on the centerline of ship at about frame #44.

Provide a circulating water-cooling system for each of the 50 cal. A.A. machine guns...

Install magazine in Hold..

Remove the fish hoist and foundation for same located on the Forecastle Deck...[10]

The memo contained additional information about reinforcing the boat structure to support the new equipment, but the template for the purse seiner conversions, including the mackerel seiners in use in eastern ports like Boston and Gloucester, was in place.

By this date in 1940, to be sure, specifics about purse seiners had already been forwarded to the navy by inspectors, who had been inspecting the boats for many months. Such specifics included lists of boats and their owners, as well as the characteristics of both the boats and their crews for duty as mine sweepers. A February 1939 memo from Admiral Hepburn, commandant of the 12th Naval District, to the Chief of Naval Operations in Washington, for example, opened by noting that "approximately 100 vessels" had been "discreetly" inspected, and their personnel evaluated by such experts as the assistant chief of the California Fish & Game Bureau, an admiralty lawyer, a manager of a fish-packing company, and others.[11] It described the physical characteristics of purse seiners including equipment, hold capacity, engine specs, radio-telephone equipment, and ended with the observation that "the ships are extremely sturdy, generally well-powered, and are adapted to naval use," except for defects such as small living quarters, inadequate sanitary facilities, and a lack of space to mount guns. Such defects did not disqualify the seiners for duty, however, since a memo the following year from the Bureau of Ships to the 13th Naval District in Seattle suggested that the conversion of purse seiners to minesweepers could proceed. After a description of ownership patterns, the last five pages of Admiral Hepburn's eleven-page memo were devoted to the most sensitive part of the matter, the personnel.

To begin with, the memo evaluates the worth of each major group of fishermen then operating—Slavonians, Italians, Scandinavians, Japanese. Then, after a short paragraph on Scandinavians, most of them Norwegians from Puget Sound and said to be "good seamen, good fishermen, good navigators, and intelligent good citizens," the memo moves on to the Italians. As a textbook case of stereotyping, it is worth quoting at length:

Italians. The Italians are sprung from the south of Italy and Sicily. Many of them are second-generation Americans. They are fundamentally paternalistic and have a tight family operation with great authority vested in the head of the family. They are volatile in nature and are therefore not completely reliable. Those who came from Italy are Italian in loyalty, although perhaps naturalized United States citizens, which would be for the purpose of avoiding payment of "light money"—more special taxes on foreign-owned vessels. Their American-born sons are loyal citizens, except that they are accustomed to doing as their fathers tell them, and their loyalty to Italy, if opposed to the United States, is probable...

The majority of the Italians are not good seamen, good fishermen, nor good navigators. They are not over-intelligent, do not know the Rules of the Road, and, in general, appear to have the characteristics of big overgrown children. However, among the captains, 15% to 20% may be selected who are considerably above the average in intelligence and leadership, and are, in general, reliable men...

The packers [who owned many of the boats, ed.] are of the opinion that the Italians, in addition to being volatile and excitable, are not energetic, would rather tie up to the dock than fish, and, as a rule, do not have the courage to prosecute an energetic naval task independently.

...The above remarks apply more generally to the crews than to the captains and the majority of the crews can be made into competent deckhands who will obey orders with moderate intelligence, but are incapable of much more.[12]

Though most of this is self-explanatory, the speculation about why Italian boat owners have become citizens—to avoid paying special taxes—is not only a slander upon the owners' loyalty, it is also likely to have been inaccurate. As other documents make clear, as early as 1936, fishermen themselves were proposing to eliminate all alien owners of boats in the California fishing fleet, a move which made U.S. citizenship not just advisable but virtually mandatory. Moreover, Peter Ferrante of Monterey wrote a letter in March 1939 on behalf of a Monterey boat-owners' group *complaining* that only a few had been asked to join a naval reserve: "Some of these men who have asked me to write to you are American-born boys of Italian descent and they feel as though they have been slighted when naturalized citizens have been asked to join the naval reserve and they have not."[13] In short, both Sicilian boat owners who became American citizens and their American-born sons were proud enough of their Americanization to complain when they were left out of their new nation's call to arms.

Nonetheless, with the dominant assessment of Italians conforming to the racism ("big overgrown children") expressed in Admiral Hepburn's memo, it is not surprising to learn that, in the end, the U.S. Navy decided *against* drafting the fishing crews along with their purse seiners. A July 16, 1940 memo from the commandant, 12th Naval District, to the chief of the Bureau of Navigation listed some of the expected problems: the reluctance of fishermen to sign a four-year contract in the naval reserve; most fishermen's need to be assured that they would serve on their own boats, with their own crews (which would force the navy to accept men with "physical disabilities and other disqualifications"); and the requirement that fishing-boat captains would have to be given petty officer ratings for which most were not qualified. The memo ended with a reference to the problem of allegedly "hyphenated" loyalties:

> American citizens may be obtained but the advisability of taking into the naval service large groups of men of hyphenated loyalty is open to question.[14]

The conclusion was obvious: "the enlistment of West Coast fishermen on a large scale in the naval reserve is undesirable and is impracticable now." It remained so for the duration of the war.

This did not end the problem for fishermen, however, for though the U.S. Navy found them personally undesirable and/or unfit, it found their purse seiners (which had always been at the core of the initiative) both desirable and fit not only for conversion, but for seizure in numbers so large as to, in the words of the Navy itself, "cripple the canning and reduction industries in Monterey and San Francisco."[15] Years later, Monterey fisherman Tom Cutino described what happened and how it had happened:

> My brother John had registered for the draft and had a prewar deferment for fishing. Then they took my father's boat. We were, I guess, desperate—there were all kinds of fears at the time, like would the block warden chastise you for having your lights on, and there was a big fear of going fishing. You were not even allowed on the wharf; there were armed guards there, and I still have my plastic I.D. card from the Coast Guard, which later allowed me to go out and fish.
>
> So these navy plainclothes guys came to our house, it was right after Pearl Harbor, a knock on the door, and they're telling my father, "Mr. Cutino, we need your boat." He was so fearful, he just said, "Go ahead, take it." No questions asked. As it turned out, in a few months they paid him for it, no depreciation.
>
> At that point, he just wanted them to take it, but they said, "We want you to bring the boat to Treasure Island." My uncle Orazio was one of the owners, but he was not naturalized. So he was afraid, my brother John didn't want to go, nobody wanted to go out there with the boat to San Francisco. But the navy pleaded with my father, gave him some patriotic talk, it's war, you know, and so finally my father and my Uncle Orazio and my brother all ran the boat up to San Francisco. And they were so fearful, of submarines and who knew what, that they nearly burned out the engine, which was pouring black smoke—they were going so fast. They finally got it to Treasure Island and left it and came back by the Del Monte Express, the train that used to run from San Francisco to Monterey in those days.[16]

Cutino Bros. in Monterey before the war.

Tom Cutino remembered that the delivery of their boat didn't end the matter, because his brother John, having subsequently joined the U.S. Navy, happened upon a fleet of requisitioned purse seiners while waiting for an assignment at Treasure Island in San Francisco Bay. A team of navy men were having great trouble removing the twenty-foot skiff from one of the seiners. John recognized the boat immediately and shouted, "Hey, that's my father's boat. I can do that." Since the navy men were having no success on their own, they agreed to let John try:

> And he says, "First thing, get everybody off the boat." The officer in charge was incredulous: "You mean you're going to get the skiff off by yourself?" John simply nodded. Then, he grabs hold of the skiff with the boom, and he maneuvers it not to the side but to the back, and lowers it over the stern, which is what you're supposed to do, and drops it gently into the water. After that they loved him, made him a second-class machinist's mate, no tests or anything, offering him whatever he wanted. So he asked to be put on his father's boat, and he was.[17]

Not long after, John Cutino, on his father's now navy-gray purse seiner, took part in tests to see if the seiners could function as sub chasers. In trying to drop depth charges, however, the seiners proved too slow to outrun their own explosives. When the mount for the .75 caliber cannon proved shaky as well, the attempt to make sub-chasers out of purse seiners was abandoned, and Cutino asked that his boat be assigned to Monterey. The navy complied, and it was employed there on patrol and for towing targets for naval aircraft—a move which allowed the elder Cutino to see his old boat, but see also that it was very far out of his reach.

Cutino Bros boat outfitted for naval duty.

Dozens of other Italian American boat owners shared the Cutinos' fate. Within a week after Pearl Harbor, sixteen Monterey purse seiners had been commandeered, including the *El Cortez*, the *Belvedere*, the *Western Star*, the *New Hope*, the *Redeemer*, the *San Giovanni*, the *Ardito*, the *Dante Alighieri*, the *Twin Brothers*, and the *Joe DiMaggio*. Two more from San Francisco and five from Berkeley and Oakland joined them. Even so, this might have left something of the sardine industry still operating, but as the 12th Naval District's history puts it, two more calls were received for additional vessels: "the first for fifteen vessels for outer patrol, and one vessel for army and mine planting." This took "the best of the Monterey and San Francisco purse seiners," probably on or about February 15, 1942. The second call was for "seventeen 'tuna clippers' and thirty-three purse seiners for use in the 15th Naval District," and came the next week, around February 23. Since the 15th Naval District included Hawaii, these latter boats would serve as far away as the Panama Canal Zone, Hawaii, and the Philippines. These were the seizures which added up to no less than forty-five purse seiners from Monterey and crippled the canning and reduction (reducing sardines to fertilizer) industries there and in San Francisco.[18]

This focus on Italian fishermen and their boats, the navy's protestations notwithstanding, left some fishermen feeling unduly targeted. Vitina Spadaro recalled the situation when her father, Giuseppe Spadaro, learned that his boat was to be taken:

> "What can we do," he said, "the government needs our boats." So he had to deliver his boat to San Francisco, to the navy. There must have been fifty boats from Monterey taken; it was a deal made by the boat owners' association. Being good Italians, they wanted to help the government, so they were willing to let the boats go. But up north they had a fishing fleet, mostly Scandinavians, and down south they also had a fishing fleet, mostly Slavonians. I feel the reason they wanted the Monterey boats was because they were Italians. They [i.e. the Italians, ed.] had to charter boats from up north and bring them down here to fish, to support their families. Why not take the boats up north?[19]

No one ever received an answer to this question. What was known was that, like many other Monterey boat owners, the Spadaros not only had to give up their boat, but because Spadaro's wife had not completed her citizenship process, had to give up their Monterey home as well. To make ends meet, Giuseppe Spadaro chartered a boat from Seattle for the next seasons until his own boat was decommissioned. But when he finally got it back, his *Marettimo* was in very poor shape: in addition to the damage from the gun mounts, the skiff (crucial for setting the sardine nets) was missing and the navy said it had been destroyed. When he said he needed funds to get the boat back in shape, the navy offered him $3,000, an amount he knew would be required just to replace the skiff. As other repairs would cost upwards of $15,000, he reported this to the navy, but they simply said, "Either you accept what we give you, or we keep your boat." Spadaro agreed to accept the $3,000, but, with a boat already chartered, he had to tie up the *Marettimo* for the season. When a huge storm swept into Monterey Bay, it wrecked the sidelined *Marettimo*, and Spadaro had to sell it at an almost total loss.

John Russo had a similar experience. His purse seiner, the *Star of Monterey*, which he had just purchased in 1940, was taken by the navy in February of 1942—at about the same time both his parents were forced to leave Monterey. Russo then chartered a boat from Seattle, but it was not easy:

> It's a loss. They took my boat, they took my job. You charter a boat, you right away have to give four shares to the boat owner. There's only eight shares for the boat and the net to begin with, so you've got four shares left. But four shares just about cover

expenses. At that time, we didn't have nylon nets, they were cotton, so we had to tan them, and every year we had to replace half the net. There goes the four shares. So essentially, I just made my own share [i.e. one of twelve crew shares, ed.]. And also, the capacity of the boat I chartered was only half of my boat, it packed only 80 tons where mine packed 145 tons, so what we make is cut in half to begin with.[20]

Like Giuseppe Spadaro, Russo found that his boat, when returned in 1943, required a good deal of work on rigging, replacing turntables, and so on, but was able to fish the next season. The coda to his story was that after the war, he managed to get the last deckload of sardines caught in Monterey.

This "last deckload" refers to the other aspect of the decimation of the sardine fleet. As noted above, World War II began for the United States smack in the middle of the great sardine bonanza. Many of the purse seiners taken by the navy had been recently purchased to take advantage of the apparently infinite schools of sardines waiting to be hauled in. But the sardines were not to last. In the first season after the war, 1946-47, the sardine catch in Monterey suddenly plummeted: from averaging around 200,000 tons in prior years, the 1946-47 catch totaled a meager 31,000 tons. San Francisco was hit even harder, recording only 2,869 tons that year. Something—overfishing, natural cycles, or some unknown combination of both—was decimating the Pacific sardine stock.[21] So not only did the navy deprive fishermen of their boats when they needed them most, but its wartime orders for naval craft overwhelmed the shipyards where boat owners, such as Sal Colletto of Monterey, were desperately trying to replace the boats taken by the navy. Though his complaints to the navy about this problem with shipbuilders did result in some speeding up of his boat order, Colletto in 1943 still had to compete with the shipbuilding bonanza created by the navy's ordering of ships for itself. The inflationary result was that he ended up paying almost twice as much for his new boat as he had for the original one he had purchased in 1939, and surrendered to the navy.[22]

Fishing Restrictions

Many of the restrictions placed on fishermen have already been noted. After the early closure of all ports, especially major ones like San Francisco, the navy and coast guard continued to issue memos outlining the rules and restrictions with which fishermen would have to comply. Some rules were uniform for all districts, while others varied with "special rules at each port." In the 12th Naval District, for example, as noted in an August 1942 Memo, the rules were phrased as follows:

All fishermen are issued licenses to fish by the Captains of the Port. On these licenses there is printed the restrictions that are placed upon them which, generally speaking, are as follows: That the fishermen have perfect freedom to fish anywhere on the coast that they see fit (except, of course, this does not include restrictions around the ports that have defensive sea areas). That they are absolutely forbidden to enter or leave any port in darkness or low visibility, or to land. Any violation of the restrictions printed on the license causes, of course, the forfeiture of the license and prosecution if considered necessary.[23]

This same memo makes clear that disagreements over the severity of the regulations persisted, especially where the Army was concerned, with naval officials more sympathetic to the need to allow fishermen to fish regardless of security fears:

The Army desires one hundred percent security and if steps are taken towards this end as desired by the Army there would be hardly a fish caught on the coast...any attempt at landing, entering or leaving any of the ports not covered by special regulations would lay the offending fisherman open to arrest or to be fired upon as he would be violating the instructions printed on his license.[24]

These instructions and regulations upon fishermen had been in place since the beginning of 1942. In February of 1942, for example, the Commander of the Patrol Force in the 12th Naval District wrote a memo warning that fishermen who violated the rules would have their licenses temporarily recalled, and that the licenses of boats that "repeatedly violate existing regulations...should be recalled and withheld for a longer period of time, to punish the owners for flagrant disregard of existing orders."[25] Shortly thereafter, on March 11, the Captain of the Port wrote back that

This office has been suspending the license of violators of the restricted areas. Violators are being notified that a second violation will result in the revocation of their licenses and such additional punitive action under existing law as the circumstances appear to warrant."[26]

Of course, to even get a license, there were hoops to jump through. In May of 1942, for example, a memo from the Commandant of the Coast Guard to District Coast Guard Officers and Captains of the Port mandated that in order to receive a license to leave local waters, the master or operator of the vessel had to be a U.S. citizen, "unless over 50% of the vessel's personnel complement are American citizens." The memo then underlined the prohibitions against enemy aliens, saying that none would be permitted to "go or remain on board any vessel unless such enemy alien is a passenger on a vessel primarily engaged in the transportation of passengers for hire." And just to make sure none would slip through, green (temporary) or pink ID cards with the stamp "Enemy Alien" prominently displayed were to be issued to all non-citizens from enemy nations. Since these restrictions applied at all ports nationwide, enemy aliens were effectively barred from all U.S. coasts (though aliens of non-enemy nations were still permitted to fish). Yet concerns about the putative danger enemy aliens posed still surfaced. A district intelligence officer, on May 6, 1942, submitted a memo to the District Coast Guard Officer requiring the periodic submission of lists to Captains of the Port throughout the 1st Naval District. The lists should include

> both citizen and alien fishermen who have participated in some suspicious activity, the evidence of which might be sufficient to warrant an indictment under the Espionage Laws, but whose continued presence on fishing vessels is undesirable because they represent potential carriers of military information or potential suppliers of fuel and food to enemy vessels....naturalized citizens who are suspected of subversive activities will have proceedings for denaturalization instituted against them.[27]

In short, it appears that officials worried that suspect fishermen might provide not only information but also actual supplies to enemy boats [see below]. Again, in October 1942, the Captain of the Port of San Francisco, responding to an inquiry from the Pittsburg CA Chamber of Commerce about the possibility of allowing Italian fishermen to operate in inland (as opposed to open ocean) waters, wrote without equivocation:

> No departure licenses shall be granted to any vessel having an enemy alien on board in any capacity, and...no vessel shall move in the local waters of the United States which has or intends to have an enemy alien on board in any capacity...Inasmuch as the Captain of the Port is governed by these Anchorage Regulations [contained in the Espionage Act of 1917, ed.] in the issuance of permits of fishing vessels, he has no authority to issue permits to boats with Italian citizens aboard in any capacity..[28]

Still, as already mentioned, the navy had reasons not to cripple the fishing industry entirely. So on January 30, 1942, it wrote that it would permit "as liberal a scope of operations as is consistent with national security." It went on to note that "crab-fishing vessels operating out of San Francisco at present do so under escort of a small Coast Guard boat, the purpose of which is to control the fishermen and serve to identify them in relation to our own forces."[29] In July of 1942, sardine fishing boats were given similar relief, when they were authorized to make passage at night, "provided they have complied with the law in all respects as to licenses, departure permits, crew lists and crew identification."[30]

As to other naval districts, and vessels other than purse seiners, the record, while not as complete, is still ample. In *Artillery at the Golden Gate*, Brian Chin writes that the

Harbor Defense Corps, commanded by Lieutenant Colonel Usis, took charge of at least sixteen crab boats, most requisitioned from Italian American fishermen in San Francisco. Chin points out that these crabbers served a private function in addition to their official one. That is, given that enemy aliens were prohibited from Fisherman's Wharf and that, according to the *San Francisco Chronicle*, the government "would rout approximately 1400 Italians from the 2,000 men employed in San Francisco's $500,000-a-year fishing industry," closing the city's commercial crabbing business, the same Colonel Usis, who now controlled the crab boats but was left without one of his favorite foods, decided on an expedient:

> Usis put the Mine Flotilla to work as a private crab fleet for the gastronomic ben-
> efit of the Harbor Defenses. The Mine Groupment commander equipped his mine
> yawls with crab pots obtained from the Coast Guard. Several recruits from the Mine
> Battalion had been crab fishermen in civilian life and they were now utilized by the
> command to do the same work in the army. When the yawls went out in the morning
> to service the mines, the crews set out the crab pots in the water. After the workday,
> mine crews hauled in the pots and headed back to the mine base at Fort Baker with
> their crab bounty.[31]

Crab boat outfitted for naval duty.

The ironic footnote to this story is that while most of San Francisco's crab fishermen were grounded and their boats taken for the national emergency—thus severely limiting the crab available for civilian consumers—Lt. Col. Usis's "emergency use" of their crab boats was providing not only a feast of abundant crab for himself and his men, but also for the "higher-ups of the Western Defense Command at the Presidio," probably including the rigidly authoritarian Lt. Gen. John DeWitt demanding ever harsher restrictions against the few fishermen still able to work.

Tony D'Amato's grandfather, Giuseppe Crivello, owned one of these crab boats, the *Virginia*, while his relatives owned no less than three other boats operating out of San Francisco. With the war, half the family's boats were requisitioned by the navy, the first to go being the *Virginia*. According to naval records, the *Virginia* was acquired on December 11, 1941, for use by the Coast Artillery, which strongly suggests it must have been one of the sixteen (the record says seventeen) boats mentioned above.[32] According to Carlo Crivello, the navy offered him $750 for the *Virginia*, but he refused the money. Instead, he told the navy, "Don't give me any money. I just want my boat back," apparently thinking he had a better chance of getting back to fishing if he didn't sell his boat outright. Though the *Virginia* was indeed returned to him, Crivello would live to regret that choice (see below).

Nor was it just west coast fishermen who endured wartime losses. Boston fishermen went through a similar ordeal. According to Frank Firicano, a long-time Boston fisherman and at one time secretary of his union, probably 300 Boston fishermen,[33] including his father, his grandfather, and several uncles, were grounded right after Pearl Harbor. Firicano also remembers that, as in San Francisco,

> They had a sub net in Boston harbor too. Because there's the Boston Navy Yard, and there were convoys leaving night and day from Boston. Eventually, they let us go fishing. We had to have a password each day, go to the Customs House to get clearance, a pass, and then on the way out, stop at a barge off Deer Island manned by the Coast Guard, and they would check out the boat to see we weren't taking provisions to the Germans. We were allowed provisions for seven, which was our crew. There was the steel gate—it opened, but no one could get out after 5 p.m. We had radio silence too; we had locks on the radios. Only in an emergency could you use it. We had to stop at the lightship, give them the password. When we returned, it was the same thing. We had to stop at the lightship, get the password of the day, and give it to the Coast Guard at the barge going in.[34]

Sal Patania, now retired from fishing, remembers the Boston requisitions as well:

> The government in those days took a lot of the boats. The guy I went fishing with after the war, he had a sixty-five footer and the government took it. There were a lot more. They took a lot of other boats; they used them for minesweepers.[35]

Sal's wife, Josie, also recalls what it was like within her family with her mother, her father, and her brothers all affected by restrictions:

> During the war, they took my father off the fishing boat. So he went to work in the spinach plant, washing the spinach. My brothers Carmelo, Angelo and Vincent were all in the service at this time. Carmelo and Vincent weren't even citizens. They swore them in before they went, Vincent to Normandy and Carmelo to the Philippines.
>
> My father had worked on a boat. He wasn't a citizen but he had a lot of children who were citizens. I went to work at age fourteen, to work in the 5 & 10, to bring some money in because they took my brothers.
>
> I remember filling up an alien card every year for my mother and father. We were witnesses. Then we made my mother go for citizenship. We taught her how to write her name and to say George Washington and Abraham Lincoln. If she saw Mussolini, we said to shoot him. They actually asked her that question. She said, "Me boom-boom."
>
> She had to leave her son, fifteen years old, in Italy, so he was drafted into the Italian service. That's why my brothers told them if they have a choice they'd rather not go to Italy. One said he wanted to go to Germany, one to the Philippines.
>
> And I remember when they took the boats. They used them to send them to war.[36]

Other fishermen recorded similarly devastating effects on their lives. These effects may be gauged by a letter written by Santa Cruz, California fisherman Giovanni Olivieri to California's U.S. Senator, Sheridan Downey, on the last day of 1941:

> Forty years ago I came to America from Italy. For the past 38 years I have been a fisherman in Santa Cruz and I have fished the waters of Monterey Bay. I am not an American citizen and cannot become one because I cannot read or write. I have been deprived of the right to fish because I am not a citizen. I have two sons in the navy and one son in the army. I have a wife and three daughters to support. I cannot get outside work because I am not a citizen. I am as loyal and devoted to this country as though I were born here. During my forty years in America I have never been arrested and have always worked from twelve to fourteen hours a day.[37]

Frances Marline Stephenson, of San Diego, also records the impact of the restrictions on her fisherman father. In a memoir titled "Promises," Stephenson reveals that her father, deprived of his ability to earn money, turned to alcohol. This, plus the threat of internment, so disturbed her American-born mother that she attempted suicide several times, and was institutionalized. Frances, working at a fish cannery, and later in an aviation plant, became the sole support of her family for a time.[38]

Boats Are Returned

World War II's impact on fishermen of Italian origin was not finished until the navy was finished with their boats. From late 1943 (after Italy joined the Allies) through 1945, it would have to decommission the hundreds of boats it had taken and either sell or give them back to the owners.[39] In the case of the purse seiner, *Cutino Brothers*, the boat was sold back for about $25,000, required another $25,000 in repairs, and ended up with the Cutinos in the black. Similarly, Anthony Bruno remembers that his father's seiner, the *St. Anthony*, was returned very well refurbished. In fact, working at the shipyards that did much of the repairs, he saw to it that the government commissioned the work his father wanted:

> Actually, it was in better shape than when they got it. It had a poop deck—a rear deck raised about a foot—so the boat could hold more fish. We found out it had been in Panama because we found the log and read it.[40]

This confirms the fact that the Maritime Commission's deal with individual boat owners varied as widely as the use to which the boats were put, the time of their return, and the condition they were in when handed back to their owners. Some boats had been purchased outright; some had been chartered with equipment, some without. The navy could do whatever it wished, for if boat owners got stubborn, a legal provision allowed the navy to simply set its own price and pay seventy-five percent of that, thereafter letting the owner sue for the rest in court—a prospect that few if any boats owners could have relished.[41] The same tactics could be used in returning boats.

The already-referred-to crab boat of Tony D'Amato's grandfather, the *Virginia*, is a case in point. It will be recalled that when the navy offered $750 to purchase the *Virginia*, Carlo Crivello told them to keep the money; he simply wanted the boat back. The navy complied, but, according to Crivello, "what we got back was a boat that was basically run into the ground. We got the shell of the boat, and an engine, and that was it." Furthermore, the navy demanded a payment of $1,000 for a boat they had been given free of charge and had then proceeded to "run into the ground." But having lost two boats to the navy and borne the stigma of enemy-alien status, the Crivello family bowed to the inevitable. They accepted the deal, never complained, and spent a good deal of money to have the *Virginia* restored.[42]

If there is a common thread running through such stories, it is surely that most fishermen of Italian descent sustained losses during World War II. If they were enemy aliens, they had been banned from fishing for nearly a year until late 1942, when newspapers announced that "alien Italians" were able to fish again—so long as they had proper I.D. cards, and were fishing on a boat with an American citizen as captain, or with a crew more than fifty percent American. Most had by this time also been allowed to return to their homes in prohibited zones. If they were boat owners, they had lost the use of their boats for periods ranging from two to four years. Whether they had been able to charter boats to use, or buy new ones, the requisition cost them money and, perhaps more important, time—for by the time they returned to fishing in full force, the sardine bonanza was about over. As to their returned boats, their condition depended on timing as well. Many fishermen maintain that the first boats to be returned were quite well restored, but that thereafter, the navy simply made a flat offer—take it or leave it—and returned the boats in varying degrees of disrepair. It could also be the case that the condition of the boats, as well as their time of return, depended upon the chance circumstance of where they had done service. Some boats, including a half-dozen from Monterey, were decommissioned as early as the spring of 1943. Others, for example the *Phyllis* and the *Dante Alighieri*, were not released until 1945. Whether this was due to the distant waters the latter had patrolled is not clear, for the record is mixed. A naval speedletter informs the 12th Naval District that the *Phyllis* was scheduled to depart from Panama for San Francisco on March 21, 1945,[43] but a similar letter about the *Dante Alighieri*, reportedly used for coastal duty near Monterey, simply says it was "delivered to war shipping administration and simultaneously returned to owner fourteen March nineteen hundred forty-five."[44] Nor does duty in distant places seem to be the deciding factor, for as earlier noted, Gus Bruno's *St Anthony* also did duty in Panama, and records indicate its "placed-out-of-service" date as May 12, 1943.[45] One must therefore attribute the varying experiences of boat owners to chance, or luck, or some as-yet-unknown level of influence, or some combination of these factors. Or perhaps to none at all. For what is apparent is that in the heat of the emergency sounded by Pearl Harbor, the navy, like the army, operated sometimes rigidly, sometimes wildly, sometimes chaotically and even comically. The fishermen were left to figure out what had happened, and why. Many of them would have concluded what Giuseppe Spadaro did when his teenaged daughter Vitina asked, "Why, why are they doing this to us?"

> "There's a war going on," he said. "People in command don't know what they're doing."[46]

---

1. *Report to the Congress of the United States: A Review of the Restrictions on Persons of Italian Ancestry During World War II,* U.S. Department of Justice, November 2001, p. 33.

2. If the shoreline were to include inner shorelines like New England's Long Island Sound, or the Chesapeake Bay, the total could reach 88,033 miles. (NB: much of the information in this chapter is derived from my essay, "A Fish Story," in *Una Storia Segreta: The Secret History of Italian American Evacuation and Internment During World War II*, ed. Lawrence DiStasi, (Heyday Books: 2001) 63-96.)

3. See Brian B. Chin, *Artillery at the Golden Gate: The Harbor Defenses of San Francisco in World War II* (Missoula, Mont.: Pictorial Histories Publishing Co. Inc., 1994), 41-42. In describing fishing for sardines outside the Golden Gate, a fisherman known as "Freckles" described what it was like during the war: "This was during the war, because we had a deadline at the Gate. You couldn't go in and out of the Gate anytime you pleased. We had a time we all had to meet as a convoy at the lightship where your identity was checked very carefully." Quoted in *Neptune's Apprentice: Adventures of a Comercial Fisherwoman,* by Marie DeSantis (San Francisco: Presidio, 1984), 69.

4. *Monterey Peninsula Herald*, February 27, 1942, p. 11.

5. Letter, Stanley Parker to Dominick Strazulo, RG 181, Records of Naval Districts and Shore Establishments, 12th Naval District (hereafter NDSE), Box 0294, NARA San Bruno.

6. At some point in early January, Elios Anderlini, the lawyer for the Crab Fishermen's Association of San Francisco, prevailed upon Earl Warren, California's attorney general, to arrange a meeting with the military authorities. An agreement emerged: "If the fishermen would assemble, the navy would convoy them out, en masse, early in the morning to fish for the day. They would then assemble at a certain time before dark to be convoyed back in." (Personal interview, Elios Anderlini, June 20, 2000. The agreement resembles a similar one forged for fishermen to pass through Boston's submarine net, see Firicano quote below.)

7. Memo, December 9, 1941, Stanley Parker to Chief of Staff, 12th Naval District, RG 181, 12th Naval District Commandant's Office, General Correspondence, Accession 58-3224, NARA SB.

8. Quoted in Louis Lyons, "Italians of Boston Lift Heads Again; 'Enemy' Ban is Off," *Boston Globe*, October 18, 1942, p. 27.

9. Memo, November 30, 1938, "Minesweeping by District Forces," RG 181, NDSE, Box S-432, NARA SB.

10. Memo, July 6, 1940, Bureau of Ships to Naval Districts, "Arrangement of Vessels Converted to Naval Auxiliaries (XAM) Mine Sweepers," with attachment, "Specifications for Emergency Conversion for Naval Use of Fish Trawlers Built by the Bethlehem Shipbuilding Co. Ltd., Quincy, Mass," RG 181, NDSE, Box S-432, NARA SB.

11. Memo, February 6, 1939, "Fishing Vessels Suitable for XAM(c)," RG 181, NDSE, Box S-432, NARA SB.

12. Ibid.

13. 1936 letter from Fishermen's Cooperative Association to the Los Angeles meeting of the American Legion; 1939 letter, Peter Ferrante & Monterey Sardine Industries, Inc., to 12th Naval District, RG 181, NDSE, Box S-432, NARA SB.

14. Memo, July 16, 1940, "Enrollment of Fishermen in Class V-6, USNR, for Service in their Own Vessels as Minesweepers," RG 181, NDSE, Box S-432, NARA SB.

15. *United States Naval Administration in World War II*, 12th Naval District, 1939-1945,

vol. III, p. 52, RG 181, NDSE, Box 1, NARA SB.

16. Tom Cutino, personal interview, July 12, 2000.

17. Ibid.

18. *U.S. Naval Administration in WWII*, op. cit., p. 52.

19. Vitina Spadaro, personal interview, October 2, 1999.

20. John Russo, personal interview, July 19, 2000.

21. Some Monterey fishermen, like Tom Cutino, maintain that the War Production Board's insistence on removing the limits on what an individual boat could catch [i.e. as a way of making up for the decrease in the overall catch its boat seizures had caused?] aggravated the problem. Before this, state-instituted limits had led to conservation: if a boat netted more fish than its limit, it would usually call another boat and share its catch rather than discard hundreds of tons of dead fish. Fishing without limits, by contrast, gave fishermen the incentive to simply discard the excess fish and race in to the cannery to unload their catch. Then, without limits, they could race out to catch another load the same night, again discarding the excess rather than taking the time to share it. The result was that far more fish were discarded during the war, fish that were destroyed to no purpose, except to decimate the stock. For a discussion, see *A History of Steinbeck's Cannery Row*, by Tom Mangelsdorf (Santa Cruz, CA: Western Tanager Press, 1986), 145ff.

22. See "A Fish Story," in *Una Storia Segreta*, op. cit., 85-86.

23. Memorandum from the Commander, Patrol Force, 12th Naval District, to Chief of Staff, 12th Naval District (Aug. 26, 1942), cited in *Report to the Congress of the United States: A Review of the Restrictions on Persons of Italian Ancestry During World War II*, (U.S. Department of Justice, November 2001), 33.

24. Ibid.

25. Memorandum from the Commander, Patrol Force, 12th Naval District, to Chief of Staff, 12th Naval District, February 26, 1942, cited in *Report to the Congress of the United States*, op. cit., 33.

26. Memorandum, Captain of Port, 12th Naval District, to Commander, Patrol Force, 12th Naval District, (March 11, 1942), cited in *Report to the Congress of the United States*, op. cit., p. 33.

27. Memorandum from the District Intelligence Officer, to District Coast Guard Officer (May 9, 1942), cited in *Report to the Congress of the United States*, op. cit., 32.

28. Letter from Captain of Port to Pittsburg Chamber of Commerce (Oct. 28, 1942), cited in *Report to the Congress of the United States*, op. cit., 34.

29. Letter from the Commander, Partol Force, 12th Naval District, to the Fish and Wildlife Service (Jan. 30, 1942), cited in *Report to the Congress of the United States*, op. cit., 35.

30. Supplementary Regulations for the Control of the San Francisco Maritime Control Area, 12th Naval District (July 25, 1942), cited in *Report to the Congress of the United States*, op. cit., 35.

31. Chin, *Artillery at the Golden Gate*, op. cit., 83-84.

32. "List of Newly Acquired Vessels," 12th Naval District, 1939-1945, vol. III, p. 52, RG 181, NDSE, Box 1, NARA SB.

33. The October 18, 1942 *Boston Globe* article by Louis Lyons referred to above, "Italians of Boston Lift Heads Again; 'Enemy' Ban Is Off," estimated that 200 Boston fishermen of Italian origin had been grounded.

34. Frank Firicano, personal interview, July 26, 2000.

35. Sal Patania, personal interview, July 25, 2000.

36. Josie Patania, personal interview, July 25, 2000.

37. Letter from Giovanni Olivieri to Senator Sheridan Downey (Dec. 31, 1941), cited in *Report to the Congress of the United States,* op.cit., 34.

38. See Teresa Fiore, "Frances Marline Stephenson's *Promises*, A Woman's *Bildungsroman*," in *Italian Immigrants Go West*, Proceedings of the 34th AIHA Conference (2001), ed. Janet Worrall, Carol Bonomo Albright, & Elvira DiFabio, (Cambridge MA: American Italian Historical Association, 2003), 25-37.

39. The 12th Naval District History cited above *(U.S. Naval Administration in WWII)* estimated that "477 small vessels would be needed to fill district requirements," including, "pleasure launches, Coast Guard vessels, pilot boats, tugs, lighters, harbor tankers, gasoline barges, river freighters, crab boats, tuna clippers, and lighthouse tenders," 34. So nearly 500 boats would have to be decommissioned.

40. Anthony Bruno, personal interview, July 12, 2000.

41. The terms cited by the U.S. Maritime Commission in a memo it sent to its district managers include the following: "By an act approved August 7, 1939, Congress amended Section 9092, Merchant Marine Act, 1936, and as so amended that section now reads as follows: Sec. 902 (a) Whenever the President shall proclaim that the security of the national defense makes it advisable or during any national emergency declared by proclamation of the President, it shall be lawful for the Commission to requisition or purchase any vessel or other watercraft owned by citizens of the United States, or under construction within the United States, or for any period during such emergency, to requisition or charter the use of any such property...(d) In all cases, the just compensation authorized by this section shall be determined and paid by the Commission as soon as practicable, but if the amount of just compensation determined by the Commission is unsatisfactory to the person entitled thereto, such person shall be paid 75 per centum of the amount so determined and shall be entitled to sue the United States to recover such further sum as, added to said 75 per centum, will make up such amount as will be just compensation therefor, in the manner approved of by section 24, paragraph 20, and section 145 of the Judicial Code (U.S.C. 1934 edition, title 28, sections. 41, 250). RG 181, Box S-434, NARA SB.

42. D'Amato interview, Aug. 9, 2000. It should be recalled, as well, that the Tolan Committee heard testimony about this same family from Tony D'Amato's mother—see Chapter 4, "Evacuation."

43. Naval speedletter, March 21, 1945, "YP 305, ex-Phyllis," RG 181, Box S-434, NARA SB.

44. Naval speedletter, March 19, 1945, "YP 370, ex-Dante Alighieri," RG 181, Box S-434, NARA SB.

45. Memo, May 24, 1943, "Vessels Under 100' Length Over-all-Placed out of Service," RG 181, 12 Naval District Commandant's Office, General Correspondence, Accession 58-3224, NARA SB.

46. Spadaro interview, op. cit., October 1999.

VII: REDUCING ENEMIES TO NULLITY

W e have seen that 600,000 Italian immigrants were branded during World War II
as both "enemies" and "aliens"—each word bearing its own weight of condemnation and shame. We have seen that there were immediate consequences to this branding in the loss of various liberties, depending on how people were categorized: loss of the
right to move freely, loss of the right to keep certain possessions known as "contraband"
(radios with shortwave band, weapons, cameras, flags, binoculars, flashlights, and more),
loss of the right to be secure within their homes (in violation of normal 4th Amendment
protections against warrantless searches), loss of the right to remain in their adopted
country if the government chose to deport them, loss of the right to constitutional protections in government hearings, loss of the right to live in or set foot in prohibited areas
including docks or shorelines, loss of the right to appear in public without the pink Certificate of Identification, and, for those formally designated as "potentially dangerous"
(internees and excludees), loss of the right to remain in the general population at all.

There were subtler consequences as well. Visible evidence of association with their
country of origin, including the use of its ways and/or its language, was interpreted as a
refusal to break with what had become an enemy nation, and hence of disloyalty or, at
the least, conflicted loyalty. The poster, "Don't Speak the Enemy's Language," graphically
underscores these subtler prohibitions. While the poster did not label speaking Italian (or
German or Japanese) a crime, its intent and implications were clear: to speak Italian was
to 'speak the enemy's language' not just in fact (i.e. speaking a language authorities did not

understand), but symbolically as well. That is, to speak Italian was to indicate, first, a con-

'Don't Speak' poster, courtesy Center of Military History

tinuing link with the politics and culture of Italy, as well as the concomitant resistance to re-shaping oneself to one's new, American culture and language.[1] It was also, by implication an intention to speak the metaphoric language of wartime Italy—the language of Mussolini and Fascism. 'Speaking the enemy's language' in this sense, therefore, meant that one was rejecting America's language of "freedom," and signaling a preference for Italy and all the negatives it now stood for: fascist dictatorship, aggression, an alliance with the vicious theories and practices of Hitler's Nazism, and the brutal persecution or elimination of those who disagreed. It was anti-American, in short; and for those immigrants unable to speak a language other than Italian, the isolation, alienation and branding could be substantial.

Whether or not it was intended by authorities at the time, the result of such language invalidation and/or stigmatizing moves toward what has been called "linguistic dispossession." As noted previously, Eva Hoffman addressed this issue in her memoir, *Lost in Translation*. There, she noted that even in her case—only thirteen when she emigrated from Poland, and thus capable of easily adapting to her new language—the deep-seated effects of linguistic dispossession left their mark. Here is how she writes about these effects:

> "...the problem is that the signifier has become severed from the signified. The words I learn now don't stand for things in the same unquestioned way they did in my native tongue. "River" in Polish was a vital sound, energized with the essence of riverhood, of my rivers, of my being immersed in rivers. "River" in English is cold—a word without an aura. It has no accumulated associations for me, and it does not give off the radiating haze of connotation. It does not evoke...This radical disjoining between word and thing is a desiccating alchemy, draining the world not only of significance but of its colors, striations, nuances—its very existence. It is the loss of a living connection."[2]

How much more traumatic such linguistic dispossession would have been for immigrants well into adulthood, and made to feel, especially during a war, that their native language was not only "foreign" but also symbolic of disloyalty, can be readily imagined. Indeed, it is perhaps remarkable that none of them, in a world gone mad with violence, actually acted on what Hoffman ultimately suggests: that "linguistic dispossession is sufficient motive for violence." Taking her cue from a short story by John Fowles, where a young man violates an elderly writer for not properly passing on the legacy of language, Hoffman puts her most radical conclusion this way:

> "Linguistic dispossession is a sufficient motive for violence, for it is close to the dispossession of one's self. Blind rage, helpless rage is rage that has no words—rage that overwhelms one with darkness."[3]

This "dispossession of one's self" via language is not something to be treated lightly.[4] Whether enforced with such dispossession in mind or not, the measures imposed on enemy aliens during the war were a serious reduction—of stature, of influence, of outlook, of the very identities of thousands of people, both individually and collectively—and invite larger questions about what underlies such measures, and why they regularly recur.

Hyphenated Americans

In this larger sense, what the branding of 600,000 Italian immigrants as "enemy aliens" initially reminds us of is that persistent American uneasiness from which such policies derive, a suspicion or fear of those often referred to as "hyphenated Americans." Notwithstanding the constant American attempt to attract immigrants, even to lure them to American shores because their labor is coveted by those in search of a large and inexpensive and "white" work force, and also notwithstanding the myth of America's welcome ("Give me your tired, your poor,/ Your huddled masses yearning to breathe free"[5]), the underlying American suspicion of foreigners has always remained active and often threatening. The negative reception given to successive waves of immigrants stands as vivid testimony to this—in the early part of the twentieth century perfectly signified by the movement known as *nativism* (see Chapter 1, above). Discrimination, including blatantly discriminatory laws like the Expatriation Act of 1907, has been directed at each newly-arriving immigrant group in turn: the Germans, the Irish, the Chinese, the Japanese, the Poles, the Jews of eastern Europe, the Greeks, the Italians, the Hispanics and so on. It takes only a glance at more-recent headlines— a Committee-of-100 Survey after a Chinese "spy plane" incident in April of 2001, which revealed that an alarming number of Americans not only had a strong dislike of Chinese-Americans, but that one-third felt they were more loyal to China than the U.S, and nearly one-half believed that Americans of Chinese ancestry would readily pass on information to the Chinese government[6]; Arizona's 2010 law, SB 1070[7], directing local police to stop and demand citizenship proof of persons based on a "reasonable suspicion" that they are illegally in the country, which critics say amounts to racial profiling; the apparently related May 6, 2010 murder of Phoenix resident Juan Varela (a third-generation Mexican-American) by his neighbor, Gary Thomas Kelley, who threatened Varela, "Hurry up and go back to Mexico or you're gonna die" while brandishing the gun with which he later murdered him[8]—to see that suspicion of foreigners remains strong. This is so even in this post-civil rights era, when pride in one's hyphenated origins has become a virtual article of faith in our "multicultural" society, and a general consensus exists (at least publicly) that racial stereotyping and/or profiling are wrong. It strongly suggests that though, on the surface, celebrating one's hyphenated origins is a mark of admirable self-esteem, below the surface there still runs a powerful river of suspicion of the immigrant. And the suspicion, as expressed in post-9/11 methods and procedures for investigating Arabs and Muslims within our borders[9], turns on the fear that most immigrants are here only temporarily (driven mainly by selfish economic needs), and that, at bottom, *the immigrant's loyalty remains with his or her race or country/culture of origin.*

Of course, this river of suspicion runs strongest during wartime. That is why the branding that took place in World War II became so pivotal for those with origins in

Italy. Prior to the war, many had borne the full brunt of the nativist anger and legislation that had been ignited by their immigration in the first place. Even so, most had managed to endure and even thrive in the years since, and were hopeful, on the eve of World War II, that their full acceptance as Americans was imminent.[10] With Mussolini's rise to power, and the entry of Italy into the war on the Axis side, however, the suspicion that Italian immigrants had not *really* become Americans was reactivated, this time among government officials as well. Recall the documents already referred to— that just prior to WWII, in 1939 and 1940, the U.S. Navy was assessing the advisability of drafting the largely-Sicilian fishing crews of the commercial purse seiners the Navy wanted for minesweepers. The Navy's 1939 report dismissed Italians as "essentially overgrown children;" its 1940 report said, in conclusion, that "the advisability of taking into the service large groups of men of hyphenated loyalty is open to question."[11]

So there it was, still—*hyphenated loyalty*. That was the problem as the Navy saw it in 1940, the problem as the entire government saw it: hyphenated loyalty; loyalty split by a hyphen. The phrase derived from a parallel phrase, "hyphenated American," that had taken root in the late nineteenth century in the midst of the very wave of migration that Italians were then dominating, and which alarmed nativists in the ways we have seen. Predictably, it took on new urgency during World War I. Theodore Roosevelt, speaking to the Knights of Columbus at Carnegie Hall on Columbus Day in 1915, had put it plainly:

> There is no room in this country for hyphenated Americanism. When I refer to
> hyphenated Americans, I do not refer to naturalized Americans. Some of the very best
> Americans I have ever known were naturalized Americans, Americans born abroad.
> But a hyphenated American is not an American at all...There is no such thing as a
> hyphenated American who is a good American. The only man who is a good American
> is the man who is an American and nothing else.[12]

"An American and nothing else," by its very nature, excluded the hyphenated ones, the ones who retained any signs of love or connection to their origins. And, as we have seen, this suspicion of "hyphenated Americans" took on equally keen urgency during the buildup to World War II.

Now the point this raises is why, in wartime, and *in whose interest*, does this suspicion of hyphenation get so seriously overblown? Obviously, the fear war arouses is primary—fear of fifth-column activity, fear of spies or saboteurs, fear of persisting loyalty to the birth country, now the enemy. But related to this fear, its obverse, in fact, is the drive for unity, negatively expressed as the struggle against disunity. Governments at war mount serious campaigns to achieve this unity, using past and future glories to rouse the nation and its people into a unified, never-give-up whole. 'We sink or swim together,' is the idea. Governments thus are driven to mount active campaigns against disunity. "A nation divided against itself cannot stand," said Abraham Lincoln in what was America's first internecine battle[13]—the Civil War—to openly and seriously campaign for preserving national unity. Indeed, Lincoln himself asserted that preserving national unity was his main intention in declaring war on the secessionist South: "If I could save the union without freeing any slave, I would do it."[14] President Woodrow Wilson expressed a related sentiment during World War I when he characterized the hyphen carried by hyphenated Americans as a "dagger that he [i.e. the hyphenated American] is ready to plunge into the vitals of this Republic."[15] Here, notably, the hyphenated American is characterized as no less than an assassin ready to eviscerate the nation itself, along with its ideals, its freedoms, its security. And Wilson's use of it reminds us of that other dagger image meant to unify a pre-war populace, the one resorted to when President Franklin Roosevelt, in June of 1940, employed it to describe Italy's alleged treachery when it attacked France: "The hand that held the dagger has struck it into the back of its neighbor." In fact, putting the latter two presidential utterances together yields a toxic equivalence: the hyphen of the immigrant is a hidden dagger; the sneak attack on an ally is a dagger that has been hidden. And though one can protest the unfairness in the hostile, and stereotypical way the metaphors merge (dagger=weapon=treachery=Italian), one must also admit that there is nothing inherently wrong with the animating suspicion itself: a government at war is obligated to take precautions, especially as regards the twin dangers of espionage and sabotage that might reasonably be thought to arise from "foreigners" in its midst, or even from those connected by birth or heritage to a nation that has become the enemy.

The problem is, in the heat of an emergency, governments rarely stop to make important distinctions. We have already noted the important distinction that is lost in the very term "enemy alien," a term which, as Earl Harrison pointed out just before the war, mistakes the immigrant—the *American alien* who is a "product of American history"—with the foreign enemy, be he undercover soldier or spy or saboteur seeking to inflict damage from within the nation's borders. Harrison, then head of the Immigration and Naturalization Service (INS), had anticipated the animosities to come and tried to head them off by warning that the American immigrant was "not at any time an enemy." But his warning was soon forgotten. For not only do governments at war tend to sweep past such distinctions, they also tend not to wait for the actual events—espionage or sabotage—to act on their suspicions. Rather, governments on the verge of war try to anticipate and control those they think *might* be disposed to engage in hostile actions in the future[16]; and that is when mental processes become the issue, that is when *beliefs* become the issue. That is, if a group is suspected of *possibly* harboring beliefs sympathetic to the enemy nation or its cause—then that person or group is seen as, is *treated* as "potentially dangerous;" in effect, as an enemy, or an enemy in embryonic form. And when this happens, when what has been called the "paradigm of prevention" becomes the basis for arrest, evacuation or internment, distinctions between what a person has done and what a person *might conceivably do* are set aside, as are the very constitutional protections which were the basis of America's revolt against an aribtrary monarch at its founding.

So it was for the three target groups in World War II—Japanese-, Italian- and German-Americans—the hyphenated Americans whose (now-enemy) nations stood at the forefront of their hyphen. These were the ones branded as 'alien enemies': both alien to the American way, and enemies to its survival. As such, they were automatically suspect (and well before the war broke out, as the evidence cited above and in Chapter 1 indicates): first, of having beliefs or *possibly* having *beliefs* that favored the enemy nations from which they derived; and second, of being so seriously out of step with American values, ideas, and aims that they threatened the unity believed to be necessary to carry out the war.

Now here it is important to stop a moment to note that in the United States of America, under its Constitution (a document which specifically extends its protections not to citizens alone, but to *all persons*), *believing* in something, however negative or misguided it might be, is *not* a crime. This is quite specific. The right to believe, and to speak up about that belief, is among the freedoms so famously trumpeted by President Franklin Roosevelt, and which his military was even then allegedly fighting to preserve. And yet, during World War II, people became suspect, and some were incarcerated, in large part because of the beliefs they were *believed* to harbor. In fact, the Italian-American writer, Jerre Mangione, who worked for the INS during the war, referred to this when, after completing his 1942 inspection tour of the internment camps where enemy aliens were incarcerated, he wrote the following: *We found ourselves in the shameful position of locking people up for their beliefs.*[17] Now aside from the question of how one determines beyond doubt what a person "believes," one of the reasons Mangione called his government's policy "shameful" is that he knew that isolating people on the basis of their beliefs is not only wrong in itself; it can easily transform into the idea that those *beliefs are inborn*, are genetic or even racial rather than cultural. And that means that such beliefs cannot be easily changed, *if they can be changed at all*. When governments do that, as the Nazis did with respect to the Jews, and as the U.S. government eventually did with respect to Japanese-Americans who were American-born citizens, they take a perilous step towards the final option to eliminate such people.

This is not to say that the United States government during World War II had anything like group elimination in mind. *It did not.* It *is* to say that especially in wartime (and also, to a lesser degree, in peacetime), the demand made of every immigrant is to fully Americanize. *Naturalize.* And it bears emphasizing that the word *naturalize* leads, on its own, to all sorts of exclusions: since *our* way is *natural*, i.e. the way nature intended humans to be; and *their* way is *unnatural*, i.e. against nature's or God's plan; then it is logically permitted to demand the excision of all evidence of unnaturalness, all signs of belief in *their* ways, including the hyphen *(... a good American is the man who is an American and nothing else).* If some individuals or groups cannot, or choose not to do this, they must be marked with identity cards (it is important to realize that "identity" is very much at issue where the immigrant is concerned, where his hyphenation is concerned, where his attempt to maintain a sense of himself in the midst of his dispossession is concerned), or isolated, or locked up, or all three.

Who Were the Enemy Aliens?

Thus we return to the targeting of those labeled "enemy aliens" in World War II. Who *were* these people? In the Italian case, they were mostly the non-citizens—the *unnaturalized* ones. No fewer than 600,000 of them registered in February of 1942 (no one knows how many thousands may simply have neglected to register at all), all of whom were obliged to carry identity cards (as symptoms of their questionable identities?) and abide by varying levels of isolation or restriction, because of *what they might possibly believe*, because of the fear of what their allegedly hyphenated loyalty might lead to. In this regard, nothing else mattered: not their pre-war behavior nor their present behavior, not their length of residence in the United States, nor the number of their children serving in the U.S. military, nor their reasons for entering the U.S. in the first place. All that mattered was their birth in that now-enemy nation, and the fact that they had *failed to naturalize*—the underlying assumption being that the failure had represented a *preference*, thus obviating any concern for *why* they might have failed, such as not having sufficient command of the English language, or sufficient time to complete the process.[18]

Then there were those who were listed as "potentially dangerous": the ones who were arrested, several hundred of whom were interned behind barbed wire for long periods. Who were *they*? Mostly they were men (and a few women) who had retained ties to Italy, including communication with relatives or business associates; or who had visited their native country too often or too recently; or who were perceived to be "too Italian": Italian language users (writers, broadcasters, journalists or newspaper publishers, teachers), members of organizations such as the *Ex-Combattenti* (Veterans of WWI), leaders of Italian social/cultural clubs—many of whom were not willing to abandon the culture or the land they were proud of, and which had become, with war, the land ruled by the enemy, by Mussolini, and hence a land to be disdained, repudiated. And of course they included those who were informed on: 'there's an Italian...a German...one who says things indicating he does not disdain his birth-land.' And beyond that, those who couldn't rid themselves of their foreign "look" because it was indelibly part of them via their skin color or habits or physical features—which latter leads inevitably to the racism that affected Japanese-Americans.

Consider just a few examples. Louis Berizzi, an importer living in New York, was listed as "potentially dangerous" by the FBI, was arrested on December 8, 1941, and was eventually brought before a hearing board to 'prove his innocence.' At his hearing, according to a letter he wrote while interned, he talked about not wanting his mother, who still lived in Italy, bombed ("When I testified before the hearing board, I was asked whether I wanted this country to win the war. I replied that I believed in democratic principles and did not believe in fascism, but naturally I did not like the idea of having my mother bombed.") It appears that the hearing board interpreted his words to mean he did not want *Italy* bombed. Berizzi was interned.[19]

Illidio DiBugnara had, just before the war, joined the U.S. Army under a provision whereby aliens, though not allowed to vote, can serve in the military. Such service often rewards the serviceman with U.S. citizenship at its conclusion. With the American entry into the war against Italy, however, DiBugnara was taken aside and questioned about whether, as a soldier, he would be willing to kill Italians. Knowing he had two brothers in the Italian army, DiBugnara said, quite truthfully, that he could not. He would serve in the Pacific Theatre with no compunctions, he said, but if he had to kill someone in his native land, he could not do it. The Army thereupon discharged him and turned him over to INS authorities as unfit, or perhaps simply as displaying conflicted, or hyphenated loyalty. The Attorney General ordered him interned.[20]

Federico Dellagatta's case has been referred to earlier, but it bears repeating here. Dellagatta's "crime" was to talk about the greatness of the Italian people and the Italian army—talk that was labeled "downright subversive activity." The logical question becomes: what was subversive about this, and subversive of what? As in all wars, government policy (propaganda) required that enemy nations like Italy be denigrated in every way possible, including its army's ability to fight, its leader's ability to lead, its people's ability to accomplish anything worthwhile. To say, therefore, as Dellagatta was reported to have said, that the Italian people were great and their army was also great was to subvert the dehumanizing of the enemy deemed necessary in war. The cartoon images in the poster, *Don't Speak the Enemy's Language*, offer visible testimony of this: Mussolini is portrayed as a bum, with stubble on his face, and band-aids covering his ineffectual shaving. To say that *his* people or *his* army was great was to subvert this depiction—and since Dellagatta had done this, verbally at least, he was branded a subversive and interned.[21]

Now, of course, no government can come right out and say this—that the enemy nation and its people are 'bums.' Indeed, when he removed the restrictions on Italian enemy aliens in October of 1942, Attorney General Francis Biddle waxed poetic about the greatness of the Italian people and their culture, especially those cultural icons most Americans could agree on: Dante, Petrarch, Michelangelo, Verdi, and their ilk. But for an enemy alien, a few months earlier, to brag in a shoeshine shop about the greatness of the same Italian people and their army—*that* was not permitted. That was "downright subversive activity." And the subversive person had to be taken out of circulation, had to be displayed as an example, a warning: *This cannot be said. Some things* are too inflammatory, too seditious *for some people* to say.

Thus we see that, at a deep level, the demand in wartime is not simply to denigrate the leaders or the political system or the battle prowess of the enemy. The demand is *to denigrate the entire culture of the enemy*; to point out that its people are fundamentally different (i.e., inferior) from our people for they are culturally disposed to unfairness, to backstabbing, to cowardice, to inhumanity. As such, they deserve whatever punishment our armies hand out to them. Indeed, handing out punishment, killing them, is precisely what both the historical moment and the natural order demand.

The trouble is, the denigration cannot be contained within strict guidelines, focused solely on those defective actors in the old country who are perpetrating the war—the political leaders, the generals, the officials, the military, the part of the population that supports them.[22] It extends to those in the new country as well, to those who have left that old country, fled from it in some cases precisely because they would not live under its dictatorial rulers, and chosen another place as their new home. That is because in wartime, simply having left one's old country is not enough. There must be the concomitant denigration added: 'The culture from which you derive is not only strange, odd, literally backward or wrong in its ways; it is also unnaturally aggressive, violent, cruel, war-like and devoted only to the aggrandizement and enrichment of the wicked few.'

Culture Nullification

These considerations touch upon a still broader issue. For what this denigration of the immigrant's culture of origin boils down to is, in effect, a nullification. Naturalization, Americanization, is at bottom a nullification—a nullification of the immigrant's old culture, indeed, a nullification of his old self; and the replacement of it with the new, allegedly superior culture, the culture that conforms with nature, that conforms with a new, 'more natural' self. The American citizen as a new type of human[23] has been a common trope for much of our history, but it involves not simply putting on the new; it requires, necessarily, a sloughing off or nullification of the old. Under normal circumstances, we may not notice this, but it is what war brings into sharp relief.

That is to say: wartime, to a greater or lesser degree, overtly and openly impels those with a link to enemy nations to become cultureless—to repudiate or disavow or cover over their links to their old country, their country of origin. All of this became very clear in the questions and restrictions imposed on Italian enemy aliens on the home front—restrictions which took the form of questions: have you returned to Italy since emigrating? How often? How often do you write to your relatives there? How often do you associate with others from that country? How involved are you with social and cultural groups promoting that association? All these and more were among the questions asked of those who registered for the Pink Certificates of Identification in 1942, those who were apprehended for any reason, those who were brought before hearing boards to judge their "potential danger." The meaning was clear: to live in America, to be "an American and nothing else," as Theodore Roosevelt put it, required that one sever that connection with the old (FBI documents reveal that letters from enemy aliens to relatives in Italy were commonly monitored).[24] To refuse to do this, to refuse voluntarily or under pressure or out of fear or shame or ignorance or incapacity or indifference or love, was to remain "something else," and that something else translated, in wartime, to being separated, segregated, excluded from certain sensitive areas. It meant being suspect—unable to be at large without an Identity Booklet. It meant being watched, surveilled, informed on, thence to be questioned, sometimes to be interned, or excluded from vast areas, or deported. To be reduced to nothingness. Nullified.

In fact, one can say that one of the major side effects of war[25] is that it drives the situation to its extreme form, to a 'catch-22.' That is, the American immigrant with roots in the enemy nation is nullified no matter what he does, for there are two basic outcomes to the wartime demand to naturalize:

a) If you refuse to, or are unable (due to skin color, racial features, and/or specific laws disallowing it, as in the Japanese case) to naturalize, you are nullified by being separated, interned, even repatriated.

b) If you yield, if you agree to naturalize, you are nullified by becoming American, by Americanizing, which is to become nullified and cultureless by default.

If this latter point seems extreme, if linking Americanization of the immigrant with culture loss and nullification seems a stretch, consider Eva Hoffman's insights again. In *Lost in Translation*, Hoffman expatiates at great length on what 'linguistic dispossession' means, and it is not, she insists, losing mere words, verbal expression. The loss involves natural gestures as well, the way one carries oneself and emotes and responds in conversation. To demonstrate this, she describes what happened in an early classroom when she tried to answer her American teacher's questions, and could not help using her normal, i.e. Polish, gestures. Hoffman's teacher finally instructed her "to sit on my hands and then try talking." Eva Hoffman, that is, was being asked to curb emotions and gestures which, in an American classroom, were seen as overly-expressive, which is to say overly-emotional, foreign, un-American. Such a style of speech and gesture could not, even in peacetime America, convey meaning accurately, naturally. And it was not simply in the classroom, Hoffman tells us, that this was so. It pervaded every relationship and situation she entered, including those with her peers, all of which led, finally, to a sense of being nullified:

> Because I'm not heard, I feel I'm not seen. My words often seem to baffle others....the back and forth of conversation is different here. People often don't answer each other. But the mat look in their eyes as they listen to me cancels my face, flattens my features. The mobility of my face comes from the mobility of the words coming to the surface and the feelings that drive them. Its vividness is sparked by the locking of an answering gaze, by the quickness of understanding. But now I can't feel how my face lights up from inside; I don't receive from others the reflected movement of its expressions, its living speech. People look past me as we speak. What do I look like here? Imperceptible, I think; impalpable, neutral, faceless.[26]

Now in Hoffman's case, as noted above, her youth came to her aid. She soon learned how to speak American and to tone down and modify (Americanize) her gestural repertoire to match those around her. At age thirteen, she could soon speak English without a trace of an accent and without those colorful, ingrained Polish gestures. But both she, and her mother, noticed the change and recognized and regretted the loss.[27]

Henry James, in *The American Scene*, once recorded a similar observation, this time referring specifically to Italian immigrants he had observed in New York City in 1904. His observation is notable because James had spent a great deal of time in Italy, and had an experiential basis for comparing the Italians in Italy with those who were even then flooding the streets of his native land. He wrote about the "white-washing" the latter seemed to undergo in the new world:

> There are categories of foreigners, meanwhile, of whom we are moved to say that only a mechanism working with scientific force could have performed this feat of making them colourless. The Italians, who, over the whole land, strike us, I am afraid, as, after the Negro and the Chinaman, the human value most easily produced, meet us, at every turn, only to make us ask what has become of that element of the agreeable address in them which has, from far back, so enhanced for the stranger the interest and plea-sure of a visit to their beautiful country. They shed it utterly, I couldn't but observe, on their advent, after a deep inhalation or two of the clear native air, shed it with a conscientious completeness which leaves one looking for any faint trace of it. "Colour," of that pleasant sort, was what they had appeared, among the races of the European family, most to have...[28]

What I think James was getting at is a cultural nullifying of Italian, and indeed of all immigrants (he referred to them as "aliens"), related to what is at issue here. Such "whitewashing" was not forced, in the sense that people would have been directly told what to do or how to behave. But it was something, according to James, "working with scientific force." This is presumably because everything in the new culture reinforces the same admonition received by Eva Hoffman from her teacher: '*we* don't make those ges-tures here. *We* don't speak in that tone of voice, or at that volume here. Such behavior is not *natural*. To become like us, to naturalize, sit on your hands. Sit on your expressive gestures. Sit on *your self*.' During wartime, of course, these messages take on even more force, take on institutional force, becoming both more explicit and more urgent—*Don't Speak the Enemy's Language. Speak American*—in every sense.

An iteration of this same message, in a slightly more institutional form, was conveyed at the Tenney Committee Hearings held in San Francisco in May of 1942 (see Chapter 5—Exclusion). The exchange that took place there is worth quoting in full once more, be-cause where Henry James had expressly regretted the loss of "colour" he observed in Ital-ian immigrants, the Tenney Committee saw the loss as necessary, as desirable, saw 'forget-ting' the 'radical difference' immigrants still maintained in their Little Italys as *imperative*:

> TUONI: As I was saying to you before, gentlemen of this Committee, the best thing is to close the papers, close the Italian broadcasting, reorganize or close the Italian organizations, they are poison—this is the time that the Italians should come into the American family and to breathe finally the free atmosphere of this country. If you do not do that, they will still persist in a campaign which finally the result will be you will

have the Italians away from the American family, and maybe tomorrow the situation
will be as to the war effort right here in San Francisco.

DR. KELLEMS: It is your opinion—or rather, I should say conviction—
that there are a special group of people whose culture and background is so different
from ours, and I think we do admit it is radically different—

A. (Interrupting) Yes.

Q. (Continuing)—and it will only be possible for them to forget that only if
they will enter the American way of life—

A. (Interrupting) they will.

Q. (Continuing)—and I believe they will. Is it not your feeling that instead
of persisting generation after generation teaching these things, creating a little Italy
here, that they will only find their own happiness and strength by forgetting...[29]

The result was that many, many Italians were constrained—by the wartime stigma
attached to Italian manners and mores and language, by what they saw happening to
neighbors and relatives for clinging to those "differences"—to do exactly that: either
forget, or suppress the cultural traits that marked them as Italian; that stigmatized them
as, at the least, *hyphenates.* They, and moreso their children, abandoned the Italian language (especially their dialect), their look (as greenhorns), and their foreign ways (what
James called "colour;" what the Tenney Committee called "radical differences")—at least
in public. Eventually, this meant an abandonment of their culture as it had developed
in those Little Italys.[30] It meant full Americanization. And, not least, it amounted to a
suppression that, for fifty years, included a virtual ban on nearly all talk of what had happened to them during World War II—the restrictions and internments and evacuations
and curfews, the wholesale stigma they had silently endured. It became a silence, collud-
ed in by the government itself, which remained intact until, as in the Japanese-American
case, the second and third generations finally uncovered it, objected to the historical loss
it represented, and ultimately violated that silence by bringing the events to light.[31]

The movement to resurrect this almost lost history continues to this day. For the
truth is that the full story has not yet penetrated the resistance of many parts of the
Italian-American community (if one can speak of such a thing anymore)—the generations following the immigrants who dispersed to the suburbs and beyond. Indeed, it is a
curious fact that what these subsequent generations take to be an interest in their heritage allows them (or induces them) to remain in the dark about this and other crucial
parts of their history in America, all the while taking trips to Italy and marveling over its
cultural "hot spots." In this, their condition tends to support what has been noted above:
the movement of immigrants and their children to abandon or forget their own culture,

in this case, Italian culture *as manifested in America*. That is to say, in a large percentage of cases, this modern willingness to embrace Italy as tourists obscures the fact that many Italian-Americans still remain neutral and ignorant, if not hostile, to their *own* history—the history of Italians in America. This is probably because Italy and its products have garnered a kind of prestige in the general population which Italian-American culture and history still have not. The result is that large numbers of Italian-Americans have remained so culturally neutral (I spoke to a friend recently who acknowledged that she, and most people she knew, *had no culture whatever*; this idea is reinforced in numerous places on the internet[32]) that they actually admit to looking to the stereotyped rendering of Italian-Americans in TV and film representations (the *Godfather*, the *Sopranos*, *Jersey Shore*) for some idea of who they are, for some link to what they have lost. They realize, if only dimly, that in succeeding in America, in becoming fully American in Teddy Roosevelt's sense, they have in fact become colorless; cultureless.[33]

Cultureless America

Why this is so, why not just Italian-Americans but many, if not most Americans feel cultureless, and, indeed, what benefit a nation of cultureless people might present to those in power (and not just in wartime), would involve another study in itself.[34] But the historical antecedents to and rationale (that is, *who benefits?*) for a cultureless America can be outlined briefly.

To begin with, it is necessary to distinguish between what social scientists mean by "culture," and what the American mythos suggests. For the former, culture is simply the sum of the ways and means whereby a population coheres and adapts to its environment. It involves the foods they typically eat and how they obtain them, the clothes they wear, the dwellings they inhabit, the festivals they celebrate, the material goods and art they create in support and reflection of all those ways. In this rendering, every human group has a culture, *is* a culture, for it could not survive without one. America is no different.

In the American mythos, however, "culture" assumes a different, less expansive meaning. For much of its Puritan-dominated period, for example, colonial Americans associated the idea of "culture" with a corrupt and privileged Europe. Kings and the nobility were viewed as those who preoccupied themselves with culture, patronizing the sophisticated entertainments of theater, opera, poetry, visual art and grandiose architecture. Such frills of life were always contrasted, by American preachers, politicians and thinkers, with the down-to-earth life of the soil engaged in by most early American settlers. Where the American pioneer was self-sufficient, content with the crude but practical home and tools he could fashion for himself, the European was decadent—dependent on artisans, serfs and slaves to provide him with the 'necessities' of life. "Culture" was thus equivalent to privilege and to the wars, decadence and enslavement associated with it. It was mired in the past.[35]

America, by contrast, had constituted itself as something new, something that needed no traditions or forms or rituals other than those it could forge on the spot, and abandon whenever they grew too encrusted with the past. The American, the new man, was distinguished not by his coat of arms or his family tree or his mastery of ancient measured modes, but by his genius for improvisation and invention, for making do with what was at hand. And improvisation depended mostly, if not entirely, on abandoning the societal rules and rituals that had hobbled Europe for centuries. The American rifleman at ease in buckskin would always triumph over the British soldier marching stiffly in his formal red coat. Town hall meetings at which the ordinary American citizen voiced his political opinions were in every way superior to a British government dominated by hereditary monarchs and nobles.

Thus, in a very real way, America has always mythologized itself as the place where culture—the rigid codes of the corrupt and unequal past—was to be abandoned. Those with enough courage to make the journey across the ocean and confront the perils and discomforts of the wilderness were also the ones most able and willing to leave behind the old and embrace the new; to say goodbye to privilege, comfort, and rules, whether they were rules of habitation, rules of land ownership, rules of learning, religion, manners, morals, or money; to say hello to the rough and ready future, to the open and expansive and infinite; to the settlement not of settled culture, but of that which is constantly on the move: The place of no place.[36] The culture of no culture.

In a sense, then, America founds itself, and then mythologizes itself as cultureless— where culture is that which America has left behind; that which Americans, as a free and equal and always evolving people, no longer have need of. And the implication is always, as we have seen, that this is *natural,* that it fulfills the type of existence that nature intends. Culture is the *unnatural* accretion of largely unnecessary frills; what is *natural* is the form of living that has no need of culture, that has moved beyond culture, that is too busy looking ahead and succeeding to bother with culture.

To be sure, there were those in the new land who did not eschew privilege and cultured goods, and who quickly established it in their new circumstances. Indeed, some of our most revered founding fathers—George Washington and Thomas Jefferson among them—were landed gentry who not only owned great estates erected on classical models, but possessed slaves and servants to rival or even outdo their European forebears. But the myth surrounding them downplayed these aspects, playing up the self-made and inventive parts of their story. And when Jefferson and his compatriots wrote the new nation's founding documents, he and they emphasized the natural, the new, the equal, the break with the tyrannies of the past:

> *When in the Course of human events, it becomes necessary for one people to dissolve the political bands which have connected them with another, and to assume among the powers of the earth, the separate and equal station to which the Laws of Nature and of Nature's God entitle them, a decent respect to the opinions of mankind requires that they should declare the causes which impel them to the separation.*
> *..We hold these truths to be self evident; that all men are created equal...*[37]

All immigrants who followed were greeted with the same set of promises, the same set of guidelines to follow: 'You come burdened not only with the poverty and hopelessness of your birthplace. You come burdened not only with the fear imposed upon you by those who have enslaved you. You come burdened also with the decadent culture of that place and its history: its privileges, its forms, its ancient ways of inequality and social, political and religious corruption. The sooner you abandon those ways, the sooner will you become American in spirit. The sooner you do that, the sooner will you be able to take advantage of what is here free and open and waiting to be exploited by your natural genius.'

Of course, one of the problems with this message is that while those who project it see mainly its positive side, many who receive it tend to notice the negative. That is, it is one thing to welcome those with talent and energy and encourage their application to personal betterment. It is another to make plain that the way of life they have brought with them is not only useless, it is corrupt, repulsive and detrimental to both those who maintain it and those who must live downwind from its corruption. For Italian immigrants at the turn of the century, to cite just one example, this meant finding themselves portrayed as barbarians who could inhabit tenements choked with garbage and squalor, eat foods like garlic that offended the nostrils, wear clothing that was unkempt and unwashed, and indulge in religious rituals that derived from paganism and devil worship. This portrayal was reinforced on every side: wages at the bottom of the income scale, jobs that forced them to be virtual pack animals, and an assessment of their moral depravity which predicted nothing but crime in their future. The end result was *shame, a shame that was reinforced, concentrated and amplified by the restrictions of World War II.* And the cure for shame—the feeling that *something is wrong with who and what I am*—is change. If what I am makes me insufficient, and incapable of participating fully in my world, then the only solution is to *change what I am.* By changing, by leaving behind or disguising or forgetting the traditional ways I came with, and by adopting, to the degree I am able, new ways, I can both blunt the criticism and counter the ostracism.[38]

This was precisely what, after World War II, many Italian immigrants and their children did, especially when the latter found accessible several ways, readymade by postwar policies, to do it: a GI Bill that allowed returning Italian American veterans to advance their education; newly emerging suburbs that allowed them, again via the GI bill, to buy a home distant from the urban villages called "Little Italys" many had grown up in.[39] Also readymade was a way of life and source of identity that had been somewhat interrupted by the war, but which was reignited with more dammed-up power than ever once World War II was over, a way which the now-liberated Italian immigrants, in their eagerness to become Americans, could hardly avoid. That way was *consumerism*, and it provides an additional answer to the question implied earlier: who benefits from a cultureless population, and how?

Consumerist "Culture"[40]

The modern 'culture' of consumerism actually began in earnest in the 1920s, shortly after World War I. At that time, the increasingly industrialized American nation was faced with both a rival movement—the communism of Karl Marx manifested in the Soviet Union—and the anticipated consequences of the mass industrial production exploding in the postwar years—i.e., the threat of *overproduction*. If, as many industrialists feared, Americans maintained their frugal ways of buying only what they needed, the accelerating output of mass-produced goods would soon satisfy and outstrip those basic needs. That would leave industry with surplus goods, surplus production facilities, and a shrunken market—a perilous situation in an economic system such as capitalism that depends on constant growth. Fortunately for the captains of industry, into this breach between an almost-unlimited supply and limited demand leaped a new industry: *public relations*. It was an industry that could induce people to consume, and among those who initiated this industry was the nephew of Sigmund Freud, Edward Bernays.[41]

Bernays had, interestingly enough, derived his inspiration from war. Working with the World War I Committee for Public Information, he noticed how effective propaganda had been in 'engineering consent' for America's entry into the war. Bernays wrote specifically that "the manipulators of patriotic opinion made use of the mental clichés and the emotional habits of the public to produce mass reactions against the alleged atrocities, the terror and the tyranny of the enemy;" it was therefore logical and even "natural that intelligent persons should ask themselves whether it was not possible to apply a similar technique to the problems of peace."[42]

As one of those "intelligent persons," Bernays wasted no time doing exactly that. Bernays was a devotee of his uncle's theories of the unconscious, especially the idea that most people (Bernays routinely referred to the "masses" as unaware and easily manipulated) were motivated by subconscious emotions and desires rather than by reason. He therefore contrived public relations campaigns designed to appeal to those emotions in a way that would induce the masses to *desire products they did not really need*. This was significant because prior to this point, American consumers (aside from the wealthy few) hardly existed as such; most Americans paid cash for what they needed, and only when they absolutely needed it. The numbers were clear: if corporate producers were not to put themselves out of business, the mass of people would somehow have to be convinced to *buy MORE than they needed*. Demand had to be increased. As Paul Maser of Lehman Brothers put it at the time:

> We must shift America from a needs to a desires culture. People must be trained to desire, to want new things even before the old have been entirely consumed. We must shape a new mentality in America. Man's desires must overshadow his needs.[43]

This job of increasing demand was precisely what public-relations experts like Bernays specialized in. In one of his most memorable campaigns, he staged an event at New York City's annual Easter Parade to change women's minds about smoking cigarettes, and thereby to open a huge untapped market for the sales of this unneeded, not to mention *unhealthful and even deadly,* product. First Bernays consulted the psychologist A.A. Brill about what cigarettes represented for women. Brill claimed that they symbolized the penis and male power, and that if Bernays could connect cigarettes with a challenge to male power, it would induce women to smoke. Bernays then persuaded a group of debutantes marching in New York's annual Easter Parade to conceal packs of *Lucky Strike* cigarettes beneath their clothes, and then, at a signal from him, to light up and smoke them as they marched. Bernays, meanwhile, had tipped off New York reporters to a rumor he claimed to have heard—that there were suffragettes who would be igniting what they called *torches of freedom* (a name Bernays had coined). The Easter Parade event, with its "torches of freedom," created a news sensation nationwide. In response, to the delight of tobacco companies, cigarette sales rose dramatically, especially among women.

As a result of these and many other campaigns, Americans in the 1920s began to do what they were being secretly "trained" to do. Responding to advertisers who presented their products not as rational necessities, as before, but as symbols that appealed to inner selfish desires, American consumers began to buy increasing quantities of clothes, cars and other objects that they were told *expressed their individuality,* their social status, their hopes about how others would see them. It had become possible to persuade people to behave irrationally (as in getting women to smoke), provided that a product was subtly connected to feelings and desires consumers hardly knew they had. As Bernays wrote:

> A man buying a car may think he wants it for purposes of locomotion, whereas the fact may be that he would really prefer not to be burdened with it, and would rather walk for the sake of his health. He may really want it because it is a symbol of social position, an evidence of his success in business, or a means of pleasing his wife.[44]

For Bernays and others, this became the new way to control and construct the economic system, people, and reality itself. Average people could not be left to themselves and their own inclinations. As Freud had revealed, humans in the mass were subject to dangerous drives and explosive aggressions. It was necessary to manage them, to divert their drives (Freud called this sublimation) into controllable channels. For Bernays and the American corporate and political leaders for whom he worked—the power elite who considered themselves, as Bernays put it, an "invisible government"[45]—this meant channeling the irrational and potentially dangerous desires of the average person into consumerism. The potentially dangerous masses, in other words, could be controlled and managed by inducing them to shop.[46] Bernays was actually quite proud of this manipulating function, considering it an absolute necessity in mass society. As he once told a group of advertising and public relations men:

> You have taken over the job of creating desire and have transformed people into constantly moving *happiness machines*, machines which have become the key to economic progress.[47]

In short, by making consumers "happy," with their inner desires satisfied, the makers of largely useless goods were performing two critical functions: they were creating an endlessly growing economy, and they were keeping the masses content. As a side benefit, of course, they were also enriching themselves. As another side benefit, they were keeping American democracy "stable," i.e. free from the dramatic and dangerous changes that historically had erupted whenever the masses became discontented with their lot. Keeping the masses docile, keeping them from gathering in strength and anger as many had done in the pre-WWI era, were, for pundits like Walter Lippmann and PR men like Bernays, key functions of the elite in any society.

The problem was that all this didn't square very well with democracy. As Stuart Ewen, a historian of public relations, assessed the situation:

> Both Bernays and Lippmann's concept of managing the masses takes the idea of

democracy and turns it into a palliative, turns it into giving people some kind of feel good medication that will respond to the immediate pain or yearning, but will not alter the objective circumstances one iota. This is not the traditional idea of democracy—changing the relations of power—but maintaining the relations of power.[48]

In the 1920s after World War I, however, and again after World War II, this would be the type of democracy that came to characterize the United States. A journalist noted this in 1927: "A change" he said, "has come over our democracy. It is called consumptionism. The American citizen's importance to his country is now no longer that of citizen, but that of consumer."[49] What he was pointing to was that at the heart of the new democracy was a new construct—a "consuming self which not only made the economy work, but was happy and docile and so created a stable society."[50] With such happy, docile consumers in place of active citizens, those in power could continue to do what they wanted.

Cultureless Consumers

It thus becomes possible to see the several advantages that inhere in rendering immigrants, and Americans in general, cultureless. People who are cultureless can be manipulated by those in power. This is because cultureless people lack a firm identity, a solid, useful place in a culture whose values they understand and in which they feel at home and secure. Instead, they are, in many senses, adrift. In such a void, the surrogate "culture" of consumerism has room to take root.

As a concrete example, it is useful to consider the observations made by Helena Norberg-Hodge[51] about the advent of consumerism (she uses the term 'development') in the tiny Himalayan kingdom of Ladakh. Living in a high Himalayan desert near Tibet, traditional Ladakhis had survived and thrived for centuries by means of a Buddhist culture perfectly suited to its terrain. Cultivating grains adapted to the thin soil and the extreme altitude, and raising the Yaks that supplied them with everything from meat to butter to clothing, Ladakhis were for centuries able to grow or make virtually everything they needed. Along with this, Norberg-Hodge found, to her surprise, that average Ladakhis, embedded in family and community, seemed to possess a happiness, a satisfaction, and a sense of worth that defied the apparently meager materials of their lives.

All this changed with the inception of "development." In the 1970s and 1980s, television sets, and tourists wearing high-tech clothing and spending wildly, introduced Ladakhis to the dazzling array of consumer goods available in the global marketplace. The effect, according to Norberg-Hodge, was not simply to instill in a previously contented people desires they had never had; it was also *to make them dis-*

contented with and ashamed of the lives that had heretofore seemed complete. Never having needed money before—because families could make virtually everything they needed, including their homes—individual Ladakhis began to search for jobs with which to earn the currency now required to buy "things." Norberg-Hodge is particularly perceptive about the underlying appeal of such consumer goods:

> Perhaps the most tragic of all the vicious circles I have observed in Ladakh is the way in which individual insecurity contributes to a weakening of family and community ties, which in turn further shakes individual self-esteem. Consumerism plays a central role in this whole process, *since emotional insecurity contributes to a hunger for material status symbols.* The need for recognition and acceptance fuels the drive to acquire possessions—*possessions that will make you somebody.* Ultimately, this is a far more important motivating factor than a fascination for the things themselves. It is heartbreaking to see people buying things to be admired, respected, and ultimately loved, when in fact it almost inevitably has the opposite effect. The individual with the new shiny car is set apart, and this furthers the need to be accepted. A cycle is set in motion in which people become more and more divided from themselves and from one another.[52] [Emphases added.]

In short, Ladakhis who are made ashamed of their own culture and induced to become modern, consuming "individuals," are estranged from their families and communities. This isolation, in turn, leads to diminished self-esteem and emotional insecurity, both of which most people find unbearable. Alleviating both the shame and the anxiety becomes paramount, with the remedy found in *more* material possessions. This new appetite for material possessions, in turn, requires that Ladakhis find paying jobs that take them ever farther from their communities and formerly self-possessed lives—and a relentless cycle sets in. As a headnote to her chapter describing these changes, Norberg-Hodge quotes a development commissioner in Ladakh, who said in 1981: "If Ladakh is ever going to be developed, we have to figure out how to make these people more greedy. You just can't motivate them otherwise."[53] The quote, did we not know its source, might have come from Edward Bernays himself.

It is the connection of shame and culture loss (including the corresponding loss of identity) with the desire for material goods that bears emphasis here. When people, like Italian immigrants during World War II, and immigrants more generally, are induced to feel ashamed of their own culture (and/or fearful of associating with it), they tend to move away from it, either physically or emotionally. Without the cultural props and community reinforcement they depend on, their insecurity and anxiety tend to rise. The pursuit of material wealth then appears to be the most direct way to counter insecurity and loss, with everything required for its pursuit functioning to reinforce the change away from the old identity and ways which have become shameful. Finally, the increasing time needed to pursue material wealth reinforces the cultural changes that began the process: the pursuit of goods to make one "feel like somebody" (i.e. to find an identity) becomes all-consuming, and requires that one spend less "old-fashioned" or family/community time, and more individual business time.

And all is done as if driven from within (or, as Henry James might have put it, as if working with 'scientific force'). Economists and advertising men routinely point out that humans are "self-interested" and so "naturally" want to change, "naturally" want to possess as many goods as possible to express their individuality, to support their new and better self-image. Of course, what Bernays and others demonstrate is that this "need" to change by possessing a plethora of largely unnecessary products is *not natural at all*, but rather the end result of carefully calculated campaigns pitched at subconscious desires.

Now we can see not just the short-term, but also the longer-term value of the cultureless or nullified individuals—in this case Italian enemy aliens and their families—whose transformation is most efficiently and rapidly accelerated by war and its aftermath. Those who are shamed or intimidated into "forgetting" their old culture lose, through the series of interlocking steps outlined by Norberg-Hodge, the security and identity that a traditional culture and community provide. They become emotionally insecure "nobodies." To regain a sense of "being somebody," they turn more and more to the pursuit of material well-being and the goods thought to provide it. They become inveterate, one might even say "addicted," consumers. To afford the increased consumption they feel they need, they spend more time earning the money required to consume and less time reinforcing old values with family and friends. Their value to the corporations who depend on such consumers to buy the mountains of goods they produce, is as obvious as the new condition that prevails: *consumption of always more goods becomes necessary for the average person's psychic and social survival.*

Wars like World War II thus accelerate and amplify the American tendency to become cultureless for a whole cluster of reasons. First, cultureless people are more easily rallied to a cause, for a cause gives such people a common reason for being. Nullified, they are more easily put into *uniform*—which word speaks for itself. Armies do not like people who know who they are, people who have a great deal invested in preserving their unique sense of self. Armies need people who can be molded into uniformly-motivated units, unthinking people willing to fight and even die in the pursuit of a common objective, however distant or questionable.

Wartime political leaders prefer nullified people as well. Those who have no sense of themselves are easier to move emotionally, to lead into hyper-nationalism and self-sacrifice. They are easier to rally against a putative enemy (as Creel and Bernays found in WWI), and easier to convince of the righteousness not only of the announced cause, but of the government's actions in pursuit of that cause. During World War II, for example, government agencies like the FBI were keen to get publicity for the work they were doing to 'control spies and prevent sabotage.' The message, more willingly received by those who needed desperately to believe, was that the government, working day and night with sophisticated methods, had the allegedly dangerous situation under control.

Equally significant, and longer term, the beneficiaries of cultureless people are the powerful forces behind and within commercial institutions and corporations, the people Bernays called the "invisible government." They are the ones who produce the products and services that, as we have seen, require always-new markets with always-more customers. Their task, therefore, is not only to produce the desired goods to be sold, but *to literally produce the people who consume them.* As Bernays himself put it:

> Mass production is only profitable if its rhythm can be maintained— that is, if it can continue to sell its product in steady or increasing quantity. The result is that while, under the handicraft or small-unit system of production that was typical a century ago, demand created the supply, to-day supply must actively seek to create its corresponding demand....*To make customers is the new problem* [Emphasis added].[54]

This 'making of customers' becomes the aim and meaning of modern life (from the corporate point of view, that is)—to produce a nation, and, finally, a world of essentially cultureless people united for and dedicated to one overriding activity: accumulating and consuming as many unnecessary products and services as possible. People who have been shamed away from their traditional culture fill this bill admirably[55]—in large part due to the sequence outlined by Norberg-Hodge, where consumerism becomes a substitute for identity. To replace knowing who you are, *you become what you possess*: your car, your house, your expensive watch or dress or running shoes or swimming pool (and throughout, the illusion of being an "individual" is played upon by the supposedly "individualized goods" offered). It is a project which instigates a never-ending search for identity—a surrogate identity in goods, grimly testified to by the spectacle of Americans, and now countless others around the world, proudly wearing mass-produced products that proclaim their "individualized" identity via the mass corporate logo printed on them.

The measures taken against Italian Americans and other "enemy aliens" during World War II can thus be seen not only as significant in their own right, *which they were.*

They can also be viewed as fitting into a longer trend in American (and global) life—the attempt to keep the mass of the population under control in the interests of the stability desired by those in power. In this regard, a cultureless population (early experiments in this area include both the destruction of all vestiges of African family life among Southern slaves, and the continuing assaults on Native American culture by the federal government) is a controllable population. With its legitimate search for identity diverted into the pursuit of material goods, it also becomes a docile population. This latter is due to the fact that when democratic societies consist of cultureless consumers (or perhaps consumers who are convinced that shopping leads to individuation and therefore is itself "culture") rather than aware and active citizens, the struggle of powerful and wealthy elites to control and maintain their superior status has already been largely won.

With respect to the Italians who were placed under restriction—and whose restrictions and internments were intended as a demonstration project for all those who knew them and were related to them—the wartime measures succeeded admirably. These restrictions not only controlled a population considered to be leaders (the ones interned) and therefore "potentially" dangerous during the war; they also accelerated the Americanization process that replaced a cohesive population clustered in Little Italys rife with ancient and well-tried modes of behavior, with modern consumers dispersed to suburbs and congratulating themselves on having "made it" into full Americanism. As noted above, the process has continued to this day. It took several generations for some—not all—of their heirs to begin to question whether the adaptation was truly worth the price paid. David Richards, for example, refers to the bargain or devil's pact whereby Italian Americans agreed to abandon their "color" (including their initial easy commerce with African Americans) in exchange for the superior status conferred by "whiteness," thus embracing and reinforcing the fundamental cleavage in American society.[56]

The end result of this de-culturalization of immigrants has been admirably expressed by Patricia Hampl. Of Bohemian (Czech) descent, Hampl writes with great penetration about the resentment expressed by white Americans over the cultural desert they find themselves inhabiting after renouncing their native culture, and is worth quoting again:

> Why should *they* get to say Black Is Beautiful—*we* didn't way back when (in 1904, 1894) get to say Bohemian is Beautiful. We had to melt, to assimilate. It's nonsense and it's ahistorical, and nobody *says* it anyway, but it's there at the heart of white society: the grudge against the past. Against those low grandmothers who thought (but they didn't think) their past and the national beauty (that is, culture) wouldn't be needed.
>
> ...Now we know what happened—on the surface. The colors faded, the differ-

ences became less distinct, and we are left with our ethnic "cuisines" as the dominant cultural legacy of our diverse past, and a murderous distinction between black and white.

This could just as easily have been written about Italian Americans, a group that has been recruited by conservatives in America to act as a bulwark against progressive moves toward a more equal and just society. Forgetting (or never having learned about; or simply dismissing) the restrictive and often racist measures once employed against their parents and grandparents, they are among the most vocal advocates of militarizing the borders against today's "illegal" immigrants; of rolling back most of the civil rights gains of the 1960s and 1970s; of cracking down on all the social programs intended to help the marginalized of society—*which they themselves once were*. Their cry is too often the one noted by Hampl: '*We* didn't get any help when we were poor and discriminated against. Why should *they*?'

This inversion becomes perhaps the most painful result of the culture loss attendant on World War II: those who are deprived of their culture tend not, as one might expect, to empathize with those who come after them and are subject to the same injustice, but to *resent* them instead. In this, the cultural nullification they have suffered bears its most pernicious fruit: it transforms formerly compassionate people and communities into isolated individuals who seem to have forgotten not only where they came from, but who they really are.

This is a loss indeed, and one that goes beyond the immediate losses of those enemy aliens who were targeted during the wartime—those who were interned, or evacuated from prohibited zones, or excluded from coastal areas, or arrested for violating the restrictions on their movement and possessions. In a direct line, it moves to their children and grandchildren; in a more indirect line, it moves sidewise to contaminate even those who, as citizens, were not targeted at all. Because in the end, who was targeted did not matter: with *all* Italianism targeted during the war, *all* Italian Americans were affected, even when they were unaware of it. Whole communities were changed, were invalidated, were induced to forget the past. The results of those changes and those losses have not been fully calculated or appreciated to this day.

———————————

1. Nancy Carnevale has recently (*A New Language, A New World: Italian Immigrants in the United States, 1890-1945*, Chicago: University of Illinois Press, 2009), presented the countless ways that Italian immigrants in pre-WWII America were met with cultural demands to forget their old, "inferior" language and Americanize by learning English. The English language, in the view of its promoters, had the capacity to so improve the moral and intellectual condition of immigrants that it could virtually change their race. Said George Gordon: "Let no American citizen hug his foreign tongue...and shut out the light of the great English language which carries all our ideals as Americans! The very vessel of the Lord it is...This tongue consecrates the immigrant who would be a citizen; he can never be a citizen of the United States without that, never." (Carnevale, 72). Theodore Roosevelt, among others, used terms ("English-speaking races") that made clear his belief in the transformative power (for European immigrants) of learning English by characterizing it as "the crucible that turns out people as Americans." (Carnevale, 56).

2. Eva Hoffman, *Lost in Translation*, (New York: Dutton, 1989), 106-07.

3. Hoffman, op. cit., 124.

4. See Carnevale, op. cit., for more on this. She cites studies documenting Italian culture's high regard for a male's linguistic dexterity—in public discourse and verbal play. For such men to be rendered child-like and nearly mute in a new setting must have been agonizing, a condition akin to castration (35). Carnevale also notes how the additional curbs America and the English language imposed on gestural freedom, which the Neapolitan in particular uses as a means of communication, had an equally crippling effect: "In psychoanalytic terms, giving up any version of Italian for English is equivalent to a kind of linguistic dismemberment" (122). See also Hoffman on this, below.

5. From the poem by Emma Lazarus, "The New Colossus," engraved on a tablet beneath the Statue of Liberty.

6. *Asian Week* May 4-10, 2001 & April 30, 2008.

7. SB 1070 was signed into law by Arizona Governor Jan Brewer on April 23, 2010. It was immediately condemned by many, including President Barack Obama as "undermin(ing) basic notions of fairness that we cherish as Americans." The law, according to the *New York Times*, "would make the failure to carry immigration documents a crime and give the police broad power to detain anyone suspected of being in the country illegally. Opponents have called it an open invitation for harassment and discrimination against Hispanics regardless of their citizenship status." (*New York Times*, "Arizona Enacts Stringent Law on Immigration," by Randal C. Archibold, April 23, 2010.)

8. *Yahoo News*, "Murder of Hispanic Man in Phoenix Classed as Hate Crime," June 18, 2010, http://re32.news.sp1.yahoo.com/s/ynew/ynew/ynew_ts2719. (accessed June 18, 2010).

9. See David Cole, *Enemy Aliens: Double Standards and Constitutional Freedoms in the War on Terrorism*, (New York: The New Press, 2005).

10. See my essay "How World War II Iced Italian-American Culture," in *Una Storia Segreta: The Secret History of Italian American Evacuation and Internment During World War II*, ed. Lawrence DiStasi, (Berkeley: Heyday Books, 2001), 303-312.

11. Memo, February 6, 1939, "Fishing Vessels Suitable for XAM(c)," and Memo, July 16, 1940, "Enrollment of Fishermen in Class V-6, USNR, for Service in their Own Vessels as Minesweepers," RG 181, NDSE, Box S-432, NARA SB.

12. Wikipedia, http://en.wikipedia.org/wiki/HyphenatedAmerican, (accessed June 6, 2010).

13. The Revolutionary War against Great Britain certainly involved a struggle for unity between loyalists and patriots, but since a formal union had not yet been formed, the issue was more one of formation or creation than preservation.

14. From http://www.cyberlearning-world.com/nhhs/html/greely1.htm. *The American Spirit*, Volume 1, "Lincoln Answers Greeley's Prayer" (1862). "Lincoln wanted to save the Union at all costs. In the letter response to Horace Greeley, Lincoln stated that he did not agree with those who would not save the Union unless they could save slavery at the same time. His stated object was to save the Union, not to save or destroy slavery. *If I could save the Union without freeing any slave, I would do it; and if I could save it by freeing all the slaves, I would do it; and if I could do it by freeing some and leaving others alone, I would also do that.*"

15. Wikipedia, "Hyphenated Americans," op. cit. See also Chris Hedges, *Death of the Liberal Class* (Nation Books: 2010), in which he discusses at length President Wilson's formation of the Committee for Public Information (CPI) one week after he declared war in April of 1917. The CPI's task was to convince an American public that was overwhelmingly opposed to entering the war to embrace it enthusiastically, and that the German enemy, known as "Huns," were bloodthirsty, savage destroyers of civilization. Thus was born modern mass propaganda, whose goal was not simply to drum up war fever, but to discredit all those (mainly socialists and progressives) who disagreed with the nation's involvement. The head of the CPI was George Creel, who later wrote a book called *How We Advertised America*. Also on the CPI was Edward Bernays, who took what he had learned about "regimenting the public mind" directly into commercial advertising, with the same effect. (See more information on Bernays below).

16. Adam Curtis, in his documentary *The Power of Nightmares*, refers to a policy called the "Paradigm of Prevention," in which governments arrest people based not on what they have done, but on what they *might* do in the future. Attorney General John Ashcroft, for example, is quoted explaining to Congress the policies the Bush Administration followed after the 9/11 attack: "We had to make a shift in the way we thought about things. So being reactive, waiting for a crime to be committed, or waiting for there to be evidence of the commission of a crime, didn't seem to us to be an appropriate way to protect the American people." David Cole comments on this policy, one similar to the policy applied to enemy aliens during WWII: "Under the preventive paradigm, instead of holding people accountable for what you can prove they have done in the past, you lock them up based on what you think or speculate they might do in the future. And how can a person who's locked up for what you think they might do in the future, disprove your speculation? It's impossible. And so what ends up happening is that the government short-circuits all the processes that are designed to distinguish the innocent from the guilty..." This should also remind us of the conclusions of the DOJ's Preliminary Report on Exclusion (see Ch. 6 cited earlier), about how impossible it is for an accused person to defend himself from charges of which he has no knowledge, speculations about what he might do in the future. In truth, not just excludees— who were American citizens—but virtually all 600,000 of those classified as "enemy aliens," were entrapped in this infinitely expansive category of "potential dangerousness." Adam Curtis, *The Power of Nightmares*, BBC documentary, London: 2004. http://wwwarchive.org/details/ThePowerOfNightmares, (accessed June 24, 2010).

17. Jerre Mangione, *An Ethnic at Large: A Memoir of American in the Thirties and Forties*, (New York: G.P. Putnam's, 1978), 352.

18. There were numerous other reasons as well. One common belief held by many immigrants was that they were already citizens via *derived citizenship*—i.e. because one or both of their parents had naturalized. I have just learned that my own parents—both of them it now turns out—operated under this mistaken belief, until each in turn found it was problematic. My father

thought he had citizenship through *his* father (my grandfather), who was naturalized in 1928. My father found out too late that since he was 26 years old and no longer a minor when his father was naturalized, he did *not* derive citizenship thereby. He had to register as an alien in 1940, was classified as an enemy alien in 1941, and was naturalized on his own in 1944. Had he realized sooner that he was vulnerable, he would no doubt have done this earlier. My mother, born in Hungary in 1914, also thought she had derivative citizenship through her father, who was naturalized in 1932. However, since the issue was in some doubt (perhaps due to her age—eighteen is the cutoff in some, but not all states—or inability to get proof of her father's citizenship—they were estranged), she, too, was forced to register as an alien in 1940, and was also considered an enemy alien. Her application for derivative citizenship through her father was finally granted in 1943—which meant that she should NOT have been classified as an enemy alien during the war—but by then it was too late; the damage had been done.

19. Berizzi letter, Jan. 1943, from Berizzi file, RG 389, Entry 4661, PMGO Records Relating to Italian Civilian Internees During WWII, 1941-46, Boxes 2-20, NARA II, College Park, MD. Cited in DiStasi, *Una Storia Segreta*, "Introduction: One Voice at a Time," (xv).

20. DiBugnara letter to J. Sexton Daniel, Jan. 30, 1943, in Illidio diBugnara file, RG 389, Entry 4661, PMGO Records Relating to Italian Civilian Internees During WWII, 1941-46, Boxes 2-20, NARA II, College Park, MD.

21. Memo for Chief of Review Section, Oct. 8, 1942, Federico Dellagatta file, RG 389, Entry 4661, PMGO, NARA II, College Park, MD.

22. The OWI, like Francis Biddle above, did try to distinguish between Italian language and culture, on the one hand, and Mussolini and fascism on the other. However, this did not match the cultural denigration that went on constantly in most public channels, and which stuck in the popular mind. It might also be pointed out that being able to point to such 'even-handedness' or lack of discrimination actually gives governments a freer hand to employ their harshest measures: they can say, or imply, "you see, we have no prejudice against the people, we are not racist, our punishment is directed solely at the malefactors." Michelle Alexander, in another context, points to the similarly beneficent face of "color-blindness" behind the mass incarceration of black men: 'all are equal here, all have the same chance for advancement, but some, the criminals we target, choose paths that require imprisonment.' Here is Alexander's conclusion: "We, as a nation, seem comfortable with 90% of the people arrested and convicted of drug offenses in some states being African American, but if the figure were 100%, the veil of colorblindness would be lost....In short, the inclusion of some whites in the system of control is essential to preserving the image of a colorblind criminal just system.." See Michelle Alexander, *The New Jim Crow*, (New York: The New Press, 2010), 199.

23. See, among others, Cotton Mather in *Magnalia Christi Americana*, "In short, the *First Age* was the Golden age: To return unto *That* will make a Man a *Protestant*, and I may add, a *Puritan*;" or Henry David Thoreau, "If we do not succeed this time, there is perhaps one more chance for the race [i.e. to leave the Old World behind], before we reach the banks of the Styx..." in "Walking," *The Portable Thoreau*, ed. Carl Bode, (New York: Penguin, 1957), p. 604. This "new man" idea found its most famous expression in the concept of the "natural rights of man" with which Thomas Jefferson began the Declaration of Independence: "We hold these truths to be self-evident, that all men are created equal, that they are endowed by their Creator with certain unalienable Rights, that among these are Life, Liberty and the Pursuit of Happiness."

24. See p. 26, Ch. 2 above, the case of Mrs. Emma Manfredi Lupi, arrested in October 1942 for sending a letter to her sister-in-law in Argentina, which letter was forwarded to Italy to inquire after her friend's aging mother.

25. Some, of course, might call it war's main purpose. That is, by providing a nation with an outside enemy, war provides it with the common threat needed to unify a fractious or reluctant population to accept or endorse policies and expenditures of life and treasure that would otherwise be unacceptable.

26. Eva Hoffman, *Lost in Translation*, op. cit., 147.

27. Nancy Carnevale, op. cit., notes the psychological consequences of this gestural repression: "In psychoanalytic terms, giving up any version of Italian for English is equivalent to a kind of linguistic dismemberment: one has to symbolically lose one's hands and the greater possibilities for communication that they allow" (122).

28. Henry James, *The American Scene*, New York: Penguin Classics, 1994 (first published 1907), (97-98). It should be noted that James's lament was not without its condescension—that of the traveler who finds peasant behavior when observed at a distance quite "colorful," especially when contained within a strict class system. Still, the same observation has been made by Italian Americans themselves when they compare their own Americanized, and hence impoverished range of gesture and emotion with that of relatives who remained in Italy.

29. *Assembly Fact Finding Committee on Un-American Activities in California*, transcript, (3667-68).

30. Paul Pisicano, in Studs Terkel's *The Good War: An Oral History of World War II*, (New York: Pantheon, 1984), puts the change this way: "Since the war, Italo-Americans have undergone this amazing transformation...We stopped being Italo and started becoming Americans... We had all lived in one big apartment house my father built. He built a wine cellar. The guys, after they'd worked hard all day—not in offices, in factories—they'd have their dinner, there was no TV, they'd go downstairs, during the grape season, and they would crush. *It was a communal effort.* Everybody in the apartment house worked on the harvest...After the war, nobody used the wine cellars. The whole sense of community disappeared. You lost your Italianness...Suddenly we looked up, we owned property. Italians could buy. The GI Bill, the American dream. Guys my age had really become Americanized. They moved to the suburbs. Oh God, I see the war as that transition piece that pulled us out of the wine cellar. It obliterated our culture and made us Americans. That's no fun."

31. See, among many others, Michi Weglyn, *Years of Infamy: The Untold Story of America's Concentration Camps*, (New York: William Morrow, 1976).

32. See, http://dailysok.com/wordpress/index.php/2010/04/benefits-of-being-cultureless/ whose April 2, 2010 entry, "Benefits of Being Cultureless," opens: "I was talking to my friend from India the other day about how America's youth today believes that we totally and completely lack a culture and strive for the sort of heritage that other people have;" or "Fellow Americans, Why is America so Cultureless?" http://answers.yahoo.com/question/index?qid=20100626114046 AAA84MY; or, "Cultureless America," http://activephilosophy.wordpress.com/2009/03/12/cultureless-america.(all accessed 7.2.10)

33. Patricia Hampl writes with great penetration about this in her first memoir, *A Romantic Education* (Boston: Houghton-Mifflin, 1981). Referring to Henry James' comments about immigrants in *The American Scene* (see above), she writes: "In this way, matters of ethnicity have become entangled with those of racism. And the bitterness that whites feel—often *low* whites [i.e. as James referred to immigrants]—about blacks and American Indians, is the bitterness of their own cultural, even racial, renunciation. Why should *they* get to say Black is Beautiful—*we* didn't, way back when (in 1904, in 1894), get to say Bohemian Is Beautiful. We had to melt, to assimilate. It's nonsense and it's ahistorical, and nobody says it anyway, but it's there at the heart of white society: the grudge against the past. Against those low grandmothers who thought (but they didn't think) their past and the national beauty (that is, culture) wouldn't be needed" (34).

34. See Stuart Ewen, *PR: A Social History of Spin*, (New York: Basic Books, 1996), Walter

Lippmann, *Public Opinion*, (New York: Harcourt Brace, 1922), and Edward Bernays, *Propaganda*, (New York: Liveright, 1928).

35. There is no doubt that a substantial portion of the American public still views "culture" in this way. Hence the so-called "culture wars."

36. Djelal Kedir has parsed the word America to mean *a* (as in 'not') *meri* (as in 'place') and *ge* (as in 'land'), hence, as "no-place-land." The place of no place. The place of constant movement.

37. Opening passages of the *Declaration of Independence*, generally attributed to Thomas Jefferson.

38. It probably bears mentioning that these ideas and feelings are not articulated publicly or even privately by those who experience them. Like the emotional impulses that will be noted below regarding the way people are induced to buy products, they usually operate below the level of consciousness.

39. See the comment by Paul Pisicano about this above, note 21.

40. Consumerism isn't strictly speaking 'culture' but might more properly be described as the absence of 'culture.' This is perhaps because whereas culture evolves, consumerism is imposed. It is, in brief, the antithesis of culture.

41. Information on Edward Bernays is widespread. Here I have consulted Stuart Ewen, op. cit., Bernays's book *Propaganda*, op. cit., and Adam Curtis' BBC documentary, *The Century of the Self* (Part 1), available online at: http://www.archive.org/details/AdamCurtisCenturyoftheSelf. (accessed June 20, 2010).

42. Edward Bernays, op. cit., Chapter II: *The New Propaganda*, (Google books online).

43. Quoted in Adam Curtis, *The Century of the Self*, part 1, op. cit.

44. Edward Bernays, *Propaganda*, op. cit., Chapter 4: The Psychology of Public Relations.

45. Ibid., Chapter 3: The New Propagandists.

46. It is interesting, if not alarming to note that President George W. Bush urged Americans to respond to the attack on 9/11 by doing precisely this: going out to shop. This amounted to saying that the primary duty of the American citizen, even in a national emergency, was to consume.

47. Quoted in Adam Curtis, *The Century of the Self*, part 1.

48. Ibid.

49. Ibid.

50. Ibid.

51. Helena Norberg-Hodge, *Ancient Futures: Learning from Ladakh*, (New York: Random House, 1991).

52. Norberg-Hodge, op. cit., 125.

53. Norberg-Hodge, op. cit., 120.

54. Bernays, *Propaganda*, op. cit., Chapter 5: Business and the Public.

55. They fill it except where, as we have seen in the last decade, their shame spurs them to affiliation with ethno-religious civilizations such as fundamentalist Islam. The outcome in that case is not consumerism and docility, but terrorism and violence.

56. See David A. J. Richards, *Italian American: The Racializing of an Ethnic Identity*, New York: New York University Press: 1999 (230ff). Jennifer Guglielmo, in *Living the Revolution: Italian Women's Resistance and Radicalism in New York City, 1880-1945*, Chapel Hill: University of North Carolina Press: 2010, makes a similar point, focusing on the early radical activism and solidarity of Italian and Sicilian women immigrants, which, in the face of serious repression during WWI and afterwards, was diverted into suburban quietism and separatism: "Admission into the nation was therefore contingent on Italians embracing U.S. nationalism, including whiteness and negrophobia....This "triumph of nativism," coupled with the criminalization of dissent, profoundly crippled Italian immigrant radicalism"(5-6).

SELECT BIBLIOGRAPHY

Barrett, Edward L. *The Tenney Committee* (Ithaca: Cornell University Press, 1951).

Bosia, Remo. *The General and I* (New York: Phaedra Press, 1971).

Benedetto, Umberto. *Italian Boys at Fort Missoula, Montana 1941-1943* (Missoula, MT: Pictorial Histories Publishing Co., 1991).

Bernays, Edward. *Propaganda.* (New York, NY: Liveright, 1928).

Biddle, Francis. *In Brief Authority* (New York: Doubleday, 1962).

Boehm, Randolph, ed. *Papers of the U.S. Commission on Wartime Relocation and Internment of Civilians* (Fredericksburg, MD: Government Printing Office, 1984).

Bosworth, R. and Ugolini, R., eds. *War, Internment and Mass Migration: The Italo-Australian Experience* (Rome: Gruppo Editoriale Internazionale, 1992).

California Legislature. *Report of the Joint Fact-Finding Committee on Un-American Activities in California* (Sacramento: State Legislature, 55th Session, 1943).

Cannistraro, Philip. "Fascism and Italian Americans," *Perspectives in Italian Immigration and Ethnicity,* S.M. Tomasi, ed. (New York: Center For Migration Studies, 1976).

_____ "Generoso Pope and the Rise of Italian American Politics, 1925-1936," *Italian Americans: New Perspectives in Italian Immigration and Ethnicity,* Lydio Tomasi, ed. (New York: Center for Migration Studies, 1983).

_____ "Luigi Antonini and the Italian Anti-Fascist Movement in the United States, 1940-1943," *Journal of American Ethnic History*, Fall 1985 (1985).

_____ *Blackshirts in Little Italy: Italian Americans and Fascism, 1921-1929* (Lafayette, IN: Bordighera, 1999).

Carnevale, Nancy. *A New Language, A New World: Italian Immigrants in the United States, 1890-1945* (Chicago: University of Illinois Press, 2009).

_____ "'No Italian Spoken for the Duration of the War': Language, Italian-American Identity, and Cultural Pluralism in the World War II Years," *Journal of*

American Ethnic History V. 22, No. 3 (2003).

Carter, Hugh, ed. *Administrative History of the Immigration and Naturalization Service during World War II* (Washington, DC: General Research Unit, 1946).

Chin, Brian. *Artillery at the Golden Gate: The Harbor Defenses of San Francisco in World War II* (Missoula, MT: Pictorial Histories Publishing, 1994).

Christgau, John. *Enemies: World War II Alien Internment* (Ames, IA: Iowa State University Press, 1985).

Cole, David. *Enemy Aliens: Double Standards and Constitutional Freedoms in the War on Terrorism*, (New York, NY: The New Press, 2005).

Commission on Wartime Relocation and Internment of Civilians. *Personal Justice Denied* (Washington, DC: Government Printing Office, 1982).

Conn, Stetson, Rose Engelman, Byron Fairchild. *Guarding the United States and its Outposts* (Washington, DC: Center of Military History, 1964).

Corbett, P. Scott. *Quiet Passages: The Exchange of Civilians between the United States and Japan during the Second World War* (Kent, OH: Kent State University Press, 1987).

Curtis, Adam. *The Power of Nightmares* (London: BBC Documentary, 2004).

_____ *The Century of the Self* (London: BBC Documentary, 2002).

Daniels, Roger. *Concentration Camps USA: Japanese Americans and World War II* (New York: Holt, Rinehart and Winston, 1972).

_____ *The Politics of Prejudice* (Berkeley: University of California Press, 1962).

_____ Sandra C. Taylor, and Harry H. L. Kitano, eds. *Japanese Americans from Relocation to Redress* (Salt Lake City: University of Utah Press, 1986).

Diggins, John P. *Mussolini and Fascism: The View from America* (Princeton, NJ: Princeton University Press, 1972).

DiStasi, Lawrence, ed. *Una Storia Segreta: The Secret History of Italian American Evacuation and Internment During World War II* (Berkeley: Heyday Books, 2001).

_____ "Derived Aliens: Derivative Citizenship and Italian American Women during World War II," *Italian Americana*, Winter: 2010 (Providence RI: University of Rhode Island Center, 2010).

_____ "Dis-enchanted Evenings: Ezio Pinza's Wartime Ordeal," *Ambassador Magazine*, 41 (Summer 1999).

Ewen, Stuart. *PR: A Social History of Spin* (New York, NY: Basic Books, 1996).

Fox, Stephen. "General DeWitt and the Proposed Internment of German and Italian Aliens during World War II," *Pacific Historical Review*, 57 (November, 1988).

_____ *The Unknown Internment: An Oral History of the Relocation of Italian Americans during World War II* (Boston: Twayne Publishers, 1990).

_____ *America's Invisible Gulag: A Biography of German American Internment & Exclusion—Memory & History* (New York, NY: Peter Lang Publishing, 2000).

Gardiner, C. Harvey. *Pawns in a Triangle of Hate: The Peruvian Japanese and the United States* (Seattle: University of Washington Press, 1981).

Gentry, Curt. *J. Edgar Hoover: The Man and His Secrets* (New York, NY: W.W. Norton, 1991).

Gillman, Peter and Leni. *Collar the Lot: How Britain Interned and Expelled Its Wartime Refugees* (London: Quarter Books, 1978).

Grodzins, Morton. *Americans Betrayed: Politics and the Japanese Evacuation* (Chicago: University of Chicago Press, 1949).

Guglielmo, Jennifer. *Living the Revolution: Italian Women's Resistance and Radicalism in New York City, 1880-1945,* (Chapel Hill: University of North Carolina Press, 2010).

Hampl, Patricia. *A Romantic Education* (Boston: Houghton-Mifflin, 1981).

Hedges, Chris. *The Death of the Liberal Class* (New York, NY: Nation Books, 2010).

Hillmer, Norman, Bohdan Kordan, and Lubomyr Luciuk, eds. *On Guard for Thee: War, Ethnicity, and the Canadian State, 1939-1945* (Ottawa: Canadian Government Publications Centre, 1988).

Hoffman, Eva. *Lost in Translation* (New York NY: Dutton, 1989).

Iacovetta, Franca, Roberto Perin, and Angelo Principe, eds. *Enemies Within: Italian and Other Internees in Canada and Abroad* (Toronto: University of Toronto Press, 2000).

Inada, Lawson, ed. *Only What We Could Carry* (Berkeley: Heyday Books, 2000).

Irons, Peter. *Justice at War: The Story of the Japanese American Internment Cases* (New York: Oxford University Press, 1983).

Issel, William. *For Both Cross and Flag: Catholic Action, Anti-Catholicism, and National Security Politics in World War II San Francisco* (Philadelphia: Temple University Press, 2010).

Krammer, Arnold. *Undue Process: The Untold Story of America's German Alien Internees* (London and Boulder CO: Rowman & Littlefield, 1997).

Lothrop, Gloria Ricci. "The Untold Story: The Effect of the Second World War on California Italians," *Journal of the West,* 35:1 (1996).

_____ "Shadow on the Land: Italians in Southern California in the 1930s," *California History,* 75:4 (Winter 1996-97).

Mangione, Jerre. *An Ethnic at Large: A Memoir of America in the Thirties and Forties* (New York, NY: Putnam, 1978).

McDermott, Thomas. "Aliens of Enemy Nationality," (INS Training Lecture, 1943).

Norberg-Hodge, Helena. *Ancient Futures: Learning from Ladakh* (New York, NY: Random House, 1991).

O'Brien, Ilma Martinuzzi, et. al. *Enemy Aliens: The Internment of Italian Migrants in Australia During the Second World War* (Ballarat, Australia: Connor Court Publishing, 2005).

Pinza, Ezio, with Robert Magidoff. *Ezio Pinza: An Autobiography* (New York, NY: Rinehart, 1958).

Pisicano, Paul. interviewed in Terkel, Studs. *The Good War: An Oral History of World War II* (New York, NY: Pantheon, 1984).

Pozzetta, George. "My Children Are My Jewels: Italian American Generations during World War II," in *The Home-Front War: World War II and American Society*, Kenneth O'Brien and Lynn Parsons, eds. (Westport, CT: Greenwood Press, 1995).

_____ and Gary Mormino. "Ethnics at War: Italian Americans in California during World War II," in *The Way We Really Were: The Golden State in the Second Great War*, Roger Lotchin, ed. (Urbana: University of Illinois Press, 2000).

Richards, David A. J. *Italian American: The Racializing of an Ethnic Identity* (New York, NY: New York University Press, 1999).

Salvemini, Gaetano. *Italian Fascist Activities in the United States*, Philip V. Cannistraro, ed. (New York: Center for Migration Studies, 1977).

Salvetti, Patrizia. *Corde e Sapone: Storie di linciaggi degli italiani negli State Uniti.* (Roma: Donzelli Editore, 2003.)

Scherini, Rose. "The Fascist/Anti-Fascist Struggle in San Francisco," in *New Explorations in Italian American Studies*, Richard N. and Sandra P. Juliani, eds., (Washington, DC: American Italian Historical Association, 1994).

_____ "The Other Internment: When Italian Americans Were Enemy Aliens," *Ambassador Magazine* (Fall 1993).

_____ and Lawrence DiStasi with Adele Negro. *Una Storia Segreta: When Italian Americans Were "Enemy Aliens"* (Berkeley: American Italian Historical Association, Western Regional Chapter, 1994).

Sheridan, Peter. "Internment of German and Italian Aliens as Compared with the Internment of Japanese Aliens in the United States during World War II: A Brief History and Analysis" (Library of Congress: Congressional Research Service, 1980).

Smith, Bradley. *The Shadow Warriors: The OSS and the Origins of the CIA* (New York, NY: Basic Books, 1983).

Smith, Tom. *The Crescent City Lynchings* (Guilford, CT: Lyons Press, 2007).

ten Broeck, Jacobus, Edward Barnhart, and Floyd Matson. *Prejudice, War and the Constitution* (Berkeley and Los Angeles: University of California Press, 1954).

Tintori, Guido. "New Discoveries, Old Prejudices," in *Una Storia Segreta: The Secret History of Italian American Evacuation and Internment During World War II*, ed. Lawrence DiStasi, (Berkeley: Heyday Books, 2001)

Theoharis, Athan. *Spying on Americans: Political Surveillance from Hoover to the Huston Plan* (Philadelphia: Temple University Press, 1978).

U.S. Congress. *Report of the Select Committee Investigating National Defense Migration*, 77th Congress, 2nd Session (Washington DC: Government Printing Office, 1942).

U.S. Justice Department. *Report to the Congress of the United States: A Review of the Restrictions on Persons of Italian Ancestry During World War II* (Washington, DC: Government Printing Office, 2001)

U.S. Senate. *Supplementary Detailed Staff Reports on Intelligence Activities and theRights of Americans. Book III. Final Report of the Select Committee to Study Governmental Operations with Respect to Intelligence Activities* (available online at: http://www.icdc.com/~paulwolf/cointelpro/churchfinalreportIII.htm.).

Van Valkenburg, Carol. *An Alien Place: The Fort Missoula Detention Camp, 1941-1944* (Missoula, MT: 1995).

Weglyn, Michi. *Years of Infamy: The Untold Story of America's Concentration Camps* (New York: William Morrow, 1976).

Lawrence DiStasi has been the project director of the traveling exhibit, *Una Storia Segreta: When Italian Americans Were 'Enemy Aliens,'* since its inception in 1994. The current Newsletter Editor/Curator and past President of the Italian American Studies Association, Western Regional Chapter, he works as an editor, writer and a publisher under his own imprint, Sanniti Publications. His books include *The Big Book of Italian American Culture* (Sanniti: 1996; first published as *Dream Streets* by Harper & Row: 1989), *Mal Occhio: The Underside of Vision* (Sanniti: 2008; first published by North Point Press: 1981), *Una Storia Segreta: The Secret History of Italian American Evacuation and Internment During World War II* (Heyday Books: 2001), and *Esty: A Novel/Memoir* (Sanniti: 2012). His shorter work and blogs can be seen at distasiblog.blogspot.com. He lives in Bolinas, CA.